Peterson's

MASTER THE™
AP® ENGLISH
LITERATURE AND
COMPOSITION EXAM

3RD EDITION

PETERSON'S®

About Peterson's

Peterson's®, a Nelnet company, has been your trusted educational publisher for over 50 years. It's a milestone we're quite proud of, as we continue to offer the most accurate, dependable, high-quality educational content in the field, providing you with everything you need to succeed. No matter where you are on your academic or professional path, you can rely on Peterson's for its books, online information, expert test-prep tools, the most up-to-date education exploration data, and the highest quality career success resources—everything you need to achieve your education goals. For our complete line of products, visit www.petersons.com.

For more information about Peterson's range of educational products, contact Peterson's, 3 Columbia Circle, Suite 205, Albany, NY 12203, 800-338-3282 Ext. 54229; or find us online at www.petersons.com.

ISBN-13: 978-0-7689-4182-1

Printed in the United States of America

10 9 8 7 6 5 4 3 2 1   19 18 17

Third Edition

OTHER RECOMMENDED TITLES

Peterson's Master AP English Language & Composition

Peterson's Master AP U.S. History

Contents

Before You Begin vii

How This Book is Organized vii

Special Study Features.. vii

How to Plan For Your Test Using This Book....................................viii

You're Well on Your Way to Success viii

Give Us Your Feedback viii

Works Referenced... ix

Top 10 Strategies to Raise Your Score... xii

PART I: AP® ENGLISH LITERATURE AND COMPOSITION EXAM BASICS

1   All About the AP® English Literature and Composition Exam...............3

The AP® English Literature and Composition Exam: An Overview 4

Registration Essentials for the AP® English Literature and
      Composition Exam 9

Getting Ready for Exam Day... 10

Building an Effective Study Plan 11

Summing It Up..17

PART II: AP® ENGLISH LITERATURE AND COMPOSITION EXAM STRATEGIES

2   Poetry Questions on the AP® Literature and Composition Exam 21

Format of the Multiple-Choice Section 22

How to Read a Poem on the AP® Exam 23

Elements of Poems 30

Classifying Poems Into Genres 32

Sound and Rhyme 40

Language, Word Choice, and Diction 43

Poetry by the Century 47

Practice Sets.. 56

Sample Passage 1 57

Sample Passage 2 60

Answer Key and Explanations 63

Summing It Up 69

3   Prose Questions on the AP® Literature and Composition Exam 71

Breadth and Depth of the Prose Section...................................... 72

How to Read a Prose Passage on the AP® Exam........................... 72

Situating Yourself within a Passage: Elements of Prose 81

How to Read Nonfiction Prose 94
How to Read Dramatic Prose... 96
Practice Sets... 105
Sample Passage 1 106
Sample Passage 2 109
Answer Key and Explanations 113
Summing It Up 118

**4   Free-Response Questions on the AP® Literature and
      Composition Exam... 119**
Format of the Free-Response Section 120
Learning a New Language... 120
Essay Section Scoring... 121
How to Spend Those 40 Minutes Per Essay................................... 123
Moving Beyond the Five-Paragraph Essay...................................... 125
Breaking Down the Composition Process 128
Home Stretch: The Last 5 Minutes of Each Essay.......................... 136
Common Reader Pet Peeves... 137
The Smallest Details Count 138
Poetry and Prose Essay Walkthroughs.. 138
How to Approach the Open Essay.. 170
Open Essay Walkthroughs..177
Summing It Up... 187

PART III: THREE PRACTICE TESTS

5   Practice Test 1 191
Answer Sheet Practice Test 1 193
Practice Test 1 197
Essay Question 1 212
Essay Question 2 214
Essay Question 3 216
Answer Key and Explanations 217

6   Practice Test 2 243
Answer Sheet Practice Test 2 245
Practice Test 2 249
Essay Question 1 265
Essay Question 2 267
Essay Question 3 269
Answer Key and Explanations 270

7   Practice Test 3 297
Answer Sheet Practice Test 3 299
Practice Test 3 303
Essay Question 1 318
Essay Question 2 320
Essay Question 3 322
Answer Key and Explanations 323

Before You Begin

HOW THIS BOOK IS ORGANIZED

Whether you have five months, nine weeks, or just two short weeks to prepare for the exam, Peterson's *Master the ™ AP® English Literature and Composition Exam* will help you develop a study plan that caters to your individual needs and timetable. These step-by-step plans are easy to follow and remarkably effective.

- **Top 10 Strategies to Raise Your Score** gives you tried and true test-taking strategies.
- **Part I** includes the basic information about the AP English Literature & Composition test that you need to know.
- **Part II** provides the review and strategies for answering the different kinds of multiple-choice questions on prose and on poetry and numerous opportunities to practice what you are learning. It is a good idea to read the answer explanations to all of the questions because you may find ideas or tips that will help you better analyze the answers to questions in the next Practice Test you take. You will also find "quick" reviews of grammar and literary terms.
- **Part III** includes three additional practice tests. Remember to apply the test-taking system carefully, work the system to get more correct responses, and be careful of your time in order to answer more questions in the time period.

SPECIAL STUDY FEATURES

Peterson's *Master the ™ AP® English Literature and Composition Exam* was designed to be as user-friendly as it is complete. It includes several features to make your preparation easier.

Overview

Each chapter begins with a bulleted overview listing the topics that will be covered in the chapter. You know immediately where to look for a topic that you need to work on.

Summing It Up

Each strategy chapter ends with a point-by-point summary that captures the most important points. The summaries are a convenient way to review the content of these strategy chapters.

Bonus Information

You will find three types of notes in the margins of the *Master the™ AP® English Literature and Composition Exam* book to alert you to important information.

NOTE

Margin notes marked "Note" highlight information about the test structure itself.

TIP

Tips draw your attention to valuable concepts, advice, and shortcuts for tackling the exam. By reading the tips, you will learn how to approach different question types, pace yourself, and remember what was discussed previously in the book.

HOW TO PLAN FOR YOUR TEST USING THIS BOOK

This books consists of a section on the content, structure, scoring of as well as useful strategies for success on the exam followed by three chapters of content review and three full-length practice tests with full explanations. Each content chapter also provides review exercises and walkthroughs designed to help you get up to speed.

You may already know what you know and don't know. If not, and frankly even if you think you do, we'd recommend taking any of the three full-length tests first, without studying, as a "diagnostic test" (with the proper timing, using a bubble sheet, at 8AM, in a testlike environment, etc.) in order to see where your weaknesses lie. Let your results guide your use of this book. After reviewing your test results, note what content you need to work on and study for first.

For more specific test-prep timeline information, see our "Building an Effective Study Plan" section on page 11.

YOU'RE WELL ON YOUR WAY TO SUCCESS

Remember that knowledge is power. You will be studying the most comprehensive guide available, and you will become extremely knowledgeable about the exam. We look forward to helping you raise your score.

GIVE US YOUR FEEDBACK

Peterson's publishes a full line of books-test prep, education exploration, financial aid, and career preparation. Peterson's publications can be found in high school guidance counselor offices, college libraries and career centers, and your local bookstore and library.

We welcome any comments or suggestions you may have about this publication. Please call our customer service department at 800-338-3282 ext. 54229 or send an email to custsvc@petersons.com.

WORKS REFERENCED

The following list represents all the works of literature discussed in this book, broken out by chapter.

Chapter 2

Excerpt from "Don Juan," by Lord Byron (Canto 11)

Excerpt from "Ode to a Nightingale," by John Keats

Excerpt from "Philomela," by Matthew Arnold

Excerpt from *Romeo and Juliet*, by William Shakespeare

Excerpt from "Amoretti LXXV," by Edmund Spenser

Excerpt from "London, 1802," by William Wordsworth

"Villanelle," by Edmund Gosse

Excerpt from "The Bells," by Edgar Allan Poe

"I Am!," by John Clare

Excerpt from "My Last Duchess," by Robert Browning

"Sonnet 116," by William Shakespeare

"The Tree" by Anne Finch, Countess of Winchilsea

"Long-Legged Fly," by William Butler Yeats

Chapter 3:

Excerpt from *House of the Seven Gables*, by Nathaniel Hawthorne

Excerpt from *Autobiography of an Ex-Colored Man*, by James Weldon Johnson

Excerpt from *The Mysteries of Udolpho*, by Ann Radcliffe

Excerpt from *Oroonoko*, by Aphra Behn

Excerpt from *Karain: A Memory*, by Joseph Conrad

Excerpt from The Haunted Mind," by Nathaniel Hawthorne

Excerpt from *Persuasion*, by Jane Austen

Excerpt from *Middlemarch*, by George Eliot

Excerpt from *English Hours*, by Henry James

Excerpt from *King Lear*, by William Shakespeare

Excerpt from *The Rivals*, by Richard Brinsley Sheridan

Excerpt from *The Story of an African Farm*, by Olive Schreiner

Excerpt from *Gulliver's Travels*, by Jonathan Swift

Chapter 4

Excerpt from *Robinson Crusoe*, by Daniel Defoe

Excerpt from Confession to a Friend in Trouble, by Thomas Hardy

Excerpt from *Mardi*, by Herman Melville

Excerpt from *The Custom of the Country*, by Edith Wharton

Excerpt from "The Wanderer," by Richard Savage

"Sonnet LXX," by Charlotte Smith

"Bluebeard," by Edna St. Vincent Millay

Chapter 5

"Written with a Slate Pencil on a Stone, on the Side of the Mountain of Black Comb," by William Wordsworth

Excerpt from *The Moonstone*, by Wilkie Collins

"Candle-Lightin' Time" and "Confirmation" by Paul Laurence Dunbar

Excerpt from *The Female Quixote*, by Charlotte Lennox

"Volpone," by Ben Jonson

Excerpt from *The Song of the Lark,* by Willa Cather

Chapter 6

"A Japanese Wood-Carving," by Amy Lowell

Excerpt from *New Grub Street*, by George Gissing

Prologue of *She Stoops to Conquer*, by David Garrick on Oliver Goldsmith

Excerpt from *My Brilliant Career*, by Stella Maria Sarah Miles Franklin, known as Miles Franklin

"Lines Composed in a Concert Hall," by Samuel Taylor Coleridge

Excerpt from *The Library Window*, by Margaret Oliphant

Chapter 7

"Delight in Disorder," by Robert Herrick

Excerpt from *Shadowings*, by Lafcadio Hearn

"On Recollection," by Phillis Wheatley

Excerpt from *Villette*, by Charlotte Brontë

"The Word of an Engineer," by James Weldon Johnson

Excerpt from "Against Thinking," by Vernon Lee

TOP 10 STRATEGIES TO RAISE YOUR SCORE

When it comes to taking an AP, some test-taking skills will do you more good than others. There are concepts you can learn and techniques you can follow that will help you do your best. Here are our picks for the top 10 strategies to raise your score:

1. **Create a study plan and follow it.** The right study plan will help you get the most out of this book in whatever time you have.

2. **Choose a place and time to study every day,** and stick to your routine and your plan.

3. **Complete the diagnostic and practice tests in this book.** They will give you just what they promise: practice—practice in reading and following the directions, practice in pacing yourself, practice in understanding and answering multiple-choice questions, and practice in writing timed essays.

4. **Complete all of your assignments for your regular AP English class.** Ask questions in class, talk about what you read and write, and enjoy what you are doing. The test is supposed to measure your development as an educated and thinking reader.

5. **If the question is a *main idea* or *theme* question,** look for the answer that is the most general and can be supported by evidence in the selection.

6. All elements in an answer must be correct for the answer to be correct.

7. **Don't rely on your memory; refer to the passage.** For poetry, read a line or two above and a line or two below the reference.

8. **With *not/except* questions, ask yourself if an answer choice is true about the selection.** If it is, cross it out, and keep checking answers.

9. If you aren't sure about an answer but know something about the question, eliminate what you know is wrong and make an educated guess.

10. **Finally, don't cram.** Relax. Go to a movie, visit a friend—but not one who is taking the test with you. Get a good night's sleep.

PART I

AP® ENGLISH LITERATURE AND COMPOSITION EXAM BASICS

CHAPTER 1   All About the AP® English Literature and
Composition Exam

All About the AP® English Literature and Composition Exam

OVERVIEW

- **The AP® English Literature and Composition Exam: An Overview**
- **Registration Essentials for the AP® English Literature and Composition Exam**
- **Getting Ready for Exam Day**
- **Building an Effective Study Plan**
- **Summing It Up**

We understand *exactly* why you're here and why you're reading this book—you're a high-achieving student with a goal to get your best possible score on the AP® English Literature and Composition Exam. Your reasons for setting this goal are likely two-fold:

- Getting a good exam score (typically a score of 3 or higher out of a range from 1 to 5) will help you earn valuable college credit while still in high school, allowing you to potentially place out of introductory-level undergraduate courses in that subject area.

- A good exam score looks great on your college application and will allow you to be more competitive and stand out among the qualified applicants to the schools you're applying to.

These are great reasons to take your AP® Exams *seriously*—which means making the most of your preparation time between now and exam day to ensure that you do your best.

You've undoubtedly taken your academic career seriously thus far, which is why you decided to take this AP®-level course in the first place. The last thing you want to have happen now is to get this close to your goal of acing the AP® English Literature and Composition Exam and to not do your absolute best because of a failure to plan appropriately!

We *completely* get it—and if this description sounds like you, then here's some great news: you have already made an excellent decision and have taken a wise step forward in your AP® Exam preparation by deciding to purchase this book. We're here to help make your goal of a great score on the AP® English Literature and Composition Exam a reality. So keep reading!

Peterson's Master the AP® English Literature and Composition Exam is your comprehensive study resource, all-in-one test-prep coach, effective preparation guide, and indispensable companion on your journey to getting a great AP® Exam score. Every facet of this book is designed by AP® Exam experts with one singular purpose: to help you achieve your best possible score on test day.

This effective test-prep tool contains all of the following helpful resources—and more:

- Complete coverage of the AP® English Literature and Composition Exam: You'll get a thorough insight into every aspect of this important exam—from structure and scoring to what to expect on exam day and how to effectively tackle every question type. After reading this book, there will be no confusion or surprises about the exam, and you'll have a great head start on the test-taking competition!

- Comprehensive AP® Exam review: This study guide will take you step-by-step through the entire AP® English Literature and Composition Exam, with a rigorous analysis of each section of the exam, along with helpful sample passages and questions that mirror those you'll encounter on test day.

- Effective strategies, tips, and advice from AP® experts: You'll be ready for anything on test day once you're equipped with the expert tools this book provides for crafting an unbeatable study and attack plan and achieving test success. The creators of this book know exactly what it takes to earn a top score on the AP® English Literature and Composition Exam—and now that knowledge is in your hands!

- Proven AP® Exam practice to build your test-taking skills: This book provides sample questions for every section and question type you're likely to encounter on test day, along with comprehensive answer explanations that will help you learn from your mistakes, build your skills, and get you in elite test-taking shape.

- Practice tests that mirror the actual exam: Chapters 5, 6, and 7 of this book are full-length practice exams with detailed answer explanations that look and feel just like the exam you'll take in May. In addition, this book gives you access to two online exams. You'll be more than ready to take the real thing after you've made your way through these practice tests and read over the detailed explanations for every answer choice.

We know how important doing well on this high-stakes exam is to you—and we're here to help. Rest assured, you've come to the right place to prepare for this exam and we are right here with you along this journey. The tools you need for test-day success are in the helpful pages that follow—so let's get started!

THE AP® ENGLISH LITERATURE AND COMPOSITION EXAM: AN OVERVIEW

It's perfectly natural if you're eager to skip over this chapter and get straight to the test prep—we completely understand! However, we suggest that you take some time to review the information here. Gaining a clear understanding of test fundamentals and of the structure and format of the AP® English Literature and Composition Exam is an important first step along your journey to exam success.

EXAM ESSENTIALS

Test Focus: This exam is designed to test your ability to effectively analyze prose and verse literary texts; to read critically and thoughtfully engage with questions involving issues of content, form, and style; and to compose written essay responses that analyze and interpret a variety of literary texts.

Length: 3 hours (with a break between Sections I and II of the exam)

Format: 2 sections

Section I (1 hour; 45 percent of your exam score): 55 multiple-choice questions

- You'll encounter a variety of published excerpts in prose fiction, poetry, and drama.

- Each excerpt will include a set of multiple-choice questions or prompts based on what you've just read.

- You'll be given an answer sheet to record your answers to the questions on this section of the exam.

Section II (2 hours; 55 percent of your exam score): 3 free-response questions

- You'll encounter 3 essay prompts and will be tasked with crafting written responses. Expect to encounter prompts based on the following:

  o A literary analysis of a prose fiction passage

  o A literary analysis of a poem

  o An analysis of a student-selected work of literature that examines a specific issue, element, or concept

- In this section of the exam, you will write your essay responses in the exam booklet.

Now that you know that you'll have 3 hours to complete the two sections that comprise the AP® English Literature and Composition Exam, we recommend that you devote some time between now and test day to get comfortable with the timing, in order to develop an effective test-taking pace.

A great way to do this is to take the practice tests in this book under simulated and timed test-like conditions and to get comfortable with completing each exam section in the time provided. You certainly don't want to be caught by surprise and hear "Time's up!" on test day before you've had the chance to finish!

AP® Exam Question Types—A Closer Look

Now you know that on exam day you'll be tasked with utilizing what you've learned throughout your academic year—along with the breadth and scope of knowledge you've acquired throughout your academic career—to demonstrate that you've successfully mastered the skills covered in your AP® course.

As mentioned, the exam consists of two sections—a multiple-choice section and a free-response section. Subsequent chapters will delve deeply into each section and will provide comprehensive review, practice, strategies, and advice for earning your best possible score on exam day. Here, we'll take a quick look at each question type, so you'll have a better idea of what to expect when you face the exam.

Section I—Multiple Choice

Section I of the exam will consist of 55 multiple-choice questions based on a variety of published excerpts in prose fiction, poetry, and drama. You may or may not recognize the passages and authors that you'll encounter on exam day; you'll have 60 minutes to complete this section and you'll need to use your critical reading and analytical abilities to full effect.

Answer All Multiple-Choice Questions!

Your score on the multiple-choice section of the AP® Exam will be based on the number of correct answers you provide.

This means that you should make *every effort* to answer each question on exam day. If you're stumped by a question, use effective strategies, including eliminating incorrect choices and educated guessing, in order to increase your chances of answering it correctly—and to increase your score!

Let's take a look at a sample passage and question:

I'm Nobody! Who are you?

I'm Nobody! Who are you?
Are you—Nobody—too?
Then there's a pair of us!
Don't tell! They'd advertise—you know!

How dreary—to be—Somebody!
How public—like a Frog—
To tell one's name—the livelong June—
To an admiring Bog!

—Emily Dickinson, 1830–1886

1. Which of the following lines from the poem is an effective example of the use of simile?
   A. I'm Nobody! Who are you?
   B. Then there's a pair of us!
   C. Don't tell! They'd advertise—you know!
   D. How public—like a Frog—
   E. To tell one's name—the livelong June—

This passage, a famous short lyric poem from Emily Dickinson that was published in 1891, highlights the challenges and emotions humans often face when feeling like an outsider. Dickinson employs a variety of literary techniques in this short piece of writing, including *simile*, which effectively compares two things using a connecting word such as *like*, *than*, or *as*. Were you able to recognize the example of simile among the answer choices? Choice D is the correct answer; it expresses Dickinson's feeling that being "Somebody," a public figure, would be dreary, like being a frog.

Use What You *Don't* Know!

Use the questions in this book—especially the ones you answer *incorrectly*—to help you focus and refine your study plan as you prepare for test day. Incorrect answers will help you determine the subject areas with which you need more practice. Make time in your study plan to address those weaknesses and build your skills!

Section II—Free Response

Section II of the exam will consist of 3 free-response questions. You'll have 2 hours to answer the 3 questions. You'll be presented 3 essay prompts that will assess your ability to effectively analyze various works of literature—either provided or student-selected.

Let's take a look at a sample prompt:

Question

(Suggested time—40 minutes. This question counts
as one-third of the total essay section score.)

Select a novel, play, or poem that features a significant character who is facing the challenge of achieving a clear sense of personal identity. Then construct an essay in which you analyze how the events that occur in the writing help shape how this character ultimately shapes and defines his or her sense of self. Do not merely summarize the plot.

You may choose a work from the list below or one of comparable literary merit.

1984	*The Great Gatsby*
A Portrait of the Artist as a Young Man	*I Know Why the Caged Bird Sings*
The Bluest Eye	*Invisible Man*
The Bell Jar	*Jane Austen*
The Brief and Wondrous Life of Oscar Wao	*Metamorphosis*
Catch-22	*Middlesex*
Crime and Punishment	*Moby Dick*
Dracula	*The Namesake*
For Whom the Bell Tolls	*The Stranger*
Frankenstein	*White Teeth*

Your written responses on the AP® English Literature and Composition Exam will be evaluated by expert exam readers for **content**, **style**, **organization**, and **mechanics**.

A high-scoring essay will offer an effective, well-constructed, and persuasive analysis of the literary selection, with a convincing point of view that thoughtfully considers a variety of relevant perspectives. Appropriate references and examples will be utilized to support the written piece. A mastery of English language usage and mechanics will be evident, and, overall, the piece will be well edited and largely free of errors.

Bottom line: Make sure your essay writing skills are *razor sharp*—which means practicing writing well-crafted essays as much as possible between now and test day.

Scoring

Your AP® English Literature and Composition Exam score is designed to reflect the knowledge you've acquired as a result of taking this college-level course and how well you can apply this knowledge to the questions you encounter on the exam. Your score will be a weighted combination of the scores you achieve on the two exam sections—the multiple-choice section and the free-response section—and will be based on the following 5-point scale:

> 1 = no recommendation
>
> 2 = possibly qualified
>
> 3 = qualified
>
> 4 = well qualified
>
> 5 = extremely well qualified

The multiple-choice questions in Section I of the exam will be machine scored, and your free-response essays in Section II will be scored by expert AP® Exam readers.

So, what exactly do these scores mean? The colleges you have decided to apply to, and to which you'll send your official AP® score, will use your score to determine whether or not you qualify for course credit and have achieved advanced placement—allowing you to skip over the equivalent college course.

Typically, a score of 3 or higher indicates that you have achieved a sufficient level for advanced placement and course credit consideration.

Earn an AP® Scholar Award!

The College Board and the AP® Program have created the AP® Scholar Awards in an effort to recognize talented students who have demonstrated exemplary levels of achievement by doing well in AP® courses and exams. For more information, visit the official AP® Exam website.

Register for a College Board account via the official website in order to access your score, which will only be available online. You'll also receive an email update regarding when you can access and review your score, typically in July of the year you take the exam.

Once you access your score report via your account, you'll have the option to view and send your score to the college indicated on your answer sheet. You can also select additional colleges to send your score report to, for a fee.

You will have several options for reporting your scores to the schools and scholarship programs you hope to pursue. In addition, each college has its own set of criteria for granting course credit and advanced placement. For a complete set of guidelines, options, and fees for score reporting and earning college credit, visit the official AP® website.

REGISTRATION ESSENTIALS FOR THE AP® ENGLISH LITERATURE AND COMPOSITION EXAM

We know that you're undoubtedly focused on making sure your English literature and test-taking skills are at peak form for test day. However, you also need to have a good handle on the test essentials—from registering to fees to what you can and cannot bring on test day and everything in between—in order to be fully prepared.

This section provides a comprehensive rundown of exactly what you need to know, so keep reading.

Registration

AP® Exams are typically administered in May each year. The 2018 exam date for the English Literature and Composition Exam is Wednesday, May 9.

Once you register for an AP® course at your school, it is the responsibility of your school's AP® exam coordinator to keep you informed regarding exam essentials and to notify you when and where to report for the official exam. Your AP® Exam coordinator is also responsible for collecting all exam fees and ordering the exams. He or she will also help with scheduling if you are planning to take multiple AP® Exams that are scheduled for the same time period.

Speak to your AP® Exam coordinator or visit the official AP® website for additional information if you have special circumstances that need to be addressed or accommodated, including a disability or if you are home schooled or are an international student.

Fees

The current basic fee for taking an AP® Exam in the United States is normally $94. There are options available for fee reductions and wavers, typically based on financial need.

To determine if you're eligible for a fee adjustment, contact your school's AP® coordinator. For a comprehensive list of fees, guidelines, and available options, please visit the official College Board website for AP® students.

AP® score reports are cumulative, which means that they will include all scores from every AP® Exam you've taken, unless you have specifically requested that one or more scores be withheld or canceled.

Currently, there is no limit to the number of AP® Exams you can take, and you are not required to take an AP® course prior to taking an AP® Exam—although it is strongly encouraged for test-day success.

GETTING READY FOR EXAM DAY

We know that after preparing diligently and making the most of this study guide you'll be totally ready to tackle every AP® test section and question. But this book doesn't just take you halfway along the journey to test-day success—we take you all the way. Knowing test-day fundamentals, including what to expect when you arrive for the exam, what to bring, and what to leave home, will help you avoid surprises, reduce anxiety, and stay ahead of the competition.

First Steps

Make sure you arrive for the test early, with plenty of time to spare in case there are any unforeseen delays. When you arrive on exam day, you'll be asked to review the policies and procedures regarding test security and administration—which include everything from maintaining exam integrity and good conduct to your right to have a fair and equal testing experience and more. You'll be asked to complete and sign your registration answer sheet, indicating that you have reviewed and agree to all of the AP® Exam policies and procedures.

Test-Day Checklist: What to Bring on Exam Day

Use this helpful checklist to know what you should bring with you on the day of your AP® English Literature and Composition Exam:

- Your AP® Student Pack, which you should receive from your AP® Exam coordinator
- A school-issue or government-issue photo ID (if you are taking the exam at a school you do not currently attend)
- Your Social Security card or Social Security number (used by some colleges as a primary student identification tool)
- A few sharpened No. 2 pencils, with erasers
- A few pens with dark blue or black ink
- A watch (optional)—not a smartwatch or a watch that beeps, makes noise, or has an alarm set to go off during the exam
- Your 6-digit school code
- If you've requested a specific testing accommodation, your SSD Student Accommodation Letter

What Not to Bring on Exam Day

Just as important as what you should bring on test day, here's a list of items that you should *not* bring to the test room, in order to avoid any issues or delays that could negatively impact your testing experience:

- A computer
- Books or reference materials of any kind
- Scratch paper or note paper

NOTE

On exam day, be sure to complete your registration answer sheet completely and accurately to avoid any potential score reporting delays! If you'd like to get a jumpstart and read the exam procedures before test day, visit the official College Board website for AP® Exams.

- Phones of any kind
- Portable listening devices or headphones
- Electronic equipment or recording devices of any kind
- Cameras or photographic equipment
- Any device that can access the Internet
- Food or drink of any kind
- Earplugs
- Smartwatches or watches that beep or have alarms
- Clothing with subject-related information
- Office supplies, including compasses, protractors, mechanical pencils, correction fluid, highlighters, or colored pencils

BUILDING AN EFFECTIVE STUDY PLAN

We know you're on the hunt for your best possible score on exam day, and we're here to help you develop an effective study plan for making that goal a reality.

Making sure that your writing skills are in peak form on exam day is essential—remember, the free-response essay section of the exam will count for 55 percent of your total exam score. Here are a few tips for making sure your writing skills are where they need to be:

- Practice: Make sure you practice writing persuasive essays on a wide variety of literary genres and texts. For most things in life—including writing—the best way to build your skills is through practice and repetition.

- Remember the fundamentals: Topics, focus, and points of view may vary, but some things that don't shift are the core tenets of essay writing—content, style, organization, and mechanics—on which the exam readers will be grading you. Make sure that your essay effectively delivers in all of these fundamental areas.

- Get feedback: It can be tough to judge the merits of your own writing. Your best approach as you practice for exam day is to have someone whose writing abilities you respect review and provide critical feedback on your work.

- Target your weak areas: As you practice for exam day, look critically at your writing and identify the areas that you need to focus on in order to get your writing skills in peak condition. Then, make sure your subsequent writing attempts address these weak areas—in an effort to eradicate them!

As a high-achieving student, you've likely had your fair share of successes during your academic career. You know which study habits work for you—and which don't—and you know the value of careful preparation for an important test. Make good use of this knowledge as you prepare for the exam.

Of course, your **critical-reading** and **analysis** skills also need to be strong for test day—these skills are essential for success on both sections of the exam. Here are a few tips for making sure your reading skills are where they need to be:

- Practice: Be sure to make time between now and exam day to practice reading a variety of literary texts thoughtfully and critically. As always, practice makes perfect.

- Pace yourself: Whether you're reading for pleasure or for a high-stakes exam, rushing through what you're reading only increases your chances of missing critical information. Between now and exam day, practice building an effective reading pace—one that lets you thoroughly and critically read and analyze passages similar to the practice passages you'll encounter in this book and on exam day—so that you can complete the exam before time runs out.

- Think it through: When you read a practice passage, always keep the "5 Ws and an H" in mind: who, what, where, when, why, and how. Think carefully about the intent and purpose of the piece and what the author is trying to convey. These critical questions will help you discern the core elements of the writing and successfully tackle any question on exam day.

AP® English Literature and Composition Test: *Not* a Cram Exam!

Doing well on this AP® Exam is *not* a race to memorize as many facts as possible between now and test day—especially since you won't know what passages and pieces of writing will appear until the day of the exam!

The exam is designed to test your ability to think critically, utilize your reading comprehension skills, and construct effective, targeted written responses.

Your *best* tools on exam day will be the knowledge and skills you've acquired throughout your academic career and during your AP® English Literature and Composition course.

You may have a fully fleshed out study plan already devised. However, if you'd like some guidance or are open to advice for constructing an effective plan of attack, we suggest the following possible strategies for using this book and making the most of the time you have between now and test day.

The Full-Review Strategy

This approach gives you an *equal* amount of time for each section of the exam, for comprehensive review and skill building. It also factors in time for you to do some independent reading and writing; keeping your brain and skills sharp by practicing reading and writing on a variety of subjects is excellent preparation for this exam.

- Step 1: List the number of days you have until test day: _____ days
- Step 2: Read this chapter thoroughly and carefully to learn the AP® English Literature and Composition Exam basics, including registration scoring, and to help you get comfortable with the general format of each test section.
- Step 3: Build your study plan. Divide the number of days you have to prepare equally between each of the two test sections, splitting that time (days or hours) between topic review and question/essay practice, using the chapters and practice tests in this book.

Multiple-Choice Section

Topic review: _____

Question practice: _____

Free-Response Section

Topic review: _____

Essay practice: _____

- Step 4: Factor in some time each day to do some independent reading and/or writing. After all, this is a test of your ability to read critically and write effectively, so getting as much practice as possible can only prove helpful! Consider breaking up the days of the week so that you'll have a few days for independent reading practice and a few days for independent writing practice. These independent review sessions can be as short as a few minutes or as long as you like, depending on how much time you have available and how much skill-building and practice you need.

  We suggest you practice with a variety of literature genres, from prose fiction to poetry and dramatic excerpts—and mix it up as much as possible to keep things interesting!

  Independent Reading Practice Days/Hours: _____

  Independent Writing Practice Days/Hours: _____

- Step 5: Structure your study calendar. Now that you know the number of days you have to devote to topic review and question practice for each section of the exam, take some time to fill in a study calendar so you'll know exactly what prep you'll be tackling each day between now and test day. Structure your calendar to suit your study style—devote each day to a single test section or divide your days so you can work on one section for a set number of hours and switch things up with the other test section—whatever keeps you interested, focused, and on track. Make sure to include independent reading and writing practice on your study schedule.

- Step 6: Adjust your study plan as needed. Remember, this is your study plan and no one knows what works best for you better than you do. As you work through your study calendar and as your test strengths and weaknesses shift, adjust your study plan accordingly.

The Weakness-Targeting Strategy

This approach lets you allocate the time you have between now and test day to target your weak areas and build your skills where you need to most.

- Step 1: List the number of days you have until test day: _____ days

- Step 2: Read this chapter thoroughly and carefully to learn the AP® English Literature and Composition Exam basics, including registration scoring, and to help you get comfortable with the general format of each test section.

- Step 3: Assess your strengths and weaknesses. Rank each test section based on your strengths and weaknesses. We recommend you use your class grades as a guide. Are you great at answering questions but struggle with essay writing? Is the reverse true? Rank the test sections accordingly, giving a 1 to your strongest section and a 2 to your weakest section.

Multiple-Choice Section: _____

Free-Response Section: _____

- Step 4: Build your study plan: Divide the number of days/hours you have to prepare among the test sections, splitting your time (days or hours) based on your rankings. You can divide your time however you see fit, as long as you're dedicating the majority of your time to improving your weak spots. One example for allocating your time is as follows:

  o 75 percent of your time for the section you ranked 2

  o 25 percent of your time for the section you ranked 1

  o Once you're comfortable with your initial study plan percentage allocations, fill in your initial number of study days for each test section.

  Multiple-Choice Section: _____

  Free-Response Section: _____

  o Now, decide how you want to divide your time for each section between *topic review* and *question/essay practice*. This should be based on your current skill set and needs.

  Multiple-Choice Section
  Topic review: _____
  Question practice: _____

  Free-Response Section
  Topic review: _____
  Essay practice: _____

- Step 5: Factor in some time each day to do some independent reading and/or writing. After all, this is a test of your ability to read critically and write effectively, so getting as much practice as possible can only prove helpful! We recommend that you devote your available time for independent reading and writing based on your current strengths and weaknesses. Of your available skill-building time, 75 percent should be used for your weaker of the two areas and 25 percent should be used for your stronger of the two areas.

  These independent review sessions can be as short as a few minutes or as long as you like, depending on how much time you have available and how much skill building and practice you need. We suggest you practice with a variety of literature genres, from prose fiction to poetry and dramatic excerpts—and mix it up as much as possible to keep things interesting!

  Independent Reading Practice Days/Hours: _____

  Independent Writing Practice Days/Hours: _____

- Step 6: Structure your study calendar. Now that you know the amount of time you have to devote to topic review and question practice for each section of the exam, take some time to fill in a study calendar so you'll know exactly what prep you'll be tackling each day between now and test day. Feel free to structure your calendar to suit your study style—devote each day to a single test section or divide your days so you can work on a section for a set number of hours and switch—whatever will keep you interested, focused, and on track!

- Step 7: Adjust your study plan as needed. Remember, this is your study plan and no one knows what works best for you better than you do. As you work through your study calendar and as your test strengths and weaknesses shift, adjust your study plan accordingly.

The Quick-Review Strategy

Perhaps you're short on time between now and test day—maybe you have just a few days—and need to make the most of them. This quick and efficient approach helps you make the most of the small amount of time you have left to earn your best possible exam score!

- Step 1: Quickly read this chapter to learn the AP® English Literature and Composition Exam basics. Don't spend too much time on it—you have some serious test preparation to get to!

- Step 2: Take and score the first practice test in this book. Carefully review the answer explanations for the questions you got wrong, making sure that you understand why you answered them incorrectly. Use your results to help gauge your strengths and weaknesses.

- Step 3. Review the book chapter material that focuses on the areas in which you are weakest, based on the results of your first practice test. Make careful use of the time that you have, spending time on the areas in which you most urgently need to build your skills.

- Step 4: Take and score the second practice test in this book. Carefully review the answer explanations for the questions you got wrong, making sure that you understand why you answered them incorrectly. Once again, use your results to help gauge your strengths and weaknesses. Hopefully, your list of weak areas is shorter this time!

- Step 5. Review the book chapter material that focuses on the areas in which you are weakest, based on the results you obtained on the second practice test. Make careful use of the time that you have, spending time on the areas in which you most urgently need to build your skills.

- Step 6: Take and score the third practice test in this book. Carefully review the answer explanations for the questions you got wrong, making sure that you understand why you answered them incorrectly. Once again, use your results to help gauge your strengths and weaknesses. Hopefully, your list of weak areas is now even shorter!

- Step 7. If time permits, review the book chapter material that focuses on the areas in which you are still showing weakness, based on the results of your third practice test. Make careful use of the time that you have left, spending time on the areas in which you most urgently need to build your skills.

- Step 8. Once again, if time permits, factor in some time each day to do some independent reading and/or writing. It's a great way to build your skills and get your mind sharp for exam day!

A Note for Parents and Guardians

If you're the parent or guardian of a student who is planning to take the AP® English Literature and Composition Exam, your support and encouragement can go a long way toward test-day success!

Help your student stay on track and focused with his or her study plan between now and test day, and make sure that his or her needs for effective test preparation are well met!

The path to a great score on the AP® English Literature and Composition Exam is *not* an easy one. The knowledge and skills you've obtained in your AP® course will be fully put to the test and will need to be razor sharp on exam day. That's where this book comes in!

Consider this your indispensable guide along your test-preparation journey. It includes a comprehensive review of the most frequently tested concepts on the exam and helpful practice for all of the question types you can expect to encounter. Make the most of the resources in the following pages as you craft your study plan and move closer toward achieving an excellent score.

Best of luck!

SUMMING IT UP

- The AP® English Literature and Composition Exam tests your ability to analyze literary texts; read critically and answer questions on content, form, and style; and compose essay responses that analyze and interpret literary texts.

- Section I of the exam is comprised of 55 multiple-choice questions about published excerpts in prose fiction, poetry, and drama. This section lasts 1 hour and makes up 45 percent of your exam score.

- Section II is comprised of 3 free-response questions. Expect to face prompts that require you to analyze a prose fiction passage, a poem, and a work of literature of your choice. This section lasts 2 hours and makes up 55 percent of your exam score.

- The complete AP® English Literature and Composition Exam is 3 hours long, with a break between Sections I and II.

- Take the practice tests in this book and online under simulated and timed test-like conditions to become comfortable with the pacing of the exam.

- Your score on Section I of the exam is only based on the number of correct answers you earn. Answer every question on exam day—you will not lose points for incorrect answers.

- Your written responses in Section II will be evaluated by expert AP® Exam readers for content, style, organization, and mechanics. The highest-scoring essays present a well-constructed, persuasive analysis of the given prompt, with a clear point of view that offers a variety of perspectives.

- Your final score will be a weighted combination of your scores on Section I and Section II and will be based on a 5-point scale:
  o 1 = no recommendation
  o 2 = possibly qualified
  o 3 = qualified
  o 4 = well qualified
  o 5 = extremely well qualified

- Each college has its own set of criteria for granting course credit. For a complete set of guidelines, options, and fees for score reporting and earning college credit, visit the official AP® website.

- The 2018 exam date for the English Literature and Composition Exam is Wednesday, May 9.

- Your AP® Exam coordinator will collect all exam fees and order your exams. He or she will also help with scheduling if you are planning to take multiple AP® Exams that are scheduled for the same time period.

- Arrive early on test day. Make sure to complete your registration answer sheet completely and accurately to avoid any potential score reporting delays.

- Make sure your writing, reading, and critical analysis skills are in peak form on exam day. Practice writing persuasive essays on a wide variety of literary genres and texts, and make time to practice reading a variety of literary texts. Target your weak areas as the main focus of your study plan.

PART II
AP® ENGLISH LITERATURE AND COMPOSITION EXAM STRATEGIES

CHAPTER 2   Poetry Questions on the AP® Literature and Composition Exam

CHAPTER 3   Prose Questions on the AP® Literature and Composition Exam

CHAPTER 4   Free-Response Questions on the AP® Literature and Composition Exam

Poetry Questions on the AP® Literature and Composition Exam

OVERVIEW

- **Format of the Multiple-Choice Section**
- **How to Read a Poem on the AP® Exam**
- **Elements of Poems**
- **Classifying Poems into Genres**
- **Sound and Rhyme**
- **Language, Word Choice, and Diction**
- **Poetry by the Century**
- **Practice Sets**
- **Sample Passage 1**
- **Sample Passage 2**
- **Answer Key and Explanations**
- **Summing It Up**

"What is poetry?" is a gigantic question, one that has been puzzled over by countless poets (and their readers, sometimes with much befuddlement) over the centuries. It is not a question that the College Board is asking you to answer in a 1-hour multiple-choice exam. You have a much more defined task: demonstrate that you can read and analyze poems and answer multiple-choice questions about how their language, formal features, and other literary qualities help you understand their meaning. This chapter cannot answer the grand question, but it can give you some tools for reading and analyzing the kinds of poems you'll find on the exam and answering the kinds of questions you'll encounter.

Because the exam has a limited purview, its definition of poetry is restricted to something more manageable: poems in English, written during or after the seventeenth century, which are short enough and self-contained enough to fit on an exam without the need for historical context, elaborate footnotes, or other kinds of explanatory information. They do not count lyrics from popular songs from the twentieth century as poetry, even if you could make the case for the high quality of wordplay, witty rhymes, or important themes. They do not use poems that break the bounds of formatting on the printed page or contain other kinds of media. They are not trying to trick you by hiding secret meanings in the poems—if there's a deeper meaning to the poem, the questions will proceed in such a way that you have the information to analyze it.

FORMAT OF THE MULTIPLE-CHOICE SECTION

In Section I of the AP® English Literature and Composition Exam, you will answer 55 multiple-choice questions in 1 hour. This section is worth 45 percent of your total score.

Here is the key information to keep in mind.

SECTION I ESSENTIALS

You have 1 hour to complete this section.

- You will answer sets of multiple-choice questions.
- Each set is based on a published work of drama, poetry, or prose fiction.

This chapter will give you tips about how read a poem on the exam and understand the kinds of questions the exam asks about a poem's structure, style, tone, diction, and themes. Even when those questions ask you to make inferences, the format of the question will be familiar to you so that you can feel confident in your interpretations. We will explain some of the basic building blocks of poetry and how to analyze these features, and then we will walk you through some important movements in Anglophone (English-speaking, mostly British and American) poetry over the past four centuries. In these overviews, we will explain some important literary concepts, identify a few important poets, and recommend some of their poems that best illustrate those formal features and concepts associated with the movements.

Continuing Your Studies Beyond This Chapter

It's important to remember that these are overviews; they are not a substitute for reading the poems themselves or for taking the initiative to read related poems you find by studying these concepts on your own. The College Board website provides a list of most frequently included poetry and prose authors that it recommends AP® English Literature and Composition teachers consult in making a syllabus, and you are welcome to consult it, too. That list of about fifty names is not a guarantee or a prediction that those poets will be on the exam, nor does it mean that other poets won't be on the exam. Likewise, the recommended poems in this book are good illustrations of important concepts, but they're intended for you to study so you can recognize the concepts. The concepts may take different shapes in different poems, across different periods.

When you take the exam, it may be the case that one of these recommended poems shows up and you've devised some sample questions about it over the course of your studying. That would be serendipitous!

If that doesn't happen, but you still recognize a concept like "the sublime" or a feature like "the heroic couplet," you'll still have a good start because you've read similar poems and practiced analyzing them. Indeed, the practice tests contain examples of poets who are similar to those mentioned in

TIP

You can't study every poem by the recommended authors in hopes that one will show up on the exam. Instead, study concepts and formal features, so that you can recognize them even when you aren't familiar with the poem or poet.

the book, but they may be slightly less familiar to you. This chapter gives you strategies for reading the poem if you recognize the author, genre, or historical period. There are also ways to answer the exam's questions about the smaller building blocks, such as rhyme or diction, so that you can gain confidence in interpreting the poem by letting the exam guide you through its questions and answer choices that will give you some analytical language that may start to look familiar. As you practice with poems from our recommendations, you'll develop familiarity with the terminology and also interpretation strategies that work best for you.

HOW TO READ A POEM ON THE AP® EXAM

First, read the poem all the way through. Underline any words or phrases that seem unfamiliar to you, but don't panic about them. You may be able to come back to them and figure out some clues from context, or you may realize that one unknown word isn't a big deal because you've found the more important elements. On this first read, just try to understand the basic idea of the poem.

Then, read the poem again, noting the places where that basic idea appears in the language and structure of the poem.

On this second read-through:

Pay more attention to...	Don't get hung up on...
Genre of poem (sonnet, ode, free verse; if you don't know the exact name, identify how many stanzas it has, its basic rhyme scheme)	The poet's intention in writing the poem
Who is the speaker and is that speaker addressing anyone in particular? (This question may help you figure out the type of poem.)	Any possible hidden meanings
Diction (Does the speaker use simple or complex, multi-syllabic words?)	One word you don't understand
Repeated words, metaphors, images—anything that seems to form a pattern	A single obscure symbol that you don't understand—the questions in the exam will likely give you some help in figuring it out
Punctuation in the sentences of the poem, not the line breaks	The meaning of a single line
Tensions that recur throughout the poem	The poet's intention

Intention vs. Meaning

Note that we've repeated the warning to set aside the poet's intentions on these initial readings. You may ask: aren't you asking for the meaning of the poem? Who else but the poet is the expert on what they meant to say? Here, there's a distinction to be made between *intention* and *meaning*. Intention seeks to discover what was going on in the poet's head during composition, but those thoughts may

NOTE

A note on our terminology: We will be referring to "features" and "elements" of poems as the building blocks for interpreting poems. A feature is a word choice, a rhyme, a metaphor, or some other element of the poem that helps convey its meaning. Feature and element are mostly interchangeable here; we'll move on to identifying specific devices in subsequent pages.

be different from the actual language that appears on the page. On the other hand, you can interpret the meaning of language and other poetic features on your own, without asking the poet. When you ask about intention, you're asking the poet "*why did you do that?*" and he may not be able to answer because he was born four centuries ago, doesn't remember, or doesn't have a direct answer. When you look for meaning, you're asking the poem, "*How does this element work in the poem?*" For instance, you may be seeking to discover the following:

> **How** *does this rhyme scheme work? The poet has a regular couplet rhyme scheme in this sonnet, but the last two lines have a half-rhyme that doesn't fit as it conventionally would. The final couplet of a sonnet is usually a formal element that emphasizes resolution and unity, but here it's not doing that. I can't ask the poet why (or if it's just poetic license), but I can infer that this change from the sonnet's usual conventions is important.* **How** *does this irregularity let me see other signals that something is amiss in the poem? What other fractures in the poem do I see when I start looking for a* **pattern** *of slightly altered conventions?*

> **How** *does this word choice work in this line? It seems too lofty and elevated for the simpler language that the speaker is using—what does it reveal about the speaker's aspirations or inner conflicts about how to behave in a society that shuns him? Does it show some* **ambiguity** *in how the speaker wants to belong and use that fancy language, while staying true to the speaker's humbler background? In the next line, the speaker returns to simpler language, so he hasn't made a definite choice, and I should keep looking for* **patterns** *of this inner conflict...*

Your interpretation will be a good one if it helps you make sense of other elements in the poem to find patterns or larger themes. The exam questions will keep you focused on justifying your interpretations by looking at how small elements of the poem fit together; the exam builders want you to *focus on the poem itself*, what you can see on the page, rather than on the poet's intentions that you can't see on the page.

In the multiple-choice questions, you may be asked to make inferences, but that's not the same as intuiting the poet's beliefs, finding secret meanings, or guessing. Inferences will always be backed up by elements of the poem: with inference questions, the exam is testing how well you can test and assess the value of interpretations. There will often be an answer choice or two that pushes way beyond what's on the page: you can be conservative and stick with answers that you can back up with features you've identified in the poem itself.

Questions Will Help You Read the Poem

The questions on the exam will tell you what to look for, so you should use them: being pointed to a metaphor or being asked the meaning of a specific word will often help you orient yourself, enabling you to find other related elements to guide your reading. Likewise, the answer choices will often give you some of the analytical language that's right on the tip of your tongue. There are often red herrings, or choices that are too good to be true, but you can often find patterns of interpretation among multiple questions and answer choices, which may help you get some idea of what you're supposed to be looking for.

TIP

Don't try to come up with elaborate secret intentions for the poet or get bogged down in endless ambiguities. (This is especially tempting in Romantic poetry, for some reason.) The goal is to answer the exam questions, not to discover a totally original, mind-blowing interpretation.

Throughout this chapter, we've identified and tagged the following categories of questions you will see on test day:

- MAIN IDEA questions: test your knowledge of the central meaning of the poem

- THEME questions: test your knowledge of the larger meaning and significance of the poem

- STRUCTURE questions: test your knowledge of how a poem is organized as a genre, including but not limited to its use of stanzas, meter, and rhyme scheme. Not all poems contain all of these elements, and there are still elements of structure in blank verse (without rhymes) or free verse (without a regular meter)

- STYLE questions: test your knowledge of the language the poet uses to convey meaning in the poem, including the use of poetic devices

- TONE questions: test your knowledge of the speaker's attitude toward the poem or characters in the poem (we will discuss some possible ways to distinguish style and tone later in the chapter)

- DETAIL questions: ask you to find nuances in the poem or check to make sure you understand less obvious ideas

- VOCABULARY-IN-CONTEXT questions: test your ability to define unfamiliar words (or to use information from the poem to help you define them)

- INFERENCE questions: ask you to interpret nuances, complexities, or other information that is not directly given to you on the page but which you can answer using ideas from prior questions

Some questions may be direct; for instance, they may use the word "infer" or "tone," while others will get at the main ideas or themes indirectly. Some questions may contain elements of structural devices and stylistic devices—it's common, for example, for questions about rhyme to call your attention to the structure of a line but also the word choice that makes the rhyme. These tagged questions are for your benefit in studying: if you know you struggle with making inferences, pay attention to how those questions are phrased in the chapter and on the practice exams, and then work on devising your own versions of inference questions. They become easier when you practice answering them, to be sure, but formulating your own questions helps you internalize how and why these questions are framed the way they are, and they make you more flexible in dealing with them.

Minding Your Time

You have to answer 55 questions in 1 hour, which already makes the test a bit of a race, and you also have to read unfamiliar language. From your own practice, you know whether it takes you more time to read a long passage of prose or a shorter passage of less familiar language in the poetry sections. In either case, you'll want to spend most of your time working through the questions, because they can help you read the passage strategically so that you make the most of your time.

Here's an example poetry passage, with some tips on how to manage your time as you're reading an unfamiliar poem and preparing to answer multiple-choice questions. We recommend you do two initial quick read-throughs that may take about 4 minutes tops—you don't need to annotate these multiple-choice passages like you would if you were writing an essay, but you should make a few notes about unfamiliar words or phrases or moments that jump out at you as seeming especially important for understanding the main idea of the poem. In these initial minutes when you're making sense of it, we recommend reading the poem in sentence form, so that you're pretending there are no line breaks and you're taking your cues from the punctuation, the way you would in reading a prose sentence.

If you can't find that main idea on these quick reads, don't worry. You can look down at the first two or three questions to see what they're asking, and they may help you find some keywords repeated that might help you get your bearings.

Okay, set your timer and spend no more than 4 minutes reading this passage twice.

NOTE

Fun fact: the name of the poem and the title character are pronounced Don Joo-an, so the rhyme will work.

From Canto 11 of *Don Juan*, by George Gordon, Lord Byron

VIII
Don Juan had got out on Shooter's Hill;
      Sunset the time, the place the same declivity
Which looks along that vale of good and ill
      Where London streets ferment in full activity,
While everything around was calm and still,
      Except the creak of wheels, which on their pivot he
Heard, and that bee-like, bubbling, busy hum
Of cities, that boil over with their scum—

IX
I say, Don Juan, wrapp'd in contemplation,
      Walk'd on behind his carriage, o'er the summit,
And lost in wonder of so great a nation,
      Gave way to't, since he could not overcome it.
"And here," he cried, "is Freedom's chosen station;
      Here peals the People's voice nor can entomb it
Racks, prisons, inquisitions; resurrection
Awaits it, each new meeting or election.

X
"Here are chaste wives, pure lives; here people pay
      But what they please; and if that things be dear,
'Tis only that they love to throw away
      Their cash, to show how much they have a-year.
Here laws are all inviolate; none lay
      Traps for the traveller; every highway's clear;
Here—he was interrupted by a knife,
With—"Damn your eyes! your money or your life!"

Line

5

10

15

20

First, let's underline the unknowns or confusing parts: There are a few confusing words just in the first stanza here, like *declivity* and *vale*. You may find some others that trouble you as well.

As you're reading in sentence form, you'll see that the first sentence doesn't end until the middle of stanza IX and has a lot of semicolons and commas. It frequently runs over the line breaks, and you may have gotten annoyed at how long it takes Byron to finish his sentences. This annoyance is a great pattern to pick out! It's getting you immersed in the poet's stylistic elements, as you're paying attention to the long rhythms of the sentence, the lofty word choice, and the exalted tone to describe Don Juan's perspective on London as he arrives.

Here are some sample questions that pick up on those observations from the initial read-throughs. Because they deal with the first stanza of the poem, they appear first on the exam, right next to or under the poem. If you're stumped about the poem, look at what the questions are asking you.

1. When Don Juan is at the "declivity" in line 2, what is he doing?
   A. Looking up at the hilltop
   B. Looking down at the city
   C. Buying supplies at the store outside of the city
   D. Cursing his bad fortune at getting lost
   E. Asking directions from the local constable

2. Byron uses all of the following devices to set the London scene EXCEPT
   A. alliteration to give a sense of the bustle.
   B. metaphor of a simmering tureen full of activity that's about to spill over.
   C. apostrophe to address the king as though he were standing with him.
   D. enjambed lines and over-full sentences to give a sense of the overfull city.
   E. consonance in the v-sounds of line 21-23 to show his desire to orate for an imagined audience.

Answers and Explanations

1. So, yes, you were asked about the word you didn't know: this is obviously a vocabulary question. Even if you were stumped by the choices, you could see that the next question asks you about London and the stylistic devices that make up Don Juan's perspective on the city. With these two pieces of information, you could probably discern that he's near a city, and he has a perspective on it that allows him to see a lot. He's also looking at the sunset, so you could probably infer that he's looking down at London, even if you still weren't sure what that word meant. "Declivity" means slope or decline, so Don Juan is looking down at the setting sun over the city. **Choice B is correct.**

2. This question about poetic devices—the *style* of the poem—is asking you to find the *exception* among several good options. Four of the poetic devices in the poem are present, and the description of each one gives you a sense that these questions are pointing you to the *main idea* of the poem: this is a satire of London, and it's not clear whether the hero Don Juan is in on the satire yet. Noticing the long, winding sentence structures in the first and second stanzas paid off, even if you weren't sure what *enjambment* means. Enjambed lines are phrases that spill over a line into the next one without punctuation or an appropriate pause, as happens in line 6 with "pivot he" here. They aren't mistakes: they convey the sense that the idea can't be contained in the metrical structure or the rhyme of the poem. Apostrophe (an address to an absent person or a personified object) is the only choice among the answers that doesn't appear in the stanzas, although Don Juan does make a gesture toward government. **Choice C is correct.**

How much time did you spend on those first two questions? Track the time that you spend on each passage of prose or poetry, aiming to spend about 13 minutes on each one. That means you have less than a minute per question. If you're really not sure about a question, move on and read the next one; it can often give you some clues and aid in finding the main ideas. That information in the phrasing of the questions goes into your "known information" bank that you can use to give yourself context for understanding what you don't know. Don't rest on that bank, though, because you have a long race ahead of you.

Let's look back at some of your known elements and see how they help you with the rest of the questions. You know the title, and you know some basic information about the poem. The title tells you that there are numerous cantos and stanzas within the poem, which is often an indicator of a narrative poem because they tend to be long and organized into these formulaic structures. Oh, look, question 5 even gives you the name for it—that's nice, except it probably means they want you to do something with that info, like interpret how that stylistic, structural element relates to the larger theme of the poem. Question 5 also identifies that the poem is satirical, which might help you answer some questions about Don Juan's role in Question 3 (or it might mislead you into picking choice B for question 4, and confusing speaker and main character).

3. Don Juan plays what role in the poem?
   A. Narrator
   B. Main character
   C. Speaker
   D. Anti-hero
   E. Authorial stand-in

4. How would you describe Don Juan's tone in stanzas IX–X?
   A. Grandiose and idealistic
   B. Witty and satirical
   C. Sneering and contemptuous
   D. Naïve and fearful
   E. Oblivious and mean-spirited

5. What is the best explanation for how the complex structure of the *ottava rima* stanza structure (*abababcc*) assists in conveying the satirical qualities of the poem?
   A. The rhymes distort Don Juan's perspective so that he doesn't see the world around him.
   B. The meter allows Don Juan to be verbose and imagine things that aren't there.
   C. Narrating his vision for London in the elaborate rhyme and meter distracts him from the world around him.

D. The Italian structure exposes all of the faults of English perspective on their capital city.
E. The half-rhymes show that Don Juan is not the skilled orator that he thinks he is.

6. What do you infer is the speaker's attitude toward slant rhymes like "pivot he" (line 6) "entomb it" (line 14)?

   I. Satirical glee at getting to make such ridiculous rhymes in the narration of Don Juan's adventures

   II. Eye-rolling at Don Juan's own pompous language to narrate his own adventures

   III. Rivalry with Don Juan in a race to make the most belabored rhymes

   A. I only
   B. III only
   C. I and II
   D. II and III
   E. I, II, and III

Answers and Explanations

3. Don Juan is not the narrator (which is more commonly used for prose) or the speaker (the name for the narrator of a poem) but the main character of this narrative poem. **Choice B is correct.** This question is just to make sure that you have the terminology and the details of his role correct.

4. The previous question asked you about Don Juan's role, as a kind of implicit warning not to mix up Don Juan and the author nor Don Juan and the speaker. The speaker has a scathing, satirical view of London's filth and grime, as we saw in question 2. Don Juan, on the other hand, is described by the speaker as "lost in wonder of so great a nation," where he sees an idealistic vision of cooperation and egalitarianism. Don't mix up Byron's and the speaker's satirical perspectives with Don Juan's obliviousness. This question is asking you about Don Juan's *tone*—not the speaker's tone or Byron's style in conveying Don Juan's limited perspective. **Choice A is correct.** Byron will keep both you and Don Juan on your toes, for in his idealism, he gets interrupted by a knife-wielding robber—the very bad behavior that he believed was absent from the city.

5. This question doesn't ask you to identify a special structural element—it does that for you, meaning that it's up to you to interpret how that *structural* element helps convey the *theme* of the Don Juan's constant blundering in his pomposity and blinkered perspective. We don't know him that well yet, but we can guess that this is not an isolated incident: the satirical distortion of his belief in himself as an idealistic hero seems like it affects every stanza it touches. Choices A, B, and

E have elements of correct assessments of Don Juan's perspective, but the best answer is the most specific one that has the clearest tie between that structural element and the way it conveys its thematic meaning. **Choice C is correct.**

6. This question asks you to make an *inference* about the speaker's attitude, which we can infer by considering the speaker's *tone* and by looking at the use of a structural element in the speaker's narration in those slant rhymes. This question is asking you to pull together a lot of different evidence to make the inference: draw a connection between the speaker's tone and Byron's own probable delight in constructing such weird rhymes as structural elements of the *ottava rima*. This inference question gives you three options and asks you to pick the most appropriate combination of options. These options have to agree with, not contradict, each other. Options I and II fit with what we've been seeing in other questions, so the puzzle remains: should we infer that there's jealousy at who gets to be the more ridiculous rhymer? We don't have any evidence of Don Juan's bad rhymes from his quoted material—there may be some doozies in the very next canto, but in this passage Don Juan has a regular rhyme and meter. Even though he's wrong, pompous, and threatened with a knife, he's not a bad rhymer here. Likewise, we don't get a sense of jealousy—just satirical glee—from the speaker in these three cantos. Option III makes too big of a leap, so it can be discarded. That leaves us Options I and II, so the **correct answer is C.**

We've asked only six sample questions about structure, themes, style, tone, main idea, vocabulary in context, details, and inference so far, but don't worry. There are many more sample questions embedded in the overview of the elements of poetry, linked to poems that you can read as examples—but for which you can also generate your *own* sample questions. Generating these sample questions gets you thinking about analyzing the poetry, but it also gets you thinking about the genres of questions and the conventions they might have. In just a few pages, you'll be reading about genres of poems and how you can identify their poetic conventions in structure or style, but it's appropriate here to think about the questions themselves as having genres and conventions that you can identify through practice and generating your own.

ELEMENTS OF POEMS

Let's start with the foundational elements of the poem: syllables, lines, stanzas. The syllable word is the smallest element of the poem: it seems obvious to say that it combines with other syllables to form words, those words join other words in lines and sentences, and those lines form stanzas.

Those repetitions of small syllables give a poem a sense of sound and structure, in rhyme (if it has one) and meter (if it has a regular meter). A poetic foot is a basic unit of meter in poetry that is composed of two or more stressed and unstressed syllables. When applied correctly, poetic feet create rhythm and meter in a poem.

Types of Poetic Feet	
Iamb unstressed-stressed syllables da-DA	be-FORE to-NIGHT
trochee stressed-unstressed syllables DA-da	NEV-er SAD-ly
anapest unstressed-unstressed-stressed syllables da-da-DA	un-der-STAND in-com-PLETE
dactyl stressed-unstressed-unstressed syllables DA-da-da	FLA-vor-ful HAPP-i-ness
spondee unstressed-unstressed syllables da-da	down-town faith-ful

These feet can be repeated to form "perfect" patterns, but they can also be used to change up a line's rhythm: a trochee might show someone being wrong-footed or emphasizing a word for extra emphasis. These feet can also be repeated in lines to form metrical patterns.

The lines are identified by how many feet are present. Iambic pentameter contains five iambs (pent- means five, like *pentagon*); iambic tetrameter contains only four iambs (tetra- means four, like *tetrahedron*). You can have monometer, dimeter, trimeter… up through hexameter, heptameter, octameter, nonometer, and decameter.

The most common types of meter are used in poems to signal different moods and tones:

Iambic pentameter is used in many regular poetic forms like sonnets and Shakespearean monologues. It emphasizes order and resolution to each idea, as the line proceeds in an orderly fashion, with no extra words or syllables.	"If music be the food of love, play on; Give me excess of it, that, surfeiting," (Shakespeare, Prologue to *Twelfth Night*)
Iambic tetrameter and **trimeter** are used in ballad forms: when these lines of four and three iambs are alternated, they're called ballad meter or common meter.	"Because I could not stop for Death, He kindly stopped for me; The Carriage held but just Ourselves And Immortality." (Emily Dickinson, "Because I Could Not Stop for Death")
Dactylic dimeter can be propulsive: in the opening lines like "HALF a league, HALF a league…" but it can't be sustained or it starts to sound distorted. Eventually, they need to be balanced by extra syllables: "ALL in the VALLey of DEATH."	"Half a league, half a league, Half a league onward, All in the valley of Death Rode the six hundred." (Alfred, Lord Tennyson, "The Charge of the Light Brigade")
Anapestic tetrameter can sound like galloping horses: ba da DA ba da DA. They can impart a sense of urgency or dread. Like their reverse feet, the dactyls, they can be hard to sustain or they start to sound too sing-songy. Lord Byron used the meter in his poem about the invasion of Jerusalem, "The Destruction of Sennacherib": "The asSYRian CAME down like the WOLF on the FOLD, And his COhorts were GLEAMing in PURple and GOLD…" (This is the most famous example of sustained anapestic tetrameter in English—only Byron wanted to take the repetitive sound and turn it into an ominous feature.)	"The Assyrian came down like the wolf on the fold, And his cohorts were gleaming in purple and gold; And the sheen of their spears was like stars on the sea, When the blue wave rolls nightly on deep Galilee." ("The Destruction of Sennacherib," by George Gordon, Lord Byron)

There are many other combinations of feet and meter, but it's most likely that you'll see iambs in regular meter, with a few anapests and dactyls that might be used to unsettle the sense of regularity. The study of the rhythm and meter is called **scansion**, so you might see a question that asks you to consider the scansion of a poem and you'll know you're looking for these rhythmic elements. You'll rarely be asked to identify anything really strange, and what's most important is how you interpret these meters—more than how you might identify them. The correct answer will always be present, so you won't be making up any innovative poetic feet or meters for the exam.

Lines are then organized into stanzas:

- Two lines: a couplet, often used at the ends of poems to signal closure
- Three lines: a tercet, often found in villanelles
- Four lines: a quatrain, a common building block of many types of poems
- Five lines: a cinquain
- Six lines: a sestet, the crucial ending stanza to an Italian or Petrarchan sonnet
- Seven lines: a septet
- Eight lines: an octet, the crucial opening stanza to an Italian or Petrarchan sonnet

CLASSIFYING POEMS INTO GENRES

A genre is a classification of poem. Genres are defined by conventions, or poetic elements that you expect to see. These expectations help readers find meanings in poems when there are conventions that are missing or askew, they help the reader ask pointed questions about the purpose of those differences: *How does this poem differ from the others in the genre? How does this difference let me understand the meaning of this particular poem?*

Here are some of the main genres of poems on the exam, with their conventions and some illustrative examples.

Lyric Poetry

Lyric poetry is the general name for poetry used to express a speaker's emotions or inner thoughts; many specific genres (such as sonnets, elegies, odes, villanelles) are subsets of lyric poetry.

Because lyric poems are about an individual speaker's emotions and personal outlook, you'll want to pay attention to how that emotional outlook is expressed in word choice, style, and use of figurative language. You'll also want to look closely at the rhyme and meter and any irregularities that seem to be relevant to the content of the poem. Sometimes those irregularities might be just part of the poet's style, but it may be something to watch out for in the questions.

Because lyric poetry is such a broad category, it can often be a place to compare poets who work in the lyric tradition but who have very different styles. So, you might see a comparative question about how two different poets wrote lyrics about the nightingale. (These are just the opening stanzas to serve as examples; you would receive the full poems on the exam because these are not that long):

"Ode to a Nightingale," by John Keats

My heart aches, and a drowsy numbness pains
    My sense, as though of hemlock I had drunk,
Or emptied some dull opiate to the drains
Line   One minute past, and Lethe-wards had sunk:
5   'Tis not through envy of thy happy lot,
        But being too happy in thine happiness,—
            That thou, light-winged Dryad of the trees
                In some melodious plot
    Of beechen green, and shadows numberless,
10   Singest of summer in full-throated ease.

O, for a draught of vintage! that hath been
        Cool'd a long age in the deep-delved earth,
Tasting of Flora and the country green,
        Dance, and Provençal song, and sunburnt mirth!
15 O for a beaker full of the warm South,
        Full of the true, the blushful Hippocrene,
            With beaded bubbles winking at the brim,
                And purple-stained mouth;
    That I might drink, and leave the world unseen,
20   And with thee fade away into the forest dim:

"Philomela," by Matthew Arnold

Hark! ah, the nightingale—
The tawny-throated!
Hark, from that moonlit cedar what a burst!
Line   What triumph! hark!—what pain!

5   O wanderer from a Grecian shore,
    Still, after many years, in distant lands,
    Still nourishing in thy bewilder'd brain
    That wild, unquench'd, deep-sunken, old-world pain—

    Say, will it never heal?
10 And can this fragrant lawn
    With its cool trees, and night,
    And the sweet, tranquil Thames,
    And moonshine, and the dew,
    To thy rack'd heart and brain
15 Afford no balm?

We won't go through an in-depth analysis of the two poems, but here are some sample questions that make you consider the differing structural elements of the two poems.

First, a sample question about theme and tone:

> Keats's speaker mentions disorientation multiple times in the first four lines of the poem, yet the rhyme structure and meter are perfectly regular. Where do you see elements of diction that may signal disorientation?
>
> **A.** The repetition of happy and happiness in lines 5-6 that shows him protesting too much that he is not envious of the nightingale's song.
>
> **B.** There are missing poetic feet in line 8, which is only three iambs long (instead of five).
>
> **C.** His inability to count the shadows in line 10 shows that he is not observant.
>
> **D.** He says he is unhappy and wants to die in line 19, signaling the poet's extreme depression.
>
> **E.** The word "plot" in line 8 shows that he is paranoid about the bird stealing his glory.

The repetition of happy and happiness in lines 5-6 shows him protesting too much that he is not envious of the bird, so the correct answer to the question is A. This exaggerated denial sets up a productive tension between the poet and his subject: who will have the better song? Which forms a better song: a poet's highly crafted language, with extended metaphors of intoxication and detailed allusions to Greek mythology, or a bird's mysterious call? The question asks you to pay attention to one example of diction, so that you might see the ways that Keats is locked into using every single one of his poetic devices to pay tribute to (or compete with) the nightingale.

It's worth looking at the wrong answers, too. Choice B calls your attention to meter, not the diction asked for in the question, so it's leading you astray. You can also test whether that line has the "wrong" meter by looking at whether there's a pattern in the rest of the poem: the eighth line of each stanza contains only six syllables, or three iambs, while the other lines are in iambic pentameter. So it's not a mistake—it's part of Keats' regular conventions for writing odes. Choices C, D, and E all make inferences that are not supported by the poem: they read too much of a hidden meaning to say that he's paranoid, incorrect, or depressed, and those readings are not supported by the rest of the poem—which is an ode praising the bird and shows him indulging deeply in its song, not becoming despondent. These answers may be tempting interpretations, but A is the best choice because it creates a pattern that you can find in the rest of the poem: that he is constantly comparing the songs in positive ways and trying his best to show the human gifts of poetry that might praise (and compete with) the nightingale's lyrics.

Next, a sample question about style:

> Matthew Arnold uses what poetic device to address the nightingale directly in "Philomela": "O wanderer from a Grecian shore…"?
>
> **A.** Archetype
>
> **B.** Apostrophe
>
> **C.** Ellipsis
>
> **D.** Rhetorical question
>
> **E.** Hyperbole

It's relatively common to see an address to O [person] or [object] in a lyric poem as a means of showing the speaker's desire for an immediate connection with the object of his attention. Whether that immediacy is possible is a source of much tension in this poem, because he has already shown that the connection is ruptured somehow and full of pain. The exam is asking you this basic structural question about an obvious device so that you can start to see the ways that there are irregularities in who gets to ask and answer all of the rhetorical questions being addressed in the poem. Choice D is tempting because of all of the rhetorical questions in subsequent lines, but this question is asking you about the use of "O" in line 5. This sample question has a factual answer: if you know that O is a signal of apostrophe, you've got it. The correct answer is B.

Let's frame a question that asks you to make an inference about the use of the rhetorical questions, which might help you start building connections between different poetic devices in the poem:

> What do you infer is the effect of the rhetorical questions in lines 9 and 15?
> **A.** The speaker wants to silence the nightingale with all of his talking.
> **B.** The speaker is insensitive to the nightingale's pain at not being able to answer.
> **C.** The speaker and the nightingale can communicate without language.
> **D.** The nightingale will reveal all in a response poem.
> **E.** The speaker is exposing broken channels of communication that cannot be bridged.

This is a poem about power dynamics that are constantly seesawing, as you may see from the different forms that the stanzas of blank verse take. The rhetorical questions lend it a one-sided quality: there are many questions, but no answers, and yet the nightingale's inability to answer the questions shows the depth of the pain. Choices, A, B, and D are not supported by the excerpt of the poem in front of you: the question would never ask you to imagine another poem (or the rest of this one), and we don't have any indications of the speaker's intentions as being negative. Choice C is also not a good choice, because the poem is given to us in language, so that's all we have to analyze. The correct answer is the only one left; choice E is the best answer.

This question is harder than the previous one because it asks you to interpret the meaning of a device, rather than just naming it. However, the two questions reinforce each other. The apostrophe becomes unusual because the speaker is addressing the nightingale with so many rhetorical questions, so both answers need to call attention to the way the formal elements become strange. The other answer choices make wild inferences that don't match up with specific formal elements under consideration in these questions. There are some subtle hints that it's the right answer from its more sophisticated, nuanced phrasing compared to the other answers—when you're given an answer with a more complex verb and a compelling phrase like "broken channels of communication," you're getting a clue that can guide you toward the most intellectual answer.

You may have circled the title "Philomela" as an unknown: you don't know the Greek myth of the woman who's transformed into a nightingale by a cruel tyrant, but this ruptured apostrophe and rhetorical questions without answers may make you think about who has control over speaking and answering in the poem. (And you should go and look up the story of Philomela, a common story that is often retold in poetry, not just in Keats and Arnold, as it's a story about the poet's power over who gets to speak and sing lyrics…)

Elegy

Elegies are poems that commemorate someone who has died. They may have a subtitle or repeated phrasing about memorials, lamentation, meditation on death, or mourning. With these themes, it is relatively easy to identify whether a poem is elegiac—the adjective form of elegy—so the questions will likely ask you more specifically about how the poem achieves the memorial or sense of mourning. For example, in Thomas Gray's "Elegy Written in a Country Courtyard," the speaker's meditation on one man's death occasions a larger sense of loss of an entire way of rural life. So, one life stands for many (a synecdoche), for a greater sense of cultural time as time passes.

Pay attention to any complexities in the speaker's attitude toward the person being mourned, which may be quite subtle. In A.E. Housman's "To an Athlete Dying Young," the speaker is addressing a young man who dies before he achieves greatness—but also before he faces the inevitable decline of his athleticism. There's a tension between the speaker's grief for the athlete's early death and his anxiety about what it means to keep living.

Ode

Elegies, odes, sonnets, and villanelles are all forms of lyric poetry—they're just more specific forms with their own conventions. An ode pays tribute to a person, animal, or object and is often a way for the poet to deploy many devices as a signal of the breadth and quality of the praise. As you saw in Keats' "Ode to a Nightingale," there's a tension between the speaker and the nightingale as competing "lyricists." That tension generates more poetry as the poet trots out all of his tricks to show the human praise for a bird's natural poetry.

Sonnet

Sonnets are easy to identify: they are fourteen lines long and have a regular metrical scheme of iambic pentameter. An English or Shakespearean sonnet has a rhyme scheme of *abab cdcd efef gg*. There may be a "volta" or a "turn" right before the final couplet, *gg*, to show a revelation or a resolution that solidifies the meaning.

Consider the prologue to *Romeo and Juliet*, a perfect example of unity in the theme and structure of the sonnet:

> Prologue to *Romeo and Juliet*, by William Shakespeare
>
> Two households, both alike in dignity,
> In fair Verona, where we lay our scene,
> From ancient grudge break to new mutiny,
> *Line*   Where civil blood makes civil hands unclean.
> *5*   From forth the fatal loins of these two foes
> A pair of star-cross'd lovers take their life;
> Whose misadventured piteous overthrows
> Do with their death bury their parents' strife.
> The fearful passage of their death-mark'd love,
> *10*   And the continuance of their parents' rage,

> Which, but their children's end, nought could remove,
> Is now the two hours' traffic of our stage;
> The which if you with patient ears attend,
> What here shall miss, our toil shall strive to mend.

We can bring some of our outside knowledge to help us understand the underlying tensions between form and content in this sonnet. The two families are compared in line 1—"both alike in dignity"—but this comparison is undone by the repeated warnings about their warring grudges. The English sonnet's *abab cdcd* format is rendered in perfect rhyme and rhythm here, but those disconnects in the quatrains seem especially foreboding here, as though we know that there's no pairing possible. We can test this pattern by looking at the ending words in the rhymes, which switch back and forth from "dignity" to "mutiny" (1, 3), pair "foes" with "overthrows" (5, 7), and mix love with rage in lines 9 and 10. The prologue's speaker is anxiously aware of so much disconnection and strife that is insufficiently mended with the "toil [the poet may] strive to mend," an attempt that ultimately will be unsuccessful. The poem is at once a love poem and a poem that shows strife at every opportunity for pairing—a perfect way to introduce the play.

On the other hand, a Spenserian sonnet is a variation on the English sonnet form that emphasizes connections among the quatrains, so that pairings are emphasized at every structural level. It takes the form *abab bcbc cdcd ee*:

"Amoretti LXXV," by Edmund Spenser

> One day I wrote her name upon the strand,
> But came the waves and washed it away:
> Again I wrote it with a second hand,
> *Line*   But came the tide, and made my pains his prey.
> 5   "Vain man," said she, "that dost in vain assay,
> A mortal thing so to immortalize;
> For I myself shall like to this decay,
> And eke my name be wiped out likewise."
> "Not so," (quod I) "let baser things devise
> 10   To die in dust, but you shall live by fame:
> My verse your vertues rare shall eternize,
> And in the heavens write your glorious name:
> Where whenas death shall all the world subdue,
> Our love shall live, and later life renew."

If the speaker in *Romeo and Juliet* was anxious about writing as "toil" that could insufficiently mend family feuds, the speaker here finds felicity in every rhyme, as though the composition of the poem signaled the perfection of the pairing, "eternize[d] in verse." Even the erasure of the lines by the ocean waves does not disturb the pairing, for the rhyme braids through when it's rewritten in the next quatrain. There is a constant sense of "renew[al]" in the poem's waves of rhyme.

As always, any changes in the conventions of rhyme and meter are important to consider in your analysis. Such variations really stand out in sonnets, because they have such a strong sense of conventionality.

An Italian or Petrarchan sonnet splits those fourteen lines into an octave (eight lines) and a sestet (six lines); the octave's rhyme scheme goes *abbaabba*, and the sestet can go *cdcdcd* or *cdecde*. There is usually a "volta" or a "turn" at the break between octave and sestet, where the shift in rhyme scheme signals a shift in tone or meaning.

"London, 1802," by William Wordsworth

Milton! thou shouldst be living at this hour:
England hath need of thee: she is a fen
Of stagnant waters: altar, sword, and pen,
Line   Fireside, the heroic wealth of hall and bower,
5   Have forfeited their ancient English dower
Of inward happiness. We are selfish men;
Oh! raise us up, return to us again;
And give us manners, virtue, freedom, power.
Thy soul was like a Star, and dwelt apart:
10   Thou hadst a voice whose sound was like the sea:
Pure as the naked heavens, majestic, free,
So didst thou travel on life's common way,
In cheerful godliness; and yet thy heart
The lowliest duties on herself did lay.

But this poem is critical and negative, you say, and a sonnet is supposed to be a love poem! Sonnets are more flexible than they seem: perhaps it is worth framing a question of the sort that might be on the exam to address this challenge to your expectations about the conventions of the poem.

Here is a sample question about structure and theme:

William Wordsworth combines elegy and sonnet in his poem "London, 1802," which addresses John Milton as a poet for the ages. What is the most important poetic element in unifying the two types of lyric poem?

A. The direct address to Milton in line 1, which shows him as the subject of admiration

B. The naming of lost culture in the "ancient English dower" in line 5

C. The apostrophe "Oh" in line 7 that asks for Milton's help in saving London

D. The volta at line 9, which bridges the degraded present with the admirable poet from the past

E. The final couplet (lines 13-14) that poses a solution to the city's moral degradation

The question is asking you for a poetic or structural element that builds a bridge between the structural and thematic elements at the same time. Thematically, we can see how Wordsworth bridges admiration (a form of love) and a look backward at the past with this line, so this line is the most important signal of how he's mixing two kinds of poetry here. Structurally, there's one obvious device that acts as a bridge in a sonnet. The correct answer is D, the volta.

Villanelle and Roundel

If you've ever tried to compose a villanelle, you know how hard they can be to get right. A villanelle is a nineteen-line poem containing five tercets that repeat and slightly adapt refrains in an intricate pattern of repetition and reformulation.

That particularity of their structure makes them easier to analyze, because their repetitive qualities tend to illustrate vivid themes like the cycles of seasons, the nature of lessons that need to be learned over and over again, or the recurring spikes of obsessive love affairs.

In Edmund Gosse's "Villanelle," the cycles of the seasons become linked to the ebb and flow of human hopes and desires: fall and winter appear and reappear in the poem, each time bringing reminders of death, waste, and the rapidly shrinking number of shrinking cycles in a human lifespan. It's a sad poem that continues posing that recurring worry about mortality.

> "Villanelle," by Edmund Gosse
>
> Wouldst thou not be content to die
> When low-hung fruit is hardly clinging,
> And golden Autumn passes by?
>
> *Line*   Beneath this delicate rose-gray sky,
> 5   While sunset bells are faintly ringing,
>   Wouldst thou not be content to die?
>
>   For wintry webs of mist on high
>   Out of the muffled earth are springing,
>   And golden Autumn passes by.
>
> 10   O now when pleasures fade and fly,
>   And Hope her southward flight is winging,
>   Wouldst thou not be content to die?
>
>   Lest Winter come, with wailing cry
>   His cruel icy bondage bringing,
> 15   When golden Autumn hath passed by.
>
>   And thou, with many a tear and sigh,
>   While life her wasted hands is wringing,
>   Shalt pray in vain for leave to die
>   When golden Autumn hath passed by.

You'll know it's a villanelle when you see the tercets and refrains—just don't bother trying to compose one yourself, because it's deceptively difficult to manage all of those slight reformulations for nuanced meanings in each tercet. The most famous is known for its refrain: Dylan Thomas's "Do Not Go Gentle Into That Good Night."

Narrative Poetry

Narrative poems tell a story. They may be quite long, so you'll receive an excerpt from a canto or book (what poets call the sections or chapters of longer works). They are stories about characters with extensive backstories, and the events of the poem take place in elaborately described settings.

Epic poems are narratives, like Edmund Spenser's *The Faerie Queene* or John Milton's *Paradise Lost*, both difficult seventeenth-century poems that require a lot of context and footnoting to understand their many obscure references and allegorical elements. You're not going to have to answer trivia about historical details in the narratives, however; any information that you need to understand the historical context will be given to you, and the authors of the exam don't want to bog you down with those kinds of footnotes.

It's more likely that they could be selections from less difficult poetic language that have self-contained cantos from which it would be easier to excerpt about thirty lines, such as Alfred Lord Tennyson's *The Charge of the Light Brigade* or John Keats' *The Eve of St. Agnes*. If you're looking to prepare these poems for the exam, you probably don't need to study every line of the poem. They repeat structural elements like rhyme and meter within stanzas, and the repeated structural elements help give a sense that you're listening to a story. To prepare them, get a sense of what happens in the poem in summary form, and then key into stanzas and cantos where the repeated formal elements shift a little bit to call your attention to crucial moments in the story.

A **ballad** is a narrative that was meant to be sung—you can imagine them being passed down in families or being retold over the years with slight variations. Poets may use them to evoke the sense of heroism of a long-ago time or to tell a doomed love story that still resonates, like Edgar Allan Poe's "Annabel Lee." Because a ballad is a subset of a narrative, you won't be asked to distinguish between them; it's more likely that you'll receive questions about the musical or dialect qualities, as seen in many Scottish ballads like Robert Burns's "John Barleycorn," which show pride in Scottish voices, language, and history.

Because the poet uses repetition in rhyme and meter to sustain the progression of the narrative, it can be tempting to get lulled into the repetition. There may be moments with broken rhymes or meter that show a rupture, or the repetitiveness may be a feature worth analyzing itself. The repetition in Poe's narrative "The Raven" (which is significantly shorter than those other narratives) is rhythmic to the point of being sing-songy, and it lends the poem a kind of taunting quality as it goes along, before finally signaling the speaker's madness.

SOUND AND RHYME

Now that we know the forms that the poems may take, we can pay attention to the sounds they make. We've been paying attention to rhyme mostly as a structural element, but now we can pay close attention to how poetic sounds work inside the lines to convey nuances of meaning. Alliteration, assonance, and consonance refer to the repetitions of sounds in proximity to each other.

Alliteration is the easiest to spot: it's the repeated first sound or syllable of a word, whether vowel or consonant. For example, Samuel Taylor Coleridge's "Rime of the Ancient Mariner" has qualities of a narrative tale that is being told propulsively on its own accord: "The furrow followed free; / We were the first that ever burst / Into that silent sea." There is a kind of cascade of alliteration here, with many more repetitions of the device to come, which signal the mariner's need to keep telling his terrible tale.

Assonance refers to repeated vowel sounds like the *ur* sound in the Ancient Mariner example above ("the f**ir**st that ev**er** b**ur**st"), or the repetition of *o* and *ee* sounds in William Wordsworth's "The Daf- fodils" (also known as "I Wandered Lonely as a Cloud"): "A h**o**st, of g**o**lden daff**o**dils; / Beside the lake, ben**ea**th the tr**ee**s, / Fluttering and dancing in the br**ee**ze." The clusters of vowel sounds are like the clusters of flowers he encounters.

Consonance, on the other hand, refers to repeated consonant sounds inside of words, like the lilting line of l-sounds in the the title of Shakespeare's play *All's Well That Ends Well*.

Alliteration, assonance, and consonance may be combined together to form a wall of repetitive sounds and **internal rhymes**, as in "Ancient Mariner" or Edgar Allan Poe's "The Raven": "**s**ilken **s**ad un**c**ertain ru**s**tling of each **p**ur**p**le **c**ur**t**ain," with the repetition of the s sounds in silken, sad, uncertain, rustling for both alliteration and consonance, then followed by the *ur* sound in purple curtain. The repetition of *s* sounds is sometimes called **sibilance**, like whispers, but you would never be asked to choose among consonance, alliteration, internal rhyme, and sibilance: you'd get one of those options and it would be clear which was the right choice.

Onomatopoeia is a word that represents a sound: *babble, buzz, meow, sizzle*. These words sound like their action; many animal sounds are onomatopoeic (*bark, ribbit, neigh*), but we also use them to talk about the sounds of everyday life (*honk, screech, slam*). From the rhyming mind of Edgar Allan Poe, is it any wonder that we get one of the weirdest, most flamboyant examples of onomatopoeia in American poetry?

Here is an excerpt from "The Bells," where the word *bells* gets repeated like a carillon or the repeated tolling of bells in a church:

> From "The Bells," by Edgar Allan Poe
>
> Keeping time, time, time,
>   In a sort of Runic rhyme,
>   To the throbbing of the bells—
>   Of the bells, bells, bells—
>   To the sobbing of the bells ;
>   Keeping time, time, time,
>   As he knells, knells, knells,
>   In a happy Runic rhyme,
>   To the rolling of the bells—
>   Of the bells, bells, bells—
>   To the tolling of the bells,
>   Of the bells, bells, bells, bells—
>   Bells, bells, bells—
>   To the moaning and the groaning of the bells.

Line

5

10

Poe's poem illustrates in a creepy, sort of ridiculous way, that those sounds we hear in everyday life can become strange and unfamiliar when they're repeated—and that makes us pay attention to them in new ways.

Slant rhymes, eye rhymes, near rhymes, half rhymes, and **oblique rhymes** are rhymes that aren't perfect. They might just be a poet's license to stretch the sound of a word into something useful for their rhyme scheme, but they may also signal something intriguing about that stretch.

Someone like Emily Dickinson uses slant rhymes all the time in stanzas like:

> "Hope" is the thing with feathers
> That perches in the soul
> And sings the tune without the words
> And never stops at all...

Her slant rhyme in the not-quite rhyme of "soul" and "all" shows her acting like the bird in the poem: it sings a tune without stopping, even to correct itself. These imperfections aren't flaws, but rather indications of personal style and aural perspective.

Like Dickinson, the Romantic poet John Clare uses half rhymes to express his own idiosyncratic rhyming sensibility in his poem "I Am!":

> "I Am!" by John Clare
>
> I am—yet what I am none cares or knows;
> My friends forsake me like a memory lost:
> I am the self-consumer of my woes—
> Line   They rise and vanish in oblivious host,
> 5   Like shadows in love's frenzied stifled throes
> And yet I am, and live—like vapours tossed
>
> Into the nothingness of scorn and noise,
> Into the living sea of waking dreams,
> Where there is neither sense of life or joys,
> 10   But the vast shipwreck of my life's esteems;
> Even the dearest that I loved the best
> Are strange—nay, rather, stranger than the rest.
>
> I long for scenes where man hath never trod
> A place where woman never smiled or wept
> 15   There to abide with my Creator, God,
> And sleep as I in childhood sweetly slept,
> Untroubling and untroubled where I lie
> The grass below—above the vaulted sky.

Try this sample question about style and theme:

> In "I Am!" John Clare describes the tension he feels in his desire for isolation in the bustle of public life. How do his rhyme choices show that he has unsettled feelings about his private and public selves?
>
> I.   The slant rhymes of "lost," "host," and "tossed" in the first stanza show his uncertainty about how to resolve these endings in rhyme and personal interaction alike.
> II. The regularity of the rhymes in his communion with God in the final stanza show his sense of peace in that relationship where he can "abide" companionship.
> III. The use of consonance in the v-sounds in lines 4-6 show the evanescent patterns of his interactions; each v-sound is attached to something that evaporates.
>
> A. I only
> B. II only
> C. I, II, and III
> D. I and II
> E. II and III

This sample question is asking you to examine multiple possibilities and assess whether they fit into a larger pattern of interpreting Clare's use of sounds and rhyme in the poem. Each possibility in this sample question is a reasonable one, backed up with specific evidence cited in the lines of the poem. In other questions where you're asked to choose among three options, there might be options that contradict each other, but this one shows three possibilities that back each other up! The correct answer is choice C.

LANGUAGE, WORD CHOICE, AND DICTION

Just what is "diction" anyway? We use the term to mean a lot of different things—including the size, creativity, or aptness of one's word choices—which means you'll have to be more specific when you use it in your own essay-writing for the exam (more on that in chapter 4). When you're thinking about word choice and diction, you'll be answering questions about how those specific choices let you understand the poet's style, tone, and vocabulary. That doesn't mean you'll never see the word "diction" again or that it might not pop up inside a question. But with specific terms like "tone," "style," and "vocabulary" we can be more precise about what qualities of the word choice we're considering and why.

Style vs. Tone

If the word "diction" seems like it could mean anything, the terms "style" and "tone" also seem like they mean different things to different people. They could indicate the feeling you get from reading a poem—but how would you translate that feeling into a question and answer that could be accessible for thousands of test-takers who might all have different reactions and feelings?

We need to limit and clarify the two words and draw some distinctions to help us see when you might use them to answer different kinds of questions:

- Style is the poet's word choice (also known as diction), sentence structure, use of poetic devices, and other elements that make up the poem's language.

- Tone is the speaker's attitude toward the events inside the poem. A poet's tone might be loving, uncertain, excited, ironic, careless, crazed, or sociopathic, while style is the poet's use of particular words, poetic devices, and figurative language that conveys the speaker's tone.

If the tone is *anxious* . . . the style might be *frenetic, haphazard, flitting all over the place.*

If the tone is *friendly* . . . the style might be *intimate, informal, closely observed.*

If the tone is *ironic* . . . the style might be *sharp, witty, playful* in use of language, *distancing oneself from the situation.*

You can see that there are overlaps between tone and style, as there may be overlaps in how we think of the relationship between a poet and speaker. For Romantic poets or heavily personal poets like Emily Dickinson, Walt Whitman, and Robert Lowell, there may be a very little distinction between poet and speaker. For other poets and poems, the distinction is more necessary (and obvious)—in Robert Browning's "My Last Duchess," for example. These distinctions are not hard and fast, nor are they supposed to give you a single correct answer. Rather, they show us the importance of looking at poems closely, of not assuming that the style and tone might be the same thing, or that the speaker and poet are the same: they make us slow down and ask *how do these distinctions work in this particular poem?*

Let's look at how the exam might ask you to examine style and tone differently in considering Browning's "My Last Duchess." Here is a selection from the poem:

> . . . Oh, sir, she smiled, no doubt,
> Whene'er I passed her; but who passed without
> 45   Much the same smile? This grew; I gave commands;
> Then all smiles stopped together. There she stands
> As if alive. Will't please you rise? We'll meet
> The company below, then....

And here is a sample test-like question about tone:

How would you describe the Duke's tone in these lines?
- **A.** Smoothly sociopathic
- **B.** Anxiously avoidant
- **C.** Deeply grief-stricken
- **D.** Loving and dutiful
- **E.** Calm and open

Browning's style of omitting the interlocutor's responses heightens the effect of the speaker's blank tone—it exposes the gap between his empty fantasy of control and the reality of the violence he has committed. The horror at the Duke's behavior mounts as the poem goes on. The revelation "then all smiles stopped together" shows us that he and the Duchess did not have a loving, mutual relationship, but that he controlled every aspect of her life—and death, as her painting "stands/ as if alive" behind the curtain. That line break on "as if" gives a sense of his break with reality: he sees no difference between the painting and the person, because they are both objects to control. The correct answer is A. We get a sense of the sociopathic *tone* from the spare, bland *style* of his language in the explanation that matches with Browning's style of rendering the dramatic monologue where the speaker seems not to even register his interlocutor's realization or horror.

The tone in the poem is about the speaker's affectless emotions in his empty performance; that tone is conveyed by Browning's style in eliminating the interlocutor's responses, his elimination of adjectives and any vivid nouns, so as to heighten the sense of the emptiness of the scene.

Here's another "My Last Duchess" question that might help you see how you have to pay attention to where the exam is directing your focus. This question is more about style.

> What is the effect of Browning's use of the unclear antecedent "this grew" in line 45?
> A. It shows his inability to put into language his grief.
> B. It shows his strategic vagueness that he uses to distract the guest from the reality of the situation.
> C. It obscures the horror with a bland article, similar to how the curtain obscures the painting.
> D. "This" is not an unclear antecedent--the pronoun refers to their careful, distant smiling interactions.
> E. It reveals his losing touch with reality.

Because of how the question was framed around the *poet's* choices, we want to focus our attention on how the *poet* chose an element of grammar to create a literary pattern with other obscurantist themes in the poem. The focus isn't on *why* the *speaker* chose the word, but on how these devices convey the themes of the poem. The correct answer is C. Choice C is an answer about the meaning of *Browning's* language and grammatical choices—not the speaker's tone, which was already addressed in the previous question.

Again, you're never going to encounter an exam question that asks you to make a black-and-white demarcation about what counts as style and what counts as tone. Nevertheless, the exam may ask you to distinguish speaker and the poet in a question, or it may ask you about the speaker's attitudes and tone as distinct from an author's choices in how to convey those attitudes in word choice and other stylistic elements. We're just working on refining those tools for understanding the differences among those kinds of questions.

Figurative Language

Another way that poets convey themes in their poetic style is to use figurative language. Figurative language can be any kind of poetic device that encourages the reader to find a deeper meaning than the literal meaning of the words on the page.

A poet uses metaphors and similes to suggest comparisons between unrelated objects, by substituting one for the other and revealing the previously unrealized connections or resemblances. A **simile** sets the two compared objects next to each other and says they are like each other; a metaphor says that one *is* the other.

The Scottish poet Robert Burns uses two similes when he writes:

> O my Luve's like a red, red rose
> That's newly sprung in June;
> O my Luve's like the melodie
> That's sweetly play'd in tune…

On the other hand, Burns uses a **metaphor** calling the years of one's age grains of sand in an hour-glass when he promises, later on in the poem, "I will luve thee still, my dear, / While the sands o' life shall run." He's not saying that years are *like* grains of sand, he's saying they're the same—and they are commensurate with the amount of time he will love her.

As you may be anxious about hearing so often, these distinctions are not as clear-cut as some might say they are. Many would say that a simile is a type of metaphor, a subset, and so you would never be asked an exam question that asked you to distinguish them, unless there was a very clear reason for making such a distinction.

Metonymy, synecdoche, synesthesia, personification, and objectification are also forms of substitution that heighten the figurative, nonliteral meaning of a poem.

In general terms, **metonymy** is a device in which a writer substitutes a word with a closely associated word, like we sometimes call all of movie culture "Hollywood," even though only some movies are filmed there, and movie culture exists worldwide. We associate movies and Hollywood with one another, so the latter gets substituted for the former.

Synecdoche is a device in which a writer substitutes a word for a whole with a word for a part of it. For instance, you might call your car "your wheels," because wheels are part of a car. As with similes and metaphors, the distinctions between these devices are also somewhat subjective. Some writers don't make a strong distinction between metonymy and synecdoche or say that synecdoche is a special case of metonymy, so, again, you wouldn't be asked to distinguish between the two unless it were absolutely clear. You probably would not get both answer choices on a question: you'd get one or the other, and your choice would be much easier to pencil in!

Synesthesia is the substitution of one sensory experience for another, creating a sensory confusion. A poet might describe a "yellow smell" or "tasting the cacophony of the city." These elements can add charming idiosyncrasies to show an artist's take on the world, or they can emphasize uncertainty and a speaker's inability to trust her own senses.

Sometimes, poets substitute people for objects or concepts (**personification**), or objects for people (**objectification**). We tend to see the poetic tradition of personification more positively; after all, it's comforting to think of Mother Nature or Father Time—personifications of the natural and temporal world. We're somewhat less comfortable objectifying people: after all, that's a slippery slope toward thinking of them as, say, paintings to be moved around, like Robert Browning's Duke in "My Last Duchess."

Shakespeare uses a number of poetic devices in "Sonnet 116," tracing the theme of constancy with an extended metaphor about a compass point that stays fixed and steady. Shakespeare personifies Love and Time in line 9, and then extends the personification to turn them into full-fledged characters in the compass's circle.

"Sonnet 116," by William Shakespeare

Let me not to the marriage of true minds
Admit impediments. Love is not love
Which alters when it alteration finds,
Line   Or bends with the remover to remove.
5   O no! it is an ever-fixed mark
That looks on tempests and is never shaken;
It is the star to every wand'ring bark,
Whose worth's unknown, although his height be taken.
Love's not Time's fool, though rosy lips and cheeks
10   Within his bending sickle's compass come;
Love alters not with his brief hours and weeks,
But bears it out even to the edge of doom.
If this be error and upon me prov'd,
I never writ, nor no man ever lov'd.

Love and Time get personal pronouns here to show the full scope of the personification and extension of the metaphor. There's an interesting shift in the volta at the end of the poem: what happens to those personifications when I/me steps in to take their place?

Apostrophe is a direct address to a person or thing in a poem, as if it were a character in the poem, present and listening to your praise or lament. It is often signaled with an O or an Oh!, as we saw with Matthew Arnold's address: "O, wanderer from a distant Grecian shore . . . ."

On that note, when a poet makes an **allusion**, she is referring to something outside of the text without mentioning it directly—another work of literature, a historical event, some other idea—and this reference helps convey additional meanings in the poem. The indirect reference heightens the sense of figurative, nonliteral layers to the poem's themes and main ideas. In Arnold's "Philomela," the apostrophic allusion to a character, "O, wanderer from a distant Grecian shore," calls up the story of Philomela, who was turned into a nightingale (objectified, we might say) as punishment by her sister's angry husband (the many retellings of the story have slightly different details).

The allusion exposes the speaker's disingenuousness in asking rhetorical questions to the nightingale he admires: he's making the allusion, so he knows the myth, and he knows the source of her pain and transformation. He doesn't need to ask her the questions, yet he wants to hear her song. The allusion solidifies the significant power dynamic between the two: one can communicate not only in language but also in poetic allusion. The allusion, objectification, and apostrophe each contribute to the poem's exploration of broken communication channels between the speaker and the nightingale. As we have seen in the examples from Shakespeare and Matthew Arnold in this section, elements of figurative language often work together to build layers of nonliteral, thematic meaning in a poem.

POETRY BY THE CENTURY

This very abbreviated overview of historical periods and "schools" is not a replacement for studying these poems or similar ones by these authors. They will be less helpful if you study just these descriptions, for the exam isn't going to ask you to identify authors, titles, or periods separate from the language of the poem itself. Every poem in this book is in the public domain, so you have many resources for reading these poets through the beginning of the twentieth century. For more contemporary poetry, you can find examples online or anthologies in your library.

The Seventeenth Century

Poets to know:

- John Milton
- George Herbert
- John Donne
- Andrew Marvell
- Aphra Behn

Familiarize yourself with:

- Their use of wit and irony
- Their many-layered spiritual meditations that may use extended metaphors and obscure language (especially Donne)

Poetry doesn't begin in the seventeenth century, but the College Board recognizes that there's only so much you can study, and many medieval poems require more translation of archaic language and explanation of context than can fit on a timed exam. John Milton's *Paradise Lost* may be too long and difficult to study, but many of his shorter lyric poems and sonnets are easier to read and can give a sense of how English poets were attempting to tie together many different older poetic traditions into a polished form. Take a look at Milton's "On Shakespeare," "On His Blindness," and the longer poem *Lycidas*, a pastoral elegy for his friend that becomes a meditation on the loss of the ideals of rural life.

It's also important to study some examples of the Metaphysical Poets like John Donne and George Herbert, since their shorter works are good choices for the exam and their language and context may be the most unfamiliar to you from a distant century. Herbert is known for his shape poems "Easter Wings," "The Collar," and "The Altar," where the line breaks give the poems the title shapes. Donne's poetry is dense but rewarding, and it's worth reading through some kind of annotated analysis of poems like "A Valediction: Forbidding Mourning," "Holy Sonnet X (Death Be Not Proud)," and "Love's Alchemy" to see the many layers of spirituality *and* irony in the poems. Once you start reading these poems, you'll start to recognize lines and phrases that have become part of our everyday language: "for whom the bell tolls" and "no man is an island" are but two examples. An annotated edition of these poems will help you not just for understanding those particular poems, but it will let you see his strategies for creating extended metaphors that pop up in multiple poems.

These seventeenth-century poets were not only concerned with spiritual crisis and deep soul-searching; they could also be quite bawdy and satirical. Andrew Marvell's "To His Coy Mistress" and "Upon Appleton House" are compelling uses of Metaphysical elements to frame social satire of relations between the sexes: who knew that metaphysics could be so physically attuned? (Actually, many of the Metaphysical poets knew it—we just need annotated editions to help us trace the ways they hid their sexual frankness.) The novelist, dramatist, and poet Aphra Behn cared little for covering up her bawdiness; in poems like "The Disappointment," "Love Arm'd," and "The Dream," she lays all kinds of sexual dissatisfaction, insults, and sarcasm out there.

The Augustan Age

Poets to know:
- John Dryden
- Alexander Pope
- John Gay
- Samuel Johnson
- Phillis Wheatley

Familiarize yourself with:
- The use of satire and wit
- Play with scale as a means to expose moral faults and comment on society
- Appeals to the classical tradition to claim authority as a poet

These poets may sound stuffy at first, with their strict rhymes and meter, but many of them are deploying that talent for clever rhymes into some wicked satires. Dryden, Pope, and Gay were all champions of the "heroic couplet," two lines rhymed in iambic pentameter and called back to classical forms of poetry from the Greeks (indeed, Dryden and Pope both translated—and improved, they believed—classical poetry). They used that form to create "mock-heroic" poems that played with scale: a grandiose form of poetry to "celebrate" silly achievements—that is, to mock them. They loved to play with these paradoxes and subversions of expectation: to make what was small into something so grandiose that it became ridiculous.

Using the same format and style as classical poems like Virgil's *Aeneid*, Pope created an elaborate tale about the heroism of stealing a lock of hair in "The Rape of the Lock." ("Rape" means stealing, in this context.) Dryden satirized the dubious achievements of a lesser poet in "Mac Flecknoe." They are very funny poems, once you start to understand the references (so use an annotated edition) and the way that they use couplets to settle you to a rhythm of reading so they can sneak in a joke. John Gay's "Trivia" is a basically a stand-up comedy routine of observational comedy, rendered in rhyme. They could also use satire in more serious ways, to comment on politics, the function of poetry, and the qualities of great art. Dryden's "Absalom and Achitophel" is a satire of then-contemporary political intrigue in the court. Pope wrote "An Essay on Criticism" and "Windsor Forest" to scold lesser poets but also to explain what poets should and could do with the form.

Samuel Johnson's poetry does less lampooning and mocking of people; in poems like "London" and "The Vanity of Human Wishes," his satire is more subtle in commenting on moral failings in society, so that readers might correct their vanities or snobberies without humiliation. All of these poets were interested in using these classical forms to claim authority for poetry as a force that could correct failings—-whether in jest or in seriousness. Phillis Wheatley was no satirist, but she used her position as the first published author of African descent in the Americas to both claim extraordinary authority for a freed slave and to comment on the continued inhumanity of the slave trade, as in "To S.M. A Young African Painter, Upon Seeing His Works" and "Imagination."

There are many more poets and styles of the eighteenth century—as you'll see in the next section—but these authors may give you a sense of how language that seems old-fashioned or formulaic in repetitive rhymes might be using those features in clever, not just stilted, ways. They can help us understand how poets might look backward to traditional forms but also use them as vehicles for irony—and even subversiveness.

The Romantic Poets

Poets to know:

- William Blake
- William Wordsworth
- Samuel Taylor Coleridge
- John Keats
- George Gordon, Lord Byron
- Percy Shelley

Familiarize yourself with:

- A poet's claiming a position as an isolated Genius
- The concept of "the sublime," in which one finds both wonder and terror in the natural world
- Meditations on the insufficiency of poetic language to express deep feelings about nature and mortality (which means they were often writing poems about the difficulty of writing)

For many people, the word "poet" conjures up an image of a solitary artist struggling over just the right words to describe an extraordinary thunderstorm crackling over a mountain. Sure, other poets had feelings before them, but William Wordsworth, Samuel Taylor Coleridge, Percy Shelley, and John Keats were sure that they were remaking poetry into a vehicle for the deepest kind of emotional communication.

These poets often referred to a concept of "the sublime," or the feeling of being so awed by a natural scene that one trembled with a sense of the smallness of humanity in the magnitude of the universe. If you look back at the Metaphysical Poets and the Augustans, you see that poets are often using poetry as a form to experiment with scale: the confines of a metrical line or the structure of a fourteen-line sonnet give them a confined space, a poetic container, to express spiritual awe, doubt, fear, love, and other too-large ineffable feelings. They may treat that play with scale ironically or satirically, or they may create an identity of the Genius Poet who can help society contend with these large feelings through reading and writing poetry. The Romantic Poets "invent" the sense of artistic genius—the gifts they give are both small and contained (a few lines of poetry) and large and expansive (in the sense of explaining nature, spiritual, and wonder in portable, quotable forms).

In "Ode: Intimations of Immortality" and "Lines Composed a Few Miles Above Tintern Abbey," Wordsworth wrote poems about writing poems, about being so transported by the natural world that he simply had to express his deep feelings about nature and art in poems. Coleridge's poems took on similar themes, although sometimes they took those anxieties about man's position in the natural world to strange and surreal places, as in the narrative poem "The Rime of the Ancient Mariner," "Kubla Khan," and "This Lime Tree Bower My Prison."

Poets like John Keats often indulge in paradoxes: in poems like "To Autumn," "On First Looking into Chapman's Homer," and "Ode on a Grecian Urn," the poet struggles with finding exactly the right language, worries that language is insufficient, yet finds he must write the poem about this insufficiency. Percy Shelley builds on Keats's paradoxes of writing about insufficient language in "Adonais—An Elegy on the Death of John Keats," sharing his own feelings of inadequacy to write poetry after Keats had died tragically early.

Lord Byron had no such anxieties about his own talent; his reputation preceded him in his adventures on the Grand Tour in Europe, and his characters became a type—a brooding, sexy, trouble-making Byronic hero. The Byronic hero shows up in the narrative poems *Childe Harold's Pilgrimage* and *Don Juan*, as well as the poem-play *Manfred*. Byronic heroes lived out that poetic fascination with scale: how bad could they be? How tempestuous? How could a small rumor fill up many, many cantos as it took on a life of its own in narrative form. For shorter works, you may try "She Walks in Beauty Like the Night."

19th-century American Poets

Poets to know:

- Henry Wadsworth Longfellow
- Walt Whitman
- Emily Dickinson
- Stephen Crane
- Edgar Allan Poe

Familiarize yourself with:

- Conflicts between public and private life
- Poetic perspectives on the Civil War
- The poet's sense of responsibility for chronicling the changing American landscape in the face of expansion west onto Native American lands and industrialization
- Responses to new technology and media

To continue our examination of how poets played with scale across national boundaries, we look now to nineteenth-century America, which looked unfathomably large and expansive to poets like Henry Wadsworth Longfellow and Walt Whitman, who proclaimed that "America is the greatest poem," and wrote in "Song of Myself": "*Do I contradict myself? Very well then I contradict myself, (I am large, I contain multitudes.)*" We can think of Longfellow, Whitman, and Stephen Crane as poets who were assessing the ways that America contained multitudes as a nation accounting for its legacies of slavery and displacement of Native Americans due to westward expansion, in the midst of the Civil War. Longfellow's *The Song of Hiawatha* and *Evangeline* give a sense of how nineteenth-century Americans understood their own place in history—and how quickly that sense of place was changing. Crane's novel *The Red Badge of Courage* is a classic Civil War novel, but he also wrote short, half-funny, half-philosophical poems like "In the Desert" and "A Man Said to the Universe," which almost seems like an answer to Whitman:

> A man said to the universe:
> "Sir I exist!"
> "However," replied the universe,
> "The fact has not created in me
> A sense of obligation."

The Amherst poet Emily Dickinson appears to be the opposite of Whitman's immensity, but it's better to say that her sense of perspective could be unusual, too, in poems like "The Angle of a Landscape" or "I Saw No Way—The Heavens Were Stitched," we see a different kind of perspective on the world. You may also look at other Dickinson poems mentioned in this chapter for more illustrative works. As you see in any of her poems, her sense of perspective was singular and private, where Whitman was public and infinite—but the two most original American poets of the nineteenth century have much to say when you examine them together.

We tend to think of Edgar Allan Poe as isolated in a space of horror or weirdness, but his poems give us a sense of American dislocation and anxiety in their own way. You might challenge yourself to think about familiar poems like "The Raven" in contrast with Whitman's use of poetic repetition in "Song of Myself," where his repetitions may start to sound as strange as the speaker's tap-tap-tapping in Poe's poem. Or you may find something interesting when you pair "The Raven" with Dickinson's "Because I Could Not Stop for Death…" What do we learn about the speakers when we try that provocative pairing? The AP® Exam may not ask you to make these kinds of pairings of poets in the essay section, and it's unlikely that they'd pick exactly such a pairing for the poetry multiple choice options. Yet it's still an interesting way to study poetry by making unusual juxtapositions that take you out of your familiar readings of a poem. Many of us remember "The Raven" so clearly from memorizing the rhyme and annoying meter, so we cease seeing its poetic potential. But there may be ways for that poem to teach us something all over again!

Pre-Raphaelites and Other Victorian poets

Poets to know:

- Dante Gabriel Rossetti
- Christina Rossetti
- Alfred Lord Tennyson
- Robert Browning
- Elizabeth Barrett Browning

Familiarize yourself with:

- Mutually generative relationships between poets and painters in the period
- Poetic responses to colonialism and political upheavals
- Poetic responses to changing ideas about women's roles in the family and in public life
- The tensions between private and public in Victorian society
- The role of publicity and fame in a poet's life
- Poetic responses to industrialization and new technologies

We have already discussed Robert Browning's "My Last Duchess" as an example of how a poem conveys meaning through a speaker's (creepy) tone and the style of language used. In that poem, as well as in "Fra Lippo Lippi," Browning joins a number of Victorian poets who either wrote extensively about painting and art or who were artists themselves. The poetic work of describing a work of art is called **ekphrasis**, and Victorian poets especially were interested in the limitations of—but also the extraordinary possibilities in—describing visual images. They do so because they're in an extraordinary moment of technological change, as they see the invention and popularization of photography, telegraphy, sound recording, and other forms of transmitting information and ideas. That spread of information matched the spread of colonialism and nationalism in the period, too, and poets could be seen celebrating the imagery, languages, and spiritual ideas that seemed new and "exotic" to them. In both ekphrasis and the vogue for translating poetry in other languages, we see the ever-present poetic question of what language can and can't do to communicate deep emotions and vivid images.

Some were anxious about these innovations and looked backward to earlier times to romanticize those moments. The Pre-Raphaelite poets looked backward to the medieval period as a time of lore and legend. In poems like "Ave" and "The Blessed Damozel," Dante Gabriel Rossetti translated and imitated medieval Italian poets like Dante—so taken with his namesake, he even painted portraits inspired by Dante's life and poetry. Alfred, Lord Tennyson's "Lady of Shallott" and "Morte d'Arthur" retell medieval tales of knights and conquests and were enormously popular. The medieval characters of Lancelot and Guinevere appeared both mythic and modern, for they adhered to Victorian ideals of powerful, conquering men and chaste women.

Modernist Poetry

These twentieth-century movements don't need the same historical background as, say, the Metaphysical poets do. For these schools of poetry, we will give some names and suggestions of illustrative poetry, but you have probably studied more of these figures in your classes, and the language and references may be closer to you. (Their poems are often not in the public domain, either, which makes reproducing their work inside this book impossible, hence the emphasis on Romantic poets.)

Poets to know:

- William Butler Yeats
- T.S. Eliot
- Wallace Stevens

- William Carlos Williams
- W.H. Auden
- Marianne Moore

Familiarize yourself with:

- How these poets rendered their growing sense that modern life is fragmented and hyper-mediated and that communication has become impossible (sound familiar?)
- Calls to break with the past and invent new forms of communication and art
- Existential crises about the decline of civilization in the face of World War I
- Responses to technological change

Harlem Renaissance

Names and texts to look for:

- Langston Hughes's "Theme for English B," "Montage of a Dream Deferred," "I, Too, Sing America"
- Claude McKay's "The Tropics in New York" and "If We Must Die"
- Paul Laurence Dunbar's "Majors and Minors," "Frederick Douglass," and "We Wear the Mask"

Familiarize yourself with:

- Collaboration across the arts, notably in painting, jazz, blues, theater
- Deep, conflicted consideration of how to construct African-American cultural identity as part of, or distinct from, larger American cultural identity
- Meditation on family and individual African-American identity in the longer histories of the Great Migration and the legacy of the slave trade
- Community identity formation in a neighborhood, city, nation

Beat poetry

Names and texts to look for:

- Lawrence Ferlinghetti's "A Coney Island of the Mind"
- Allen Ginsberg's book-length poem, Howl
- Gregory Corso's "Marriage"
- Gary Snyder's Turtle Island and Sustainable Poetry for his interest in environmentalism that led to his founding of eco-poetry as a new school of thought

Familiarize yourself with:

- The role of travel and migration in constructing a poet's identity
- The role of jazz, mass media, drugs, and sexuality in facilitating metaphysical experiences that one could then record and publicize through one's poetry
- The self-mythologizing poet, who bore some resemblance to Romantic poets who claimed the role of Wanderer

New York School of Poets

Names and texts to look for:

- Frank O'Hara's "Having a Coke with You," "Poem (Lana Turner Has Collapsed)," "Why I Am Not a Painter"
- John Ashbery's "Self-Portrait in a Convex Mirror," "And Ut Pictura Poesis Is Her Name," "Some Trees"; he also writes Confessional poetry in his 365 short poems, The Dream Songs
- Kenneth Koch's "The Circus," "You Were Wearing"

Familiarize yourself with:

- Cross-fertilization between poetry, art, popular culture, music, theater, and other forms of artistic expression
- Imitation of and responses to the modernist poets and artists they admired
- Imitation of Surrealist art and poetry
- City life as an inspiration for poetry
- Poetry about poetry, or poetry about the difficulty of defining poetry and art

Confessional Poetry

Names and texts to look for:

- Robert Lowell's "For the Union Dead," "The Quaker Graveyard in Nantucket," "Sailing Home from Rapallo"
- Anne Sexton's "The Double Image" and "The Black Art"
- Sylvia Plath's "Lady Lazarus," "Blackberrying," "Ariel," and "Daddy"
- Elizabeth Bishop is not exactly a Confessional poet, although she was friendly with Lowell (and she is frequently included on the AP® English Literature curriculum). Look for her famous villanelles, "One Art," "The Fish," and "Sestina"

Familiarize yourself with:

- Unsettling emotional frankness
- Poetic explorations of trauma, psychological distress, abuse, grief

- Confessions that make a poet "unlikable" or "unrelatable" for their ugly feelings—and how readers then recognized elements of their own lives and found them both very relatable and also scary to see things they wished to keep hidden
- Mythologizing the poet's biography after his or her death

Black Arts Movement

Names and texts to look for:

- Gwendolyn Brooks's "The Bean Eaters," "Still Do I Keep My Look, My Identity," and "We Real Cool"
- Amiri Baraka's "Legacy" and "Incident"

Familiarize yourself with:

- Poetry as social and political commentary during the Civil Rights movement
- Separation of Black identity as a political statement
- Collaborations with artists, musicians, political organizers, journalists, activists

As we've noted before, these lists are useful as a starting place in your study. You can't predict that any one poet will appear on the exam, not even if you count frequencies from previous years. The exam questions won't ask you trivia about a poet's biography or historical facts. Everything you'll need to know about the poems will be there on the page. This background knowledge is helpful for you to build your own sense of context that will make poetic language seem more manageable, because you see the poets as people who are responding to their time and culture—just as we try to do today. All of these poets are commenting on the world around them; they just happen to be using styles, tones, structures, and detailed allusions that can look weird if you don't have that sense of context. When looking at the structure used by a poet, you are looking at the way they build on a previous genre tradition and how they are making it their own. When you look at the style used by a poet, you are observing how the poet is responding to historical events or popular culture of that time period.

PRACTICE SETS

Now you can practice answering these sample questions. You may not be familiar with the first poet, Anne Finch, who wrote during the seventeenth century—she's not listed in the overview, but she is still representative of some of the same Metaphysical themes we were tracking. William Butler Yeats is listed among the Modernist poets, and you may be able to see some of the familiar themes and concepts from that listing in his poem here. As you're answering the questions, think about how the questions give you some necessary context, but they also remind you that you have everything you need inside the poem and questions. The best preparation allows you to have confidence in that reminder.

SAMPLE PASSAGE 1

"The Tree," by Anne Finch, Countess of Winchilsea

Fair tree! for thy delightful shade
'Tis just that some return be made;
Sure some return is due from me
Line   To thy cool shadows, and to thee.
5   When thou to birds dost shelter give,
Thou music dost from them receive;
If travellers beneath thee stay
Till storms have worn themselves away,
That time in praising thee they spend
10   And thy protecting pow'r commend.
The shepherd here, from scorching freed,
Tunes to thy dancing leaves his reed;
Whilst his lov'd nymph, in thanks, bestows
Her flow'ry chaplets on thy boughs.
15   Shall I then only silent be,
And no return be made by me?
No; let this wish upon thee wait,
And still to flourish be thy fate.
To future ages may'st thou stand
20   Untouch'd by the rash workman's hand,
Till that large stock of sap is spent,
Which gives thy summer's ornament;
Till the fierce winds, that vainly strive
To shock thy greatness whilst alive,
25   Shall on thy lifeless hour attend,
Prevent the axe, and grace thy end;
Their scatter'd strength together call
And to the clouds proclaim thy fall;
Who then their ev'ning dews may spare
30   When thou no longer art their care,
But shalt, like ancient heroes, burn,
And some bright hearth be made thy urn.

1. To what genre does this poem belong?
- **A.** Pastoral ode
- **B.** Ballad
- **C.** Satire
- **D.** Monologue
- **E.** Free verse

practice sets

2. What is the effect of repeating the word "return" in lines 2 and 3?
   A. Wondering how to write a nature poem that's unique
   B. Shifting emphasis from the general to the personal
   C. Indicating her guilt at not being able to offer anything back to the tree
   D. Showing the cycle of life
   E. Indicating that time has passed

3. From context, what are "chaplets" (line 14)?
   A. Garlands
   B. Books
   C. Birds
   D. Kisses
   E. Hands

4. How does the speaker feel about what the other visitors have offered the tree?

   I. The tree is a constant presence, so she wonders if the ephemeral gifts left by humans are enough.
   II. The offerings they provide are worthless compared to what the tree provides.
   III. Others have left symbols of their own use, so she will leave a poem.

   A. I only
   B. II only
   C. III only
   D. I and II
   E. I and III

5. What is the best way of characterizing the speaker's reflections on the notion of "return" when she repeats the word yet again in line 16?
   A. She is aware of a tension between constancy and ephemerality, and wonders how her gift, her poem, fits along that continuum.
   B. She has been heartbroken and now only thinks of the tree as a site of painful memories.
   C. She feels sad that humans can never repay fully what the earth has given them.
   D. She is planning her wedding underneath the tree.
   E. Her nostalgia for the past makes her return to the tree both sweet and painful at the same time.

6. What is the shift in tone at line 19?
   A. From loyal to bitter
   B. From simple to prognostic
   C. From romantic to rejected
   D. From happy to grief-stricken
   E. From young to old

7. That tonal change allows the poet to explore what kinds of themes in lines 23-32?
   A. A call for rebellion against land-owners who encroach upon the shepherds
   B. A deeper sense of the connection between women's bodies and the earth
   C. An impending sense of loss and cultural change
   D. A rejection of the material world for a spiritual calling
   E. A Gothic interest in death and decay

8. The elements of what other poetic genre have risen to prominence in the second half of the poem?
   A. Satire
   B. Ballad
   C. Fable
   D. Epic
   E. Elegy

9. The regular meter in the couplet form emphasizes which of the following?
   I.   The intertwined relationship between the tree and those who receive its shade
   II. The tree's sturdiness and steadfastness
   III. The tension between the speaker's sense of poetic duty and her disillusionment with poetry

   A. I only
   B. III only
   C. I and II
   D. II and III
   E. I and III

practice sets

SAMPLE PASSAGE 2

"Long-Legged Fly," by William Butler Yeats

That civilization may not sink,
Its great battle lost,
Quiet the dog, tether the pony
Line To a distant post;
5 Our master Caesar is in the tent
Where the maps are spread,
His eyes fixed upon nothing,
A hand under his head.

Like a long-legged fly upon the stream
10 His mind moves upon silence.

That the topless towers be burnt
And men recall that face,
Move most gently if move you must
In this lonely place.
15 She thinks, part woman, three parts a child,
That nobody looks; her feet
Practice a tinker shuffle
Picked up on a street.

Like a long-legged fly upon the stream
20 Her mind moves upon silence.

That girls at puberty may find
The first Adam in their thought,
Shut the door of the Pope's chapel,
Keep those children out.
25 There on that scaffolding reclines
Michael Angelo.
With no more sound than the mice make
His hand moves to and fro.

Like a long-legged fly upon the stream
30 His mind moves upon silence.

10. What natural phenomenon is Yeats referring to in the refrain of this poem?
    A. Spontaneous generation, the belief that insects could generate from non-living material
    B. Sublimation, passing from the gaseous stage directly into physical matter
    C. Diffusion, the spreading of particles (and ideas) widely
    D. Surface tension, or the cohesion of water molecules that minimizes surface area so that it may resist external forces
    E. Crystallization, as when dew forms on a spider web and then freezes overnight

11. What is Julius Caesar doing in lines 1-10, as he appears to be staring off into space?
    A. Contending with a humiliating battlefield loss in private
    B. Building a brilliant new military strategy in his head
    C. Meditating before a strenuous military campaign
    D. Punishing his subordinates with the silent treatment
    E. Trying to block out all the noise inside and outside his head

12. The three-part poem focuses on stories of genius and extraordinary achievement. Why do the opening two lines sound so uncertain, and why are the first figures we meet dogs and ponies?
    A. The delay in revealing Caesar builds tension.
    B. The delay in revealing Caesar shows his diminished authority because of his eccentric behavior.
    C. The dogs and ponies show the importance of these heroes inter-acting with everyday people.
    D. Upon realizing it's Caesar, the reader begins to question first impressions and what's happening on the surface of a scene.
    E. It shows Caesar contending with his own doubts, to humanize a genius and show his emotions beneath the steely surface.

13. Although she is not named directly, the subject of the second stanza is Helen of Troy. We know this because Yeats uses the phrase "the topless towers be burnt" from the Renaissance dramatist Christopher Marlowe, who wrote in the play *Doctor Faustus*: "Was this the face that launched a thousand ships/And burnt the topless towers of Ilium?" This reference to another piece of writing is an example of what rhetorical device?
    A. Allusion
    B. Ellipsis
    C. Paraphrase
    D. Synesthesia
    E. Synecdoche

14. What is the relationship between the rhetorical device in the second stanza and the mention of the "tinker shuffle" in line 17?

    I. It shows the poet's disdain for the common people who dance in the streets and who could not understand *Doctor Faustus*.

    II. Both the rhetorical device and Helen's adoption of the tinker shuffle are examples of crafting something out of the tools at hand.

    III. It shows the genius's ability to move between highbrow and lowbrow culture strategically.

    A. I only
    B. II only
    C. III only
    D. I and III
    E. II and III

15. Helen of Troy is more often objectified as "the face that launched a thousand ships," not a mastermind. What is the most striking source of Helen of Troy's genius, as Yeats has rendered her here?

    A. She can manipulate people into doing what she wants, like Caesar.
    B. She manifests extraordinary beauty, like Michelangelo can do as an artist.
    C. She can manipulate surfaces to conjure her own power.
    D. She disguises herself as an everyday person, like a spy would.
    E. She has transcended her objectification and become a feminist hero.

16. The third stanza opens with the pubescent girls giggling at the Sistine Chapel. All of the following interpretations of their presence are plausible EXCEPT

    A. they're distracting Michelangelo from his art with their chattering.
    B. they thought they were alone in the silent room and were startled by noticing him.
    C. they are rebelling against dictates for silent reverence and rules for who can be present in the Sistine Chapel.
    D. they are paying attention only to the obviousness of Adam's nakedness and don't see the genius in his art.
    E. they echo Helen's nonchalance in walking down the street, drawing a connection between the two stanzas.

17. Yeats is not claiming to be a genius in the same category as Caesar, Helen of Troy, and Michelangelo, but how is the poet's work similar to the talents of the figures described in the poem?

    I. The poet works on the surface of the page.

    II. The poet must work in silence in order to be productive.

    III. The poet uses language to craft illusions, like these geniuses who make something out of nothing.

    A. I only
    B. II only
    C. III only
    D. I and III
    E. I, II, and III

ANSWER KEY AND EXPLANATIONS

1. A	**5.** A	**9.** C	**12.** D	**15.** C
2. B	**6.** B	**10.** D	**13.** A	**16.** C
3. A	**7.** C	**11.** B	**14.** B	**17.** D
4. E	**8.** E			

1. **The correct answer is A.** Even if you don't know what "pastoral" means, you can probably tell that this poem is some kind of poetic tribute to the tree, so it's some kind of ode. "Pastoral" means that it takes place in nature; the appearance of the shepherds and nymphs are conventional in the pastoral tradition. If you didn't see nature or tribute in the poem, then you could also eliminate many of the other choices: there's no sharp edge of criticism that you'd find in a satire, so choice C is unlikely, nor are there repeated refrains that you might find in a ballad (choice B). The poem follows a regular meter and rhyme, so it's not free verse (choice E). Finally, one gets the sense of a private communion with the tree in paying tribute, so there's no sense of self-conscious performance that one might find in a dramatic monologue, so choice D is also out. This question about genre appears first among the test questions, so it must help us see something about the main idea and larger themes of the poem: we will have to pay attention to the concepts of poetic tribute and nature in this pastoral ode.

2. **The correct answer is B.** This is a tough poem to analyze because it seems so simple. Are there even any ambiguities or tensions to analyze here? In the early lines of the poem, she sees the return gift to the tree as conventional: she and others owe the tree something small for all it has given them over the years. She establishes the convention first for them, then for herself: "'Tis just that some return be made; [by others] / Sure

some return is due from me." Moving from the general to the personal lets her reflect on the nuances of this conventional act of offering something in return. Choices D and E are too vague to be helpful; she may be seeing the cycles of life as time passes, but those answers don't help us understand the repetition.

Choice A is pointing in the right direction, but her reflection on the conventions of nature poetry are larger than worrying about her own uniqueness. Reflecting on the conventionality of returning tributes to the tree's steadfastness gives the speaker the idea that she may use the conventions she knows—the conventions of the ode—to give her own special return. But this act of reflection actually makes her think critically about the limitations of those conventions, both in poetry and in life. She writes a pastoral ode, but the second half of the poem pushes beyond those conventions of shepherds and love for nature, to meditate more deeply on what constancy actually means in a time of change. The poet Anne Finch was exiled from her home during the English Civil War in the seventeenth century, giving her a crucial perspective on the value of returning to assess change.

3. **The correct answer is A.** "Chaplets" are garlands that hang on the boughs of the tree. Even if you've never heard of a chaplet before, you can get the sense of something flowery hanging from lines 13-14: "bestows/ Her flow'ry chaplets on thy boughs." If you noticed the boughs in the poem, then you

might have guessed that they were birds perched among flowers (choice C), but you would be wrong. They may sound like "chapters," but they are not hanging books on the tree (choice B). It's not kisses or hands (choices D and E), although of course one would use one's hands to hang the garlands. The shepherd's chaplets are a conventional feature of pastoral poetry.

4. **The correct answer is E.** Among the three options, you have to decide which ones agree with each other and which ones may be contradictory. Option II is too negative and judgmental for this poem: she is not saying that these small gifts are worthless, but rather noting that their ephemerality makes her consider the ephemerality of any gift, including the gift of her poetry. Striking Option II means that you can eliminate choices B and D. Both options I and III leave room for the ambiguities of that consideration, so they are the best pair of answers. That pairing in choice E is a good way to phrase the tension at the heart of the poem: she has written a poem as a tribute because that is the best kind of "return" she can give, but she has inscribed in it a worry about the ephemerality of any kind of tribute.

5. **The correct answer is A.** Question 2's sensitivity to the repetition of the word "return" has, well, returned again, and like the speaker, we're asking: what's different? We can eliminate choices B and D—the speaker hasn't mentioned them in the poem, so they're not good choices. Choices C and E are very tempting because they're partly right in identifying thematic elements of the poem: insufficiency and nostalgia, respectively. The question asks you to find the best answer, however, and choice A gives you the analytical language of finding a *tension* between those thematic elements; it basically

sets up a great essay topic for writing about this poem. Choices C and E might be okay answers in another set of answer choices, but they're not the best, most sophisticated answers for this particular question.

6. **The correct answer is B.** For a poem about change, there was bound to be a question about how to interpret how those changes are reflected in tone and mood. The best way to approach this question is to strike out the wrong answers first. Let's look at how the choices describe where the poem ends up tonally, since the descriptions of the opening tones are all fairly bland and similar. We don't see a sense of bitterness, rejection, or grief, so choices A, C, and D are not good options. Choice E is too general to be helpful, and we don't really have a way to assess what a young or old tone might sound like. Choice B is the only one left, and the word "prognostic" may be a bit surprising at first read. Where do we see elements of her prognostication? Well, we see her looking forward into the future and imagining more change, even death and a final act of commemoration. Choice B gives a good way of understanding where the poem is heading, and it will help answer some later questions about how the poem changes genre.

7. **The correct answer is C.** By the end of the poem, Finch has taken up some heady themes of cultural loss and decay. Actually, the poem has been pointing toward this commentary on cultural change from the very beginning, for many poems about shepherds and the pastoral life have a built-in sense that such a happy rural life cannot be sustained. Those chaplets we looked at earlier in the poem were symbols of ephemerality not just of a flower, but of an entire lifestyle. Finch is writing at a moment after a Civil War, when England was pervaded with senses of death, loss, and cultural change. Choice C is the correct answer, but you may have

been tempted also to consider choice A if you were really feeling the call not just to write poetry, but to effect change. Finch is OK with writing poetry that hints at its ephemerality: no revolutionary is she. There are elements of spirituality (choice D) and death imagery (choice E) in these lines, but they are not the best answers here—we don't have a sense of decay, really, and we don't see any plans for Finch herself to renounce the material world. That final scene of destruction will be the ultimate tribute to the tree. The concept of a tribute has changed significantly over the course of the poem, from a poem to an urn—a symbol of loss embedded in that sense of tribute.

8. **The correct answer is E.** The previous question asked you to identify the themes that Finch addresses at the end of the poem, which sets up this question about what genre typically picks up those themes. The elegy is defined by its sense of loss, and it often registers cultural change—as in Thomas Gray's "Elegy Written in a Country Churchyard," written about a hundred years later than this poem, but which takes up many of the same themes about the loss of a rural lifestyle. The elegy also serves as a form of commemoration, so it pairs well with the ode form in paying tribute. It might be possible to see her attention to cultural change as a call for satire (choice A), but the sense of loss is stronger than a sense of critique or mockery. We don't see any characters who might populate a ballad or an epic (choices B and D). Those elements are not present in the more mournful elements of axes and urns showing the destruction of a cultural ideal.

9. **The correct answer is C.** This question asks you to interpret the ways that the structural elements underscore the themes of the poem. There are many themes listed among the options, and most of them are deeply relevant to the ways that Finch uses, and then transforms, the pastoral ode into a reflection on cultural change. We have already answered several questions that identify Option I as a basic theme of the poem that matches the structure: the couplets show an interrelationship. We can eliminate any choices that don't contain Option I (choices B and D). The real question, though, is how these structural elements reflect the shift in theme later in the poem. Finch continues to use the couplet to express her sense of loss, never wavering from these formal elements. Is it a sense of dutifulness, as Option III suggests, or does the couplet work just as well for her elegiac reflections on cultural change? Your thoughts on Option III largely depend on whether you see *poetic* disillusionment in Finch's poem. We say no: there may be cultural disillusionment, but she uses her poetic talents to adapt her genre, which hardly suggests that she's lost confidence in her poetic identity. Option III is too big a leap, while Option II is a more nuanced take on how Finch uses her talents to meditate on change. You can mark the answer choice that contains both Option I and II: choice C.

10. **The correct answer is D.** This is not a science exam, so brief definitions of those natural phenomena are included among the answer choices. The long-legged fly appears to walk on water because of surface tension (and some other physiological factors that aren't relevant to poetry). Although the title gives us an insect, we're not discussing spontaneous generation of insects (choice A) or the way that a spider-web collects dew in beautiful radiating shapes (choice E, and we know that spiders aren't insects too). It might be tempting to read any of these natural phenomena as metaphors for the creative process: of how ideas seem to spontaneously generate, diffuse into the wider culture, or

leap from idea into realization, as we might describe creative sublimation (choice C), skipping the stage of painstaking craft and revision. All of these would make excellent poems, but Yeats has chosen the metaphor of surface tension, and that attention to surfaces is crucial to pay attention to in the rest of the questions.

11. **The correct answer is B.** Julius Caesar is a military dictator who is being celebrated for his genius in this poem, so he must be shown doing what geniuses (and dictators) do: strategizing. In its refrain, the poem draws connections between these geniuses and the long-legged fly, who appears to be walking on nothing that can support him, but is mastering the forces of surface tension. When Caesar is staring at nothing, he is manipulating an idea, a strategy, in that apparent absence—he appears to be making something out of nothing. He doesn't even need maps to make his plans. The other tempting choice is choice E, because the refrain also mentions the importance of silence for the genius. Yet choice E locates the noise "inside and outside his head," and we don't really have that Caesar is blocking out his own doubts or negative self-talk. There's no noise in his head that we can determine, only pure military strategy genius. So, choice E knocks itself out by making too deep an inference—and this is a set of questions all about surfaces. You may also eliminate the other choices here: we don't see any emotional markers of humiliation (choice A) or shame (choice D). Because the poem is celebrating his genius, it will call attention to what he makes and crafts, not his sense of inner peace and calm, so choice C is a better bet for a different kind of man.

12. **The correct answer is D.** This is a tough question that you may want to come back to after you've seen how the exam is asking you to interpret Yeats's presentation of the

other geniuses in the poem. He seems to be pointing you toward considering the role of surfaces in the poem, and how geniuses appear to people, but it's not totally clear yet. This question asks you to interpret that sense of uncertainty that's rippling from the very first lines of the poem. Choice A is very tempting because you've just answered a question about surface tension and you're attracted to analytical language about tension. It's too superficial and vague a statement, however, because we don't know what the tension is, what it's between. Choices B and C don't have enough evidence to support them, as we don't see the men or any interactions with other people. Choices D and E also use the language of surfaces that we've seen in question 10, so they seem like they could be good choices. Yet we don't really see any emotions from Caesar, so choice E doesn't seem as likely. Choice D is the right answer, and it will point you to answering other questions about this thematic motif of surfaces in the poem.

13. **The correct answer is A.** The question defines the rhetorical device for you: "this reference to another piece of writing," so if you've studied your lists of devices, you'll know it right away. It might be possible to think of this reference as a paraphrase of Christopher Marlowe, as choice C suggests, but the better answer is that it's an allusion because it doesn't mention the source directly. If you blank on the name of the device, yet you remember some other rhetorical devices, you can eliminate the obviously wrong answers. The reference to Helen's beauty is not an example of sensory confusion in synesthesia (choice D), nor is the allusion a form of synecdoche, which might substitute Helen for the entire Trojan War or something like that (choice E). The best advice for this question is to take the gift of the definition and don't think too hard about it.

14. **The correct answer is B.** While the previous question gave you a lot of extra information, this question asks you to make some inferences. The three options suggest a number of unusual inferences and interpretations that may either rouse your skepticism or lead you astray. It's tempting to interpret that allusion in all sorts of ways, but we don't really have enough information to assess the possibility of Options I or III. There is some confusion in those Options about who has access to the allusion: Yeats, the speaker, or Helen herself. We don't have a sense of who the speaker is, which makes it hard to assess his attitudes in Option I. Yeats has called Helen a genius, but it's not because she knows Renaissance drama and can make allusions—that rhetorical device exists separately from her. Thus Option III is out because she's not engaging with highbrow literary culture—she's just doing a dance in the street. Rather, Yeats suggests that Helen's genius comes from her ability to craft something out of thin air—just like a poet might pick out a literary allusion from his mind. The allusion appears in the poem, floating on no reference point but its own language, like the long-legged fly on water.

15. **The correct answer is C.** This question dials back the far-fetched inferences of the previous question and points you toward analyzing the most important theme of the poem: the manipulation of surfaces. Choices A and B are technically correct, but they're superficial connections—as you might expect, superficial connections lead you astray in this question, too. You can't really choose between the two, as they're both basically true, so that probably means that neither one is the *best* answer. It might be tempting to choose choice D or E, because they could be examples of Helen's manipulation of superficial judgments about her; nevertheless, they are too specific and

aren't supported by the details of the poem. Better to stick with the analytical language about surfaces in choice C, because you know that the exam has been guiding you toward this kind of thematic interpretation over the course of the questions.

16. **The correct answer is C.** You are looking for the outlier here, the one wrong answer among several correct ones. As stanzas 1 and 2 were linked with references to military strategy, this poem gets its link in the reference to beauty. As choice E suggests, we see echoes of Helen's eternal youth in the teenage girls, but it is distraction in stanza 3—just as Helen's youthful beauty was a strategic distraction in the Trojan War. Choice A recalls Caesar's need to work in the silence away from his men, and we see that Michelangelo was being quiet as a mouse in line 27, so choice B is also a plausible interpretation. Choice D is the most sophisticated thematic explanation of their presence—although choices A, B, and E are also fine—in how they highlight the poems' interest in surfaces and illusions. Adam is merely a titillating illusion to them, not an extraordinary example of genius. Choice C may look like it's of a piece with choices A, B, and D in its references to noise and silence, but we don't have any sense of rebellion or purposeful irreverence from the poem—they are just being teenage girls, Yeats is saying. Their presence isn't provocative; it's annoying for the genius artist. Because you've been able to confirm that A, B, D, and E are all good choices, you must choose the misleading interpretation in choice C as the outlier answer.

17. **Choice D is correct.** Think about Yeats' many poetic devices deployed in this poem: to name just two we've discussed in the questions so far, we've seen an extended comparison to surface tension and a strategic allusion to classical literature. This is

a show-offy poem about geniuses who craft illusions and strategies of their own. Options I and III echo the language used to describe Caesar's, Helen's, and Michelangelo's own interests in surfaces, so it's not a leap to say that the poet works on the surface of a page and uses illusory words to make his craft. Option II is a possibility, but it seems like a leap. The word "must" seems like a tip-off that it's asking too much of the inference. Do we know that all poets work in silence? We could probably debate this question with some biographical information about Yeats's working and socializing habits, but we don't have those in front of us. Let's go with Options I and III only, and choose D.

SUMMING IT UP

- Section I of the AP® English Literature and Composition Exam features fifty-five multiple-choice questions based on published works of drama, poetry, or prose fiction. You will have one hour to answer all questions, and the section is worth 45 percent of your total score.

- Your first step should always be to read a poem the whole way through to understand its basic idea. Then read it again to get a sense of its genre, diction, and style—do not get caught up in the author's intention in writing the poem. You want to know why an author uses certain devices. Ask yourself how styles, word choices, and tone serve to convey a feeling or a meaning.

- AP® English Literature questions will test you in many of the following categories: main idea, theme, structure, style, tone, details, vocabulary-in-context, and inference.

- Time matters more than you might think, so practice timing yourself to see what your habits are and how you can read passages and questions most efficiently. Our tips are only as good as how you use them to get to know your own test-taking habits and adapt them to your needs.

- We recommend looking for patterns when you read passages so that you can identify the conventions. Exams have conventions for asking questions and framing answers, too, so if you practice taking them, you will become an expert at identifying patterns and conventions, which will allow you to work more quickly at eliminating wrong answers because you know their tricks.

- You don't need to know the name every device or structural element in the poem, but you do need to be able to identify how these elements affect the meaning of the poem.

- Style, or diction, is the author's word choice, while tone is the speaker's attitude toward the events that occur within a poem.

- Use the structure of the questions to help guide your reading of the poem strategically. The questions will give you analytical language and repeat thematic elements that appear in many answers, so you can use them to help you if you're really not sure what's going on.

- Use the overviews of each era in this chapter to make a reading list for the time leading up to your exam, and then practice generating possible multiple-choice questions about tone, theme, etc. Thinking about the questions you will see on test day as you read poems in preparation is a great way to close-read poetry. By the time you face the poems on your exam, you will know precisely what to expect.

Prose Questions on the AP® Literature and Composition Exam

Chapter 3

OVERVIEW:

- Breadth and Depth of the Prose Section
- How to Read a Prose Passage on the AP® Exam
- Situating Yourself Within a Passage: Elements of Prose
- How to Read Nonfiction Prose
- How to Read Dramatic Prose
- Practice Sets
- Sample Passage 1
- Sample Passage 2
- Answer Key and Explanations
- Summing It Up

Students tend to think that poetry is harder than prose because of the formatting: the line breaks, rhymes, and meter all make it look unfamiliar. One of our recommendations in the poetry chapter has you reading those poetry passages as prose: as you're reading, pretend you're reading sentences so that you can get a sense of what's going on before you attend to the qualities of that rhyme or meter. We figure that reading prose is more natural, because you read lots of prose every day, whether it's prose in an email, a novel, a textbook, or even a test-prep book.

Yet, literary prose is not without difficulties of its own: it is *not* the same as reading an article, an email, or a textbook. The beauty of literature is in how it shows us different points of view, places we had never imagined, places we thought we knew well but which are trans-formed by an author's unusual perspective—ideas that can't be expressed in just an email or a summary in a test-prep book. You won't have time to appreciate the strangeness or beauty of that prose while you're taking the exam, but, whether you like it or not, the questions will cue your attention to those beauties and ask you to take a closer look at them. So, as you're strategizing, keep in the back of your mind that what's challenging here is also what's rewarding about these books.

This chapter will give you tips on how read a prose passage on the exam and understand the kinds of questions the exam asks about the style, structure, and themes of that passage. We will explain some of the basic building blocks of prose narration, such as setting, characterization, and dialogue, and how to analyze these narrative features, and then we will walk you through some important thematic groupings of the Anglophone (English-speaking) literary world, including some thoughts on how the novel has become an important form of literature in world literature.

It's important to remember that these are overviews and summaries, not substitutes for studying the novels themselves. The College Board website provides a list of most frequently included poetry and prose authors that it recommends AP® English Literature teachers consult in making a syllabus, and you are welcome to consult it, too.

Likewise, the recommended novels, prose nonfiction, and drama in this book are good illustrations of important concepts, such as composing the American landscape, novels of manners and morals, satirical fiction, unreliable narrators, and communicating the immigrant experience, but the beauty and power of these novels is how they tell these stories. Each one is different.

BREADTH AND DEPTH OF THE PROSE SECTION

The scope of possibility in the AP® English Literature and Composition Exam's prose section is somewhat different from the poetry section. It would be impossible to read all of the novels, plays, and essays by all of the authors who have written in English. It would be even more impossible to remember all of the details from those texts. The exam gives you a much more manageable task: read a passage of about 600-800 words and analyze its formal and thematic qualities. It's asking you to read one short passage deeply, rather than to test your knowledge of a huge, unmanageable breadth of literature. At the same time, being familiar with a wide variety of types of literary fiction will help you dig deeper, faster, because you'll have some awareness of those forms and themes already.

Your AP® English class will prepare you for a wide variety of texts by giving you a syllabus of representative works. Even if you had years to study, it's unlikely that you'll be familiar with the exact passages given to you on the exam. They may be less well-known works by an author or works by an author who writes in the same tradition or style.

Therefore, your study can be tactical so that you learn how to read the literature, of course, but also how to read the *exam* quickly and strategically. There are genres and styles of questions, as well as familiar patterns that red herrings use to distract you. When you learn how to read these, you'll gain an advantage that enables you to get through the race with fewer distractions.

HOW TO READ A PROSE PASSAGE ON THE AP® EXAM

You'll always feel short on time in such a condensed timeframe on the test. You have to answer fifty-five questions in 1 hour and read at least four passages that may be as much as 800 words in length. You have to read these prose passages strategically, because you don't have time to annotate them as you would in reading them for a class. We recommend you do an initial quick read-through that may take about 6 minutes tops. Circle any unfamiliar words or phrases, and underline words, phrases, or events that jump out at you as seeming especially important for understanding the main idea.

Master the™ AP® English Literature and Composition Exam

TIP

A specific novel recommendation on these lists will give you a representative sense of the author's work, so that when a less well-known work pops up on the exam, you'll already have some context for understanding that author's main preoccupations and styles.

Pay more attention to...	Don't get hung up on...
What's going on in the passage, the main idea?	Is this relatable?
Who is the narrator?	The author's intention
What is the setting and how is it described so that you get a sense of how the narrator feels about it?	Judging the quality of the descriptive language
How does the author use language? (Does the speaker use simple or complex, multi-syllabic words?)	One word you don't understand
Repeated words, metaphors, images—anything that seems to form a pattern. These repetitions may be called **motifs** and they often show you the way a small detail, repeated, illustrates a theme in the passage	Any possible hidden meanings
Tensions that recur throughout the passage that might give you a sense of the themes	The author's intention

If you can't find that main idea on these quick reads, don't worry. You can look down at the first two or three questions to see what they're asking, and they may help you find some repeated keywords that can help you get your bearings.

Questions Will Help You Read the Passage

As we discussed in the poetry chapter, the questions on the exam will tell you what to look for as you read the passage. The questions about details and vocabulary are not random trivia questions; most likely, they're there to give you a clue about what to pay attention to, or even to help students who may not know a word and need some suggestions about what it could mean in context. The questions about the structure, style, and tone will give you a sense of how those elements illuminate the themes and main ideas of the passage. You might get asked about a shift in style or tone that indicates a few lines to pay particular attention to, as you're being clued in that the shift is significant. Think of the questions as a guide to your reading—not just as multiple-choice enemies to be vanquished.

Once again, here are the question types you will face on the text. For a more thorough review of these types, refer back to Chapter 2. Once again, throughout this chapter, we've identified and tagged these categories of questions you will see on test day:

- Main idea questions
- Theme questions
- Structure questions
- Style questions
- Tone questions

- Detail questions
- Vocabulary-in-context questions
- Inference questions

Some questions may use this language directly ("What can you infer about the author's feeling toward the narrator?"), while others will get at the main ideas or themes indirectly, without those specific words. You may be asked about a narrator's attitude toward the scene, which you'll know is a question about tone, and you'll be looking for adjectives and perhaps figurative language they use to show their perspective on the events they're describing. You may be asked about the genre, so that you can better understand how the author deploys conventional elements—symbols, character types, structural elements—in a surprising way.

These tagged questions are for your benefit in studying: if you know you struggle with distinguishing between the author and the narrator, pay attention to how those questions are phrased in the chapter and on the practice exams, and then work on devising your own versions of style and tone questions.

Eliminating the Wrong Answers

So, the questions are helpful for guiding you—but that doesn't mean they're entirely benevolent, as often they want to teach you a lesson on your racing journey through the exam.

Beware of...	Watch for...
Answer choices framed as overstatements, with words like "always," "never," "completely," and other phrases that don't leave room for the nuances that the exam is often asking you to discern. The exam might try to trick you into judging or exaggerating, instead of analyzing.	Phrases like "tensions between x and y," "both idea x and idea y" (to show the possibility of holding two opinions at the same time)
Answer choices framed as generalizations that are usually true and aren't specific to the passage For example, "the use of imagination" is rarely a good answer to describe a piece of fiction-writing because it's usually a given that fiction is imaginative.	Answer choices that are keyed to the particular style and themes of the passage and don't seem like they'd be applicable to any passage

Beware of...	Watch for...
Answer choices that are judgmental, unless you're being asked to analyze a narrator's tone and that narrator has a very clear disapproving perspective For example, "the narrator should do x" is rarely a good answer because it's imposing your own outside judgment on the passage, rather than reading the narrator's own perspective.	Answer choices that explain a reasonable, open-ended theory to understand why a narrator uses a particular tone or stylistic device—not just whether it's good or bad
Answer choices that are speculative about what happens in the rest of the book or what could happen if characters acted differently	What's actually in the passage; the answer will be among the choices, and even if it's asking you to infer an interpretation, it won't be outlandish or deeply psychological about inner motives you don't know about
Answer choices that speculate about the author's opinion, unless you're asked directly about it and given a reasonable amount of information for choosing a good answer Don't speculate about the relationship between author and narrator unless you have enough information to do so.	Answer choices that allow you to understand the narrator's idiosyncratic choices better These choices will help you turn "this is a weird word choice" into "I see why this word choice illuminates the narrator's perspective…"

These patterns of help and occasional misdirections become most apparent when you practice working through a lot of multiple-choice questions. That's why we give you so many sample questions and practice exams in this book: you start to internalize the logic of the test's questions. The goal isn't to read every book and know it backward and forward but to know the *test's* quirks backward and forward.

So, set your timer and let's try out a passage. Remember to read through it quickly and make notes about any unfamiliar words or what seems to be the main idea of the passage. This example is long and may have some frustratingly long sentences in it… so beware of *The House of Seven the Gables*!

From *The House of the Seven Gables*, by Nathaniel Hawthorne (1851)

> In almost every generation, nevertheless, there happened to be some one
> descendant of the family gifted with a portion of the hard, keen sense, and
> practical energy, that had so remarkably distinguished the original founder.
> His character, indeed, might be traced all the way down, as distinctly as if the
> Colonel himself, a little diluted, had been gifted with a sort of intermittent
> immortality on earth. At two or three epochs, when the fortunes of the family
> were low, this representative of hereditary qualities had made his appearance,
> and caused the traditionary gossips of the town to whisper among themselves,

"Here is the old Pyncheon come again! Now the Seven Gables will be new-shingled!" From father to son, they clung to the ancestral house with singular tenacity of home attachment. For various reasons, however, and from impressions often too vaguely founded to be put on paper, the writer cherishes the belief that many, if not most, of the successive proprietors of this estate were troubled with doubts as to their moral right to hold it. Of their legal tenure there could be no question; but old Matthew Maule, it is to be feared, trode downward from his own age to a far later one, planting a heavy footstep, all the way, on the conscience of a Pyncheon. If so, we are left to dispose of the awful query, whether each inheritor of the property—conscious of wrong, and failing to rectify it—did not commit anew the great guilt of his ancestor, and incur all its original responsibilities. And supposing such to be the case, would it not be a far truer mode of expression to say of the Pyncheon family, that they inherited a great misfortune, than the reverse?

We have already hinted that it is not our purpose to trace down the history of the Pyncheon family, in its unbroken connection with the House of the Seven Gables; nor to show, as in a magic picture, how the rustiness and infirmity of age gathered over the venerable house itself. As regards its interior life, a large, dim looking-glass used to hang in one of the rooms, and was fabled to contain within its depths all the shapes that had ever been reflected there,—the old Colonel himself, and his many descendants, some in the garb of antique babyhood, and others in the bloom of feminine beauty or manly prime, or saddened with the wrinkles of frosty age. Had we the secret of that mirror, we would gladly sit down before it, and transfer its revelations to our page. But there was a story, for which it is difficult to conceive any foundation, that the posterity of Matthew Maule had some connection with the mystery of the looking-glass, and that, by what appears to have been a sort of mesmeric process, they could make its inner region all alive with the departed Pyncheons; not as they had shown themselves to the world, nor in their better and happier hours, but as doing over again some deed of sin, or in the crisis of life's bitterest sorrow.

The popular imagination, indeed, long kept itself busy with the affair of the old Puritan Pyncheon and the wizard Maule; the curse which the latter flung from his scaffold was remembered, with the very important addition, that it had become a part of the Pyncheon inheritance. If one of the family did but gurgle in his throat, a bystander would be likely enough to whisper, between jest and earnest, "He has Maule's blood to drink!" The sudden death of a Pyncheon, about a hundred years ago, with circumstances very similar to what have been related of the Colonel's exit, was held as giving additional probability to the received opinion on this topic. It was considered, moreover, an ugly and ominous circumstance, that Colonel Pyncheon's picture—in obedience, it was said, to a provision of his will—remained affixed to the wall of the room in which he died. Those stern, immitigable features seemed to symbolize an evil

influence, and so darkly to mingle the shadow of their presence with the sunshine of the passing hour, that no good thoughts or purposes could ever spring
up and blossom there. To the thoughtful mind there will be no tinge of super-
stition in what we figuratively express, by affirming that the ghost of a dead
progenitor—perhaps as a portion of his own punishment—is often doomed to
become the Evil Genius of his family.

First, let's underline the unknowns or confusing parts: What could "intermittent immortality" mean?
There are a few confusing words, such as "tenure," "mesmeric," and "immitigable." The narrator mentions a "vague impression"—why are things so deliberately unclear in this passage? Are we supposed
to know what's going on with several generations of a family, when we don't even meet anyone who's
still alive? There's a wizard?!

You are likely either befuddled or annoyed at Hawthorne and his unnamed narrator—or both. Strange
as it may seem, this annoyance is a great pattern to pick out! You are entering the House of Seven
Gables, where every sentence twists and turns like the corridors of a haunted house, deliberately
disorienting you. Pay attention to this sense of disorientation. It's not just you; it's not that you're
a bad reader or that Hawthorne was a bad writer. No, this effect is very deliberately mirroring the
sense of strangeness in the house. Importantly, the strange *style* reveals the *theme* of the passage: that
every event that transpires in the house has generations of complicated history behind it. No wonder
the sentences are so long—there are much gossip, doubt, myth, and bad feelings underneath every
idea. You will undoubtedly be asked about this style and these themes in the questions, so get ready
to turn the frustration into careful attention.

Here are some sample questions that pick up on those observations from the initial read-throughs.
If you're stumped by Hawthorne's thorny prose, check out the contextual information provided to
you in the very first question.

1. The story of the House dates back to the seventeenth century, when Colonel Pyncheon wanted
   to build a house on land that belonged to Matthew Maule. Pyncheon accused Maule of witch-
   craft and had him hanged, and Maule was said to put a curse on the house that has stayed with
   it for generations. The passage exhibits all of the characteristics of the Gothic genre EXCEPT
   A. a sense of history that repeats itself in twisted ways.
   B. a house that is disputed among family members, revealing past indiscretions and
      betrayals.
   C. an open question as to whether there's a supernatural element present.
   D. the sense that characters are doubles of one another, even if they don't know it.
   E. heavy-handed symbolism and figurative language about shadows and darkness.

You may still be annoyed at Hawthorne, but you should be thanking your test writer. This question is
a great example of how the questions help you read the passage. The relationship between Matthew
Maule and the Colonel is not fully explained in the excerpted passage, and it's shrouded in so much
myth, uncertainty, and difficult language that it's hard to tell what's going on. The question gives
you a clearer sense of their identities.

This question gives you contextual information for understanding the main source of conflict
between Pyncheon and Maule. It also gives you the genre of the Gothic novel, so you can apply

TIP

When you're
struck by
something weird
or disorienting,
underline it for
later. These
moments may be
places where the
author is using
style to show
you a *theme*.
The words on the
page reflect the
abstract idea
behind them.
The exam will
highlight these
features that
call attention to
themselves, and
it will help you
work through
it with possible
interpretations
in the answer
choices.

your knowledge of its conventions to help you orient yourself in the haunted house. In the structure of the question, it spells out many of the structural and stylistic elements in the passage, clarifying some of the features that might have seemed confusing underneath all of that verbiage. It's testing you, but in its answer choices, it's giving you the language you can use to find something to grasp onto in the passage.

Which convention from that list is missing from the passage? You might take a look at the choices and think, well, all of them are there. There's definitely a haunted house, a twisted sense of history, and the possibility of a curse and charges of witchcraft. You might look at two bitter old men fighting and figure that they must be doubles of each other, both fixated on cursing each other in life and death—but that's actually an overgeneralization that would mislead you into misunderstanding the important distinctions between the two men. As we warned you in the first pages of the chapter, beware of overgeneralizations about characters. Even if you feel like this answer is not obvious from the other choices, you do have to pick one exception here, and remember how much you were complaining about the heavy-handed language and crazy twists and turns of the sentences? The only exception that makes sense is choice D, so it is the correct answer.

The next questions are also helpful in orienting you to the difficult language and style of the passage, in the effort to link style and the theme.

2. What does the Pyncheon family's "tenure" refer to?
   A. Their denial of responsibility for the Colonel's misdeeds
   B. Their rights to own the house
   C. Their great sense of responsibility for their ancestor's unconscionable behavior
   D. Their quarrels over family ownership that have left the house unoccupied
   E. Their research into ancestry and genealogy

This is a question that asks you a somewhat difficult vocabulary word that comes from specialized legal vocabulary about Pyncheon's will and how property is passed down through generations. If you know French, Spanish, or another Romance language, you'll be familiar with *tenir* or *tener*: to have, to own. The correct answer is choice B.

The question isn't only useful for checking off a vocabulary word, however. It sets up the information that may be helpful—and possibly misleading—for the next two questions. Keep noticing how the answer choices repeat ideas; some of them (like C and E) are incorrect, but at the very least they give you a sense of the main concerns of the passage: family, responsibility that travels through generations, curses…

3. What is the rhetorical question at the end of the last paragraph asking?
   A. Do ancestors bear responsibility to make reparations for their ancestors' ill-gotten gains?
   B. Does evil travel along family lines to successive generations?
   C. Can a house be truly evil because of the sins that were committed on the property in earlier times?
   D. Who is the architect of a house that has been added on to with so many additions?
   E. How do you apologize for a grievous sin you committed years earlier, without realizing it?

This question is asking you to articulate the main idea of the passage: the sins of forefathers bring suffering and punishment on their descendants. It's a rhetorical question, so it will be asked repeatedly, and without resolution, throughout the novel. In thematic terms, this is original sin, or the Christian idea that Adam's fall in the Garden of Eden affects all of mankind, who must suffer for his sins. Hawthorne applies this idea of original sin to key events in American history, as Colonel Pyncheon's sin dates from the colonial America's witch trials, when he used that political and religious controversy to advance his own material needs by illegitimately taking property from a poor man. The titular House of Seven Gables holds the legal, spiritual, familial, and even supernatural legacy of this sin. As in *The Scarlet Letter*, Hawthorne is asking about the legacy of colonial policies, spiritual troubles, social stratifications, and political maneuverings. That's a lot to assess in this question, but it's useful for understanding why the question is so important.

Choices B and C might be tempting if you are following along the Gothic theme, but the best answer uses the language of reparations and responsibility—recall the focus on legal words from question 2. "Evil" is too general to be helpful in untangling those strands of family and ownership, for it flattens all complicated questions under a black stamp of EVIL. The correct answer is choice A.

4. What is the literary device used in the phrase "they clung to the ancestral house with singular tenacity of home attachment" and what theme does it reveal?
    A. The metaphor of clinging creatures shows the house's connection to the natural world
    B. The redundancy of words about attachment reveals how enmeshed the generations are with their history
    C. The dissonance of the sounds exposes how ugly the house is because of its sordid history
    D. The personification of the house shows how it has become a member of the disgraced family
    E. The sibilance of the words about its inhabitants shows its haunted qualities

Question 2's vocabulary builder about tenure and holding rights becomes relevant here, for the sense of holding is amplified to mean clinging *tenaciously*—that is, with great attachment. Basically, there are so many references to holding in that sentence that the word becomes over-determined: it seems overstated and too obvious. They hold, they cling, they attach, yet they can't detach themselves from history. The correct answer is B.

But again, this style doesn't mean that Hawthorne is a bad writer who needs an editor to cut two or three of these references to holding; rather, this redundant sentence is like the Seven Gables on the house: an odd, lopsided number of architectural features. These features—in architecture and in writing style—are too numerous, overelaborate, and rooted in some obscure past that keeps getting in the way.

5. What is the tone of the word "venerable"?
    A. Ironic, as the house is disgraced
    B. Admiring, for the house is a landmark in the town
    C. Sad, for the house is now in disrepair
    D. Incantatory, to ward off the curse of the house
    E. Scathing, for the narrator despises the house

Here is another vocabulary question that is also asking you about the narrator's tone. We've already seen that the narrator has an overelaborate style, but can we figure out anything about his attitudes toward the house or the family in the passage? We've already noticed the narrator's use of a rhetorical question about whether the family bears responsibility for Colonel Pyncheon's sins, as they benefit by getting to live in the house he built on the land he took from Maule. We also noticed in the previous question that there are certain redundant features on the house. With that context in mind, why does the narrator call the house venerable, if it's cursed and ugly? Venerable usually means grand, but this house is anything but that—it may be large, but it's ostentatious and the subject of town gossip. We can see the irony in a respectful adjective being applied to a cursed house, so the answer is choice A.

6. The word *immitigable* gives the sense that the portrait of Colonel Pyncheon is
    A. a forgery.
    B. decaying.
    C. horrifying.
    D. forbidding.
    E. haunted.

This question focuses your attention on the mysterious portrait that is conventional in Gothic novels. (Think of Oscar Wilde's *The Portrait of Dorian Gray*, for one.) This detail is a kind of microcosm of the character himself, so you need to pick the best definition of "immitigable." Many of the answer choices are similar enough in meaning that it seems like you're out of luck if you don't know what that word means. But if the portrait and the Colonel's character are supposed to be mirrors of each other, we should pick an adjective that clearly applies to humans and objects alike, not just objects. "Forbidding," choice D, is the best adjective choice to describe a face in portrait and in human personality. (Arguably, one could have a haunted personality, but we know that the Colonel is more of a jerk than a tortured soul.)

7. The narrator mentions "a large, dim looking glass" that used to hang in one of the rooms. How is the "dimness" of the mirror reflected in the novel's language?

    I.   The narrator keeps mentioning the obscurities of the house's secrets that can never be fully revealed.
    II.   The narrator's style backtracks on itself so often that it's hard to understand the story clearly.
    III. The narrator is affected by the curse on the house and cannot fully explain its secrets.

    A. I only
    B. III only
    C. I and II
    D. I and III
    E. I, II, and III

This question asks you to link the style and the theme in the passage, as you've done in other questions, but it's notable for how it delineates those themes and asks how they complement (or contradict) each other. You have to pick the best combination of options here: what are the most believable interpretations of the "dim" or unclear style? We definitely noticed Option II on the initial read, so let's circle that one. We've been clued in to those obscurities in previous questions about the use of ironies, rhetorical questions that don't have answers, and redundancies that have no use beyond overdetermination. Therefore, Option I looks like a good bet, too. Option III is the puzzler: do we have enough information to assess anything about the narrator, beyond our annoyance? No. As it turns out, the narrator's presence remains indeterminate throughout the novel, but there's no explanation for it. Option III jumps to conclusions. Therefore, the answer is Options I and II, or choice C.

8. There are parallels between the mirror and the novel itself because
   A. the novel has been recovered as a lost object from the House, to be puzzled over by those who encounter it.
   B. both have been partially distorted by the ravages of age.
   C. both have frames: the literal frame of the mirror and the "found object" motif of this narration.
   D. both reflect negatively on their creators.
   E. the generations of Pyncheons appear in a hazy picture that's difficult to determine clearly.

You may be tempted to say that his novel is unreadable in the twenty-first century because it's no longer relevant or even readable in our contemporary time of simpler language. The other answers make interpretations that aren't supported by the language in the passage. The better answer here is the one that echoes the descriptive language about the mirror, which includes words like "hazy" and "vague." The narrator tells you he can't offer a "magic picture" that accounts for these generations, but he's telling a story about them, so his narration serves as just that magic picture. (Interestingly enough, photographs and engraved images become very important in the novel, so the mirror is a hint at that thematic element.) The correct answer is choice E

Track the time that you spend on each passage of prose or poetry, aiming to spend about 13 minutes on each one. That means you have less than a minute per question. If you're really not sure about a question, move on and read the next one; that can often give you some clues about finding the main ideas. In this example from Hawthorne, you see how the passage became significantly more understandable with each question because those questions gave you ways to focus in the midst of so many shadowy words and Evil Genius sentences. Maybe we did this on purpose, to get you on our side as we continue to many, many more literary concepts to study about prose: next to Hawthorne, anyone looks familiar and comforting.

SITUATING YOURSELF WITHIN A PASSAGE: ELEMENTS OF PROSE

When you read a passage, make a quick inference about where you might be in the story. Are you at the beginning, as characters are being introduced (as in the prior passage from *The House of the Seven Gables*)? Are you in the middle of the action? Are you near the end of the story, as characters are reflecting on what's happening?

The elements of the plot can be broken down into stages. You can almost think of these as you would a piece of drama; there may be dramatic passages on the exam, and these same structural elements hold for those staged stories, as well (we'll talk more about drama later). Those stages are:

Exposition

Exposition is the introduction of the characters and the situation (Act I). Pay attention to the following:

- How the narrator's point of view is established
- How the setting in time and place is described
- How characters are introduced

Conflict

Conflict is the situation that the narrator must deal with, the obstacle that causes characters to engage with one another, often in disagreement (Act II or the early middle of the drama). Pay attention to the following:

- How the narrator expresses desires and the obstacles that may be in the way of attaining the objects of those desires
- How characters' conflicting motives are described
- How characters' conflicts are expressed in dialogue

Rising Action or the Complications

This is how the conflict plays out among multiple characters (Acts III and IV). Pay attention to the following:

- Competing desires that seem to cause more conflict than pleasure
- Disputes between characters that reveal tensions that can't be fully resolved
- Larger social and cultural themes that resonate with these ongoing conflicts
- What causes the climax or major confrontation?

Resolution (Act V)

Resolution is the outcome of the conflict, whether desires have been attained and conflicts have been resolved, and where changes have occurred in the relationships among the characters and/or in their perceptions of themselves.

Pay attention to the following:

- How does the author register how a character has changed? Do they reflect directly by saying something like: "Now that I look back on it…" Or are these changes only noticed by the narrator?
- How does the narrator try to sum things up? What's been clarified? What's more complicated?
- How have the themes taken on a deeper, more complex meaning?

One passage isn't going to be able to answer all of those questions, and you may not be able to tell where you are, exactly. It would be a challenge to get thrown into a passage at the very end of a novel, when you didn't even have a way of assessing how things had changed or what the initial obstacle was. It's more often the case—but not always so—that you're introduced to characters from an earlier part of a story because that's where the author is building context, creating the thematic elements in the creating and personal introduction of the narration.

Now that we're situated in the general structure of prose fiction, let's immerse ourselves in the key aspects of the narrative: the setting and the point of view.

Setting

The setting is the time and place of a novel. The location may be a landscape, a city, a home; it may be familiar or strange. Indeed, it's often the case that authors create tension in a setting by making the familiar become strange. The home becomes abnormal in *The House of the Seven Gables*, and its timeframe seems to become unstable as it stretches back to the colonial past and the character of Colonel Pyncheon achieves "intermittent immortality" in haunting the house or at least making the characters uneasy.

When you're looking at the setting of a passage on the exam, pay attention to the narrator's descriptive language, which will give you a sense of the narrator's attitude, how he or she perceives it in an idiosyncratic way. To use the language of film: the narrator is directing the scene and telling you where to look.

Let's see how the narrator of James Weldon Johnson's *Autobiography of an Ex-Colored Man* directs our attention to details in the unfamiliar setting he's encountered. He's trying to find a place to stay in Atlanta, where he's new in town:

From *Autobiography of an Ex-Colored Man*, by James Weldon Johnson

I glanced around the apartment and saw that it contained a double bed and two cots, two wash-stands, three chairs, and a time-worn bureau, with a looking-glass that would have made Adonis appear hideous. I looked at the cot in which I was to sleep and suspected, not without good reasons, that I should not be the first to use the sheets and pillow-case since they had last come from the wash. When I thought of the clean, tidy, comfortable surroundings in which I had been reared, a wave of homesickness swept over me that made me feel faint. Had it not been for the presence of my companion, and that I knew this much of his history—that he was not yet quite twenty, just three years older than myself, and that he had been fighting his own way in the world, earning his own living and providing for his own education since he was fourteen—I should not have been able to stop the tears that were welling up in my eyes.

I asked him why it was that the proprietor of the house seemed unwilling to accommodate me for more than a couple of days. He informed me that the man ran a lodging house especially for Pullman porters, and, as their stays in town were not longer than one or two nights, it would interfere with his arrangements to have anyone stay longer. He went on to say: "You see this room is fixed up to accommodate four men at a time. Well, by keeping a sort of table of trips, in and out, of the men, and working them like checkers, he can accommodate fifteen or sixteen in each week and generally avoid having an empty bed. You happen to catch a bed that would have been empty for a couple of nights." I asked him where he was going to sleep. He answered: "I sleep in that other cot tonight; tomorrow night I go out." He went on to tell me that the man who kept the house did not serve meals, and that if I was hungry, we would go out and get something to eat.

Here's a sample question about detail:

What is the significance of the description of the mirror in the room?

A.   It exposes the faults of the room with embarrassing clarity.

B.   The narrator is having a hard time seeing himself inside the unfamiliar room, literally and figuratively.

C.   It shows him an ugly side of himself that he didn't realize until he met the proprietor.

D.   It shows him the reflection of all of the other guests who have passed through the room.

E.   Although he mentions the myth of Adonis, it's also alluding to the myth of Narcissus, who admired his own reflection too much.

It would be fascinating to trace these questions about self-perception in Weldon's novel, as the title suggests. For this question, though, we don't have enough information to make large thematic statements or social commentary; it's not the same kind of portentous, symbol-laden narration as in *The House of the Seven Gables*. Weldon is working directly in the tradition of realism or the detailed description of everyday life without lots of figurative or abstract language. What you see in the setting is what his narrator sees, with no mystification. Even though it's realism, it's still a subjective perspective, and he shows the reader his disdain, even revulsion, for the dirty, cramped room. He doesn't want to be there. The correct answer is choice B.

Let's now look at a question about structure:

What happens to the narrator's perspective after he describes the mirror?

A.   It shrinks because he becomes so fixated on all of the disarray in the room that he can't focus.

B.   It shrinks because he becomes self-conscious.

C.   It expands to consider his position among other men who have passed through the room.

D.   It becomes distorted like the dirty mirror's reflection.

E.   It shifts to other characters.

Even as he's trying not to cry from homesickness, he compares his own lonely, precarious situation with his companion, who's also young and without a place to call home. He learns about how the lodging-house works and how African-American porters live a transient life in these kinds of establishments, where they all feel dislocated. Thus the perspective on the setting shifts somewhat in these two paragraphs, as he moves from his personal discomfort to consider the social implications of so many men's dislocation. The familiar becomes strange not just as a psychological state of mind, but as a way of using realistic description to make social commentary on everyday life. Choice C is correct.

Here's another example of how setting might reveal a character's inner state, in Ann Radcliffe's Gothic novel, *The Mysteries of Udolpho*. We discuss the sublime more in depth in the poetry chapter, when we talk about the Romantic poets, but the basic idea is that it's a feeling of intense awe of the natural world. It's often contrasted with the beautiful: you can admire a stream or meadow as a beautiful scene, but you feel so overwhelmed in front of a mountain or waterfall that you're nearly trembling with a mix of emotions. It's a very literary sensibility, one which poets deliberately sought. When authors use it as a setting in a novel, it shows the characters contending with nature in an epic way or confronting the small scale of humanity in the grandeur of nature. Settings in the sublime evoke powerful feelings and allow authors to discuss grandiose themes like spirituality, mortality, and man's relationship with nature. In this passage, we see a character's inner thoughts, as St. Aubert is narrating his reflections to himself.

From *The Mysteries of Udolpho*, by Ann Radcliffe

The rich plains of Languedoc, which exhibited all the glories of the vintage, with the gaieties of a French festival, no longer awakened St. Aubert to pleasure, whose condition formed a mournful contrast to the hilarity and youthful beauty which surrounded him. As his languid eyes moved over the scene, he considered, that they would soon, perhaps, be closed for ever on this world. 'Those distant and sublime mountains,' said he secretly, as he gazed on a chain of the Pyrenees that stretched towards the west, 'these luxuriant plains, this blue vault, the cheerful light of day, will be shut from my eyes! The song of the peasant, the cheering voice of man—will no longer sound for me!'

Here's a sample question about tone and main idea:

St. Aubert calls the mountains he sees in the distance "sublime," for they are vast and magnificent. Why does he repeat the word "cheer" in his sad musings?

I.   He is highlighting the contrast between his larger-than-life awed feelings about nature with the small wonders of human joy in the festivals

II.   Because he does not want to speak his feelings aloud, he is committing the pathetic fallacy of ascribing human emotions to nature

III.   He is challenging readers to find more positive feelings in the sublime, to get a perspective on the value of our short lives

A. I only
B. II only
C. III only
D. I and II
E. I, II, and III

This kind of setting is conventional for a Romantic novel like Radcliffe's, as she finds Gothic qualities in nature and in castles (there is a mysterious castle not two paragraphs away from St. Aubert's reflections). The question asks you to interpret a repeated word, to see what the pattern might mean. The

TIP

Pay special attention to any extra information the exam gives you as a headnote at the top of the passage, a footnote, or context in a question. That information is likely helpful in understanding the passage and answering questions.

three options throw a lot of critical vocabulary at you, from *sublime* to *pathetic fallacy*. Don't tremble in terror at that language. Fortunately, Option II defines the literary device for you: the projection of human emotions onto an object or natural world. St. Aubert seems to be doing just that, and Option II gives you a reasonable interpretation of the pathetic fallacy as a strategy of projecting, but not voicing, his feelings "secretly." Option I also looks like a reasonable interpretation for the contrast between joy and sadness, as the repetition shows the gap between what Aubert is seeing and feeling. It's Option III that's a step too far: that question is trying too hard to create a lesson in this scene. Aubert is already reading it as a representation of his feelings, so we shouldn't project any more onto it. Go with Options I and II, and pick choice D as the correct answer.

Point of View

It's crucial to understand what kind of narrative point of view you're reading. As you've already seen from Weldon and Radcliffe, the characters' perspectives on a setting affect not only how they see themselves, but also how the reader understands what's going on in the story. A narrator gives you the tone of the passage by which you can understand his or her attitude toward the situation. Consider this book's tagging system for multiple choice questions: A narrative is set up as a *structure* for you to get situated and immersed in a story, so that you understand the *main idea*. You trust (or distrust) the narrator based on linguistic *style* of introduction, description, and characterization of other figures in the story. The narrator's *vocabulary* gives you a sense of background, education, and attitudes, and more *details* are revealed gradually over the course of the narrative. The narrator causes you to make *inferences*, and their narration may clue you into *themes* of the story.

Let's take a look at some of the different types of narration so that you can get a sense of how many different ways there are to tell a story:

First-person narration: Uses "I" to tell the story

Examples of protagonist first-person narrators: Robinson Crusoe in Daniel Defoe's novel, Offred in Margaret Atwood's *The Handmaid's Tale*

Examples of side characters who are observers: Nick Carraway in *The Great Gatsby*, Nelly Dean in *Wuthering Heights*

Pay attention to these stylistic and structural features:

- The narrator may be the protagonist or main character: what are the limitations of his/her perspective? What isn't being shown, either through lack of knowledge or deliberate obscuring from the reader by the narrator?

- How does the narrator reflect on the action of the novel: is it straightforward, or does the narrator express doubts, uncertainties, or fantasies that cut into the narration?

- The narrator may be a side character who is observing the action. You can ask the same questions here—why is the action being related to the reader at a remove?

- Are there moments where you question how the narrator knows something that he didn't witness or couldn't have experienced?

When you're reading passages on the exam, you'll want to pay attention to shifts in narrative voice. A narrator might switch to the first-person plural "we" to broaden the perspective to other characters, or the narrator might switch to "you" in order to gain some distance from the story or flatter the reader into sharing the perspective. Here's one such example of first-person narration where something more unusual is happening.

Aphra Behn's 1688 novel *Oroonoko* is the tragic story of an African prince and his lover, Imoinda. It's narrated by a white woman in Surinam—sometimes thought to be a stand-in for the author herself, although that historical fact is hard to pin down.

> From *Oroonoko*, by Aphra Behn
>
> The Prince [Oroonoko] return'd to Court with quite another Humour than before; and tho' he did not speak much of the fair *Imoinda*, he had the Pleasure to hear all his Followers speak of nothing but the Charms of that Maid, insomuch, that, even in the Presence of the old King, they were extolling her, and heightening, if possible, the Beauties they had found in her: so that nothing else was talk'd of, no other Sound was heard in every Corner where there were Whisperers, but *Imoinda! Imoinda!*
>
> 'Twill be imagin'd Oroonoko stay'd not long before he made his second Visit; nor, considering his Quality, not much longer before he told her, he ador'd her. I have often heard him say, that he admir'd by what strange Inspiration he came to talk Things so soft, and so passionate, who never knew Love, nor was us'd to the Conversation of Women; but (to use his own Words) he said, 'Most happily, some new, and, till then, unknown Power instructed his Heart and Tongue in the Language of Love; and at the same Time, in Favour of him, inspir'd *Imoinda* with a Sense of his Passion.' She was touch'd with what he said, and return'd it all in such Answers as went to his very Heart, with a Pleasure unknown before.

What role does the narrator play in this passage?
A. Direct witness
B. Storyteller after the fact
C. Concealed spy
D. Whispering observer
E. Reader of his testimony

The narrator's role in the story as a mediator is complicated to untangle, as she frequently uses phrases like "'twill be imagin'd" as though she's imagining these details herself. It's not clear whether she's embellishing Oroonoko's quotation or paraphrasing him. In fact, these limitations on her perspective become more shocking as she has to relate (or skim over) violence and death; her limitations as a narrator become untenable, even if she desires to serve as a witness for this account. In turning to imagination and negotiating multiple perspectives of the king, his court, Oroonoko, and Imoinda, she's a storyteller with limited narrative perspective. The best answer is choice B. With Behn in mind, we will go on to discuss the kinds of limitations of other narrative perspectives.

First person narrators: Unreliable narrators whose perspective seems misleading or distorted

Literary examples: Tristram Shandy in Laurence Sterne's novel of the same name, the unnamed narrator of Charlotte Perkins Gilman's "The Yellow Wallpaper," Humbert Humbert in Vladimir Nabokov's *Lolita*, "Chief" Bromden in Ken Kesey's *One Flew Over the Cuckoo's Nest*, Pi Patel in Yann Martel's *The Life of Pi*

Pay attention to these features:

- Subtle shifts in tone and use of intentionally distracting or misleading qualifiers, such as "I can't tell you, but…" or "I didn't hear this from the source, but…"

- Attempts to persuade and seduce readers to believe their side of the situation—these persuasions can be stylistically inventive and charming to read! How does the narrator create tensions for the narrative between belief and doubt, or trust and distrust?

- Unreliable narrators aren't necessarily liars—they could be unreliable because they're naive, mentally unsound, gossipy, playful, under the influence of some illness, poison, or drug . . . .

- How do they serve a role like that of the clown or fool in a Shakespeare play? They may be poking holes in the idea that one could ever tell the full truth of a situation in a narrative.

Frame narratives: Narratives that have stories within stories

Frame narratives are often relayed by first-person narrators who might have contradictory accounts of a situation or who might themselves be unreliable.

Literary examples: John Bunyan's *Pilgrim's Progress*, Mary Shelley's *Frankenstein*, Emily Brontë's *Wuthering Heights*, Joseph Conrad's *Heart of Darkness*, Edith Wharton's *Ethan Frome*, the narrator and the governess in Henry James's *The Turn of the Screw*

Pay attention to the following:

- Who is the narrator of the particular passage you are reading, and what kind of relationship does he or she have with the rest of the novel?

- What structural devices in a short passage can show the narrator's peripheral perspective?

- Why is there the need for distance from the events of the novel?

- When do frame narratives introduce doubt and disbelief in the narrative, by showing conflicting accounts of the same situation?

Frame narratives are not as common on the exam because they require extensive setup, but you may get an essay question that asks you to analyze the function of such a narrative structure, or you may see a brief story within a story in someone's dialogue inside a passage—a mini frame narrative or a flashback.

First-person plural narration: Narrators who use "we" to speak for a group of people

Literary examples: William Faulkner's "A Rose for Emily," Jeffrey Eugenides' *The Virgin Suicides*, Chang-rae Lee's *On Such a Full Sea*, Julie Otsuka's *The Buddha in the Attic*

> **TIP**
>
> In a short passage, you may not be able to assess the reliability of a narrator unless there's an obvious stylistic marker—unreliable narrators can be quite sly. Watch out for misleading answer choices that make you jump to conclusions: they are the unreliable paths of the exam!

Pay attention to these stylistic and structural features:

- The first-person plural may be a way of serving a form of community testimony about something that affected an entire group, the members of which come together to tell the story as a source of collective authority

- At other times, they may serve a similar purpose as the chorus in Ancient Greek plays. They may be the conscience of the story, commenting on the characters' behavior, or the horrified onlookers who can't affect the action of those characters. In those cases, the choice of "we" will show the limitations of knowledge leading to action: it's like "we" are trapped behind glass, observing but not actually of the story.

The novels mentioned among those examples are newer and more attuned to stylistic inventiveness, but let's look at an example from Joseph Conrad in 1898, to see some of the historical uses of the "we" voice. The story takes place in the Dutch colonies of Malaysia.

From "Karain: A Memory," by Joseph Conrad

It was only on board the schooner, when surrounded by white faces, by unfamiliar sights and sounds, that Karain seemed to forget the strange obsession that wound like a black thread through the gorgeous pomp of his public life. At night we treated him in a free and easy manner, which just stopped short of slapping him on the back, for there are liberties one must not take with a Malay. He said himself that on such occasions he was only a private gentleman coming to see other gentlemen whom he supposed as well born as himself. I fancy that to the last he believed us to be emissaries of Government, darkly official persons furthering by our illegal traffic some dark scheme of high statecraft. Our denials and protestations were unavailing. He only smiled with discreet politeness and inquired about the Queen. Every visit began with that inquiry; he was insatiable of details; he was fascinated by the holder of a sceptre the shadow of which, stretching from the westward over the earth and over the seas, passed far beyond his own hand's-breadth of conquered land. He multiplied questions; he could never know enough of the Monarch of whom he spoke with wonder and chivalrous respect— with a kind of affectionate awe! Afterwards, when we had learned that he was the son of a woman who had many years ago ruled a small Bugis state, we came to suspect that the memory of his mother (of whom he spoke with enthusiasm) mingled somehow in his mind with the image he tried to form for himself of the far-off Queen whom he called Great, Invincible, Pious, and Fortunate. We had to invent details at last to satisfy his craving curiosity; and our loyalty must be pardoned, for we tried to make them fit for his august and resplendent ideal. We talked. The night slipped over us, over the still schooner, over the sleeping land, and over the sleepless sea that thundered amongst the reefs outside the bay.

What position does the group of narrators serve in the story?

A. Jury

B. Customers

C. Skeptics

D. Audience

E. Dupes in a confidence scheme

Even Karain is uncertain about who or what the narrators are, as they constantly assure him that they are not representatives of the government—so then who are the white men who are attending his ship so attentively. Sailors? Merchants? Something slightly less legal? The ambiguity of their presence troubles Karain, but not too much—its lack of resolution should trouble us, however, in creating uncertainty about their motives. The passage—indeed, the entire story—is shot through with obscurity about what happened, as though in collectively narrating, they could not get a clear perspective. The best answer among these choices is D, the audience, for they return to listen to Karain every night, and are deeply attuned to every facet of his presentation. What's complicated about thinking about Karain as a performer?

Second-person narration: "You" are the narrator of the novel

Literary examples: *If On a Winter's Night a Traveler*, by Italo Calvino; Leo Tolstoy's "(December)," from the *Sevastopol Sketches*; parts of William Faulkner's *Absalom, Absalom*

Pay attention to these literary features:

- How does the direct address to you, the reader, immerse you in a scene? Where are the moments where you're taken out of it abruptly because the "you" conceit doesn't work?

- Are all readers the same kind of "you"? Who isn't included among the readers implied by the second-person voice? Who can or can't participate in the events of the novel?

- How is the direct address to the reader immersive but also disorienting, misleading, or otherwise tricky?

- Why are you being asked to stand in for a more specific character? What is the point of generalizing a character like "you"?

From "The Haunted Mind," by Nathaniel Hawthorne

What a singular moment is the first one, when you have hardly begun to recollect yourself, after starting from midnight slumber! By unclosing your eyes so suddenly, you seem to have surprised the personages of your dream in full convocation round your bed, and catch one broad glance at them before they can flit into obscurity. Or, to vary the metaphor, you find yourself, for a single instant, wide awake in that realm of illusions, whither sleep has been the passport, and behold its ghostly inhabitants and wondrous scenery, with a perception of their strangeness, such as you never attain while the dream is undisturbed. The distant sound of a church clock is borne faintly on the wind. You question with yourself, half seriously, whether it has stolen to your waking ear from some gray tower, that stood within the precincts of your dream. While yet

in suspense, another clock flings its heavy clang over the slumbering town, with
so full and distinct a sound, and such a long murmur in the neighboring air, that
you are certain it must proceed from the steeple at the nearest corner. You count
the strokes--one--two--and there they cease, with a booming sound, like the
gathering of a third stroke within the bell.

Why does Hawthorne use the phrase "unclosing your eyes so suddenly" when he could use the
more obvious phrase "opening your eyes"?

A. To show the creative impulses that arise at odd hours of the night

B. To expose the narrator's madness

C. To create assonance between the "unopening" vowels and the toll and stroke of the
church bells

D. To amplify the sense of disorientation in the passage

E. To create a form of synesthesia

This passage is full of clichés about insomnia! There's hardly a sentence that doesn't have a well-worn
phrase that's no longer shocking to describe an unsettling situation. But that's how insomnia feels,
in some ways, because you don't feel quite conscious or active enough to get out of that in-between
state. You're stuck in limbo. The word "unclosing" is a kind of *liminal* word—a word that's partway
between open and closed. The word is strange enough that it enhances the sense of disorientation,
halfway between morning and night, somewhere between sleep and wakefulness.

Third-person close (or limited) narration: The narrator tells a story about a character with access to only that character's thoughts

Literary examples: Newland Archer in Edith Wharton's *The Age of Innocence* (for most of the novel),
George Orwell's *1984*, Ray Bradbury's *Fahrenheit 451*

Pay attention to the following:

- The use of "free indirect discourse," or the ways that a narrator slips in and out of a character's thoughts in a third-person narration (see below)

- The third-person limited narration is often used to show how the character is different from
those who surround him or her. What does the limited perspective allow you to see about
the character's interactions with others, as well as the character's unshared inner thoughts?

Let's take a look at that "free indirect discourse" concept, which sounds more difficult than it actually
is. Jane Austen is one of the great novelists who create omniscient narrators *and* unforgettable individual characters who seem to speak to us through those narrators. Austen is credited with being
one of the first writers to use "free indirect discourse," or the slipping in and out of a character's
head to show the character's thoughts and feelings, while keeping a level of remove in the narration.

From *Persuasion*, by Jane Austen

Just as they were setting off, the gentlemen returned. They had taken out a
young dog, who had spoilt their sport, and sent them back early. Their time
and strength, and spirits, were, therefore, exactly ready for this walk, and they

TIP

Pay attention to
words that the
narrator appears
to have made up,
for those small
details can reflect
his attitudes,
preoccupations,
and judgments.

entered into it with pleasure. Could Anne have foreseen such a junction, she would have stayed at home; but, from some feelings of interest and curiosity, she fancied now that it was too late to retract, and the whole six set forward together in the direction chosen by the Miss Musgroves, who evidently considered the walk as under their guidance.

Anne's object was, not to be in the way of anybody; and where the narrow paths across the fields made many separations necessary, to keep with her brother and sister. Her pleasure in the walk must arise from the exercise and the day, from the view of the last smiles of the year upon the tawny leaves, and withered hedges, and from repeating to herself some few of the thousand poetical descriptions extant of autumn, that season of peculiar and inexhaustible influence on the mind of taste and tenderness, that season which had drawn from every poet, worthy of being read, some attempt at description, or some lines of feeling. She occupied her mind as much as possible in such like musings and quotations; but it was not possible, that when within reach of Captain Wentworth's conversation with either of the Miss Musgroves, she should not try to hear it; yet she caught little very remarkable. It was mere lively chat, such as any young persons, on an intimate footing, might fall into. He was more engaged with Louisa than with Henrietta. Louisa certainly put more forward for his notice than her sister.

What is the best characterization of the narrator's perceptions about Anne's behavior?

A. Anne notices more about others' social behavior than she wants to let on.

B. Anne is lost in her own world of poetical musings inside her head while others socialize.

C. Anne must be more active if she is to attract the attention of any of the gentlemen in the party.

D. Anne dislikes Captain Wentworth for his forwardness with Louisa and Henrietta.

E. Anne wants to spend time with the Miss Musgroves in private so she can talk about her secret feelings for Captain Wentworth.

This question asks you to get inside Anne's head, as the narrator is giving you access to her thoughts. We see both Anne's desires to avoid socializing with the others, as well as her keen attention to Louisa and Henrietta's conversation with Captain Wentworth. The narrator can see that she's torn between wanting to participate and wanting to flee. The correct answer is choice A. Anne spends much of the novel like this, caught between desire and action; free indirect discourse is Austen's tool to show the exquisite torture of this state of being in-between.

Third-person omniscient narration: The narrator gives you perspective on all characters and what they are thinking and seeing

Literary examples: Nathaniel Hawthorne's *The Scarlet Letter*, Charles Dickens' *Bleak House*

Pay attention to:

- Omniscient means all-seeing, so what does "all" mean in the novel? What is the scope that the narrator can account for that a limited third-person narrator might not be able to see?

These novels often have a big sprawl, as in Bleak House or Middlemarch, so what can they do with that expanded sense of scale?

- Does the narrator favor one character? Why?
- How does the narrator describe characters' perspectives during conflicts?
- What kind of character would you imagine the narrator to be if the narrator were inside the story? Is it possible to imagine the narrator inside the story?

George Eliot's *Middlemarch* is mostly narrated by an omniscient narrator, and there are even occasionally shifts into the first-person "I." Many readers see the beginnings of a modernist fragmentation and stream of consciousness in sections of the novel. As you're reading this short passage, try to imagine what's just slightly different about this characterization of Dorothea Brooke, as opposed to Anne Elliot in *Persuasion*:

From *Middlemarch*, by George Eliot

The rural opinion about the new young ladies, even among the cottagers, was generally in favor of Celia, as being so amiable and innocent-looking, while Miss Brooke's large eyes seemed, like her religion, too unusual and striking. Poor Dorothea! compared with her, the innocent-looking Celia was knowing and worldly-wise; so much subtler is a human mind than the outside tissues which make a sort of blazonry or clock-face for it.

Yet those who approached Dorothea, though prejudiced against her by this alarming hearsay, found that she had a charm unaccountably reconcilable with it. Most men thought her bewitching when she was on horseback. She loved the fresh air and the various aspects of the country, and when her eyes and cheeks glowed with mingled pleasure she looked very little like a devotee. Riding was an indulgence which she allowed herself in spite of conscientious qualms; she felt that she enjoyed it in a pagan sensuous way, and always looked forward to renouncing it.

How would you characterize the narrator's tone in the last sentence?
A. Wryly discerning
B. Sanctimonious and superior
C. Flirty and suggestive
D. Admiring of her morals
E. Nit-picky and petty

The narrator clearly has thoughts about Dorothea's religiosity and how it affects her interactions with other characters. The narrator is a bit hard on Dorothea for her piety, but the answer choices here all overstate that judgment. The narrator is more perceptive than mean, and the tone is more ironic and wry than cruel. The correct answer is choice A.

Novels that switch narrative techniques from chapter to chapter

Literary examples: Wilkie Collins' *The Moonstone*, William Faulkner's *As I Lay Dying* and *The Sound and the Fury*, James Joyce's *Ulysses*, Toni Morrison's *Beloved*

- Where are the conflicts between the different narrators?
- How do different narrators have different kinds of access to situations? How are those differing forms of access reflected in descriptions of setting and characterization?
- Is the narrative experimenting with different kinds of narration, like legal testimonies, letters, diaries, in setting up these chapters?

It's unlikely that you'd see a passage on the multiple-choice part of the exam that asks you about substantial point-of-view switching in a novel like *Ulysses*. You will probably not see such a difficult book on the exam. (Indeed, if you read *The Sound and the Fury* for school, you might have used one of the editions that prints the different points of view in different colors of ink!) It may happen that you get a passage where there's an obvious shift in point of view—keep your eye out for such an example in the sample questions—but you won't be asked a question about the large-scale disorienting point-of-view switches from those legendarily difficult novels.

Epistolary novel: A novel made up of letters

Literary examples: Henry Fielding's *Pamela*, Jane Austen's *Lady Susan*, Bram Stoker's *Dracula*, Alice Walker's *The Color Purple*

Pay attention to the following:

- From reading the correspondence in full, what do you know about the story that the correspondents don't know separately? How do the gaps in the characters' knowledge of the full situation create conflicts, suspense, or tension?
- How does the author manipulate the delay in writing and receiving letters? How does that delay create tension or further plot points?
- How does the form of correspondence change with new communications technologies?

It's possible that there could be a series of letters from an epistolary novel among the multiple-choice passages, but such a selection would likely be either very short letters, or one letter from a character to another, which you could treat more like a first-person narrative.

HOW TO READ NONFICTION PROSE

There may be a piece of nonfiction prose on the exam, taken from a literary essay or work of history, ethnography, political commentary, art criticism, or popular science. Prose nonfiction is not so different from fiction at all; it uses similar descriptive techniques and figurative language to give a sense of an author's perspective on a setting, event, or conflict. Many paragraphs of landscape description you might find in a novel like Wallace Stegner's *Angle of Repose* or Willa Cather's *My Antonia* would be just as at home in an essay about the making of the modern American landscape. Characters in contemporary novels might digress briefly to discuss their take on a popular film, just as you'd find in a piece of cultural criticism by Susan Sontag or bell hooks.

> **TIP**
>
> These are not exhaustive lists, not by any account. What books and authors would you add or change on these lists? Great, now start generating multiple choice questions and/or essay questions about these narrative features that you're thinking about!

You can use the same strategies that you would in reading prose fiction, with more focus on setting and description than on dialogue and characterization. Here, you can also collapse the distinction between author and narrator, as the author is narrating their own perspective in an essay. You may also want to think about how the author is communicating to an audience of readers, the way you would analyze a rhetorical essay on the AP® English Language Exam. Let's take a look at a sample passage from Henry James, who wrote prose fiction and nonfiction, to see how he sets his scene:

From *English Hours* (1888), by Henry James

The London year is studded with holidays, blessed little islands of comparative leisure—intervals of absence for good society. Then the wonderful English faculty for "going out of town for a little change" comes into illimitable play, and families transport their nurseries and their bath-tubs to those rural scenes which form the real substratum of the national life. Such moments as these are the paradise of the genuine London-lover, for he then finds himself face to face with the object of his passion; he can give himself up to an intercourse which at other times is obstructed by his rivals. Then every one he knows is out of town, and the exhilarating sense of the presence of every one he doesn't know becomes by so much the deeper.

This is why I pronounce this satisfaction not an unsociable, but a positively affectionate emotion. It is the mood in which he most measures the immense humanity of the place and in which its limits recede farthest into a dimness peopled with possible illustrations. For his acquaintance, however numerous it may be, is finite; whereas the other, the unvisited London is infinite. It is one of his pleasures to think of the experiments and excursions he may make in it, even when these adventures don't particularly come off. The friendly fog seems to protect and enrich them—to add both to the mystery and security, so that it is most in the winter months that the imagination weaves such delights.

Here's a sample question about main idea:

What does Henry James's use of the pathetic fallacy in the term "friendly fog" tell you about the main idea of the passage?
A. There are times when he enjoys the company of abstractions more than people.
B. He finds more comfort in nature than he does in the bustling city.
C. He is lonely during the Christmas holidays, so he searches for fellow Londoners in the misty city.
D. In the enigmatic weather, he devises mysterious stories about the strangers he doesn't know on the streets.
E. He sees the city as a landscape of social interactions.

This question asks you to identify the main idea of the passage, by locating it in a microcosm of figurative language: the two words "friendly fog" reflect the larger concerns of the passage. You don't even need to know exactly what "pathetic fallacy" means here, although you may remember from earlier in the chapter that it's the projection of human emotions onto an object or natural world. It's easy to project your feelings onto fog because it seems to envelop you, making it hard to tell where it begins and you end. You might think it's choice E, then, but that statement is too general and could apply to any description of the city. You need something more compelling as an interpretation: choices B, C, and D aren't supported by the passage and are describing the opposite of the author's ideas. Choice A is the better choice, for it describes why James prefers the abstractness of fog—it's easier to project his feelings onto it than to go through the motions of interactions with people he sees every day. The correct answer is choice A.

HOW TO READ DRAMATIC PROSE

You may encounter a dramatic passage on the exam, but you can tackle those passages by reading them as you would a page of dialogue in a novel or as you would interpret a paragraph of a narrator's inner thoughts in a first-person narration. There's an extra layer of awareness required, however, in that these monologues and dialogues were written to be performed, so the characters are often written as exaggerated, dramatic, or contrived. Even when they're not breaking the fourth wall to speak directly to the audience, as Hamlet does frequently, they're often intensely performative—because there's no extra narration to give you a sense of what they're thinking or what might be happening that you can't see on stage.

Let's take a look at two different ways that dramatic passages might be excerpted and presented to you on the exam.

From Shakespeare's *King Lear* (Act I, Scene ii)

EARL OF GLOUCESTER. These late eclipses in the sun and moon portend
no good to us. Though the wisdom of nature can reason it thus and thus, yet
nature finds itself scourg'd by the sequent effects. Love cools,
friendship falls off, brothers divide. In cities, mutinies; in
countries, discord; in palaces, treason; and the bond crack'd
'twixt son and father. This villain of mine comes under the
prediction; there's son against father: the King falls from bias
of nature; there's father against child. We have seen the best
of our time. Machinations, hollowness, treachery, and all
ruinous disorders follow us disquietly to our graves. Find out
this villain, Edmund; it shall lose thee nothing; do it
carefully. And the noble and true-hearted Kent banish'd! his
offence, honesty! 'Tis strange. *[Exit]*

EDMUND. This is the excellent foppery of the world, that, when we are
sick in fortune, often the surfeit of our own behaviour, we make
guilty of our disasters the sun, the moon, and the stars; as if
we were villains on necessity; fools by heavenly compulsion;
knaves, thieves, and treachers by spherical pre-dominance;
drunkards, liars, and adulterers by an enforc'd obedience of
planetary influence; and all that we are evil in, by a divine
thrusting on.

TIP

In drama, characters are always performing, even in intimate private moments. (That's why we have dramatic monologues.) Keep this sense of performance and playing to the audience in mind as you're reading their lines.

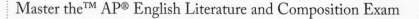

Here's a sample question about style:

What is the significance of Gloucester's and Edmund's uses of elaborate lists in this exchange? Consider Gloucester's "machinations, hollowness, treachery, and all ruinous disorders" as well as Edmund's "knaves, thieves, and treachers…, drunkards, liars, and adulterers…"?

I. The lists give a précis or summary of the kinds of events and characters that populate a tragedy, foretelling the events to come.
II. Gloucester's list is made up of abstractions, where Edmund's is individualized, showing how their characters' lofty and base perspectives intersect in villainy.
III. The lists have an incantatory quality, as though they were summoning all of these events and villains to descend onto the stage.

A. I only
B. II only
C. III only
D. I and II
E. II and III

You're not given much context for understanding these two characters in this excerpt from *King Lear*. Perhaps you've read the play before, but maybe you haven't. You may be anxious about having to interpret these characters from a well-known tragedy in the middle of their speeches. This question gives you a specific stylistic element to focus on, effectively helping you situate yourself in the language of the passage. You don't need any additional information about the characters than their use of elaborate lists.

So, what do you see among the answer choices that might give you even more context for understanding the unfamiliar passage? Option I is a general enough summary that it seems like it could account for Gloucester's lists of villainous actions, yet it's also specific enough to the tragedy that's under consideration. It's a good middle ground between general and specific—so it gives you context. Option II describes a stylistic distinction between the two characters' lists—Gloucester is speaking in abstractions, whereas Edmund is naming individuals--and then gives a reasonable interpretation of why that distinction may be important later in the play. Option III is a fascinating possibility, but it's kind of the evil twin of Option I: it's too aggressive in interpreting the passage and may mislead you by promising events that may or may not happen in the play. It's too good to be true—at least, given the brevity of the passage. Option I is the safer version of this interpretation because it sticks with what's on the page (and stage). Therefore, you can stick with Options I and II and pick choice D as the correct answer.

On the other hand, sometimes the excerpt may need some additional context so that you can get up to speed with the action of the play. That's especially true in comedies, where there may be confusion about who's who or who's in love with whom—think of how difficult it would be to explain Shakespeare's *Twelfth Night* or Oscar Wilde's *The Importance of Being Earnest* in just a sentence or two. The exam will give you enough context to show you what's going on in a dialogue.

Let's look at an example. Lydia Languish has spent the play scheming to be married: she is in love with a penniless but good-hearted man she knows as "Ensign Beverley," but she has been trying to contrive a marriage to the wealthy Sir Anthony Absolute. In this scene from Act V, scene 1, of

Richard Brinsley Sheridan's play *The Rivals*, she learns that "Ensign Beverley" is really Anthony Absolute's son, Captain Jack Absolute, and her plans are in disarray.

The Rivals, by Richard Brinsley Sheridan (Act V, scene 1)

LYDIA So, then, I see I have been deceived by every one! But I don't care—I'll never have him.

JULIA Nay, Lydia——

LYDIA Why, is it not provoking? when I thought we were coming to the prettiest distress imaginable, to find myself made a mere Smithfield bargain of at last! There, had I projected one of the most sentimental elopements!—so becoming a disguise!—so amiable a ladder of ropes!—Conscious moon—four horses—Scotch parson—with such surprise to Mrs. Malaprop—and such paragraphs in the newspapers!—Oh, I shall die with disappointment!

JULIA I don't wonder at it!

LYDIA Now—sad reverse!—what have I to expect, but, after a deal of flimsy preparation with a bishop's license, and my aunt's blessing, to go simpering up to the altar; or perhaps be cried three times in a country church, and have an unmannerly fat clerk ask the consent of every butcher in the parish to join John Absolute and Lydia Languish, spinster! Oh that I should live to hear myself called spinster!

JULIA Melancholy indeed!

LYDIA How mortifying, to remember the dear delicious shifts I used to be put to, to gain half a minute's conversation with this fellow! How often have I stole forth, in the coldest night in January, and found him in the garden, stuck like a dripping statue! There would he kneel to me in the snow, and sneeze and cough so pathetically! he shivering with cold and I with apprehension! and while the freezing blast numbed our joints, how warmly would he press me to pity his flame, and glow with mutual ardour!—Ah, Julia, that was something like being in love.

JULIA If I were in spirits, Lydia, I should chide you only by laughing heartily at you; but it suits more the situation of my mind, at present, earnestly to entreat you not to let a man, who loves you with sincerity, suffer that unhappiness from your caprice, which I know too well caprice can inflict.

Here's a sample question about vocabulary in context:

In the passage, Lydia is bemoaning how her plans for love and marriage have gone awry. A "Smithfield bargain" is a colloquial term for a marriage of convenience; Lydia is under the age of 21 and had therefore tried to obtain the blessing of a "Scotch parson" to grant the marriage, as marriage laws were more relaxed in Scotland. The "ladder of ropes" is a symbol for all of the following EXCEPT

A. the criss-crossing of identities and allegiances in the play.

B. Julia's machinations to complicate her friend's plan.

C. the convoluted contrivances of her plan.

D. the rickety foundation of mutual understanding between Lydia and her lover (and her betrothed).

E. the tortuous desire to climb to the top of the social register.

This question gives you a considerable amount of contextual information about unfamiliar vocabulary in the passage, and so it's asking you to build on that context to interpret some figurative language. Like the question about *The House of the Seven Gables*, it's giving you a lot of context so that you can situate yourself better into a complicated situation. The "EXCEPTION" format is helpful in that way; you can find four of these five answer choices in the question and the explanatory headnote at the top of the passage. Affections are indeed criss-crossed in the play, and you can tell that her plan to climb the social ladder by marrying rich is contrived. Because of the identity mix-ups, the foundations of these affections are constantly shifting. The only answer that doesn't fit is choice B, because we don't learn enough about Julia in this passage (or in the supporting information) to tell what her role is. She looks more like the trusty best friend here. The correct choice is B because it's the exception.

You may have read William Shakespeare's plays in your classes, so you're already familiar with reading drama as literature. Here are some other types of drama to pay attention to. This list is by no means exhaustive but rather a few representative plays. Of course, you'll be reading the plays in very brief excerpts, so it's best to study these as forms of prose that are consciously performable, so that the conventions of conflict, performance of one's self, and parody are especially heightened:

- Classical drama: Aeschylus's Oresteia, Sophocles' Antigone and Oedipus Rex

- Renaissance drama that's not Shakespeare: Ben Jonson's Volpone and Christopher Marlowe's Doctor Faustus

- Plays about morals and manners: Molière's Tartuffe, William Congreve's The Way of the World, Oscar Wilde's The Importance of Being Earnest

- Family dramas: Anton Chekhov's Three Sisters and The Cherry Orchard, Henrik Ibsen's A Doll's House and Hedda Gabler, Seán O'Casey's The Plough and the Stars, Tennessee Williams' A Streetcar Named Desire, Thornton Wilder's Our Town, Edward Albee's Who's Afraid of Virginia Woolf?, Arthur Miller's Death of a Salesman, Eugene O'Neill's Long Day's Journey into Night, Lorraine Hansberry's A Raisin in the Sun, Sam Shepard's True West, August Wilson's Fences

- Twentieth-century experiments in form and existential questioning: George Bernard Shaw's Man and Superman, Samuel Beckett's Waiting for Godot, Jean-Paul Sartre's No Exit, Luigi Pirandello's Six Characters in Search of an Author, Harold Pinter's The Birthday Party, Tom Stoppard's Arcadia and Rosencrantz and Guildenstern Are Dead, Bertolt Brecht's The Caucasian Chalk Circle

- Contemporary monologue and drama: Caryl Churchill's Top Girls, Tony Kushner's Angels in America, Anna Deveare Smith's Fires in the Mirror, Suzan-Lori Parks's Topdog/Underdog

Overview of Characteristic Prose Since the Beginning of the Novel

We've made a reading list with some recommended novels, plays, and nonfiction prose that represent some of the major themes that organize the study of Anglophone literature. The list isn't arranged alphabetically or chronologically, but by theme and genre. As we discussed above, a genre is a grouping of similar types of novels: a coming-of-age story is called a *bildungsroman*; a Gothic novel like Hawthorne's *The House of the Seven Gables* is full of familiar elements, like possibly haunted houses and secrets in the family tree. The conventions that make up these genres change and recombine over time, with social, cultural, technological, and stylistic adaptations.

You'll see that the thematic and generic organization is flexible, as it stretches across centuries to juxtapose books and authors in thought-provoking ways. You'll notice, for example, that Benjamin Franklin's and Frederick Douglass's *Autobiographies* are in different sections, although both might be considered part of the formation of the American identity, stories of personal development, and stories of episodic adventures (with mixtures of truth and fiction). Franklin and Douglass draw on all three genres of autobiography, novel of education, and prose nonfiction to create their stories. Franklin's could easily be moved around; we thought it would be interesting to consider it among the eighteenth-century picaresque novels and moral tales upon which it draws for its narrative conventions.

The magic of classifications is that they make you consider the structure and themes of stories closely. By all means, go ahead and question the way the lists are organized, because you'll have to examine the books more closely to argue about whether they fit or not. If you disagree with a novel's placement, move it around, add your own. Don't just mark up this book, though. How would you write a multiple-choice question or an essay question that makes you think closely about the style, structure, and themes of these novels?

- What do you learn when you think of Saul Bellow's Augie March and Benjamin Franklin as similar types of characters? How do you see the similarities or distinctions reflected in the introductions of the characters or the transitions among their adventures?

- What do you learn about the flexible, expansive genre of the bildungsroman when you think about how Kazuo Ishiguro adapts the genre into science fiction in Never Let Me Go?

- In the novel Wide Saragasso Sea, Jean Rhys reimagines the Gothic novel Jane Eyre as a story about colonialism in Jamaica—a fascinating recombination of genres and themes to make you reconsider Charlotte Brontë's novel in a new way. How does the unfamiliar vocabulary of the island affect your understanding of how the Gothic novel plays with making the familiar strange?

- How do we think differently about Transcendentalism and the visionary description of the American landscape when we think about it linked with the institution of slavery, the Civil War, or the annexation of Native lands? These are all ways that land is inherently political—is Transcendentalism also political?

You can generate multiple-choice questions that take up these questions—and many more that you generate—by finding passages that seem to illuminate ideas in such a way that you can pinpoint shifts in tone or vocabulary. This is a way to focus on what's admittedly a gigantic expanse of Anglophone literature. Again, you're not looking to conquer all novels with these summaries; rather, you can use them to help you dive deeper into a novel to explore the language used to illuminate these themes.

Picaresques and Other Episodic Narratives

Prose fiction: Cervantes' *Don Quixote*, Daniel Defoe's *Moll Flanders*, Jonathan Swift's *Gulliver's Travels*, Henry Fielding's *Tom Jones*, Voltaire's *Candide*, Mark Twain's *Huckleberry Finn*, Saul Bellow's *The Adventures of Augie March*

Prose nonfiction: Joseph Addison's *Spectator* essays from the early eighteenth century are not picaresques, but they follow in the tradition of short narratives, as does James Boswell's episodic account of the *Life of Samuel Johnson* and Benjamin Franklin's *Autobiography*.

Familiarize yourself with:

- Elements of surprise or accident that suddenly shift the fortunes of the narrator—how does an author play with tone and style to show these ups and downs?

- Narrators' self-presentations as a hero on a journey—how do they introduce themselves and explain their own behavior?

- Unreliable narration as a narrator puffs up his adventures

- Unexpected meetings and complicated interactions—how does the narrator engage with characters from different cultures, social classes, religious perspectives?

Bildungsromans or coming of age novels

Charlotte Brontë's *Jane Eyre*; Charles Dickens' *Great Expectations* and *David Copperfield*; Thomas Hardy's *Jude the Obscure*; Richard Wright's *Black Boy* and *Native Son;* James Joyce's *Portrait of the Artist as a Young Man*; Zora Neale Hurston's *Their Eyes Were Watching God*; Betty Smith's *A Tree Grows in Brooklyn*; Maya Angelou's *I Know Why the Caged Bird Sings*; Rudolfo Anaya's *Bless Me, Última*; Sandra Cisneros' *The House on Mango Street*; Sherman Alexie's *The Absolutely True Diary of a Part-Time Indian*; Kazuo Ishiguro's *Never Let Me Go;* Junot Diaz's *The Brief Wondrous Life of Oscar Wao*

Familiarize yourself with:

- Variations in the first-person narrative—how does the author experiment with point of view in showing the narrator's changing perspective?

- How does the narrator's self-presentation and self-description change over the course of the novel as the narrator grows older and perhaps wiser?

- The narrator's responses to adversity or shifts in fortune

- How school and other forms of education are presented—what is the narrator's opinion of the lessons he's learning, whether formally or informally? How are these opinions reflected in the tone?

- The expansiveness of the genre, as it's the most flexible form that the novel takes over the centuries

Gothic and Southern Gothic

Horace Walpole's *Castle of Otranto*, Mary Shelley's *Frankenstein*, Charlotte Brontë's *Jane Eyre*, Emily Brontë's *Wuthering Heights*, Edgar Allan Poe's "The Fall of the House of Usher" and other short stories, Robert Louis Stevenson's *The Strange Case of Dr. Jekyll and Mr. Hyde*, Bram Stoker's *Dracula*, Oscar Wilde's *The Portrait of Dorian Gray*, Henry James's *The Turn of the Screw*, Flannery O'Connor's *A Good Man Is Hard to Find*, William Faulkner's short story "A Rose for Emily," Eudora Welty's *The Robber Bridegroom*

Familiarize yourself with:

- The way a house or natural setting takes on human characteristics to reflect the twisted family trees of the inhabitants

- Use of the sublime, or the awed feeling one gets in the forbidding expanses of the natural world

- The characters' habits of retelling and reinterpreting old stories like fairy tales, myths, and legends in fragmented, distorted forms

- Baltimore writer Edgar Allan Poe is the link between the European Gothic tradition and the American Southern Gothic tradition

- How do the conventions of the genre shift from European estates and castles to America, where the Southern Gothic takes up issues of racial and class distinctions?

Commentary on Manners and Morals

Prose fiction: Jane Austen's novels, especially *Pride and Prejudice*; Henry Makepeace Thackeray's *Vanity Fair;* George Eliot's *Middlemarch*; Edith Wharton's *The House of Mirth* and *The Age of Innocence*; Henry James's *Washington Square;* Evelyn Waugh's *A Handful of Dust*; Kazuo Ishiguro's *The Remains of the Day*

Prose nonfiction: John Ruskin's *Modern Painters*, Oscar Wilde's "The Decay of Lying," Matthew Arnold's "Sweetness and Light," Lionel Trilling's "Manners, Morals, and the Novel"

Familiarize yourself with:

- How the novels discuss class distinctions among characters and whether class mobility is possible

- Characters' senses of constricted gender, sexual, racial, and class identities—how are these structures expressed and challenged in their dialogue and narration?

- The novel's incorporation of dramatic conventions like dialogue and tableaux to stage elaborate dinner parties and other highly performative moments, to see the ways that characters perform their social roles in conflicting ways

- How a character makes distinctions between what can and can't be said out loud in company, and how those conflicted inner feelings are exposed in "free indirect discourse," or one's inner thoughts transcribed on the page

- Commentary on how changes in media and technology—the railroad, the photograph, the telegraph—affect communication for the characters

Creating a Sense of History in Fiction

Prose fiction: Sir Walter Scott's *Ivanhoe*; Nathaniel Hawthorne's *The Scarlet Letter*; Herman Melville's *Benito Cereno*; Charles Dickens' *A Tale of Two Cities*; Leo Tolstoy's *War and Peace*; Virginia Woolf's *Orlando*; Robert Graves's *I, Claudius*; Maxine Hong Kingston's *The Woman Warrior*; Toni Morrison's *Beloved*; Edward P. Jones' *The Known World*

Prose nonfiction: William Hazlitt's *The Spirit of the Age* and Virginia Woolf's *A Room of One's Own* and *Three Guineas*

Familiarize yourself with:

- The use of specialized vocabulary and period-specific details to set a scene that immerses readers in the past

- How and why authors might romanticize the past at moments when they want to preserve (or challenge) contemporary social, cultural, technological, and political change. You might see that romanticization reflected in style and tone

- Inferences you might draw about how a novel reflects both a vision of the past and its context at the time it was written—say, why Dickens writes A Tale of Two Cities (about the French Revolution) in the middle of the Victorian period

Making the American Landscape and Character

Prose fiction: Herman Melville's *Moby Dick*, Mark Twain's *The Adventures of Tom Sawyer* and *Adventures of Huckleberry Finn*, William Faulkner's *As I Lay Dying* and *The Sound and the Fury*, Willa Cather's *My Antonia*, James Weldon Jones's *The Autobiography of an Ex-Colored Man*, Wallace Stegner's *Angle of Repose*

Prose nonfiction: Frederick Douglass's *Narrative of the Life of Frederick Douglass*; Ralph Waldo Emerson's *Nature* and *Self-Reliance*; Henry David Thoreau's *Walden: Or, Life in the Woods*; W.E.B. DuBois's *The Souls of Black Folk*; Rachel Carson's *Silent Spring*; John McPhee's *The Control of Nature*

Familiarize yourself with:

- The concept of "Transcendentalism" in the works of Emerson and Thoreau, who built on the European concept of the sublime and translated it to the American landscape, where they meditated

- How conflicts between urban and rural life are described

- How regions of United States are differentiated from one another descriptively: as the wide-open West, the cramped city, the forests of New England. What's the significance of an author's challenges to those conventional descriptions or where you see a shift to see the landscape in a new way

- Novelistic commentary on slavery, the Civil War: how does the novel become a form of social commentary in America, as you might see in Harriet Beecher Stowe's Uncle Tom's Cabin or in essays and memoirs such as Frederick Douglass's Narrative?

- How might we see connections between these social commentary novels and contemporary writing on the natural world, where description of the depletion of the environment becomes a political act?

Immigration and Post-Colonialism

Prose fiction: Joseph Conrad's *Heart of Darkness*, Chinua Achebe's *Things Fall Apart*, Jean Rhys's *Wide Saragasso Sea*, Graham Greene's *The Quiet American*, Julia Alvarez's *How the Garcia Girls Lost Their Accents*, Edwidge Danticat's *Krik? Krak!*, J.M. Coetzee's *Disgrace* and *Waiting for the Barbarians*, Kiran Desai's *The Inheritance of Loss*, Arundhati Roy's *The God of Small Things*, Chang-rae Lee's *Native Speaker*, Chimamanda Ngozi Adichie's *Half of a Yellow Sun*

Prose nonfiction: Gloria Anzaldua's *Borderlands*, Edward Said's *Orientalism*

Familiarize yourself with:

- The use of specific details to immerse the reader in a scene
- Play with narrative perspective to comment on looking in at a culture from the outside
- Incorporation of different languages and cultural references
- Conflicts between characters who disagree about cultural change
- Experiments in form to incorporate myth, magic, popular culture into traditional formats
- The novel as a form of social critique, challenges to how characters have been stereotyped, caricatured, or erased in previous stories

Making Sense of Art and Literature in an Age of Mass Media

Prose fiction: Virginia Woolf's *To the Lighthouse*, F. Scott Fitzgerald's *The Great Gatsby*, Ralph Ellison's *Invisible Man*, George Orwell's *1984*, Aldous Huxley's *Brave New World*, Ray Bradbury's *Fahrenheit 451*, Vladimir Nabokov's *Lolita*, Thomas Pynchon's *The Crying of Lot 49*

Prose nonfiction: George Orwell's *Politics and the English Language*, Joan Didion's *Slouching Towards Bethlehem*, James Baldwin's *Notes of a Native Son*, Susan Sontag's *Notes on Camp*, bell hooks' *Ain't I A Woman?*, John McPhee's "The Search for Marvin Gardens"

Familiarize yourself with:

- Literary responses to mass media in the twentieth century by incorporating bits of newspapers, popular culture, film, jazz and other forms of popular music, technology
- The rapid switching of narrative perspective in a modern novel as a response to the innovations of film and television, where switching perspective feels more intuitive
- Critiques of "literature" as a term that is too limited to account for the many different forms that writing and cultural expression can take, experiments in form
- The use of the fragment (or the "note") to show the author's sense that culture is constantly in flux and everything is partial or unable to be completely grasped

A brief multiple-choice passage or an essay question can't take up all of these issues, of course. In the following sample passages and questions, try to track how these passages address the topics in these overviews. How does Olive Schreiner's experiments in perspective reveal a character's spiritual crisis? How do her descriptions of the landscape show that character's conflicted, ambivalent opinions about spirituality? How might you consider Jonathan Swift's *Gulliver's Travels* a picaresque story, in which Gulliver the narrator is both a hero and a fool?

PRACTICE SETS

Now it's time to try some questions on your own. Practice the techniques we've reviewed in this chapter and see how you do with the following practice sets.

SAMPLE PASSAGE 1

From *The Story of an African Farm* (1883), by Olive Schreiner.

The narrator of this passage is named Waldo, so we'll use "he" in the questions and explanations, although the use of the first-person plural narrative voice is significant.

At night, alone in our cabin, we sit no more brooding over the fire. What should we think of now? All is emptiness. So we take the old arithmetic; and the multiplication table, which with so much pains we learnt long ago and forgot directly, we learn now in a few hours, and never forget again. We take a strange satisfaction in working arithmetical problems. We pause in our building to cover the stones with figures and calculations. We save money for a Latin Grammar and Algebra, and carry them about in our pockets, poring over them as over our Bible of old. We have thought we were utterly stupid, incapable of remembering anything, of learning anything. Now we find that all is easy. Has a new soul crept into this old body, that even our intellectual faculties are changed? We marvel; not perceiving that what a man expends in prayer and ecstasy he cannot have over for acquiring knowledge. You never shed a tear, or create a beautiful image, or quiver with emotion, but you pay for it at the practical, calculating end of your nature. You have just so much force: when the one channel runs over the other runs dry.

And now we turn to Nature. All these years we have lived beside her, and we have never seen her; and now we open our eyes and look at her.

The rocks have been to us a blur of brown: we bend over them, and the disorganized masses dissolve into a many-coloured, many-shaped, carefully-arranged form of existence. Here masses of rainbow-tinted crystals, half-fused together; there bands of smooth grey and red methodically overlying each other. This rock here is covered with a delicate silver tracery, in some mineral, resembling leaves and branches; there on the flat stone, on which we so often have sat to weep and pray, we look down, and see it covered with the fossil footprints of great birds, and the beautiful skeleton of a fish. We have often tried to picture in our mind what the fossiled remains of creatures must be like, and all the while we sat on them, we have been so blinded by thinking and feeling that we have never seen the world.

The flat plain has been to us a reach of monotonous red. We look at it, and every handful of sand starts into life. That wonderful people, the ants, we learn to know; see them make war and peace, play and work, and build their huge palaces. And that smaller people we make acquaintance with, who live in the flowers. The bitto flower has been for us a mere blur of yellow; we find its heart composed of a hundred perfect flowers, the homes of the tiny black people with red stripes, who move in and out in that little yellow city. Every bluebell has its inhabitant. Every day the karoo[1] shows us a new wonder sleeping in its teeming bosom.

On our way back to work we pause and stand to see the ground-spider make its trap, bury itself in the sand, and then wait for the falling in of its enemy.

Further on walks a horned beetle, and near him starts open the door of a spider, who peeps out carefully, and quickly pulls it down again. On a karoo-bush a green fly is laying her silver eggs. We carry them home, and see the shells pierced, the spotted grub come out, turn to a green fly, and flit away. We are not satisfied with what Nature shows us, and we see something for ourselves. Under the white hen we put a dozen eggs, and break one daily, to see the white spot wax into the chicken. We are not excited or enthusiastic about it; but a man is not to lay his throat open, he must think of something. So we plant seeds in rows on our dam-wall, and pull one up daily to see how it goes with them. Alladeen buried her wonderful stone, and a golden palace sprung up at her feet[2]. We do far more. We put a brown seed in the earth, and a living thing starts out—starts upward—why, no more than Alladeen can we say—starts upward, and does not desist till it is higher than our heads, sparkling with dew in the early morning, glittering with yellow blossoms, shaking brown seeds with little embryo souls on to the ground. We look at it solemnly, from the time it consists of two leaves peeping above the ground and a soft white root, till we have to raise our faces to look at it; but we find no reason for that upward starting.

---

[1] The South African desert.

[2] In the Aladdin story from the *Arabian Nights*, Aladdin uses his magic lantern to conjure a palace out of enchanted stones.

1. What does the first-person plural narrative voice emphasize in this passage?
   A. The narrator's attempt to negotiate a sense of self in the wider world after some kind of identity crisis
   B. The author's experimentation with language and structure to create a new kind of imaginative writing
   C. The narrator's delusions of grandeur in trying to control the natural world
   D. The author's ability to mix dry scientific writing and the conventions of fiction
   E. The narrator's social commentary on how society has rejected a scientific worldview

2. What is the effect of the momentary shift to second-person narration in the second paragraph?
   A. It shows the narrator's total rejection of prior identity.
   B. It intensifies the narrator's sense of delusion and disorientation.
   C. It exposes a lack of focus and attention to detail.
   D. It reveals a desire to theorize new ideas from these kinds of knowledge.
   E. It criticizes family members who have stuck to older beliefs.

3. How would you assess the narrator's dilemma in this passage?

    I.   The passage is set up like a debate, with the narrator trying out different perspectives to see which one is the most persuasive.

    II. The passage reveals that the narrator's ideas about spirituality and scientific observation are in tension, generating thought and reflection.

    III. The narrator wishes to return to a time when the world seemed easier to understand, before the desire for scientific observation took hold.

    A. I only
    B. II only
    C. III only
    D. I and III
    E. I, II, and III

4. What is the narrator's tone in the two paragraphs about seeing the details of the rocks and flowers?

    A. Scientific and detached
    B. Curious and intimate
    C. Loving and maternal
    D. Imaginative and fantastical
    E. Dutiful and unenthusiastic

5. In observing the details of flowers and ants, the narrator uses personification to describe ants as people and cities thriving inside of flowers. What is the most important idea that this technique reveals?

    A. The narrator's use of imagination to describe the natural world
    B. The narrator's insistence on ranking humans over the natural world
    C. The narrator's wish to join this tiny world and reject humanity
    D. The narrator's philosophizing about the scale of mankind in the universe
    E. The narrator's projection of human anxieties onto nature as a pathetic fallacy

6. Where is the likely source of the phrase "a man is not to lay his throat open"?

    A. The Bible
    B. A Latin scholar the narrator read in one of his books
    C. A folk saying from earlier in the narrator's life
    D. An ecologist who studied man's impact on the natural world
    E. The narrator's grandfather, who studied poetry

7. The reference to Aladdin and the golden palace made of a single stone serves all of the following thematic purposes EXCEPT

    A. the tale of many small rocks reinforces the narrator's interest in scale.
    B. it ties back to the stones on which the narrator had written figures and calculations.
    C. the narrator attempts to synthesize older knowledge of imaginative stories with newer knowledge of science.
    D. the narrator is making connections to the books he saved money to buy at the beginning of the passage.
    E. both Aladdin and the ants build palaces.

8. When the narrator says, "we find no reason for that upward starting," what is the effect of that lack of resolution to the examination of the flowers?

    A. The narrator rejects science because it cannot sate his desire for meaning.
    B. There is an ever-present tension between the narrator's desire to observe small details and find larger meaning.
    C. The narrator is hypothesizing about why the plant has stunted growth.
    D. The narrator is struck dumb by a visionary revelation of meaning in the face of the flower.
    E. There is no morality to be found in the natural world.

SAMPLE PASSAGE 2

Gulliver's Travels, by Jonathan Swift

I had hitherto seen only one side of the academy, the other being appropriated to the advancers of speculative learning, of whom I shall say something, when I have mentioned one illustrious person more, who is called among them "the universal artist." He told us "he had been thirty years employing his thoughts for the improvement of human life." He had two large rooms full of wonderful curiosities, and fifty men at work. Some were condensing air into a dry tangible substance, by extracting the nitre, and letting the aqueous or fluid particles percolate; others softening marble, for pillows and pin-cushions; others petrifying the hoofs of a living horse, to preserve them from foundering. The artist himself was at that time busy upon two great designs; the first, to sow land with chaff, wherein he affirmed the true seminal virtue to be contained, as he demonstrated by several experiments, which I was not skilful enough to comprehend. The other was, by a certain composition of gums, minerals, and vegetables, outwardly applied, to prevent the growth of wool upon two young lambs; and he hoped, in a reasonable time to propagate the breed of naked sheep, all over the kingdom.

We crossed a walk to the other part of the academy, where, as I have already said, the projectors in speculative learning resided.

The first professor I saw, was in a very large room, with forty pupils about him. After salutation, observing me to look earnestly upon a frame, which took up the greatest part of both the length and breadth of the room, he said, "Perhaps I might wonder to see him employed in a project for improving speculative knowledge, by practical and mechanical operations. But the world would soon be sensible of its usefulness; and he flattered himself, that a more noble, exalted thought never sprang in any other man's head. Every one knew how laborious the usual method is of attaining to arts and sciences; whereas, by his contrivance, the most ignorant person, at a reasonable charge, and with a little bodily labour, might write books in philosophy, poetry, politics, laws, mathematics, and theology, without the least assistance from genius or study." He then led me to the frame, about the sides, whereof all his pupils stood in ranks. It was twenty feet square, placed in the middle of the room. The superfices was composed of several bits of wood, about the bigness of a die, but some larger than others. They were all linked together by slender wires. These bits of wood were covered, on every square, with paper pasted on them; and on these papers were written all the words of their language, in their several moods, tenses, and declensions; but without any order. The professor then desired me "to observe; for he was going to set his engine at work." The pupils, at his command, took each of them hold of an iron handle, whereof there were forty fixed round the edges of the frame; and giving them a sudden turn, the whole disposition of the words was entirely changed. He then commanded six-and-thirty of the lads, to read the several lines softly, as they appeared upon the frame; and where they found three or four words together that might make part of a sentence, they dictated to the four remaining boys, who were scribes. This work was repeated three or four times, and at every turn, the engine was so contrived, that the words shifted into new places, as the square bits of wood moved upside down.

Six hours a day the young students were employed in this labour; and the professor showed me several volumes in large folio, already collected, of broken sentences, which he intended to piece together, and out of those rich materials, to give the world a complete body of all arts and sciences; which, however, might be still improved, and much expedited, if the public would raise a fund for making and employing five hundred such frames in Lagado, and oblige the managers to contribute in common their several collections.

He assured me "that this invention had employed all his thoughts from his youth; that he had emptied the whole vocabulary into his frame, and made the strictest computation of the general proportion there is in books between the numbers of particles, nouns, and verbs, and other parts of speech."

9. During the eighteenth century, the Royal Society of England undertook many experiments just like the "advancers of speculative learning" mentioned in the first passage, including a "universal language" that could generate sentences anyone could read without laborious translation. What kind of commentary do you infer that Jonathan Swift is making about the connection between fiction and real life here?

    A. Promoting the work of these scientists and artists as visionaries

    B. Reporting objectively on these experiments

    C. Satirizing these projects as vainglorious and foolish

    D. Puffing up these accomplishments in a fantasy travelogue

    E. Making sense of a confusing situation where he feels unsure about what he's seeing

10. What is the best description of Gulliver's position as a narrator?

    A. Gulliver is a stand-in for the author.

    B. Gulliver is too credulous an observer.

    C. Gulliver is a satirist.

    D. Gulliver is an impartial witness.

    E. Gulliver is biased against the scientists in his skepticism.

11. The experiment to "sow the land with chaff" is a metaphor for

    A. the ingenuity of the projectors and universal artist to make such helpful inventions.

    B. the prescience of their recycling plan.

    C. the lesson that hard work pays off when you keep trying even after you've failed.

    D. the worthlessness of the hard work they're investing in these projects.

    E. the inefficiency of reading fiction when others are gaining knowledge about science.

12. Swift clues the reader into Gulliver's limited understanding of the scene in front of him in all of the following phrases EXCEPT
    A. "One illustrious person more, who is called among them 'the universal artist'"
    B. "Rooms full of wonderful curiosities"
    C. "Which I was not skillful enough to comprehend"
    D. The teacher's phrase, "every one knew how laborious the usual method is of attaining to arts and sciences…"
    E. "Broken sentences, which he intended to piece together"

13. What are the two meanings of "speculative" that are being put into tension here?
    A. Theoretical and far-fetched
    B. Future-oriented and hopeful
    C. Imaginative and socially conscious
    D. Rational and predictive
    E. Creative and wishful

14. If you were going to adapt *Gulliver's Travels* for a contemporary setting, what kind of organization or institution would Gulliver visit in the passage?
    A. A museum that preserves past artifacts
    B. A technology start-up for entrepreneurs to pitch ideas
    C. A kindergarten with lots of activities
    D. An artist's studio devoted to artisanal woodworking
    E. A big box store where you could find anything you wanted

15. Why is the word "improved" important to understanding the theme of this passage?
    A. Gulliver feels smarter after having learned from the scientists and universal artists.
    B. The scientist's many years of reflecting on these issues are beginning to pay off, slowly.
    C. It raises the question as to which is more important to society: arts or sciences?
    D. Gulliver feels morally improved after having experienced the social and emotional benefits of education.
    E. It raises the paradox of whether these institutions meant to generate knowledge are teaching ignorance.

16. The description of the engine takes up several paragraphs for which of the following reasons?
    I. The long description exposes its contrived nature.
    II. It satirizes the grand scale of the scientist's tiny, silly contributions to the world.
    III. The middle paragraph's many commas in one sentence approximate—but exceed in sense—the broken sentences generated by the machine.
    A. I only
    B. II only
    C. I and II
    D. II and III
    E. I, II, and III

17. What is the best explanation of the engine's larger meaning in the early science fiction novel/travel narrative *Gulliver's Travels*?

   A. There is pathos in the sad fact that none of the sentences generated by the machine will be the equal of Swift's own prose.

   B. There is the delicious possibility that one of the sentences generated will surpass the author's own writing.

   C. The machine has a structure with different legs and posts, just like there are different segments to Gulliver's journey.

   D. Swift is provocatively asking what separates authors from machines in a land that celebrates projecting ideas more than realizing them.

   E. Swift is like the universal artist in being able to devise so many different creative ideas.

ANSWER KEY AND EXPLANATIONS

1. A	5. D	9. C	12. E	15. E
2. D	6. C	10. B	13. A	16. E
3. B	7. D	11. D	14. B	17. D
4. B	8. B			

Sample Passage 1

1. **The correct answer is A.** It's somewhat unusual to see a first-person plural narrator, so this question is asking you to consider the ways that this structural and stylistic choice reflects the major themes in the passage. You don't know what happened to make the narrator, Waldo, feel as though "a new soul crept into this old body," but some sort of existential and/or spiritual crisis seems to have occurred. Waldo is now trying to reconcile past spiritual outlooks and a newfound curiosity about scientific observation of the natural world. That "new soul" is not fully integrated, so "we" emphasizes the ongoing, in-process negotiation of this new identity. Choices B and D are too general to be good answers about what's being emphasized in this particular passage. Because the rest of the questions are focused on the narrator and the narrator's feelings, it's a good bet that this question is meant to narrow your focus on the narrator. The narrator is not so focused on the rest of society, as choice E suggests, so it's not a good choice. There is ambivalence and uncertainty in the passage, but there aren't any hints of delusion, so choice C is also not correct. (For clarity, we will refer to the narrator as Waldo, and use he/him/his pronouns for the rest of the explanations.)

2. **The correct answer is D.** This question builds on the ideas of the previous one and asks you to consider the effect and meaning of a shift into the second-person narration. It happens only briefly, and then the narrative shifts back to first-person plural, so

we can assume that it's significant. Many of the answer choices here may be tempting. First, you can eliminate the obvious wrong answers: remember to beware of overstatements like "total loss of identity," for this passage is more of a struggle to reconcile past and present identities. Choice A is too strong a statement to help you see the nuance of a stylistic choice like this shift in voice. There are no family members mentioned, so choice E is out. As you noted in question 1, the passage is full of uncertainty, but it's not delusive, so choice B is not a good choice. The passage shows intense attention to detail, so choice C is incorrect. That leaves choice D: a desire to theorize new ideas. Even if you weren't sure initially, you've eliminated other overstatements and judgments and you're left with a more open-ended idea of the narrator's desire to synthesize new knowledge. You can take this idea with you as a guide to the rest of the passage.

3. **The correct answer is B.** This question asks you to choose among the best options, and with the possibility that only one option may be correct or that there may be more options that reveal the narrator has several dilemmas. The passage is not organized as a debate (Option I) because there's no resolution about which perspective is "better": the passage ends on an uncertain note about what can be known and understood about the growth of the flower through observation or fairy tales. Yet Waldo doesn't see a way back to erase all of these new ideas, as Option III suggests; it might have been

easier to live without doubt in the past, but there are enough lines in the passage about the wonder of this new world that you don't get a sense of renunciation. The best option among these is Option II, which resists the one-sidedness that Options I and III present. Neither of those options is a good partner or collaborator with the other options; they are mutually exclusive in their black-and-white hardline stances. Option II is the most open-ended answer that fits with the answers to 1 and 2, about negotiation of identity and new theories, so choice B is the correct answer.

4. **The correct answer is B.** This question has a few red herring answers that might initially seem attractive. Waldo is overwhelmed by testing the scientific worldview of studying geology, paleontology, and ecology for the first time—yet these observations are hardly detached, as choice A offers, so it is incorrect. Waldo describes Nature as a woman, newly observed even though she's been there all this time, so you might pick choice C as a possibility—yet we don't really see a "loving" sensibility. Choice D may also be tempting because the descriptions are so vivid and they use figurative language like personification, but they are not exactly fantastical in building a new world as in a fantasy novel. Choice B is the middle ground between C and D and more precisely describes the intimacy of the comparison of Nature to a wife/mother, as well as the interest in these tiny new details that you only see when you look closely. Waldo claims a lack of interest in a later paragraph (choice E), yet this idea seems to be part of the ambivalence; indeed, Waldo claims a lack of enthusiasm at the same time as he's crafting a comparison to a fairy tale, that we may be somewhat skeptical of that claim.

5. **The correct answer is D.** This question names the literary device for you and asks you to interpret its meaning in the passage. As with the other questions, there are a few tempting choices that you can entertain briefly before you reject them for being overstatements or generalizations. Choice A is way too general to be helpful, as it could describe any kind of figurative language and isn't specific to personification. The phrases "insistence on ranking" in choice B and "reject humanity" in choice C don't give a sense of the richness of personification as a device, nor do they help you analyze the extent of the passage's use of the device in so many natural descriptions. Choice E could be a good option, but we don't really see anxieties here. The best choice (D) interprets the link between personification and the narrator's questions about man's place in the universe. The universe is limitless, and man is as tiny as the ants and tiny elements of the flowers.

6. **The correct answer is C.** This question asks you to make an inference about the source of an unusual adage. We don't have any specific evidence, such as a footnote or a traceable allusion to some piece of literature, so we have to work from context. It sounds most like a folk saying that the narrator has heard in the desert, where there are few resources and one must fend for oneself. (Although the narrator has now realized that there's far more to the desert than he imagined.) It doesn't sound like it's from the Bible or a Latin grammar (choices A or B), and, more important, such a precise answer requires more specific evidence. Likewise, there's no one mentioned who fits the bill as an ecologist or a poet (choices D or E), for the narrator is more of an autodidact who's teaching himself about all of these subjects. Choice C is the only choice that's supported by the context of the passage, and it fits better within the narrator's language of personifying nature and trying to spiritualize

it at the same time in phrases like "embryo souls."

7. **The correct answer is D.** This question asks you to find the one exception among four correct answers. If you were unsure about the answer to question 5 and the importance of perceiving scale (choice A), this question gives you that correct answer among its choices, so it reinforces the previous answers. Choices B, D, and E refer to details mentioned earlier in the passage—except that D is incorrect, as the narrator buys math and Latin books because he is attempting to gain a wholly rational take on the world. Choice C explains that such a hard swerve toward rationalism and empiricism has been unsustainable for the narrator, for he seeks some kind of larger meaning in the universe. The narrator doesn't believe in Aladdin (sometimes rendered as Alladeen, as in the passage), but rather in the potential for imaginative stories to feed his desire for philosophical musings on the unknowable.

8. **The correct answer is B.** This is a summing-up question that asks you to express how the final sentence indicates the theme in the clearest way. You can almost immediately pick choice B for its nuanced analytical language of "tension" between two poles between which the narrator has been vacillating throughout the passage. As with prior questions, you can reject the answer choices that have overstatements: the narrator doesn't reject science (choice A) because he continues looking closely at the natural world, yet he also continues trying to find some kind of morality in it (choice E). The flower does not have stunted growth (choice C); it's taller than the narrator and he has to turn his face up at it. If only there were a visionary revelation in the face of the flower that might give the narrator some sense of resolution—but instead there are only more details to observe. In the best possible way, all of this close observation is a boon for the narrative work of description in the novel. If there's one thing we can say about this passage, it's that Waldo gives you a kind of model for looking closely and trying to find deeper meanings. You can be more decisive on the exam, however, and less ambivalent and tormented.

Sample Passage 2

9. **The correct answer is C.** *Gulliver's Travels* is a combination of several genres, including the travelogue, picaresque tale, and the satire. As you learn from the contextual information in the question, he's also incorporating real examples from scientific journals that were published at the time, in which scientists would share their experiments and ideas for inventions. It's kind of cool to imagine a pillowy form of marble—but would that even qualify as marble anymore? What makes a substance a substance when we recombine all of its features? This is a fascinating question in a novel that innovates a form by recombining features from prior genres, including science, and leaving them recognizable, yet strange and fantastical. The biggest clue to the satire arrives in the long description of the Engine, where we realize that they've devoted an enormous amount of foolish energy into trying to eliminate the human part of creativity, "without the least assistance from genius or study." Gulliver himself may believe that he's promoting the scientists' work (choice A), reporting objectively (choice B), or writing a travelogue (choice D) but keep in mind that his perspective is separate from Swift's (see the next question). Choice E is too vague to be helpful here, so it's not a good choice. Choice C gives you

the language of satire that you can take with you to the next questions.

10. **The correct answer is B.** This question builds on the previous one to focus on Gulliver's relationship to the narrative: does the narrator realize that he's in a satire? Swift recombines the conventions of the picaresque's naive hero and the travelogue's descriptive observer, by asking what would happen if those genres, which depend so much on detailed observation, had a narrator who didn't understand what he was seeing. He's not an unreliable narrator who's deliberately obscuring elements from readers; he simply doesn't understand them fully. Therefore, he is not a stand-in for the author or a satirist (choices A and C)—two ways of saying the same thing in this case. He is a dupe, a too-credulous observer, who can't be impartial or unbiased (choices D and E) because he believes just about anything they tell him.

11. **The correct answer is D.** This question asks you to read a particular use of figurative language through the lens of satire: how does this metaphor reflect the main idea of Swift's satire? Choices A, B, and C don't work for a satire, for they invest value in the scheme, yet the scheme is pretty clearly a scam for "sowing" the non-seed parts of seeds. There's a reason the phrase "separate the wheat from the chaff" is used: the chaff is the stuff that you don't want. Choice E doesn't bear any relation to the metaphor, so it's not a relevant choice. Choice D tells you exactly what chaff is: worthless, so it's silly to devote so much intense labor to it.

12. **The correct answer is E.** This question pulls out fragments of quotations from the passage and tests how closely you've read them. You can tell the tone from many of the adjectives like "illustrious" and "wonderful" (choices A and B), both of which indicate Gulliver's gullibility. We can tell Gulliver's

lack of understanding of the teacher's claims by his lack of commentary on the teacher's phrase about generating knowledge and art without work—he doesn't realize the silliness of that claim, so choice D is out. He believes that his lack of understanding is because the contraptions are too complex (choice C), but they are perhaps more complicated (and contrived) than complex. After eliminating those choices, you're left with choice E, which actually shows Gulliver's correct assessment of the situation, so it's the outlier. It's the example where Swift is not showing Gulliver's limitations—it's just an explanation of the stuff the engine makes.

13. **The correct answer is A.** These answer choices give you many synonyms for "speculative" and ask you to pick out the best pair with a satirical edge to them. When you see it that way, you can cast out any of the choices that are wholly positive—because they have no tension in them, no contrast in the two meanings offered. Choice B has two similar meanings related to the future, both positive. Both choices C and E focus on speculation as a form of creativity and world-building, as in speculative fiction, but they too lack tension. Choice D's rationalism does not describe the experiments in the passage. The best answer is choice A, where you can see the language of speculation in the form of generating ideas—which is admirable—but also in gambling, like speculating on land or the stock market. This form of speculation is riskier because it banks everything on imagining a future—the theory doesn't actually relate to reality.

14. **The correct answer is B.** As we saw in the previous question, *Gulliver's Travels* is a story about investing—investing time, interest, and money into these contraptions. At the end of the passage, they are trying to "raise a fund for making and employing five hundred such" engines in Lagado. Such activities would not happen at a kindergarten (choice

C), and while both artists and museums look for funding, they are not creating or displaying the kinds of speculative ideas described in this passage. The answer choices give you "past artifacts" (choice A) and "artisanal woodworking" (choice D) that would be hard to scale in such a way as is being promoted here. The best answer is choice B, where the entrepreneurial scientists would be able to pitch their ideas—for the engine sounds a lot like predictive text algorithms, right?

15. **The correct answer is E.** Like "speculative," the word "improved" takes on a satirical meaning in this passage—for what's seemingly improved is actually made worse by these contrived inventions. Who would want a wool-less sheep or seeds that didn't grow? These aren't improvements. You can eliminate choices A, B, and D because they don't account for the satire; they *believe* in these improvements. Choice C is too general to be helpful, and the question isn't posing that black-and-white distinction between art and science. It's more like a distinction between knowledge and folly or wisdom and foolishness. Choice E's statement of a paradox gives you a good statement of the passage's theme.

16. **The correct answer is E.** This question asks you to tie together a stylistic element (language) with structure (how that language is arranged in paragraphs) to understand how they help Swift create his satire. Satire depends on playing with scale and distorting the small flaw into a large exposure of a social problem; here, the small flaws in the engine's conception and execution are magnified into a seemingly never-ending presentation of a bad idea. All three of the options listed are excellent examples—especially option III, which draws a connection between the long, winding sentence and the work that the machine can't do in putting such broken pieces together. Only a satirist has the

ability to take those fragments and put them together under the critical distorting lens to create commentary on how knowledge is produced. The other answer choices (A, B, C, and D) leave you with only one or two options, but Options I and II work well with that inspired reading in Option III, so the answer is choice E.

17. **The correct answer is D.** This question asks you to interpret the possibility that the engine is a commentary on the practice of writing itself, as both are about putting words into different combinations. The scientists have been engaged in experiments to "write books in philosophy, poetry, politics, laws, mathematics, and theology, without the least assistance from genius or study." That is: these scientists want to replace authors with machines that will automate writing. You know from previous questions that Swift has written a satire, and many questions in this section have asked you variations on Swift's lampooning of the scientists. This question asks something a little different, a little more sophisticated; it asks you to infer the larger meaning of Swift's satire beyond lampooning silly ideas.

Choice B seems to believe that Swift and other authors could be surpassed by the engine, while choices A and E don't take the passage's satirical perspective into account. Swift doesn't consider it sad, and he's satirizing the "universal artist," not comparing himself to him. Choice C is not the best answer because that connection between the word "leg" doesn't reveal anything other than a coincidence. That leaves choice D: Swift is using the genre of science fiction to generate new worlds to travel to, and the engine is also a generator. Both the author and the engine are generators and creators: if all that matters is the speculation on the idea, then does the painstaking work of authoring a book matter anymore?

SUMMING IT UP

- On Section I of your exam, you will have to answer fifty-five multiple-choice questions; at least four passages will be prose excerpts that are up to 800 words in length.

- Do an initial quick read-through: circle any unfamiliar words or phrases, and underline moments that jump out at you.

- Skim through the test questions—they will give you hints as to what is important within the passage.

- Observe your own reading habits as you work through sample passages: what trips you up in reading? As you observe, then study, then refine your own habits, you'll start to feel more comfortable reading and assessing passages quickly.

- Look for thematic motifs and other patterns in the passages to help you assess the thematic elements and how they're reflected in small details like word choices and larger abstractions.

- Eliminate the wrong answers quickly so that you can focus on fewer choices to read and assess.

- The earlier questions will give you some analytical and thematic language. If you hit on a good answer about themes and main ideas early in the questions, circle it so you can remember to look for later answers that use similar expressions of that language, because they're more likely to be correct.

- Also pay attention to significant shifts in tone and narrative voice, because they tend to signal parts of the passage that are important for understanding larger themes in the passage.

- When you read a passage, make a quick inference about where you might be in the story. Your analysis of the text might change, depending on whether you're in the beginning, middle, or end.

- When you're looking at the setting of a passage, pay attention to the narrator's descriptive language. Ask yourself how the narrator describes the place, which will give you a sense of how he or she perceives it.

- After reading a passage, make note of the author's point of view. Who is narrating? What is his/her perspective on the situation? How does any bias affect this point of view? The narrator's vocabulary gives you a sense of background, education, attitudes, and more, which allow you to make strong inferences.

- In dramatic prose, characters are often extra-performative—there is no narration to give you a sense of inner thoughts. The exam will always give you enough context to show you what's going on in a dialogue.

- Use the overviews of thematic groupings in this chapter to make a reading list, and then practice generating possible multiple-choice questions about tone, theme, etc.

- Use the sample prose passages and questions in this chapter to devise possible essay prompts for yourself in subsequent chapters.

Chapter 4: Free-Response Questions on the AP® Literature and Composition Exam

OVERVIEW

- **Format of the Free-Response Section**
- **Learning a New Language**
- **Essay Section Scoring**
- **How to Spend Those 40 Minutes Per Essay**
- **Moving Beyond the Five-Paragraph Essay**
- **Breaking Down the Composition Process**
- **Home Stretch: The Last 5 Minutes of Each Essay**
- **Common Reader Pet Peeves**
- **The Smallest Details Count**
- **Poetry and Prose Essay Walkthroughs**
- **How to Approach the Open Essay**
- **Open Essay Walkthroughs**
- **Summing It Up**

Forty minutes of reading, thinking, and writing—multiplied by three—is a lot of work! It may be tempting to seek a foolproof formula to follow. Fair warning: this chapter won't give you such a formula. Furthermore, it will cast doubt on the five-paragraph essay you might know from other classes: state a basic idea in an introduction; then name three discrete features of diction, imagery, rhyme, etc.; then restate the ideas of each of the preceding four paragraphs in a conclusion. Five-paragraph essays can be useful when you need to dump a lot of information quickly, but the very thing that makes them simple and formulaic (and thus easy to write) also makes them boring to read. AP® exam readers will be reading hundreds of student essays, all about the same literary passages. They don't want to read the same body paragraphs over and over again. A formula might help you get through it, but it won't help you get a high score.

TIP

Plan to spend about 40 minutes per essay, with minimal outlining and rewriting, so you're spending the majority of your time composing.

TIP

Bring a watch so you can keep track of the time. You cannot use your phone, smartwatch, or other Internet-connected device

With that bad news out of the way, here's some good news: there are ways to *adapt* that formula into more flexible, compelling essay structures—and quickly, too. In this chapter, we'll explain how to work through the prompts in such a way that you can write a dynamic essay, rather than a predictable, mechanical one. These essays will show you how to think and work through the complexities of the prompt as you write your paragraphs. Your readers will be impressed by how your ideas develop over the course of the essay, instead of feeling like they're following a schematic diagram or a script. They want to be surprised, even challenged by your work—in a good way, of course. Read on to learn how to impress them!

FORMAT OF THE FREE-RESPONSE SECTION

In Section II of the AP® English Literature and Composition Exam, you will write three short essays in the span of 2 hours. This section is worth 55 percent of your total score, so it's weighted slightly heavier than the multiple-choice questions.

Here is the key information to keep in mind.

SECTION II ESSENTIALS

You have 2 hours to complete this section.

In those 2 hours, you will write three essays based on prompts relating to the following:

- An analysis of a prose passage from a novel, short story, creative nonfiction, or play
- A literary analysis of a poem
- An open topic about a literary concept or theme, in which you choose a literary work from your own study that you believe best illuminates the prompt

---

LEARNING A NEW LANGUAGE

A large part of passing the AP® exam depends on understanding its language. In Section I, the exam writers interpret (and strategically, sometimes trickily, *misinterpret*) passages and ask you to assess the best possible answers in multiple-choice format. You can apply strategic guessing or elimination, or you may know the answer before you read it among the answer choices. The best answer, as determined by the College Board, is present on the page—you just have to find it.

That's not the case in Section II: it's up to you to write interpretive essays about two passages of prose and poetry and then to write a third essay about an assigned theme or concept by discussing your own choice of literary text. In each of the three essays, you are responsible for doing the work of generating ideas and insights and then guiding your reader through your literary analysis in a clear, thoughtful essay.

Some prefer the structure of the multiple choice, while others prefer the creativity of the essay section. It's possible, though, to take some strategies for reading and writing from Section I with you into Section II—if you're not too exhausted from those fifty-five questions. You won't be able to take notes with you from section to section, but you can pay attention to how the exam questions have asked you about finding themes in a passage, or analyzing a literary device. That's the language ETS recognizes for interpreting literary texts, so you can use it as a model for your own writing for this exam. (ETS, or Educational Testing Service, is the company that administers AP® and other exams on behalf of The College Board.)

The previous sections of this book helped you analyze how questions are framed, to learn how to answer them. In the essay section, you can use that same language you're now so attuned to, in order to frame your own analysis with analytical vocabulary terms they're sure to recognize. You can adapt their language for your own use.

The key to this chapter is *adaptability*. You will learn strategies for framing introductory paragraphs, analytical paragraphs in the body of your essays, and thoughtful conclusions that show how your idea has developed over the course of the essay. Within the sample essays, there are breakdowns of specific kinds of sentences that may be useful for you to study and adapt for your own uses. These are not formulas, but rather "moves" or "plays" such as one might find in a basketball or football playbook or a jazz piano fakebook. On a football or basketball team, players learn set plays that they can call out during a game to move the ball forward; after running drills repeatedly in practice, they've internalized the plays and can adapt them at game time.

In the following sections, we've outlined, modeled, and debriefed thinking and writing strategies that you can internalize, so you'll have the power (and perhaps even the interest!) to adapt them in your own exam essays.

ESSAY SECTION SCORING

But you didn't come here just to learn new language for interpreting literary essays. The essays you write for the AP® English Literature and Composition Exam are different from any essays you may have written for school. They are essays that are narrowly defined enough to be composed in 40 minutes and are focused on two main skills: close literary analysis and clear organization of your interpretations. They are essays that are meant to be read quickly for a score, not for thoughtful personal feedback about what you can do differently in future essays. So, let's get down to the thing you're most worried about: scoring.

Each essay in Section II is scored on a scale of 0-9, for a possible total of 27 points. The majority of the scored essays fall into the 5-6 range, while very few essays are scored with a 9. Exam readers are not trying to artificially keep the essay grades on a specific kind of distribution curve; rather, the middle is large because it's hard to distinguish among many essays that adhere to a simple format and end up sounding somewhat mechanical, superficial, or both.

Readers don't use a checklist to look for specific items in your essays; instead, they use a rubric that describes the features of top-scoring, middle-range, and low-scoring essays. This method is called "holistic" grading or looking at the whole essay rather than awarding discrete points for various features you might find in an essay. The Educational Testing Service staff trains its readers by giving them sample essays that they've determined are representative of top, middle, and low scores, so exam readers can see how the rubric works in practice, among other graders, and they submit samples of their grades to make sure that they're scoring consistently. Each essay you write will be graded by a different reader who is focused on a specific category, or, in the case of the open essay, who has read

TIP

This book not only gives you strategies for taking the test, it also gives you many examples of the exam's interpretive language that you can internalize. Underline phrases that you might wish to adapt for your own uses in the practice exam, the sample essays in this chapter, and the sample questions from the prose and poetry questions. Also underline phrases that seem unfamiliar and that you want to understand better.

Don't strive to be an objective essay-writing machine; instead, be a compelling human writer with flashes of creativity and originality.

the particular work of literature you've selected. Readers will not see the others' scores, so your three essays will not be compared to each other.

The idea of a holistic rubric may sound subjective to you: it is. Assessing writing is a subjective process. Reading is a subjective process. That's why we read literature: to get into other people's heads and explore ideas that are different from our own. Literary analysis isn't about using a specific set of tools to process texts in order to find a single meaning; it's about examining a literary work from your personal perspective to determine what that work means *to you* and how you view both the author's intent and the degree to which he or she accomplished his or her objectives. The trick is that, since there's some subjectivity involved, your job on the essay section is to analyze the author's work and *support* your views about that work.

What follows is a description of what the rubric looks like in general. The rubrics used from test to test are similar enough to give you this overview, but keep in mind that different readers might differ on the distinction between "effective" or "successful" work.

Top-scoring (8-9 range)

Essays in the top range answer the question with clarity, attention to detail, and compelling ideas. The writer has a strong idea to guide his essay and develops depth by analyzing rich material from the passage. The analysis feels motivated by an idea, not by a checklist of devices to be identified dutifully. The writer engages with specific quotations (or examples in the open essay) and gives clear, detailed context and analysis of their formal elements and meaning, beyond simple restatement and summary. These essays may have a couple of superficial errors, but they are more notable for their command of a rich vocabulary, a variety of sentence structures, and for the essay's coherent fluency.

Above average (7 range)

Essays in the above average range have a good idea to guide them, but they have less robust textual analysis. Some of that analysis may be more of a summary than an analysis of rich details. They may read somewhat mechanically, with less fluency and a more formulaic sentence structure and vocabulary than a top-scoring essay. They are solid essays, but they lack the sophistication and depth of a top-scoring essay.

Middle-range essays (5-6 range)

Middle-range essays have limited insights because they are superficial, generic, judgmental rather than analytical, and/or use formulaic organizational methods that leave the paragraphs disconnected and mechanical. These essays often rely on generalizations or on superficial gestures to analyzing devices. That is, their writers may know they need to mention devices like "diction" or "imagery," but they don't build anything with the tools other than to refer to them once generally and move on. The writers may simply restate the prompt, or they may stay at the level of what was given in the question, rather than developing ideas of their own.

Below average (3-4 range)

Essays that are below average show a reader and writer who struggled to understand the passage and question being asked. They may address an unrelated idea in the passage, or they may show a misunderstanding of how to analyze what they're examining. They may show some of the same judgmental, formulaic, and superficial qualities of a middle-range essay but with more errors and fragmented ideas. They often lack specific textual references and rely on generalizations or tangentially related ideas. They are often short and abbreviated, like an outline that wasn't finished. They usually contain significant errors that affect the reader's understanding.

Low-scoring (1-2 range)

Low-scoring essays show a reader who did not understand the question or the passage. They may be too short to understand—for a writer who ran out of time and attempted to get a something brief on the page, or for someone who struggled to understand what was being asked. The writing is difficult to understand because of significant errors, fragmented ideas, or a poor command of writing skills.

No score (0)

No response registered, or the essay does not relate to the essay prompt at all.

Exam readers will send the combined score (0-27) to the College Board, where it will be converted, along with your Section I score, into a number on the AP® point scale. You may see how these numerical scores were converted in prior years on the College Board website. Although it's tempting—and perhaps comforting—to try to treat this test as a numbers game, you can't control some of the scoring quirks across the entire nation of test-takers in a given year. It's best to treat this part of the exam *as a writing exam*, and learn how to write the best essays that will stand out among the readers' large stacks of similar work.

HOW TO SPEND THOSE 40 MINUTES PER ESSAY

With that goal of clear, personal writing in mind, let's figure out the best strategy for tackling the three essays in the time allotted. You have 2 hours for Section II, so aim to spend 40 minutes per essay. You may feel more or less confident about the essay types, but each essay is worth the same number of points, so plan to spend roughly the same amount of time on each one.

If you have some weeks to practice before the exam, practice writing 40-minute essays so that you can see what proportions of reading, planning, writing, and review work best for you. You may think that you need a lot of time to plan and outline, but if you get in the habit of writing a 40-minute essay every day, you'll find that your planning time will decrease significantly because the reading and writing process will feel more habitual—which is not the same as formulaic. You'll hear that warning reiterated multiple times throughout this chapter—there's no formula to follow every time—but you'll feel more capable and flexible in generating and organizing ideas if you practice often. That way, you'll know how to turn an abstract idea about a theme or concept into a clear essay based on textual analysis. You'll know how to take apart a difficult passage. You'll also know what kinds of analytical "moves" or strategies are your favorite building blocks to stack together into interesting sequences.

TIP

Writing a relatively painless 40-minute essay takes hours of repetitive practice.

You can start with the following general guidelines for timing and then adapt them based on the habits you develop.

8-10 minutes of reading the passage and making notes

- Read the prompt, and underline the main task it's asking you to perform.
- Read the passage, and underline and make annotations about
  - ○ words or phrases you don't understand.
  - ○ words or phrases that are footnoted and may help you understand other unknowns.
  - ○ phrases that seem directly related to the main task that you identified in the prompt.
  - ○ phrases that surprise you because they seem out of place or to challenge your expectations—they may even seem confusing, unsuccessful, or wrong in some way.
- Identify a *tension* or *conflict* that seems to be present in the passage: how does your surprising/challenging element expose that tension? Briefly note it in the margin and tag the sections of the passage that seem relevant to exploring that tension further.

25-27 minutes of composing the essay

- Write your introduction. Explain
  - ○ the main idea of the passage with the vocabulary from the prompt, but don't restate the prompt completely.
  - ○ the tension or conflict that you've identified within that main idea, which isn't stated in the prompt but which you've identified from your own close reading of the language in the passage.
  - ○ the preliminary so-what question: why that tension helps you see a new facet of the main idea.
- Write your body paragraphs.
  - ○ Start with straightforward ideas to build a foundation for your analysis—both for yourself to gain confidence and for your reader to have somewhere clear to start understanding how you're thinking about the passage.
  - ○ After that first body paragraph about the straightforward example, start looking at the surprising, unconventional, annoying, or ambiguous quotations you've annotated so that you're not just analyzing obvious examples.
  - ○ Using your annotations of relevant and surprising phrases, incorporate quotations into your own sentence.
  - ○ Analyze those quotations—don't just restate them or summarize them—and give them ample context for how they relate to your argument.
  - ○ Keep track of explaining the "so what" of your analysis at the end of each paragraph.
  - ○ It's okay to make paragraph breaks if you feel you're losing track of an idea—your readers will thank you.
- Write your conclusion.
  - ○ Make sure to include a conclusion, even if it's short.

o   Use the first sentence of your conclusion to explain how the main idea has become more nuanced through your analysis.

o   But don't just restate what you said in the previous paragraphs—it's a short essay, so repetition is unnecessary.

o   Look back at your so-what statements in the body paragraphs and make one more even loftier claim for the importance of your analysis.

5 minutes of editing

- Read through the sentences and clearly cross out any extra words or ideas you didn't finish.

- Make sure that you have clear topic sentences (and no placeholders) for each paragraph that show what your main idea is.

- Check for repetitive sentences that you can tighten up quickly by crossing out unnecessary words.

- Check for usage, punctuation, and spelling errors.

MOVING BEYOND THE FIVE-PARAGRAPH ESSAY

Notice how we've broken down the basic mechanics of literary analysis into some guidelines: start with a foundation and then find the more ambiguous, surprising, and complicated passages. But know that those are guidelines, not a specific formula. We don't recommend always dividing a paragraph into three separate devices like diction, metaphor, and tone. We also don't recommend writing a formulaic thesis statement that lists those devices. Those formulas are comforting: they give you a pre-made structure and you just have to fill in the blanks. However, the formulaic, three-pronged structure doesn't let you explore the nuances in the passages, because it breaks up the ideas into discrete, single-use tools: first I will look at diction, then I will move on to metaphor. Those two items aren't related . . . are they? Of course they are! The problem with a three-pronged thesis that breaks things up into pre-made boxes is that the tensions and conflicts you're analyzing in these passages have interrelated pieces; you may not be able to (or want to) separate them.

Your Trusty, Rusty Toolbox

You may be most comfortable framing your thesis and topic sentences in terms of "tools" you'll be using to analyze the text. It's more compelling to explain what you realize when you *use* these tools. You can and should still use those familiar tools; just focus your explanations on what they reveal, not just that you paid attention to buzzwords such as *rhyme*, *metaphor*, *diction*, etc.

For example, compare the difference between these sentences:

> *The diction in this passage is convoluted, which shows that the narrator is confused about what he is witnessing. The narrator's sensory language is clearer, however, showing that the two narrative features are contradictory.*

> *The narrator's convoluted diction signals his confusion at the scene in front of him; as his words fail him, however, his sense of smell becomes sharper and he startles to recognize the clue that's been sitting right in front of him.*

> **TIP**
>
> If you find that you struggle with topic sentences, leave two lines of space as you start your paragraphs—many people find that they're ready to write their best topic sentences at the *ends* of the paragraphs because they've just realized what they want to say.

The second sentence uses stronger verbs: *signals, fail, startles* vs. *shows, is, showing*. The stronger verbs let you re-tell the story in your own analytical language by focusing your attention on *how and what* the tools reveal in the passage, not just that you are using them and stating what's "clearer." Show, don't tell. Use strong verbs. You've heard these guidelines before, but you probably thought they referred just to writing fiction. Not necessarily. Narrate your analysis like you're re-focusing your director's camera on the scene to highlight the features you want the reader to notice in your survey of the passage.

To continue with the earlier sports metaphor, when you throw a ball as part of play, you don't explain: "I am throwing the ball in order to advance the ball." The act of throwing is less important than where it ends up, and how that play generates the next play. When you're practicing those plays, you may be reciting to yourself, "Now I am throwing the ball" (or not), but eventually it becomes a habit and you think about higher-order stuff. When you're chopping onions for a dish and then you present the complete dish after several other steps, the chopping part becomes less important than how the onions support the other flavors. But while you're learning to chop onions, it's a lot of focus and tears. We hope there are fewer tears with this strategy, even if your eyes water at our insistence that you try something new.

You may see the word *analysis* and figure that it's up to you to get inside the narrator's or main character's head and analyze their feelings, then solve their problems or say what they should do. You will pretend you're a psychologist and "read" the patient in the passage. Avoid the "should" statements: you're here to consider the author's use of language, not to diagnose or fix the characters.

You may also want to judge or assess what's effective, successful, or confusing in the passage and give the author advice about what could be different, in your opinion. You will pretend you're an editor and try to fix the passage. Those judgments will limit you, the writer, because you will spend all of your reading time trying to find "evidence" to support your dislike, confusion, or frustration. You will pretend you're a lawyer and try to make a case for what's wrong, what could be better, and what the characters need to do differently.

You're neither psychologist, editor, nor lawyer. You're a reader. The task here is to read the passage through the lens that the prompt gives you, and then record your readings of specific language from the passage in an organized, thoughtful form that takes the exam reader through your interpretations. You're both readers: first of the passage, then of the essay. Just two readers, communicating via essay.

The Benefits of the Open Thesis

Your first line of communication is your introduction, where you're expected to write a thesis statement that helps orient the exam reader. Instead of the three-pronged or judgment/opinion-based thesis, it's a better idea to work with an open thesis. The open thesis gives an idea of what you will be analyzing in the passage and a preliminary explanation as to why that's important. It may be more than one sentence long—the potentially frustrating thing about it is that it's open and adaptable to your ideas.

The open thesis may:

- reveal a deeper way of considering the main idea of the passage, by exposing a hidden tension or conflict that you will analyze in depth.

- point out the surprising element of the passage that your analysis will illuminate in order to help you reconsider the main idea in greater depth.

- propose an initial hypothesis for understanding a tension or conflict from the essay prompt and to indicate a surprising way of reconsidering that tension.

It's open-ended, so you can surprise yourself as you're writing and generating new ideas as you analyze passages. If you're thinking deeply as you write, you may surprise yourself when you find a new facet of your idea that you hadn't thought about in the introduction. Because your open thesis has promised the reader that there are depths you'll explore in your analysis, you'll have room to develop those insights. A judgment or a three-pronged essay doesn't have these dynamic qualities or adaptability because they tend to be inflexible; they predetermine the kinds of work you're going to do in the essay.

Here are some comparisons between three-pronged theses, judgments/opinions, and open theses. (Note that the works of literature in question don't matter for these examples.)

Three-pronged thesis: *The protagonist's family background influences his behavior as an adult, as is evidenced by his disconcertingly interrelated uses of violence, pity, and humor.*

Judgment/opinion: *The protagonist's sadistic sense of humor is a product of his family background, which makes it hard to relate to his jokes.*

Open thesis: *The most disconcerting element of John's narration is the violence underlying his humor, creating a push-pull sense of intimacy with the reader, where one is tempted to laugh and be repulsed in successive sentences.*

What might follow the open thesis: *The unexpected outcome of this oscillating attraction and repulsion is not relatability but pity for what he cannot understand about himself. This pity combines with the violence to deepen the sense of moral ambiguity in the novel.*

Three-pronged thesis: *The speaker of the poem deals with disappointment in love in destructive ways that are reflected in the form and language of the poem, as seen in the broken rhyme, the irregular meter, and the mixed metaphors.*

Judgment/opinion: *The speaker's heartbreak is clear from his use of broken rhyme and meter, but his use of metaphors is less successful in showing his disillusionment because they are cliched.*

Open thesis: *The speaker rejects not only love but also the act of writing love poetry itself. Each "broken" mode of rhyme, meter, and metaphor shows his distrust of any form of human coupling— or linguistic pairings. He turns each sonnet convention against itself to show the insufficiency of language to form bonds between distinct entities, be they humans or words.*

What might follow the open thesis: *Yet he has also left room for some hope in the flawed attempt at composition. The poem asks, what does one do with flaws, if one cannot correct them?*

These are just examples from (missing) sample passages, but they indicate the ways that you can explore a passage to find its hidden depths, and then use the essay form to guide the reader through that exploration. The open thesis opens up that space for exploration and provides an initial signpost. Let's work through a real passage and prompt to see how to do all of that exploration in less than 40 minutes.

BREAKING DOWN THE COMPOSITION PROCESS

Your first step should always be to read the prompt. The prompt will give you the primary vocabulary, the words that you can use to focus your attention on the passage. It may outline a tension or conflict for you to examine; it may suggest a few analytical tools to focus your attention. Your primary goal for the essay is to answer the question, so the most important thing is to make sure that you know what you're being asked to do.

Let's start with a prose prompt.

Read the following passage carefully. Write a well-organized essay in which you discuss how the shipwrecked sailor experiences disorientation on the island, to the extent that even familiar features of the island become unfamiliar to him.

from *Robinson Crusoe*, by Daniel Defoe

I was now at a great loss which way to get home with my boat! I had run so much hazard, and knew too much of the case, to think of attempting it by the way I went out; and what might be at the other side (I mean the west side) I knew not, nor had I any mind to run any more ventures; so I resolved on the next morning to make my way westward along the shore, and to see if there was no creek where I might lay up my frigate in safety, so as to have her again if I wanted her. In about three miles or thereabouts, coasting the shore, I came to a very good inlet or bay, about a mile over, which narrowed till it came to a very little rivulet or brook, where I found a very convenient harbour for my boat, and where she lay as if she had been in a little dock made on purpose for her. Here I put in, and having stowed my boat very safe, I went on shore to look about me, and see where I was.

I soon found I had but a little passed by the place where I had been before, when I travelled on foot to that shore; so taking nothing out of my boat but my gun and umbrella, for it was exceedingly hot, I began my march. The way was comfortable enough after such a voyage as I had been upon, and I reached my old bower in the evening, where I found everything standing as I left it; for I always kept it in good order, being, as I said before, my country house.

I got over the fence, and laid me down in the shade to rest my limbs, for I was very weary, and fell asleep; but judge you, if you can, that read my story, what a surprise I must be in when I was awaked out of my sleep by a voice calling me by my name several times, "Robin, Robin, Robin Crusoe: poor Robin Crusoe! Where are you, Robin Crusoe? Where are you? Where have you been?"

I was so dead asleep at first, being fatigued with rowing, or part of the day, and with walking the latter part, that I did not wake thoroughly; but dozing thought I dreamed that somebody spoke to me; but as the voice continued to repeat, "Robin Crusoe, Robin Crusoe," at last I began to wake more perfectly, and was at first dreadfully frightened, and started up in the utmost consternation;

but no sooner were my eyes open, but I saw my Poll sitting on the top of the hedge; and immediately knew that it was he that spoke to me; for just in such bemoaning language I had used to talk to him and teach him; and he had learned it so perfectly that he would sit upon my finger, and lay his bill close to my face and cry, "Poor Robin Crusoe! Where are you? Where have you been? How came you here?" and such things as I had taught him.

However, even though I knew it was the parrot, and that indeed it could be nobody else, it was a good while before I could compose myself. First, I was amazed how the creature got thither; and then, how he should just keep about the place, and nowhere else; but as I was well satisfied it could be nobody but honest Poll, I got over it; and holding out my hand, and calling him by his name, "Poll," the sociable creature came to me, and sat upon my thumb, as he used to do, and continued talking to me, "Poor Robin Crusoe! and how did I come here? and where had I been?" just as if he had been overjoyed to see me again; and so I carried him home along with me.

The Prompt

What the Prompt Asks

The prompt is asking you to find elements of disorientation and unfamiliarity in the passage. This task is simple enough in the opening paragraphs: he gets lost. The passage continues for several paragraphs after he finds his way back to his "country house," where he encounters his pet parrot, Poll, speaking to him in his own words. One way of asking this question in a pointed way is this: *Why does the unfamiliarity follow him home?*

Some of the challenges of this prompt are: Resist summarizing the events of the passage, dig deeper than the obvious examples, resist summarizing the challenging examples. This passage appears to be simple, but that means you have to work harder to distinguish your analysis and to progress beyond the basics in that analysis.

Read the passage for the main idea

First, find the most straightforward examples of disorientation in the passage. In the early paragraphs, Crusoe's disorientation is characterized by long strings of clauses and digressions that highlight the fact that he doesn't know where he's going. Here's one example:

I had run so much hazard, and knew too much of the case, to think of attempting it by the way I went out; and what might be at the other side (I mean the west side) I knew not, nor had I any mind to run any more ventures; so I resolved on the next morning to make my way westward along the shore, and to see if there was no creek where I might lay up my frigate in safety, so as to have her again if I wanted her.

It may be tempting to register a judgment opinion about the style of narration here: those semicolons could be periods. First, that's a stylistic device that's more common in the eighteenth century (although you wouldn't be expected to know that). More importantly, the feature that grabs your attention with its digressiveness is also the main idea of the passage: *the somewhat disjointed style highlights the main idea.* You may remember that link from Section I of the exam: style and theme are often linked.

Mark similar passages that show this kind of digressiveness or tendency to wander about or depart from the main subject. In other words, these passages mirror the character's own disorientation. Of course, they're so long that you won't be citing them in full in your essay—this is where fragmentary quotations will come in useful—but it's important to mark the examples so you can see the patterns in the style.

Because we're paying attention to digressive sentences, this one seems striking in how it makes the order of words more complicated than it has to be: "...for I always kept it in good order, being, as I said before, my country house." If we're thinking about how even his home becomes unfamiliar to him, it's useful to note that his language to introduce his "country house" is out of syntactical order, even if he claims, interrupting himself, that it's always in order.

Read a passage for its confusing and challenging parts

What are some other ways that Defoe signals disorientation in the passage? He is disoriented when he is awakened by the sound of a voice mimicking him. Poll's dialogue is strange because he is repeating Crusoe's own language back to him: "Poor Robin Crusoe! and how did I come here? and where had I been?" He thought he was alone, but what challenges him is not the presence of another human, but of a mimic that repeats his own language.

Identify tensions and conflicts

Thus, what's most disconcerting about Poll's language is *how familiar it is.* That's a fascinating irony to explore in your essay: what's most familiar to Crusoe are his own thoughts, but they become disorienting when he hears them repeated back to himself in the imitative voice of a parrot. You can call that unsettling experience an example of the *uncanny*—when the familiar becomes strange. There is a tension between familiarity and strangeness.

We reframed the essay prompt as: *what happens when disorientation follows him home . . .* That provocative framing makes it seem like a horror movie, and the talking parrot who repeats his own voice only adds to such a creepy re-envisioning of the scene.

You can now write an introduction and an open-ended thesis about the passage:

> *We thought it was an adventure story of a shipwreck, where Robinson Crusoe's getting lost is part of the conventional means of exploration. In the later paragraphs of the passage, the story becomes more like a horror tale or a Gothic novel, where Crusoe's "country house" becomes a site for the uncanny, where he encounters a double of himself in parrot form. Both Crusoe and the reader are disoriented by the way familiar features become strange.*

The introduction is the most important part of the essay because you're setting up your reader's expectations, and this introduction certainly challenges them to reconsider the passage in a new way. This essay promises to analyze the passages that you've underlined first as conventions in an adventure story, and then flip them around to show how they may also be conventions in a horror story.

(Note: This is not the only way that you could frame this essay; it's just an example. What would you do differently in exploring that tension between familiarity and strangeness in the passage?)

Body Paragraphs

Straightforward Example

Write the first body paragraph about the most straightforward textual examples of the idea you're exploring. This way, you can start with analysis that you feel confident in explaining, and your reader will have a firm foundation for understanding where you're coming from. You can start with the clear examples of digressiveness you underlined. You can explain how the stacks of clauses become disorienting and difficult to follow and how Crusoe himself gets lost in his explanations.

Examples of Surprise

Write the next body paragraph about a textual example that has a surprising element that makes you have to dig deeper into the tension you've uncovered. This may be a detail that doesn't quite fit your expectations and makes you reassess what was straightforward in the previous paragraph.

Here, you can find two different examples of surprise from your reading: You can note the example of the disordered sentence in describing his home (mentioned above as something you could annotate). That example is a short sentence fragment that locates the disorientation not just in the lost parts of the island but in his "old bower," "his country house." In that way, it's the first step to showing how the disorientation follows him home.

Here you could start to build the case that even the home is strange to him, a common convention in a horror story or a Gothic novel. (Indeed, you wouldn't be responsible for knowing this, but the "country house" poem by such poets as Andrew Marvell in the seventeenth century is sometimes thought to be a forerunner to the Gothic novel because it describes an estate and, as we see here, it's only a slight shift in perspective that turns such a description into something strange.)

The second example is Poll's repetition of his own language. We've noted that it's uncanny because it's both familiar to him (his own words) and strange (because it comes from a parrot—and one he hadn't expected to see). You can identify the tension between familiarity and strangeness in this pet who talks to its owner; indeed, it's a pet that reminds its owner of his loneliness and self-pity, which we don't always expect pets to do!

Using Quotations

In order to analyze quotations in depth, you need to quote enough of the passage that you have something substantial to work with. A sentence or most of a sentence is more useful than a single word or two; you can zoom in and focus on particular words after you've given the context and explanation. Such analysis might look like this:

> Crusoe explains the twists and turns of finding his way home in exhaustive detail, so that the reader can barely follow him: "In about three miles or thereabouts, coasting the shore, I came to a very good inlet or bay, about a mile over, which narrowed till it came to a very little rivulet or brook, where I found a very convenient harbour for my boat . . . " The clear details about estimated distance and direction are narrated with frequent interjections to correct himself slightly with phrases like "or thereabouts" and "about a mile over." Why does he need this much detail? Is he explaining the route to himself so he may find it again? The description is both realistic and disorienting in its immersive detail.

This analysis mixes longer quotations with more focused attention to patterns in single words and phrases. The passage is introduced with enough context to explain what's going on, but it's not mere summary or description. The introductory phrase "the reader can barely follow him" signals how to pay attention to details in the quotation after the colon. When you introduce these longer quotations, use a colon to set them off from your own language.

You might introduce quotations in context like this:

> Crusoe is awakened from his slumber when he hears a strange voice that sounds both familiar and strange: "Robin, Robin, Robin Crusoe: poor Robin Crusoe! Where are you, Robin Crusoe? Where are you? Where have you been?"

> Defoe slyly reveals Crusoe's self-pity and loneliness, by having Poll proclaim it in mimicking his master: "for just in such bemoaning language I had used to talk to him and teach him; and he had learned it so perfectly. . ."

It's best to balance these sentences with your own words at the front and to use the quotation as the end of the sentence. Don't try to cram your own analysis after the quotation as part of the same sentence. You can just start a new sentence to give your analysis a chance to breathe.

Fragmentary quotations are useful after you've worked with the more substantial sentence form, to draw attention to single words or phrases that you really want to highlight.

> The "bemoaning language" becomes ghostly in Poll's repetitions, like an echo of Crusoe's own voice on the island that is not quite "sociable," for it is only a repetition that the animal has "learned . . . perfectly."

Explain the so-what question.

Why does your analysis of the passage help you explore your surprise or challenge to your expectations? It would be difficult to over-explain the significance of your analysis; most people skimp on this section either because they think it's obvious, or they aren't really sure why they've just analyzed this passage. Either of those possibilities will be transparently obvious to your readers, so keep writing these sentences until you think you've come up with an insight about *why* that analysis helped you see a new element of the passage. Writing is a process of thinking, so it's normal, even admirable, to come up with ideas and insights even as you're writing these sentences. It's gratifying to see an author hit on an idea, especially if it shows them reconsidering and reflecting on previous paragraphs. We call this *thinking on the page,* and it shows that you're a sophisticated reader and writer, able to communicate that reflection in such a short span.

For this passage, you've taken the reader on an unexpected journey into what they thought was a deserted island but is actually a deserted island that is haunted with echoes and disorder. Why does this shift in expectations matter? Is it just a clever reading?

You might answer the so-what question like this:

> The haunted parts of the island show Crusoe's horror at his loneliness. When repeated back to him, the phrases "Poor Robin! . . . how did I come here? and where had I been?" expose the fact that he has been searching for existential answers to his condition. He wants answers; he encounters only a voice repeating his worries back at him. His "country house" will never be his home, for he is apparently permanently displaced. All of his explanations about distance and direction lead him only to temporary spaces in which he can camp out. He is left to make sense of the accident that left him shipwrecked, with no hope of an answer. He thought he was in an adventure story, but he is also a ghost on the island.

Say what you will about that example: it's not boring. It interprets the passage in a creative, surprising way. It doesn't have to be a perfect essay; rather, it needs to show why your analysis lets us see something about the passage we hadn't seen before. The prompt asked you to discuss how Crusoe experiences disorientation on the island and back at his home, so we've given an interpretation about how the disorientation warps the sense of generic conventions and expectations in the passage. We (and he) are supposed to be in an adventure story, but the conventions become strange, unfamiliar, and scary, as if we were instead in a horror story. The horror is not due to monsters but to existential loneliness. That's an intense so-what answer!

The sample essays in prose and poetry are coming up next, which is where we'll get to breaking down these strategies into specific sentence forms. We won't write out the full essay; rather, we'll show how you can apply the reading and thinking strategies to poetry with some minor adaptations.

Read this poem by Thomas Hardy carefully. Then write a well-organized essay in which you discuss how the speaker reconciles his conflicted feelings about his troubled friend. By looking at the formal elements of the poem, show how he arrives at this reconciliation.

"Confession to a Friend in Trouble," by Thomas Hardy

Your troubles shrink not, though I feel them less
Here, far away, than when I tarried near;
I even smile old smiles—with listlessness—
Line   Yet smiles they are, not ghastly mockeries mere.

5   A thought too strange to house within my brain
Haunting its outer precincts I discern:
—That I will not show zeal again to learn
Your griefs, and, sharing them, renew my pain . . . .

It goes, like murky bird or buccaneer
10   That shapes its lawless figure on the main,
And each new impulse tends to make outflee
The unseemly instinct that had lodgment here;
Yet, comrade old, can bitterer knowledge be
Than that, though banned, such instinct was in me!

What the Prompt Asks

The prompt asks you to analyze how Hardy reconciles his conflicted feelings about his troubled friends, by looking at the formal elements of the poem. This poem is a sonnet, so we may be looking at the sonnet's structure, rhyme, meter, and also Hardy's direct address to the distant friend. How do these formal elements illuminate his ambivalent feelings and perhaps give him a bit of solace about the irrevocably changed friendship?

Read the passage for the main idea

Thomas Hardy's "Confession to a Friend in Trouble" is a sonnet with a conflict at its center: the poet loves his friend, yet he is unsure how to express those feelings to a friend who is flailing for help. We don't have access to knowledge about what's wrong with the speaker's friend or what we might find in Hardy's biography to see any deeper connections to his life.

The ambivalence is baked into every line of the poem: the rhymes in the first paragraph are all about missed connections, even if they rhyme in a superficial way: "less"/"listlessness" and "near"/"mere." Even as he's making a poetic attempt at connection, he's highlighting the superficiality of the exercise.

Identify Surprising, Unconventional, Challenging Qualities

One surprising element is that even though the poem is addressed to his friend, the word "you" is mentioned only twice. The poet seems to be avoiding his friend even in the language of the poem. This absence is not conventional in a sonnet, but then, this sonnet's subject itself is unconventional.

We also have the sonnet form, the rhyme scheme of which takes the form *abab cddc eeffgg*. This structure is not conventional for sonnets, either in English or Petrarchan forms. This shift from the sonnet's conventions is surprising, for it makes us pay attention to how the speaker resolves rhymes in different schemas in each stanza.

In both of these "challenges," it may be tempting to tell Hardy and his speaker what to do to resolve the friendship: show more empathy, cut the cord, try to talk it out in a conversation instead of in a one-sided poem. The thing is, the ambivalent sonnet is all we have to analyze; the "flaws" in the sonnet form and rhyme are what make it compelling to read. Those frustrating elements, both formal and emotional, that we might be able to advise or fix are the stuff that makes the poem so powerful. Analyze the struggle on the page instead of trying to solve it off the page.

Why are these important for exploring the tensions in the poem?

Can a poem actually reconcile a troubled friendship? The prompt is asking you how Hardy reconciles the conflict, but many features of the poem suggest that these feelings are in fact irreconcilable. They will constantly shift their forms, for the feelings "like murky bird or buccaneer / That shapes its lawless figure on the main" (9-10). The speaker is using the structural, rhythmic, and conventional limitations of poetic form to give a shape to his diffuse feelings; the limitations of the sonnet's form also enable him to express ambiguities. Thus, the major tension in this poem is what reconciliation might look like.

Body Paragraphs

Straightforward Examples

In analyzing poetry, it's a good idea to build your foundation by looking at the largest structural elements, like form. In this case, we were surprised that the sonnet had unconventional rhyme endings. We might interpret the unconventional stanza structure to say that it shows him struggling to figure out the best way of making connections. The uncertain, shifting approaches to pairing formal elements reflect his personal ambivalence about pairing and connection in the friendship.

Develop Complexity

We were also surprised that the word "you" is conspicuously absent from the sonnet. "Your troubles" and "your griefs" appear in lines 1 and 8, but they are marked with negations: they "shrink not" and the speaker "will not show zeal again to learn" about them. The friend himself is missing from the poem, replaced by the "pain" the speaker feels at that friend's overwhelming troubles. In the speaker's mind, the friend has been eclipsed by his troubles.

Using Quotations

In analyzing poetry, you can introduce quotations the same way you would with prose passages and signal a line break with a backslash (/). Then cite the lines in parentheses at the very end of the sentence.

The format looks like this:

> *The speaker gestures to his attempt to contain his ambivalence when he voices "a thought too strange to house within my brain" that can only "haunt the outer precincts" (5-6). Yet he sets off this troubling thought in italics, to record its devastating ambivalence:* "I will not show zeal again to learn / Your griefs, and, sharing them, renew my pain" (7-8).

So-What Question

This is a poem about the insufficiencies of the poetic form. Each conventional element—from structure to rhyme—is about trying to make a connection with words and formal structures that might contain his ambivalent feelings. The final couplet is not a loving reconciliation of two old friends who have solved their problems, but a record of the "bitterer feelings," or the "unseemly instinct that had lodgment here" in the poem (12-13). The reconciliation, then, is with the realization that pain and ambivalence are constants.

This is another intense so-what conclusion! It answers the question by first showing that the simple reconciliation isn't possible and by then suggesting a darker interpretation of the request for resolution. The poem ends on an unsettled note, so our conclusion must take stock of that irresolution, instead of trying to tie it up neatly.

HOME STRETCH: THE LAST 5 MINUTES OF EACH ESSAY

As you're composing your essay, try to leave yourself a few minutes to check over your work to make sure you haven't left any sentence fragments or left out any topic sentences or words.

Edit Your Ideas

Because writing is a process of thinking, you may have repeated yourself as you were writing toward an idea. You may have come up with your best idea at the end of a paragraph. Don't make the exam reader work too hard to decipher your sentence order, but do go back and tighten up any repetitions that you can cross out quickly and cleanly. Your essay doesn't need to be perfect, but it does need to be legible, so make sure that you've crossed out stuff clearly and not left any ambiguous stray marks or fragments.

Check for Usage Errors

The score is holistic, so you're not being marked down for particular errors; no one expects you to be perfect on a timed exam, but readers may get frustrated when they see a pattern of mistakes. They often read looking for what's called a "hierarchy of mistakes": they care most about pervasive

TIP

It may be helpful to underline particular words you want to emphasize, as though you were italicizing them on the computer. Don't overuse this strategy and underline everything or your reader won't know which ones are the most important. If this strategy appeals to you, you can use it once or twice an essay— at most.

patterns that affect their ability to understand what you're saying. They won't pay as much attention to an extra comma that doesn't affect their comprehension of your work.

Commas, semicolons, and periods are easier to edit than whole words or sentences, so if you have a tendency to write long, winding sentences, go back and add some clarifying punctuation. Remember Daniel Defoe's *Robinson Crusoe*, searching for familiarity in those long digressions; remember how he encountered only repetitions and echoes of his ideas? Remember how disorienting those sentences were? Try to make your writing seem more familiar, so that it doesn't sound like you're parroting back fragments of phrases, like Poll.

COMMON READER PET PEEVES

All teachers or readers have their own pet peeves, and of course, you can't know what idiosyncrasies your exam readers are bringing to the table. Here are a few very common errors that seem like they're small but which actually reveal larger thinking problems that readers will notice.

Empty Transition Words

You may have learned the value of transition words like *moreover, therefore, thus, nevertheless, however,* and other phrases. Their value is relative to how frequently you use them: use them *sparingly*, to emphasize important transitions. When they're overused, it starts to look as if you're using them to disguise the emptiness of the connection you're drawing between paragraphs and sentences. In cases of overuse, either strike them out as you're editing, or, better yet, take a moment to write out a transition based on the actual connection between your ideas, rather than patching a gap in your logic.

Unclear Antecedents

An unclear antecedent is an ambiguous reference to *this, that, these, those, them,* and other pronouns where your reader isn't sure which noun is being specified.

Examples:

> *This shows how the speaker is wavering in his affections.*
>
> *The protagonist isn't sure how to feel about this.*

Specifying a noun after "this" in a sentence like "this shows . . ." is a great way to build a transition without using empty transition words.

Example: *The speaker reiterates her loyalty to her family in the final stanza; this loyalty is tinged with ambivalence...*

Related to the unclear antecedent problem is the sloppy connection: when you drop in a quotation and say "this connects because . . . (reasons)," you're not explaining what "this" refers to. Show, don't tell the connection.

TIP

Make sure that you've spelled characters' and author names correctly—those silly errors stick out like sore thumbs. (See what we did there?)

TIP

As you scan your work one last time, make sure that you haven't used the word "interesting" or "unique" or any similarly overused words. Show, don't tell: choose a more specific adjective that indicates what *makes* it interesting or unique.

THE SMALLEST DETAILS COUNT

We've focused a lot on essay content, but let's take a minute to discuss the nitty gritty of essay mechanics.

If you are hand writing your essay, use legible handwriting. The reader will only score what he or she can read without too much scrutiny or frustration. They know you're rushed for time, but you should know that they're reading hundreds of essays and don't have time to spend deciphering tiny, illegible scrawl.

Make visible indentations. The reader's eyes will glaze over if they're reading long paragraphs.

Vary your sentence lengths. Especially in sentences where you want to emphasize your main ideas, try using short, punchy sentences to make them stand out. Because writing is a process of thinking, it's common to stack up many compound sentences with *and, but, or, yet, so* as you string together ideas. Make sure that you're not just endlessly stringing clause after clause together with little variation. Likewise, check for places where you've joined together independent clauses with just a comma—called a comma splice.

Make sure that you're using vocabulary from the question in your answer. This is the commonsense way to make sure that you're answering the question that ETS is asking: are you using, adapting, and refining the terms they've given you? You don't want to just restate or summarize; you want to show that you're building on the work they've done in framing the question for you.

Follow the order that works best for you. Start with the essay that most interests you, but remember to number it with the corresponding number and label (prose, poetry, open). Make sure to spend about 40 minutes on each one, as each one counts the same.

POETRY AND PROSE ESSAY WALKTHROUGHS

Let's look at a sample question and three sample responses: one high-scoring, one middle-range, and one low-scoring. For the high-scoring essays, we've broken down the paragraphs into tables that show some of the strategies you might adapt for your own writing.

Sample Prose Prompt 1

Herman Melville wrote the novel *Mardi* in 1849, two years before *Moby-Dick*. Like that epic tale, Mardi contains elements of philosophical musing about the relationship between humans and the natural world of the sea. Read the passage carefully. Write an essay in which you analyze how Melville's narrator combines scientific observation with figurative language in his encounter with the strange creatures in the sea. What is the purpose or function of combining those two modes in this passage? Are there tensions between science and metaphor? Are there unexpected correspondences between observation and figurative expression?

From *Mardi*, by Herman Melville

There is a fish in the sea that evermore, like a surly lord, only goes abroad attended by his suite. It is the Shovel-nosed Shark. A clumsy lethargic monster, unshapely as his name, and the last species of his kind, one would think, to be so bravely waited upon, as he is. His suite is composed of those dainty little creatures called Pilot fish by sailors. But by night his retinue is frequently increased by the presence of several small luminous fish, running in advance, and flourishing their flambeaux like link-boys lighting the monster's way. Pity there were no ray-fish in rear, page-like, to carry his caudal train.

Now the relation subsisting between the Pilot fish above mentioned and their huge ungainly lord, seems one of the most inscrutable things in nature. At any rate, it poses poor me to comprehend. That a monster so ferocious, should suffer five or six little sparks, hardly fourteen inches long, to gambol about his grim hull with the utmost impunity, is of itself something strange. But when it is considered, that by a reciprocal understanding, the Pilot fish seem to act as scouts to the shark, warning him of danger, and apprising him of the vicinity of prey; and moreover, in case of his being killed, evincing their anguish by certain agitations, otherwise inexplicable; the whole thing becomes a mystery unfathomable. Truly marvels abound. It needs no dead man to be raised, to convince us of some things. Even my Viking marveled full as much at those Pilot fish as he would have marveled at the Pentecost. But perhaps a little incident, occurring about this period, will best illustrate the matter in hand.

We were gliding along, hardly three knots an hour, when my comrade, who had been dozing over the gunwale, suddenly started to his feet, and pointed out an immense Shovel-nosed Shark, less than a boat's length distant, and about half a fathom beneath the surface. A lance was at once snatched from its place; and true to his calling, Jarl was about to dart it at the fish, when, interested by the sight of its radiant little scouts, I begged him to desist.

One of them was right under the shark, nibbling at his ventral fin; another above, hovering about his dorsal appurtenance; one on each flank; and a frisking fifth pranking about his nose, seemingly having something to say of a confidential nature. They were of a bright, steel-blue color, alternated with jet black stripes; with glistening bellies of a silver-white. Clinging to the back of the shark, were four or five Remoras, or sucking-fish; snaky parasites, impossible to remove from whatever they adhere to, without destroying their lives. The Remora has little power in swimming; hence its sole locomotion is on the backs of larger fish. Leech-like, it sticketh closer than a false brother in prosperity; closer than a beggar to the benevolent; closer than Webster to the Constitution. But it feeds upon what it clings to; its feelers having a direct communication with the esophagus.

The shark swam sluggishly; creating no sign of a ripple, but ever and, anon shaking his Medusa locks, writhing and curling with horrible life. Now and then, the nimble Pilot fish darted from his side--this way and that--mostly toward our boat; but previous to taking a fresh start ever returning to their liege lord to report progress.

A thought struck me. Baiting a rope's end with a morsel of our almost useless salt beef, I suffered it to trail in the sea. Instantly the foremost scout swam toward it; hesitated; paused; but at last advancing, briskly snuffed at the line, and taking one finical little nibble, retreated toward the shark. Another moment, and the great Tamerlane himself turned heavily about; pointing his black, cannon-like nose directly toward our broadside. Meanwhile, the little Pilot fish darted hither and thither; keeping up a mighty fidgeting, like men of small minds in a state of nervous agitation.

Presently, Tamerlane swam nearer and nearer, all the while lazily eyeing the Chamois, as a wild boar a kid. Suddenly making a rush for it, in the foam he made away with the bait. But the next instant, the uplifted lance sped at his skull; and thrashing his requiem with his sinewy tail, he sunk slowly, through his own blood, out of sight. Down with him swam the terrified Pilot fish; but soon after, three of them were observed close to the boat, gliding along at a uniform pace; one on each side, and one in advance; even as they had attended their lord. Doubtless, one was under our keel.

"A good omen," said Jarl; "no harm will befall us so long as they stay."

Sample 8-9 Essay

The narrator of Herman Melville's *Mardi* is a detailed, inspired observer of the sea around him, and he uses elaborate metaphors to show how small pilot fish attend to their protector shovel-nosed shark, as well as how the remora fish attaches to the shark. These symbiotic relationships, or "reciprocal understanding[s]," among animals are instructive for him, for they model the collaborative relationships on board the ship. Scientific language and metaphors are not as distinct as they may seem, for they both rely on models and comparisons for comprehending distinctions among details. The narrator's figurative language about dictators and democracies in the water helps him understand power and authority on board his ship, so that the crew can understand their own collaborative duties. The fish provide a biological and metaphorical model for collaborative authority, but that model is dynamic and subject to change—much like human nature itself.

At first, the narrator is mystified by the interactions between the gigantic shark and the bright tiny school of fish that swim around it, calling the scene "one of the most inscrutable things in nature." Yet he combines observation with elaborate metaphor in order to make them seem more like human societies, with a clear distinction in roles between master and servant. The shark is "like a surly lord, [who] only goes abroad attended by his suite," and the pilot fish are servants who carry "flambeaux like link-boys lighting the monster's way" and who attend "their liege lord to report progress." In these metaphors, the behavior becomes not just understandable, no longer "inscrutable," but natural. Scientific language is full of metaphors that are used as models for understanding: schools of fish, say, or the language of kingdoms, classes, orders, and families for classifying species. These terms provide us a way of thinking about hierarchies and relationships. They are thus functional metaphors for understanding the natural world in human terms.

It is strategic for a captain to organize the world around him this way—not just on board his ship, where crewmen like Jarl will listen to him, but outside the ship as well. Indeed, the very structure of moving from "inscrutable" to the natural order of things is a way to make the human extension of the metaphor seem more like a natural observation of how the world works, not an imposition: following leaders is natural, and collaboration is beneficial. One piece of figurative language, such as the pilot fishes' luminescent flambeaux-of-the-sea, might sound silly, but the repetition of the language of "sparks" and "radiant little scouts" makes the metaphor seem less artificial and more like just an observation of what the fish are and do. The description of the pilot fish becomes playful, so that you'll smile at the comparison rather than being confused by it, as "a frisking fifth pranking about his nose, seemingly having something to say of a confidential nature." The repetition of the shark as a "lord" may sound excessive at first, but the repetition and elaboration of the metaphor makes it seem natural. It sets up the most elaborate metaphor of all, in which the shark becomes the dictator Tamerlane, who roams over his domain, laying waste to those in his way. Even if you don't know exactly who he is, the narrator's repetition makes his power obvious. The narrator uses the literary historical example of Tamerlane twice, so that the possibly unfamiliar comparison becomes just a name that sounds reasonable—what was inscrutable becomes a historical reference. These comparisons become natural; they transform from figurative language into data.

The remora that ride the shark are the reminder that the master-servant relationship is more complicated than it appears to be. "Leech-like," they ride the shark without providing any obvious benefit to their host. Here Melville makes an unusual series of comparisons that are more "inscrutable" than anything else in the passage: the remora "sticketh closer than a false brother in prosperity; closer than a beggar to the benevolent; closer than Webster to the Constitution." Even with a footnote, that three-part comparison is unwieldy: first a comparison to the Biblical proverb, then a seemingly satirical comparison to a historical figure. Even the middle comparison, "a beggar to the benevolent" is unsettling because it inverts the structure of power. One expects the benevolent to act out of the power to do good, but the language here makes it seem like the beggars are just taking without giving back. Benevolence doesn't seem as authoritative when its beneficiaries are accused of being freeloading remoras. These ambiguities and conflicts are the stuff of democracy—not the rigid autocracy of Tamerlane. Even without deep knowledge of Melville's thoughts on Webster and the Constitution, we know that ongoing legal discussions about the Constitution show the ways that power and authority are subject to debate and adaptation in a democracy. Fundamentally, they are subject to <u>interpretation</u>--the way that figurative language is also subject to interpretation, or how scientific observation changes with new data.

This is why Jarl's observation at the end of the passage is so important: they show him interpreting a change in the pilot fishes' behavior, as they adopt the ship as their new master, the new "shark" they will follow. Jarl interprets their behavior as an omen, a sign that links human imagination with the natural world. The crew member, not the captain, gets the final word in the passage, showing the ways that the collaboration on the ship is less autocratic and more flexible than one might have thought. The ship itself is the master here—as the pilot fish understand—not any one person.

Reader Comments for the 8-9 Essay

(For clarity, Herman Melville is the author referred to in this explanation, and the exam writer—the student who presumably wrote the essay—is the writer.)

This is a clear, compelling essay with a lot of depths—fittingly so for an essay about sea exploration. The writer has identified three layers of symbiosis in the passage from *Mardi*: the scientific observation of symbiosis among the sea creatures, the metaphorical extension of that symbiosis to a ship's crew who must collaborate, and finally to the interrelationship between the modes of scientific observation and metaphor in the passage. In this way, the writer has addressed the essay question about how Melville combines those two modes, and makes a clear argument that they complement each other, and that it's a false dichotomy to say that they're at odds.

In the work with *Tamerlane* and Daniel Webster, the writer bites off a bit more than s/he can chew (like a shark), but the writer is also to be commended for diving deep into those difficult passages. (Sorry—the sea puns are irresistible!) The writer doesn't try to make a wacky interpretation here; these ideas about Melville's references to dictatorial and democratic authority seem compelling and would be fascinating to trace in a longer essay. Revision would let the writer be clearer about what's meant by "we know that legal discussions about the Constitution show . . ." means specifically for this argument.

The struggle to interpret those references leads the writer to a fascinating insight about how Melville himself discusses interpretation in both science and metaphor. The obvious idea would be that metaphors are subjective and scientific observation is objective, but Melville has shown throughout the passage that the narrator is interpreting the shark's behavior subjectively, through the lens of his own human organizational methods. The writer makes a sophisticated point here about the role of interpretation in both modes of scientific observation and metaphorical language. Arguably, such an insight wouldn't have surfaced if not for some fumbling around in interpreting the unknowns in *Tamerlane* and Webster, just like a scientist might do in investigating a new piece of unusual data.

Here is an outline of the first paragraph, the introduction, of the 8-9 essay, where you can see how the writer used strategies for explaining the main idea about the three layers of symbiosis among animals, shipmates, and formal scientific and metaphorical elements of the narration.

What the writer says (sentence copied from the essay)	What the writer does in the sentence (explanation of the strategy) **Note:** Adapt these strategies to your own uses, but don't try to follow them in a rigid order.
The narrator of Herman Melville's Mardi *is a detailed, inspired observer of the sea around him as he uses elaborate metaphors to show how small Pilot fish attend to their protector Shovel-nosed shark . . .*	• Names the author and title of the excerpted work in a conversational way • Uses the vocabulary from the exam question (observation, metaphor) to show the connection between the two modes

What the writer says (sentence copied from the essay)	What the writer does in the sentence (explanation of the strategy) Note: Adapt these strategies to your own uses, but don't try to follow them in a rigid order.
These symbiotic relationships, or "reciprocal understanding[s]," among animals are instructive for him, for they model the collaborative relationships on board the ship.	• Briefly explains the main idea of the passage • Integrates fragmentary quotations into the explanation to indicate how that main idea is conveyed in the language of the passage. No analysis yet—these fragments are for you to practice narrowing your focus onto small examples of the language as you explain the main idea of the poem, as if you were scanning your camera over the poem to find the details on which to focus. • Briefly explains the **so what**: the animal symbiosis is an organizing metaphor for collaboration among humans • Cites line numbers to help the reader find the quotations
Scientific language and metaphors are not as distinct as they may seem, for they both rely on models and comparisons for comprehending distinctions among details.	• Makes a link between the passage's main idea (symbiosis of animals) and writer's own idea about the link between formal qualities of the scientific and metaphorical modes mentioned in the prompt (symbiosis of science and metaphor)
The narrator's figurative language about dictators and democracies in the water helps him understand power and authority on board his ship, so that the crew can understand their own collaborative duties. The fish provide a biological and metaphorical model for collaborative authority, but that model is dynamic and subject to change—much like human nature itself.	• Builds on the so-what idea from the earlier sentence to show how it's developing complexity already • The final clause about how these interactions are subject to change guarantees that the essay will be dynamic as the writer assesses these changes in different parts of the passage.

The introduction may seem a bit long—it's a bit repetitive and could be tightened up if it were a revisable essay. Nevertheless, it's a sophisticated insight, so the writer seems to be working out some of the so-what idea during the writing process. Remember, you can modify these strategies on your own and see what works best for you.

Here are some exemplary, even ambitious, sentences and strategies from the body paragraphs of the essay.

What the writer says (sentence copied from the essay)	What the writer does in the sentence (explanation of the strategy) Note: Adapt these strategies to your own uses, but don't try to follow them in a rigid order.
At first, the narrator is mystified by the interactions between the gigantic shark and the bright tiny school of fish that swim around it, calling the scene "one of the most inscrutable things in nature."	• Introduces the idea of "inscrutability" as a theme worth considering next to the analysis of the symbiotic relationships • This key idea lays the groundwork for later paragraphs in the essay in which the writer develops complexity by looking at "inscrutable" passages, so it's a clever way to insist that the passage has complexity at its very core.
The shark is "like a surly lord, [who] only goes abroad attended by his suite," and the pilot fish are servants who carry "flambeaux like linkboys lighting the monster's way" and who attend "their liege lord to report progress."	• In this early paragraph, picks relatively straightforward (yet interesting) material from the passage to analyze • Incorporates fragmentary quotations from the text into own sentences, to show how focusing on metaphorical language illuminates the scientific observation • Note: picking the liege/lord example wasn't just the most straightforward example of metaphor; it will also become useful as the discussion turns to power and authority
Scientific language is full of metaphors that are used as models for understanding: schools of fish, say, or the language of kingdoms, classes, orders, and families for classifying species. These terms provide us a way of thinking about hierarchies and relationships. They are thus functional metaphors for understanding the natural world in human terms.	• Explains the so-what of the analysis of the metaphorical language, then draws in how scientific language also contains metaphors • The so-what allows the writer to explore the connection between the two modes. Note that the writer doesn't just say *that* they are connected—that's clear from the first paragraph—but rather explains HOW they're connected. The author is developing complexity and not just repeating the basic point made in an earlier paragraph.

What the writer says (sentence copied from the essay)	**What the writer does in the sentence** (explanation of the strategy) **Note:** Adapt these strategies to your own uses, but don't try to follow them in a rigid order.
The repetition of the shark as a "lord" may sound over-determined at first, but the repetition and elaboration of the metaphor makes it seem natural. It sets up the most elaborate metaphor, in which the shark becomes the dictator Tamerlane, who roams over his domain, laying waste to those in his way. Even if you don't know exactly who he is, the narrator's repetition makes his power obvious. The narrator uses the literary historical example of Tamerlane twice, so that the possibly unfamiliar comparison becomes just a name that sounds reasonable—what was inscrutable becomes a historical reference. These comparisons become natural; they transform from figurative language into data.	• Continues to find complexities in the initial example, by building in later material from the text. • Makes a daring move, analyzing an unfamiliar term—Tamerlane—from the footnotes. The writer uses the material from the notes and actually makes a concession to not knowing the full depth of the reference. The writer flips that ignorance into an insight by discussing how the reference is "naturalized" by repetition—the shark's name just becomes Tamerlane, and so it takes on enough context to understand that it's a connotation of authority and power. • Uses a short sentence at the end to show the so-what of the somewhat rambling/convoluted analysis.
The remora that ride the shark are the reminder that the master-servant relationship is more complicated than it appears to be.	• Write a hybrid topic-transition sentence that builds the master-servant idea from the previous paragraph and introduces the new element: when symbiosis fails • Deal with the contradiction or challenge to your main idea, to show how it becomes more complex
Here Melville makes an unusual series of comparisons that are more "inscrutable" than anything else in the passage: the remora "sticketh closer than a false brother in prosperity; closer than a beggar to the benevolent; closer than Webster to the Constitution." Even with a footnote, that three-part comparison is unwieldy: first a comparison to the Biblical proverb, then a seemingly satirical comparison to a historical figure.	• Engages a complicated passage that frustrates or confuses the writer • Uses that "inscrutability" not as a block, but as a theme that has been under consideration since paragraph 1 • Attempts to parse the quotation by highlighting the difficulty, so that it's not just restating but is explaining the difficulty in understanding as a feature

What the writer says (sentence copied from the essay)	What the writer does in the sentence (explanation of the strategy) Note: Adapt these strategies to your own uses, but don't try to follow them in a rigid order.
These ambiguities and conflicts are the stuff of democracy—not the autocracy of Tamerlane. Even without deep knowledge Melville's thoughts on Webster and the Constitution, we know that ongoing legal discussions about the Constitution show the ways that power and authority are subject to debate and adaptation in a democracy.	• Finds the ambiguity in the passage and argues for its value. • Makes a big so-what claim. This sentence may be the fuzziest idea in the essay, but it's also remarkable for its ambition and interest in ambiguity.
Fundamentally, they are subject to <u>interpretation</u>—the way that figurative language is also subject to interpretation, or how scientific observation changes with new data.	• Makes a large-scale so-what claim about the deepest connection between scientific and metaphorical language: they are both subject to interpretation.

If you do not feel confident leaning into the difficult passages, then tread in safer waters. It can be rewarding to explore those confusing, frustrating moments because your insights and attempts will show the dynamism of your interpretation. You won't just be explaining and summarizing; you'll be generating ideas. The writer is "thinking on the page" about what these references might mean, and the ambition in reaching for these interpretations is obvious. It makes for a sympathetic read, even when it's a little bit fuzzy and unclear.

The writer must tie these ambitions together in the conclusion.

What the writer says (sentence copied from the essay)	What the writer does in the sentence (explanation of the strategy) Note: Adapt these strategies to your own uses, but don't try to follow them in a rigid order.
This is why Jarl's observation at the end of the passage is so important: they show him interpreting a change in the pilot fishes' behavior, as they adopt the ship as their new master, the new "shark" they will follow. Jarl interprets their behavior as an omen, a sign that links human imagination with the natural world.	• The topic-transition sentence builds from the insight at the end of the previous paragraph • Carrying forward the idea about "interpretation" and the omens shows the value of the so-what statement in the previous paragraph and builds on it further to analyze the last lines of the passage
The ship itself is the master here—as the pilot fish understand—not any one person.	• Ends with a memorable image that shows the dynamics of power that were traced throughout the paragraph

The 8-9 essay is quite long, and you may be intimidated by its length. Think of these 8-9 essays as aspirational essays: if you practice writing them often, they won't seem as daunting. Let's look at some middle- and low-scoring essays so that you can see what readers might more typically see and score.

Sample 5-6 Essay

In Herman Melville's novel *Mardi*, the narrator combines scientific observation and metaphorical language to show the philosophical relationship between man and the natural world around him. There are tensions between metaphor and science because the similes and metaphors often distract from the description of the sharks and fishes, so that it's difficult to understand what they're doing, which is important for understanding animal behavior. This problem in the narration is evident in Melville's use of uncommon diction that may be unfamiliar to all readers, his confusing metaphors that do not aid understanding, and his bias as a fisherman that can never have an unbiased relationship with animals because of his job. For these reasons, science and metaphor cannot be reconciled.

Some of the metaphors and similes Melville uses are interesting, but mostly they just add confusing language to his observations. For example, he describes the pilot fish swimming around the shark as a "suite," which is somewhat clear for understanding their proximity, and how they all travel together. The sentences become less clear as he goes on to call it a "retinue," when it would be easier to just say that they are trailing the shark. If he is trying to give a clear picture to show the symbiotic relationship between the large and small animal, that word is too unusual. He makes the description even more convoluted in the next sentence. "(The fish are) flourishing their flambeaux like link-boys lighting the monster's way. Pity there were no ray-fish in rear, page-like, to carry his caudal train." He is being clever by saying that the illuminated fish carry "flambeaux" in the water, which is an example of a paradox, but that figurative device is not useful for scientific understanding. This description is not a good example of scientific observation because it mentions animals (ray-fish) that aren't there, which does not help with the explanation of what the pilot fish are doing. He does not explain a "caudal train," either, so it's not clear if that is part of the metaphor or the scientific observation, showing the problematic conflict between them.

The example of the remora is the most confusing simile in the passage, and it demonstrates the problem of mixing science and figurative language. He quotes: "Leech-like, it sticketh closer than a false brother in prosperity; closer than a beggar to the benevolent; closer than Webster to the Constitution." First, it is confusing to compare an animal to another animal that it is not, he could have used a simile of a vacuum or something else. It doesn't help to understand the remora by comparing it to a different animal that isn't remotely related. It's misleading biology. The quotation from the Bible about how it "sticketh closer than a brother" mixes up science and religion, which is a slippery slope. Finally, the comparison to Webster is confusing because some readers might think it refers to Webster's dictionary or something else, the comparison is too unfamiliar.

These choices of diction are a reminder that Herman Melville's narrator is biased in his account. It is clear that even he gets mixed up in using these metaphors because he calls it "a mystery unfathomable." If it is unclear why the pilot fish swim with the shovel-nosed shark, he should investigate instead of clouding the mystery further with references to the Bible, American history, and overly complicated metaphors. These word choices show his bias toward philosophical readers or readers of literature, and not for readers interested in scientific observation. The fisherman wants to control nature with language so that he can turn it into a "mystery," not by understanding it as a disinterested observer. The example of Moby-Dick being written after this passage is a clear piece of evidence that he is more interested in mystery and language than science.

In conclusion, it is possible that the metaphors and science are locked in a kind of battle of the wills, just like the fishermen and the sharks. Who will win? The author, Herman Melville, finally wins because he is in control of the story and he likes to show off his ability to make these kinds of long-winded descriptions of the sea. The scientific work will be up to other writers who can write more concisely. The conflict will rage on.

Sample 1–2 essay

The author is showing the cooperation between the shovel-nosed shark and the pilot fish, as well as the unequal relationship between the ramora and the shark. These are examples of interspecies collaboration, of species together because they feed off and protect each other. Interspecies collaboration happens often in the sea because the hierarchy among predators is strong, and they have to adapt to find ways of existing. This passage is a good explanation of how that collaboration works, and how sailors were the first to see that kind of interaction in nature, like Darwin and other scientists did. It is interesting that this occurred at the same time or thereabouts.

This passage is interesting because it shows interspecies collaboration in a vivid way with unfamiliar language. It is supposed to be clear and scientific, but there is a tension with the unknown words, and that tension is hard to understand.

Reader Comments for the 5–6 and 1–2 Essays

The 5-6 essay is significantly constrained by the way the writer has turned the essay prompt into a judgment-based contrast: which is better, science or metaphor. That black-and-white judgment limits the writer to insisting that science is better than metaphor in each paragraph, flattening all of the ambiguities, playful elements, and unusual references in Melville's language. It looks like the writer underlined passages that "proved" the argument that scientific language is "better," but the "evidence" for such a point leaves out everything that makes this novel interesting. Novels don't tend to prove arguments like a polemical argument would; instead, they are for exploring complexity and ambiguity. It can be hard to see all of that richness in a short passage, but the College Board selects these passages because they are rich, not because they are arguments to take apart as right or wrong.

The word "proved" and "evidence" got scare-quotes above because it can be limiting to think that you're proving a point in these literary analyses—instead, it's more like you're exploring the idea by analyzing in depth. You don't have time to assemble an air-tight "case," and it's more dynamic to show how your idea becomes more complex over the course of the essay, rather than trying to prove it in repetitive paragraphs, as this author does. The author uses words like "problem" and "cannot be reconciled," but the essay question has actually indicated that it's looking more for "correspondences" and something more dynamic like a "tension," rather than absolute judgment. Those words—"reconcile," "correspondence, and "tension"—indicate that you should find how they play off each other or interrelate in unexpected ways, as we saw in the 8-9 essay.

Furthermore, the attempts to edit Melville and suggest what he "should have said" are not the best way to frame your literary analysis. Your opinions about word choice don't matter as much as your analysis of why the word choice is important. Even—especially—when it's most frustrating or confusing, the author's choices are there for you to interpret, not to judge as good/bad. That judgment limits you to a narrow range of ideas—which may be tempting to do to manage the material—but it doesn't help you write an essay with much complexity.

There are also a number of comma splices that show the author cramming together opinion and analysis. These flawed sentence structures highlight the superficiality of the analysis and repetitiveness of the judgments.

The 1-2 essay is severely limited by its misunderstanding of the question and brevity. This is a writer who ran out of time or had some other problem reading and understanding the passage.

Here's another set of high-, middle-, and low-scoring essays. We won't go through each sentence of this top-scoring essay about Edith Wharton's *The Custom of the Country*, but you can annotate the essay yourself by noting those places where the author executes some of the thinking and writing strategies outlined in this chapter.

Sample Prose Prompt 2

Read this passage from Edith Wharton's novel *The Custom of the Country*. Write a well-organized essay in which you analyze the narrator's relationship to the main character, Undine Spragg. Where do you detect hints of moral judgment, irony, or some other subtle hints of a complicated relationship between narrator and protagonist? Why is that narrative tension important for understanding the larger complexities of social status and ambition in the passage?

> Undine's white and gold bedroom, with sea-green panels and old rose carpet, looked along Seventy-second Street toward the leafless tree-tops of the Central Park.
>
> She went to the window, and drawing back its many layers of lace gazed eastward down the long brownstone perspective. Beyond the Park lay Fifth Avenue—and Fifth Avenue was where she wanted to be!
>
> She turned back into the room, and going to her writing-table laid Mrs. Fairford's note before her, and began to study it minutely. She had read in the "Boudoir Chat" of one of the Sunday papers that the smartest women were using the new pigeon-blood notepaper with white ink; and rather against her mother's advice she had ordered a large supply, with her monogram in silver. It was a disappointment, therefore, to find that Mrs. Fairford wrote on the old-fashioned white sheet, without even a monogram—simply her address and telephone number. It gave Undine rather a poor opinion of Mrs. Fairford's social standing, and for a moment she thought with considerable satisfaction of answering the note on her pigeon-blood paper. Then she remembered Mrs. Heeny's emphatic commendation of Mrs. Fairford, and her pen wavered. What if white paper were really newer than pigeon blood? It might be more stylish, anyhow. Well, she didn't care if Mrs. Fairford didn't like red paper—SHE did! And she wasn't going to truckle to any woman who lived in a small house down beyond Park Avenue . . .

Undine was fiercely independent and yet passionately imitative. She wanted to surprise every one by her dash and originality, but she could not help modelling herself on the last person she met, and the confusion of ideals thus produced caused her much perturbation when she had to choose between two courses. She hesitated a moment longer, and then took from the drawer a plain sheet with the hotel address.

It was amusing to write the note in her mother's name—she giggled as she formed the phrase "I shall be happy to permit my daughter to take dinner with you" ("take dinner" seemed more elegant than Mrs. Fairford's "dine")—but when she came to the signature she was met by a new difficulty. Mrs. Fairford had signed herself "Laura Fairford"—just as one school-girl would write to another. But could this be a proper model for Mrs. Spragg? Undine could not tolerate the thought of her mother's abasing herself to a denizen of regions beyond Park Avenue, and she resolutely formed the signature: "Sincerely, Mrs. Abner E. Spragg." Then uncertainty overcame her, and she re-wrote her note and copied Mrs. Fairford's formula: "Yours sincerely, Leota B. Spragg." But this struck her as an odd juxtaposition of formality and freedom, and she made a third attempt: "Yours with love, Leota B. Spragg." This, however, seemed excessive, as the ladies had never met; and after several other experiments she finally decided on a compromise, and ended the note: "Yours sincerely, Mrs. Leota B. Spragg." That might be conventional. Undine reflected, but it was certainly correct.

This point settled, she flung open her door, calling imperiously down the passage: "Celeste!" and adding, as the French maid appeared: "I want to look over all my dinner-dresses."

Considering the extent of Miss Spragg's wardrobe her dinner-dresses were not many. She had ordered a number the year before but, vexed at her lack of use for them, had tossed them over impatiently to the maid. Since then, indeed, she and Mrs. Spragg had succumbed to the abstract pleasure of buying two or three more, simply because they were too exquisite and Undine looked too lovely in them; but she had grown tired of these also—tired of seeing them hang unworn in her wardrobe, like so many derisive points of interrogation. And now, as Celeste spread them out on the bed, they seemed disgustingly common-place, and as familiar as if she had danced them to shreds. Nevertheless, she yielded to the maid's persuasions and tried them on.

The first and second did not gain by prolonged inspection: they looked old-fashioned already. "It's something about the sleeves," Undine grumbled as she threw them aside.

The third was certainly the prettiest; but then it was the one she had worn at the hotel dance the night before and the impossibility of wearing it again within the week was too obvious for discussion. Yet she enjoyed looking at herself in it, for it reminded her of her sparkling passages with Claud Walsingham Popple, and her quieter but more fruitful talk with his little friend—the young man she had hardly noticed.

"You can go, Celeste—I'll take off the dress myself," she said: and when Celeste had passed out, laden with discarded finery, Undine bolted her door, dragged the tall pier-glass forward and, rummaging in a drawer for fan and gloves, swept to a seat before the mirror with the air of a lady arriving at an evening party.

Sample 8-9 Essay

Undine Spragg, the protagonist of Edith Wharton's novel *The Custom of the Country*, is indecisive, superficial, and vain. These qualities sit on the surface of the novel's narration, where the narrator details her conflicting desires to be "fiercely independent and yet passionately imitative" and details the silly choices that she labors over, like which color of paper is most fashionable, or which dress suits her best. It is easy to judge her. The narrator has presented these details almost like a lawyer would in assembling a case against Undine. Yet underneath these surface details, so cunningly arrayed for the reader's negative judgment, is a tension between narrator and protagonist about authorship. Undine is an unacknowledged author of her own life and reputation in this passage, which creates a power struggle between the third-person omniscient narrator and the protagonist who is not omniscient, but is trying to craft her own story.

Undine quibbles over the color of writing paper and the particular words to choose—but these are just a shade removed from how an author might puzzle over the specific details to illuminate in a passage. She has chosen "pigeon-blood notepaper . . . with her monogram in silver," and she will write with white ink. These choices are unusual, and the narrator points the way toward thinking of them as tacky because Mrs. Fairford uses "the old-fashioned white sheet, without even a monogram—simply her address and telephone number." Mrs. Fairford's identity is blank, registered only by her address—a signal that people should recognize her by subtle cues of her social status. Undine makes a decision to show off her still-in-process style: "Well, she didn't care if Mrs. Fairford didn't like red paper—SHE did!" The narrator is casting aspersions on her with the capitalized letters, but these are Undine's choices of self-presentation: her initials, her personal style. Undine is trying to make her mark on the page, on New York society, by authoring her own personal style. That style is "fiercely original and yet passionately imitative," because all authorship is a mixture of acknowledging and tweaking of conventions.

Authors participate in genres by imitating previous styles, then adding in little details of their own. Edith Wharton imitated the "silver fork" novels of earlier novels like Thackeray's *Vanity Fair*, but she established her own style, her own "monogram in silver," by including details from her own social experience in New York. Undine may not be the sophisticated author that Wharton is, but she is trying to pick out evocative details to narrate her life to herself from her own window in her "white and gold room," which shows a similar attention to fashionable, aspirational colors like sea green. She is trying to narrate the life she wants to have by creating a "perspective . . . [b]eyond the Park lay Fifth Avenue—and Fifth Avenue was where she wanted to be!" In this way, she struggles with the narrator over who controls the perspective: is it the narrator's perspective that satirizes the conventions of upper-class New York, or is it the up-and-comer's perspective of how she aspires to imitate and then personalize these conventions. The narrator is authoring a satire; Undine is authoring a dream.

Indeed, we might see her indecisiveness about how to sign her mother's name as a signal of her confusion about her own identity. She is trying on styles, trying on names: "but when she came to the signature she was met by a new difficulty." What kind of woman should she be--like her mother, like Mrs. Fairford, like herself? Her struggles to define her identity are written on the page, where Mrs. Fairford's remain invisible on her clean white paper. She delights in trying on the author's persona, even in writing a short note. "It was amusing to write the note in her mother's name," the narrator writes of Undine's behavior, trivializing the activity. The narrator infantilizes the girl who is trying to figure out her identity with or separate from her mother and her mother's friend's. The narrator details how Undine "giggled as she formed the phrase 'I shall be happy to permit my daughter to take dinner with you' ('take dinner' seemed more elegant than Mrs. Fairford's 'dine')." Undine's writing process, though, is understandable for testing the waters of authoring her social identity: she is imitating her mother, then making distinctive choices of her own. The narrator may see these choices of Undine's self-presentation as silly and meaningless, but they are also details about how she should identify as a young woman who is at the cusp of adulthood.

The satirizing narrator wants to have it both ways: Undine's behavior is trivial, yet her decisions matter to her social standing. The narrator is satirizing Undine in judgments like "the impossibility of wearing it again within the week was too obvious for discussion," yet Undine herself is in a context where authoring those details correctly, strategically, confers social status. She is authoring her self-presentation; she is editing her dress collection. She lacks the luxurious perspective of standing outside the story as an observer; instead, she aspires to the luxurious perspective above Park Avenue, and she is inside a confined social space in which to create her identity. Strikingly, they are both outsiders--the narrator is only an observer, but Undine resents her West End observer status and wants into the inner circle. Why can't we see her as a strategist and an author, instead of an indecisive, silly fool?

If we see her strategically, the choice of words, names, and style become more important decisions for authoring one's self-presentation. The reason that we think of these details as superficial and trivial is because we associate them with women's choices. They are gendered judgments. The notepaper, decor, and dress are the ways that women could author their own position in society; we don't think of Wharton's attention to those strategic social details as silly, so why are we so hard on Undine?

Reader Comments on the 8-9 Essay

We won't go through each sentence of this top-scoring essay about Edith Wharton's *The Custom of the Country*, but you can annotate the essay yourself by noting those places where the author executes some of the thinking and writing strategies outlined in the earlier chapters of the book.

The writer answers the prompt by arguing that the tension between narrator and protagonist is about the concept of authorship. The essay makes a strong argument for seeing Undine as the author of her social standing who is trying out the details of her self-presentation. Undine struggles with the satirist narrator because they scrutinize these details from different perspectives: as an outsider and as an aspirant to the inside track.

What's impressive about the essay is how it models "retelling" the story through the analytical lens of authorship. Talk about a power struggle: The writer seizes control of the story from the narrator to recast the details about Undine's choices as authorial choices. What had seemed to be silly details about "pigeon-blood notepaper" and monograms now become choices about writing and authorial identity. (Strangely enough, the pigeon's-blood color detail will come back later in the book as pigeon's-blood rubies, as Undine has authored her destiny in very strategic ways. Yes, the color was called "pigeon's blood," and not just "dark red.")

The writer retells the paragraph about signing her mother's name as a moment of identity formation: what kind of woman will she be, even if she's play-acting. This is an admirable moment of interpretation that helps the writer develop the theme of identity and self-presentation in a thoughtful way. Likewise, the writer has convincingly framed the interpretation of Undine's desire for a Fifth Avenue "perspective" as a story about finding her own authorial perspective.

What remains a little bit fuzzy is the role of the "real" author here: the writer makes some comparisons between Undine and Edith Wharton. Wharton has created the satirical narrator, who comes in for much criticism in the essay. The writer never makes the mistake of conflating Wharton and this narrator, yet it's still confusing to see Wharton and Undine conflated, or at least compared, in the conclusion. Still, it's an interesting, engaging essay, convincing in its reinterpretation of Undine Spragg as an author and editor of her own life.

Sample 5-6 Essay

This passage from Edith Wharton's *The Custom of the Country* shows the protagonist Undine Spragg's snobbery and superficiality. The narrator disapproves of these qualities, as demonstrated by the narrator's use of moral judgments, subtle cues of diction, and use of irony. The relationship between narrator and protagonist is clear, that the narrator is using her to criticize how society makes superficial judgments about social standing. Undine is a figure who represents the problems with social judgment.

The narrator sees qualities in Undine Spragg that she does not see in herself. "Undine was fiercely independent and yet passionately imitative. She wanted to surprise every one by her dash and originality, but she could not help modelling herself on the last person she met, and the confusion of ideals thus produced caused her much perturbation when she had to choose between two courses." These sentences show that Undine has negative qualities that affect the positive ways she sees herself. She thinks she is fashionable, but she is just copying what she thinks is trendy. She thinks she has good judgment, but actually she is indecisive. Most importantly, she thinks that her snobbery is due to her "ideals"—positive feelings—and not just basic social climbing that is not admirable. The narrator exposes all of these faults in one paragraph, and they affect how the reader sees Undine for the rest of the passage, when the narrator is just speaking through her perspective. The moral judgments in this paragraph make it clear that Undine is not admirable at all.

To pay attention to particular words that show the narrator's perspective peeking through outside of that paragraph, it shows in sentences like "It gave Undine rather a poor opinion of Mrs. Fairford's social standing, and for a moment she thought with considerable satisfaction of answering the note on her pigeon-blood paper." This quote contains words like "rather" and "considerable" that show Undine's inner thoughts, but the narrator is making them seem silly and judgmental. That's because she IS silly and judgmental to try to judge someone based on the paper they use. Words like "rather" and "considerable" show her "confusion of ideals" that was mentioned in the previous paragraph, because they show her own judgments but also how she has been affected by other people's judgments, and she can't decide which is correct. Social standing is confusing because who can tell whether one color of paper is more fashionable. The narrator doesn't directly voice an opinion about the color, but it is clear that Undine's indecisiveness, as shown by words like "rather" and "considerable" are being judged by the narrator.

This is even more clear in the ironic use of the word "certainly." The word is used twice in the passage. First, Undine cannot decide how to sign her mother's name to a letter on her too-trendy writing paper. She can't decide whether it's the right color, or how to show her mother's social class with signing her name. She has to "choose between two courses," as has already been mentioned. She decides on "Yours sincerely, Leota B. Spragg." "That might be conventional, Undine reflected, but it was certainly correct." The word certainly is ironic there because she has just exhibited so much uncertainty. She is following an etiquette book that she seems to be making up herself. This is seen again when she cannot decide between dresses. "The third was certainly the prettiest; but then it was the one she had worn at the hotel dance the night before and the impossibility of wearing it again within the week was too obvious for discussion." She is "certain" here, as seen also with words like "too obvious for discussion," but ironically this makes her even more indecisive because she refuses to pick the best option. Undine is always uncertain—never certain. The narrator uses "certainly" in an ironic fashion to show the gap between her beliefs about herself and the way she really is in being superficial and indecisive.

The narrator can see the qualities in Undine that show how she has been affected by her desire to live "on Fifth Avenue." That is where she wants to be, "certainly," but the narrator knows that social standing is harder to achieve than just knowing she wants to be important. It is revealed in her superficiality, but not her hard work to get to "where she wanted to be."

Sample 1–2 Essay

The woman in the story named Undine is spoiled and vain. She focuses on the wrong things in society, like what to wear. The silliest thing she does is worry about how to sign her name, followed by whether people will notice if she wore a dress from a prior occasion. Superficial details don't matter for a person's worth, it matters what is inside you.

The author is showing that she is not a good person because she cares about superficial details and has not shown that she cares about other people. She treats her maid like a servant and is "careless" with how she treats her things. This shows that she does not have a good personality.

This is seen most clearly when she looks in the mirror at the end. She is vain like an evil queen. She cares only about herself, that's why she spent so much time worrying about how to sign her name. She doesn't have anything else to think about.

She is like a princess locked away in a castle, as seen in the quotation about her "perspective." She doesn't know what the rest of the world can be. Or maybe she is the evil queen.

Reader Comments on the 5–6 and 1–2 Essays

The middle-range essay is a very clear, strongly argued essay, and if we were trying Undine Spragg for snobbery, it would be an excellent closing statement. However, the passage is asking you to find the deeper conflicts between the narrator and main character, and the writer has composed a one-sided prosecution of her that adheres very closely to the narrator's position. There is a judgment-based thesis: "The relationship between narrator and protagonist is clear, that the narrator is using her to criticize how society makes superficial judgments about social standing." This judgment doesn't become more complex or nuanced because it insists that the relationship is "clear": this idea is a starting place because it is obvious from the passage. It's a fine place to start, but the thesis needs to be more open-ended so that there's room to find the complicated elements of the relationship between the narrator and Undine. Even though this essay looks technically polished and clear, it's one-dimensional.

The 1-2 essay shows the significant limitations of the judgment-based thesis. The writer doesn't address the prompt at all, for there's no mention of any conflict between the narrator and Undine. The writer doesn't treat the passage as anything other than a story to be summarized and judged, so there's no mention of any literary elements like narration, style, or irony. The writer also glosses over the detail about Undine practicing her mother's signature, not her own. Because the writer is merely summarizing, there are no substantial quotations and no analysis of these stylistic elements. The writer ends on an intriguing note about the fairy tale qualities—and, indeed, Undine Spragg is sometimes thought of in those villainous terms—but this idea comes from a superficial reading, and not from an inquiry about narration or style.

Sample Poetry Prompt 1

Let's look at the following poetry analysis prompt and some high-, middle-, and low-range responses. The first example asks you to compare two short poems (one is a selection from a longer work). You may be asked to write such a comparative essay, but you can adapt the strategies easily to talking about two different poets. On your initial read of the top-scoring essay, note how the writer structures the analysis of the two poems in distinct paragraphs but then builds in work with both poems later in the essay. That's not the only way to organize such a comparison, but it's one strategy that allows you to build enough contextual analysis to make the comparisons compelling.

These two poems by Richard Savage and Charlotte Smith seem to be in dialogue with each other: you can nearly imagine Smith encountering Savage, the restless Romantic poet, as the "Lunatic" she has been warned about as she walks near the sea cliffs.

Read the passages carefully. Write an essay in which you analyze how these poets negotiate the antisocial qualities of the poet as a wanderer, a figure who is who is not only wrapped up . . . but also possibly frightens others. How do they register these uncertain reactions to a Wanderer's inscrutable behavior? You may want to pay attention to how the poets use formal devices such as rhyme and structure to reconcile or resolve these wandering, antisocial qualities of genius.

Selection from "The Wanderer," by Richard Savage

...O *Contemplation*, teach me to explore,
From *Britain* far remote, some distant Shore!
From Sleep a Dream distinct, and lively Claim;
Line   Clear let the Vision strike the Moral's Aim!
5   It comes! I feel it o'er my Soul serene!
Still Morn begins, and Frost retains the Scene!

Hark!—the loud Horn's enlivening Note's begun!
From Rock to Vale sweet-wand'ring Echoes run!
Still floats the Sound shrill-winding from afar!
10   Wild Beasts astonish'd dread the Sylvan War!

Spears to the Sun in Files embattled play,
March on, charge briskly, and enjoy the Fray!

Swans, Ducks, and Geese, and the wing'd, Winter Brood,
Chatter discordant on yon echoing Flood!
15   At Babel thus, when Heav'n the Tongue confounds,
Sudden a thousand different, jargon Sounds,
Like jangling Bells, harsh-mingling, grate the Ear!
All stare! all talk! all mean; but none cohere!
Mark! wiley Fowlers meditate their Doom,
20   And smoky Fate speeds thund'ring thro' the Gloom!
Stop'd short, they cease in airy Rings to fly,
Whirl o'er, and o'er, and, flutt'ring, fall and die.

Still Fancy wafts me on! deceiv'd I stand,
Estrang'd, adventrous on a foreign Land!
25   Wide and more wide extends the Scene unknown!
Where shall I turn, a *Wanderer*, and alone?
From hilly Wilds, and Depths where Snows remain,
My winding Steps up a steep Mountain strain!
Emers'd a-top I mark the Hills subside,
30   And Tow'rs aspire but with inferior Pride!

"Sonnet LXX," by Charlotte Smith
*On being cautioned against walking over a headland overlooking the sea, because it
was frequented by a Lunatic.*

Is there a solitary wretch who hies
    To the tall cliff, with starting pace or slow,
And, measuring, views with wild and hollow eyes
Line   Its distance from the waves that chide below;
5   Who, as the sea-born gale with frequent sighs
    Chills his cold bed upon the mountain turf,
With hoarse, half utter'd lamentation, lies
    Murmuring responses to the dashing surf?
In moody sadness, on the giddy brink,
10   I see him more with envy than with fear;
He has no *nice felicities* that shrink
    From giant horrors; wildly wandering here,
He seems (uncursed with reason) not to know
The depth or the duration of his woe.

Sample 8–9 Essay

The most remarkable thing about Charlotte Smith's sonnet about a wandering poet is her speaker's unexpected confession that she feels <u>envy</u> for the man that others see as a "Lunatic." She compares herself to him because they are in the same position: both are on the sea cliffs, staring at the sea in abjection. She believes the man is "uncursed with reason" (13) and thus has no faculties for understanding his miserable state; hers is self-aware depression, however, not just "hoarse, half utter'd lamentation" (7). There is something self-pitying, condescending, and self-centered about her comparison, her certainty that he lacks reason and thus can't be suffering as much as she is. How does she know how deep his woe is? Richard Savage provides a kind of corrective to this narrow perspective: his speaker is a wanderer like the one Smith might be warned about as the Lunatic. He is searching for peace, for the power of "contemplation" that might help him resolve his discordant feelings into a form that "cohere[s]" (poem 1, line 18). He is not mad, just searching for inspiration.

The unusual feature of these two poems is that Savage's wanderer is more sympathetic than Smith's observer: somehow, it is easier to relate to the wandering outsider than the observant woman who envies and condescends to him. The Romantic genius is more relatable because his feelings are familiar in their aspirational wildness, but the woman's envy is harder to digest and thus expands our notion of what the Romantic poet can be and do with unsettled, even ugly feelings.

Smith's and Savage's poems are familiar Romantic scenes of poets projecting their conflicted emotions onto the natural world, then trembling in awe at how grand those projections appear to be. For all of the claims about wildness and ineffability of their visions, they utilize rhyme and familiar poetic conventions like the sublime, the powerful feelings of awe at grand scenes of nature. Savage's speaker names what he needs to resolve his unsettled feelings: he needs to get outside of his own head and explore beyond what he knows. He calls on the poetic muse of "Contemplation" who will let him compose his troubled sleep into a poetic dream: "Clear let the Vision strike the Moral's Aim! / It comes! I feel it o'er my Soul serene" lines 4 and 5. This step onto the poet's wandering path comes to him with relative ease from a familiar convention of invoking a muse. That path is rocky and terrifying, but it's been trod before.

In this contemplative state, he encounters a jumble of discordant sounds that he must resolve into poetry—a familiar task for a poet. He is overwhelmed by their variety and volume, but even this confusion he manages with repetition: "All stare! all talk! all mean; but none cohere!" (poem 1, line 18). The "jargon sounds" are not so discordant that he cannot resolve them in rhyme at the end of each line; the evocation of "Babel" a recognizable allusion that lends coherence and familiarity to the cacophonous scene. His lines show him encountering too much meaning and significance—an excess of stimuli from the natural world around him—yet he has a specific tool for such a resolution: the theory of the sublime. When he asks "Wide and more wide extends the Scene unknown / Where shall I turn, a *Wanderer*, and alone?" he finds conventional scenes of the sublime; he even has an italicized identity of a Wanderer that is familiar from Romantic poetry.

This analysis is not meant to lessen the effects of Savage's wandering—only to note that the Wandering is a creative journey that may look incoherent but has poetic legacies and means of comprehending it. We can look at Savage's Wanderer and understand him in his loneliness, in his confusion at so much creative inspiration that he can barely contain himself. He is a type, a person whom others want to emulate in setting off on their own inspirational Romantic journeys.

Initially, Smith's scene seems no less conventionally Romantic and sublime. She spies a "solitary wretch who hies / to the tall cliff," who stares "as the sea-born gale with frequent sighs chills his cold bed upon the mountain turf" (1-6). Yet even this convention is uncertain, for it is framed as a wandering question that takes up six lines. Inspiration comes from conventional invocation for Savage's "Soul serene" and his muse; whereas, Smith's speaker seems to be addressing no one, and it's not clear what would resolve her question. She italicizes her own reply: "*He* has no *nice felicities*" that conflict with these sublime scenes (11). She does not feel the conventional sublime terror, but something less poetic: envy at his freedom. As an outsider, he is free from conventions of everyday life; he has no one to please with expectations of social graces. The comparison may sound petty or self-pitying—especially because it negates the possibility of his suffering—but the unpleasantness of the confession is bracing, even exhilarating.

Smith's speaker does not seek the Wanderer for mutual understanding, but for a means to test her anti-social feelings, an outlet for her rejection of niceties. This is a sonnet that observes the conventions of the love poem—rhyme, meter, form—while rejecting the very sense of unification and mutual dialogue that the couplet and fourteen lines promise poets. Smith's speaker and the Wanderer will not, cannot take solace in each other, for her envy separates them irrevocably. Savage's sublimity was matched with a muse who brought him contemplation; even his discord is resolved in rhymes. Smith's couplets isolate her speaker rather than unify her with the Wanderer, as seen in the enjambed, questioning lines: "Who, as the sea-born gale with frequent sighs / Chills his cold bed upon the mountain turf, / With hoarse, half utter'd lamentation, lies / Murmuring responses to the dashing surf?" (5-8). Verbs like "chills" and "lies" are destabilizing because it's not immediately clear what they refer to, or even if they are verbs. Her anti-social feelings affect the structure of her sentences: she will not be felicitous in making her questions coherent for the reader.

Envy is antisocial; it is constantly "measuring, views with wild and hollow eyes" (3) as it relentlessly compares one's position to others, rejecting sociality in favor of isolating jealousy. The admission of envy becomes a way for her to be antisocial with <u>and against</u> the Wanderer: he can roam in solitude without reason, while she can stew in loneliness without social niceties or "felicities." In this way, she plays a variation on the Romantic anti-hero in an especially provocative way that rejects female sociality, but also rejects communion with muses and poetic resolution.

Analysis of the 8-9 Essay

This is an enormous essay—it's perhaps more aspirational than realistic for writing in 40 minutes, but it serves as a model here for you to adapt.

The writer composes a two-paragraph introduction, adapting the strategies discussed earlier in the chapter. The writer reverses the analytical strategies, beginning with the surprising, challenging element of Smith's envy, and then bringing in Savage's poem to show what a more conventional "Wanderer" poem might look like. The contrast allows the writer to tease out what's so disconcerting about that element in Smith's poem, creating a new depth to what we know about envy. The key here is the *adaptability* of the strategies: you can write two shorter paragraphs if your paragraph is becoming too long, and you can start with the surprising element to kick things off with a bang.

Let's look at the introductory paragraphs.

What the author says (sentence copied from the essay)	**What the author does in the sentence** (explanation of the strategy) **Note:** Adapt these strategies to your own uses, but don't try to follow them in a rigid order.
The most remarkable thing about Charlotte Smith's sonnet about a wandering poet is her speaker's unexpected confession that she feels <u>envy</u> for the man that others see as a "Lunatic."	• Names the author and title/genre of the poem in a conversational way • Focuses the analysis immediately on a surprising or unusual aspect of the poem
She compares herself to him because they are in the same position: both are on the sea cliffs, staring at the sea in abjection. She believes the man is "uncursed with reason" (13) and thus has no faculties for understanding his miserable state; hers is self-aware depression, however, not just "hoarse, half utter'd lamentation" (7). ... Richard Savage provides a kind of corrective to this narrow perspective: his speaker is a wanderer like the one Smith might be warned about as the Lunatic. He is searching for peace, for the power of "contemplation" that might help him resolve his discordant feelings into a form that "cohere[s]" (poem 1, line 18).	• Briefly explains the subject and meaning of the poem • Integrates fragmentary quotations into the explanation to show the most obvious, basic elements of the surprising aspect you've identified. No analysis yet—these fragments are for you to practice narrowing your focus onto small examples of the language as you explain the main idea of the poem, like you're scanning your camera over the poem to find the details to focus on. • Cites line numbers to help the reader keep track of fragmentary quotations • Notice that the same strategies are repeated in the subsequent introduction of Richard Savage's poem, to give a sense of symmetry and balance to the explanation
He is not mad, just seeking inspiration.	• Surprises reader with a short sentence. • Resists summing up in general: instead, the author shows how the poem has become more complex with just a small shift in focus. The Wanderer is not the figure we thought he was; he's become more complex.

What the author says (sentence copied from the essay)	What the author does in the sentence (explanation of the strategy) **Note:** Adapt these strategies to your own uses, but don't try to follow them in a rigid order.
The unusual feature of these two poems is that Savage's wanderer is more sympathetic than Smith's observer: somehow, it is easier to relate to the wandering outsider than the observant woman who envies and condescends to him. The Romantic genius is more relatable because his feelings are familiar in their aspirational wildness, but the woman's envy is harder to digest and thus expands our notion of what the Romantic poet can be and do with unsettled, even ugly feelings.	• Explains the contrast between the two poems • Explains why that contrast illuminates the surprising or unusual quality that you will analyze in the rest of the essay. The "envy" is the surprising element identified in the first paragraph, and the contrast of finding Savage's poem more relatable amplifies what's disconcerting about Smith's envy. • Makes a preliminary claim about why that contrast and surprise challenge your expectations in the poem and makes you reconsider the meaning. There is now a tension between wanderer and envious female poet, and the author can tug at both ends in the body paragraphs.

Now let's look at the body paragraphs to see how the writer has framed the comparison and contrast between the two poems.

What the author says (sentence copied from the essay)	What the author does in the sentence (explanation of the strategy) **Note:** Adapt these strategies to your own uses, but don't try to follow them in a rigid order.
This step onto the poet's wandering path comes to him with relative ease from a familiar convention of invoking a muse. That path is rocky and terrifying, but it's been trod before. The "jargon sounds" are not so discordant that he cannot resolve them in rhyme at the end of each line; the evocation of "Babel" a recognizable allusion that lends coherence and familiarity to the cacophonous scene, rather than evoking some less poetical chaos.	• Emphasizes the conventions of Romantic poetry like references to the sublime and inner contemplation • Identifies the convention as well as its function in the story.

This analysis is not meant to lessen the effects of Savage's wandering—only to note that the Wandering is a creative journey that may look incoherent but has poetic legacies and means of comprehending it. We can look at Savage's Wanderer and understand him in his loneliness, in his confusion at so much creative inspiration that he can barely contain himself. He is a type, a person whom others want to emulate in setting off on their own inspirational Romantic journeys.	• Deepens the analysis of the ambiguities of the function of these conventions: they make the outsider figure into someone more familiar by being a type we can identify with and even emulate. • Explains the so-what of the analysis. These ambiguities don't negate the power of the Wanderer; they amplify that power into admiration • This so-what sets the stage for analyzing what's so alienating about Charlotte Smith, so it sets up the contrasts in the next two paragraphs.
Inspiration comes from conventional invocation for Savage's "Soul serene" and his muse; whereas, Smith's speaker seems to be addressing no one, and it's not clear what would resolve her question. She italicizes her own reply: "He has no nice felicities" that conflict with these sublime scenes (11).	• Directly contrasts the language from Savage's and Smith's poems. • Explains the significance of the contrast: Smith's speaker is alienated, even from the alienated figure.
The comparison may sound petty or self-pitying—especially because it negates the possibility of his suffering—but the unpleasantness of the confession is bracing, even exhilarating.	• Makes a challenging, original interpretation of the "envy" element that occasioned the analysis. • Demonstrates how the analysis of that "ugly feeling" has developed through the contrast analysis of Savage's poem and thus explains the "so what" of the contrast structure for the essay
Smith's speaker does not seek the Wanderer for mutual understanding, but for a means to test her anti-social feelings, an outlet for her rejection of niceties. This is a sonnet that observes the conventions of the love poem—rhyme, meter, form—while rejecting the very sense of unification and mutual dialogue that the couplet and fourteen lines promise poets. *Smith's couplets isolate her speaker rather than unify her with the Wanderer, as seen in the enjambed, questioning lines: "Who, as the sea-born gale with frequent sighs / Chills his cold bed upon the mountain turf, / With hoarse, half utter'd lamentation, lies / Murmuring responses to the dashing surf?" (5-8). Verbs like "chills" and "lies" are destabilizing because it's not immediately clear what they refer to, or even if they are verbs.*	• Analyzes how Smith's sonnet simultaneously adheres to conventions like rhyme and form, but it also rejects the very possibility of fellow-feeling • Analyzes the particular feature of enjambed verbs and explains the significance of their instability • Mirrors the analysis performed on Savage's rhymes, in order to underscore the contrast between them • Explains the so-what of Smith's embrace and rejection of conventions

Again, these paragraphs are quite long, and the writer may be writing toward some of these ideas in a somewhat repetitive way. One of the admirable things about the essay is the writer's sense of motivation: the writer is not just comparing and contrasting the poems because that's what the prompt asked for. The writer has a clear motivating question: what do we do with envy, when it's such a corrosive feeling? The comparison and contrast are not just tools to be used; rather, they help deepen our understanding of that question, and of the feeling itself. In these tables, we've noted the places where the writer leads with the insight, instead of just dutifully acknowledging the tool used. The writer notes how Savage repeats words like "all" to lend coherence to his poetic wandering, or that Smith enjambs her lines to destabilize the sensory experience of her own wandering experience. The contrasting use of those poetic devices to lend coherence or destabilize the senses is the meat of this essay. Yet the writer doesn't say: now I will look at rhyme, now I will look at the use of repetition, now I will look at enjambment. The writer doesn't say: I am making a contrast. The writer shows, instead of telling.

Finally, the conclusion paragraph that gives the final answer to the introductory question about Smith's envy:

What the writer says (sentence copied from the essay)	What the writer does in the sentence (explanation of the strategy) Note: Adapt these strategies to your own uses, but don't try to follow them in a rigid order.
Envy is antisocial; it is constantly "measuring, views with wild and hollow eyes" (3) as it relentlessly compares one's position to others, rejecting sociality in favor of isolating jealousy.	• States how the main idea has become more complex through analysis of the poems' language • Incorporates one final fragmentary quotation
The admission of envy becomes a way for her to be anti-social with and against the Wanderer: he can roam in solitude without reason, while she can stew in loneliness without social niceties or "felicities."	• Indicates the so-what: why it's important that Smith's speaker expresses envy and isolates herself • Articulates the so-what of the essay's main tool of comparison and contrast, in showing new insights about Smith and Savage's Wanderers
In this way, she plays a variation on the Romantic anti-hero in an especially provocative way that rejects female sociality, but also rejects communion with muses and poetic resolution.	• Ties back to the early paragraphs about Savage's use of Romantic genre conventions, showing the so-what for understanding how a female Wanderer twists the genre conventions

Some teachers may warn against using quotations in the conclusion, so that you can focus on just one task in what will probably be the most rushed part of your writing process, but you can decide what works for you. One benefit of it is that it allows you to show off the ways that your insights about the poem allow you to reread lines with a newfound depth. One drawback is that you're adding in yet another idea, when you should be finishing up. This writer clearly chose the former approach.

The writer manages to work in a so-what sentence at three different levels: the poem, the writer's own essay, the field of Romantic poetry. Level 1, the poem: why Smith's speaker confesses to an ugly feeling of envy. Level 2, the essay: why the comparison and contrast was an important tool. Level 3: why these insights give us a new appreciation of the convention of the Wanderer in Romantic poetry. Ambitious work, indeed!

Sample 5-6 Essay

In Charlotte Smith's "Sonnet XXL" she expresses "envy" for the Lunatic who she sees wandering around by the sea. She does not seem to understand that the Wanderer is suffering from mental illness, so her poem, which is supposed to be a love poem, sounds callous and self-centered. It is important to compare her poem to Richard Savage's poem, "The Wanderer," because Savage demonstrates the way to make these feelings more relatable than Smith does, by identifying with the Wanderer rather than the observer. This reduces the difference between them, so it is easier to understand the emotions involved.

The most important job of the poets in these poems is to make the Wanderer seem relatable, and Savage does this more successfully with his vivid imagery and creative rhymes. On the other hand, Smith uses more clichéd imagery and predictable rhymes, so that we don't get the sense of a Romantic genius, but an envious imitator. For example, in Savage's poem, he is very creative in describing a jumble of sounds, but he does so with rhyming lines.

For example:

> At *Babel* thus, when Heav'n the Tongue confounds,
>
> Sudden a thousand different, jargon Sounds, (15-16)

And

> Like jangling Bells, harsh-mingling, grate the Ear!
>
> All stare! all talk! all mean; but none cohere! (17-18)

The rhymes are about being "confound[ed]" and the ears being "grat[ed]" with "jangling," but the rhymes resolve those confusing or discordant sounds. Therefore, there is a creative contrast between his meaning and the form of the poem: is it a jumble, or is it a couplet, or is it both? On the other hand, Charlotte Smith uses clichéd rhyming words in couplets like:

> Who, as the sea-born gale with frequent sighs
>
> Chills his cold bed upon the mountain turf,
>
> With hoarse, half utter'd lamentation, lies
>
> Murmuring responses to the dashing surf? (5-8)

The sighs/lies lines are so obvious that they could only be more clichéd if she used a word like "eyes" or something, and the verb "lies" is very separate from its noun, which makes the sentence hard to follow. The surf/turf cliché is as remarkable as you'd find on a contemporary menu. Between the clichés and rambling word order, her poem does not make you want to know more about the speaker and it does not make the Wanderer himself seem interesting.

Smith's biggest misstep in the poem is her use of the word "envy," because it shows that even she does not want to get to know the Wanderer as a person. On the other hand, Savage shows that the Wanderer is worth understanding, for he is just a unique individual who wants to spend more time in nature than with people. This does not make him envious or isolated, but more like a genius who wants time to make his art. Savage shows this with his imagery of the Wanderer's surroundings.

He describes:

> Where shall I turn, a *Wanderer*, and alone?
>
> From hilly Wilds, and Depths where Snows remain,
>
> My winding Steps up a steep Mountain strain!
>
> Emers'd a-top I mark the Hills subside,
>
> And Tow'rs aspire but with inferior Pride!

Even though he is "alone," he takes the reader on a journey with just his vision of the scene "wide and more wide," and shows a landscape that is compelling. He describes mountains that look forbidding, but he makes "steps up" them and shows how the Hills "subside" as he walks them. This is a way of making an unforgiving landscape into something more relatable and human. He is conquering the sublime with his art, which makes him a hero or a genius. We want to salute him, even if he will shrug it off for fear of showing too much "Pride." This shows connections with him, rather than the isolation of Smith's "envy" of the Wanderer.

It should be clear that Savage's Wanderer is more interesting than Smith's speaker who does not make an effort to reach out to the person who is obviously in need of help. The goal of these poems should be to identify with the speakers, not to isolate them. Smith does not seem to consider that possibility, as she seems to deny him his humanity. She quotes:

> He seems (uncursed with reason) not to know
>
> The depth or the duration of his woe. (13-14)

Here she is not even trying to understand him, because she says he lacks the ability to understand or communicate. She makes her problems bigger than his by saying that it's worse for her to have "reason" and he is "uncursed" by it. Frankly, this is off-putting and makes the reader unsympathetic to her because she is so self-absorbed. Savage's Wanderer is self-focused for art, but Smith is just a narcissist.

Perhaps that is the theme of the poems, since they are about Romantic heroes like Lord Byron's Manfred or Mary Shelley's Dr. Frankenstein, who are flawed anti-heroes who are overly focused on their own creations, to their own detriment. We don't get the sense of that comeuppance in Smith's sonnet, so it is hard to tell. Instead of focusing on what she does wrong, we should reach across the gulf of isolation to find what Savage does right in showing his wanderer as a creator in his own right, instead of just a victim of circumstances. This is a way to claim genius from tragedy and isolation, by showing him making something out of all that discord.

Sample 1-2 Essay

The second poem, "Sonnet XXL" is a better poem than the first poem because it is more about emotions. The first poem is about an outsider, but it sounds to positive. It makes you feel strong emotions like "woe" in the second poem, which means "sadness," and that is clearly shown with other language like "wretch" and "moody."

You don't get a sense of sadness in the first one, it should have with less cliches about mountains and streams because those don't have emotions. Instead, he mentions different birds and their different calls, which isn't a clear way to show feelings. He is annoyed by their Babbling, but that is complaining, not something for a deep poem.

The second poem is also about nature, but the nature of the sea is clearly tied to the poet's "woe." That makes it makes sense as a description of her feelings. The language in the poem gives you a sense of her feelings and what she is seeing, whereas the other poem is more about cliches of being in the mountains.

In conclusion, language is important in these poems because it can be helpful for showing emotion, or it can be cliches in showing how everyone talks about nature in poems. Language is important for being creative with feelings, not cliches.

Reader Comments on 5-6 and 1-2 Essays

The middle-range essay suffers from its judgmental qualities, as the writer has taken the compare/contrast prompt literally and offered an opinion about which poem is better. The opinion/judgment-based thesis is too limiting: "The most important job of the poets in these poems is to make the Wanderer seem relatable, and Savage does this more successfully with his vivid imagery and creative rhymes." Who decided that the most important job is to make them relatable? Is a reader's job to judge "success"? We're not writing Rotten Tomatoes summaries of the poems, so you don't need to use those evaluative words that signal success or failure.

Actually, in picking out the less "successful" elements of Smith's poem, the writer has found an interesting challenge in trying to understand the concept of "envy" in the poem. The 8-9 writer uses that off-putting quality not to judge Smith, but to understand the function of that "ugly feeling" in the passage. The writer can flip that judgment into analysis by setting aside the opinion and digging into why it changes the opinion of the poem's Speaker. Why is the Wanderer "more relatable": what does "relatable" even mean to someone who wants to exist outside of society? What does "relatable" mean to a reader looking back at these Romantic-era poems? The writer has exposed a lot of possible ideas to analyze in making the judgment—but they require reflection and analysis rather than single-minded proof of Smith's inferiority.

The writer also makes few attempts to integrate the quotations into sentences, leaving them as big chunks in the middle of paragraphs. Sometimes, the writer uses fragmentary quotations to take the language in those blocks apart further, but they remain undigested—it clearly takes time to copy out those long passages, and the writer could have quoted fewer passages so as to leave time to focus on the particular phrases.

In these ways, the writer could have both expanded the focus beyond judgment about what's "successful," as well as narrowed the focus in choosing more apt, curated quotations.

TIP

If you feel repulsed or annoyed by a feature in a passage, that's probably a good sign that it's worth analyzing, not to judge its goodness or badness, but to focus on how it challenges your expectations and makes you reconsider the piece.

TIP

These essays are so short that you don't need to make generalizations about all of society, humanity, or history. You don't need to drill down from a general statement to the specifics: from the first sentence to the last, focus on the passage and prompt.

The low-range essay doesn't consistently mention the authors' names or titles, referring to them mainly as the first or second poem. Without authors' names or titles, it's hard to remember which poem is under discussion, but even then, the writer seems to switch back and forth in judging which poem is better. The limitations of the judgment-based thesis are magnified here: first, there's very little analysis because it's all opinion, and second, there are few details that distinguish the two poems. The gender pronouns may be one clue as to which poem is which, but it's not enough to show any insights about them.

The conclusion overgeneralizes, so that the two poems are no longer even present in the essay: "In conclusion, language is important in these poems because it can be helpful for showing emotion, or it can be cliches in showing how everyone talks about nature in poems. Language is important for being creative with feelings, not cliches." It's ironic that the writer warns against clichés here, yet falls into the essay-writing cliché, too. You don't need to make grand sweeping statements like this one in your conclusion (or in your introduction). They aren't helpful for showing anything specific about your reading of the passage in question or your answer to the prompt.

Sample Poetry Prompt 2

The myth of Bluebeard has been told many times in literary and popular culture: Bluebeard is a mysterious man who warns his young bride not to enter the locked room in his castle. She may go anywhere except this room, he advises her, which makes her all the more curious. When she finds a way to enter the room, she finds the corpses of his former wives. Her fate varies from telling to telling: sometimes she escapes with the help of her family, while other times the ending is more ambiguous.

Read this retelling of the story in poetic form by Edna St. Vincent Millay. How does Millay challenge and subvert the plot of the fairy tale? How does she use formal poetic devices to assist her in the subversion of a conventional tale? Why is this retelling significant?

"Bluebeard," Edna St. Vincent Millay

This door you might not open, and you did;
So enter now, and see for what slight thing
You are betrayed. . . . Here is no treasure hid,
No cauldron, no clear crystal mirroring
The sought-for truth, no heads of women slain
For greed like yours, no writhings of distress,
But only what you see. . . . Look yet again--
An empty room, cobwebbed and comfortless.
Yet this alone out of my life I kept
Unto myself, lest any know me quite;
And you did so profane me when you crept
Unto the threshold of this room to-night
That I must never more behold your face.
This now is yours. I seek another place

Sample 8-9 Essay

In her sonnet "Bluebeard," Edna St. Vincent Millay has subverted so many elements of the Bluebeard story that one can hardly know where to start counting the differences in the retellings. What is left of the story? The secret room is empty; the partner's desire for privacy and boundaries is not horrifying, but rather understandable; and there is no violence or attempted murder--only rejection for violating one's stated wishes. In rejecting what we thought we knew about the story, Millay opens up the possibility of rejecting one more closely held idea: that we are talking about essential gender identities in the poem. The "you" and "I" are not gendered in the poem; the reader brings their own preconceptions about the story about the conventionality of heterosexual marriage to the story. Millay seems to be challenging the reader: if you let go of fairy tales, you may let go of what you thought you knew about relationships and gender.

Fundamentally, the fairy tale Bluebeard is a story about forbidden knowledge. In the traditional fairy tale, the young wife seeks to know her older husband's secret in forbidding her from a locked room. Millay subverts that knowledge by having the door open to emptiness. The knowledge is not there: "The sought-for truth" is absent (5). The truth is more personal and individual; it is a desire for separateness, boundaries, and the space to know oneself in private. The word "know" is repeated as an admonition not of violence, but of autonomy: "Yet this alone out of my life I kept / Unto myself, lest any know me quite" (9-10). Millay's Bluebeard and wife have flipped the conditions of knowing each other. Knowledge is not a private horror, but a necessary one to maintain individuality.

Such desire for autonomy is not gendered; those beliefs could belong to anyone. Millay begins to more directly question the reader's notions of gender--one might say, the knowledge they think they have about gender--by including symbols in Bluebeard's room more traditionally associated with women, with witches. Or, rather, there is a conspicuous absence of those symbols: "No cauldron, no clear crystal mirroring" inside the room (4). There are "no heads of women slain" (5). These details highlight the ambiguity of the genders in the poem: the mention of the female-oriented symbols makes us trace backward to find any gender pronouns, other than the ones we thought we knew. No: there are only absences. We project our own preconceptions in those absences, and Millay is revealing that habit and subverting it. With the use of the indirect pronoun, "you," Millay broadens the address to the reader. Millay tells us: "But only what you see. . . .   Look yet again" (7). Look at your own preconceptions.

Millay is subverting the sonnet form, as well, and showing the preconceptions of the form to be too limiting. The poem follows the conventions of iambic pentameter and rhymed stanzas in *abab cdcd efefgg*. But the final couplet belies its "coupling": "That I must never more behold your face. / This now is yours. I seek another place" (13-14). The poem ends with rejection, with the end of the relationship. Even though the form is binding the rhymes, the "you" and "I" are uncoupled in the retelling of the story. The use of ellipses also signals ruptures and breaks in the iambic pentameter, for they suggest words or syllables that would subvert the regular meter. They appear as absences in the middles of the lines: "You are betrayed. . . .   Here is no treasure hid" and "But only what you see. . . .   Look yet again--" (3,7). Those syllables and words are missing, unknown, unknowable. They are like the missing symbols in the room.

In reminding the reader to look again, that second ellipsis is a reminder that "only what you see" can be deceiving because you fill in the gaps with your own preconceptions. The fairy tale of Bluebeard is about violence, but this poem shows the violence of making assumptions about what's known and what can be knowable. Everything in the old fairy tale has been elided from the original fairy tale with these ellipses. What is left but the warning that our conventions can also be more flexible, malleable, and self-reflexive than they appear to be. Those conventions are the stories we tell ourselves about relationships and gender, but also about how we define "you" and "I."

Comments on the 8–9 Essay

This is a confident, compelling essay that takes on Millay's challenges in an admirable way. It's actually a pretty conventional five-paragraph essay with an open thesis, but it uses that structure as a foundation to make some fascinating insights about conventionality, or the preconceptions that we use to set up our expectations of fairy tales, poetic genres, and social relations of marriage and gender. The so-what sentences at the ends of paragraphs are short and punchy, driving home the clarity of a complex idea.

What's important to note is that the author isn't just expressing an opinion here, or using the poem to advance a personal belief in a polemical way. Rather, the writer uses close attention to poetic devices like rhyme, structure, language, and even ellipses to test out this idea.

The writer uses a compelling, well-tested conventional move of analyzing the "absences" in the ellipses: this move is eminently adaptable for many analytical essays, as it allows writers to fill those gaps with interpretations. It's an analytical move that was so popular that it became a cliché, in a way, because people started interpreting anything to fill those gaps. But this particular analysis is grounded in the language and formal elements, so the interpretation follows from reading, not just from projecting a random idea.

Sample 5–6 Essay

There is no other way to say that this poem is anti-feminist. Women have told the story of Bluebeard for hundreds of years as a signal that women are not safe from domestic violence. It is offensive to retell it "from a different perspective" to show how the man feels, when the power of the story is in its warning to women. This is like trying to understand how men feel when they hurt women. It's very problematic that it's written by a woman, but it is possible that she has written a poem about the problem of internalized misogyny. She is subverting misogyny by showing how seductive it is. In this essay, internalized misogyny will be discussed by looking at the genre of the poem, the structural details, and the word choice.

The first indication of the internalized misogyny is in choosing a sonnet form to tell the story of domestic violence. It seems like it is supposed to be a provocative, contrarian choice "to play devil's advocate." This is shown by how she erases the important details and gives an alternative perspective, that there are no bodies, just cobwebs. Maybe he's not that bad, she suggests, and he just wants to be alone. He says "alone out of my life I kept / Unto myself, lest any know me quite," which shows that he is not violent, just solitary (9–10). The signals of the problematic language are still clear, however, when he accuses the "greedy" wife of "profan[ing]" the room with her presence (6, 11). Therefore, it is ambiguous as to whether the author believes that this is a love poem, or if she is using the form ironically.

The meter is iambic pentameter, showing that this is a conventional sonnet. The sonnet form always makes couples tied together in "couplets" or "couples." They cannot escape each other, as seen in the rhyme scheme where they always have to "finish each other's sentences," so to speak. This is seen in the rhyme scheme abab cdcd efefgg. The final couplet reads: "That I must never more behold your face. / This now is yours. I seek another place" (13-14). This is interestingly ironic because it is a couplet, yet it is about being separated.

To repeat, if it is ironic, then this irony is the author's subversion of the meaning of the original story. It is significant to retell the story as a woman poet because she can comment on how sonnets are limited forms. They are like locked rooms with significant limitations--only a key with the right sonnet rhyme scheme can "unlock" them.

The previous paragraphs said that Millay has internalized sexism and misogyny, but her project is actually subversive and very sneaky: she wants to show that all of our poetic structures have misogyny "baked" into them at their very structure. They confine their female speakers. This rejection of the poem space as sexist is seen in the final words that end the poem: "I seek another place," a room that is less limiting.

Sample 1-2 Essay

"Bluebeard" is a confusing poem, because if one did not know the story already, it would not make any sense. It is confusing to understand what is going on without the summary. The poem is addressed to the reader, you. Opening the door in the poem is forbidding, which could mean that opening the poem by reading it is forbidden, and that is why it is so confusing. You are not supposed to enter the room, you are not supposed to enter the poem.

When you enter the room of the poem, there is nothing there. What makes this a poem is the rhyming, but it does not contain any meaning.

Therefore, it is a poem about meaninglessness. It is a trick poem to make you think about how the things you want are empty and meaningless, and you will only be confused when you get them. The poem sends you away at the end because it wants to show you the meaninglessness of your desires.

Comments on the 5-6 and 1-2 Essays

The writer of the 5-6 essay starts off in the wrong direction. Confused about how to analyze gender relations in the poem, the writer makes strong, polemical claims about how there is "no other way" to see the poem than as the author's internalized misogyny. These strong judgments limit the interpretation, and the writer soon realizes those limitations in the body paragraphs.

The writer often twists the interpretations around trying to account for both a strong, over-determined reading of the poem's misogyny, and the more subtle, nuanced reading that might surface in a conversation with another reader and revision. It's like the writer realizes the limitations of the strong, polemical claims about internalized misogyny during the writing process, but isn't sure how to fix it. This is actually good evidence that writing is a process of thinking: the work of analyzing the details of the poem causes the writer to see the complexity unaccounted for in the first reading.

What would have been a good way to fix the problem? First, the writer could have written an open thesis that framed the issue as exploring the tensions between the man and his wife, instead of

TIP

Just as you were looking for the challenging, surprising, or frustrating elements of a passage or poem, you can also get good analysis out of finding significant gaps or absences: a missing foot in a poem, or the mention that something is absent. These absences are usually very significant for exploring the layers of a poem!

trying to "prove" the pervasive misogyny in the poem. If the writer then realized midway through a paragraph that such a strong judgment was off the mark, the writer could cross out some sentences and try to write a new introduction, space-permitting.

Another possibility would be to work that reflection into the essay itself. The writer could begin a paragraph with the realization: one of the subversive qualities of the poem is that it tricks the reader into judgment that they must then revise. The *Bluebeard* story is so familiar that we all bring pre-conceptions about the message and theme. The sonnet form is provocative for how it excites those preconceptions. The missing feet in the iambic pentameter clue you in that something is not quite right, and you should examine the conventions of the poem and story more closely. The writer could then write a clear, longer conclusion about that process of realizing one's own preconceptions, and how Millay's subversions work so effectively to challenge one's beliefs. That kind of reflection may be difficult to pull off in 25 minutes, but it would save this essay from a 5 grade and perhaps pull it up a few points to show the "thinking on the page."

As a stylistic note, one of the problems with the essay is that the writer over-uses scare quotes around conversational language. In fact, there are more scare quotes around the writer's own language than there are around Millay's language. It's best to avoid using scare quotes in a close reading of a passage, so that you don't mix up your own ironic use of a word and your analysis of an author's use of irony!

The 1-2 essay is very general and vague, although there's something unusually, if incompletely, compelling about the fumbling analysis. There are indeed poems and prose passages about meaning-lessness on the AP® English Literature and Composition Exam, but you still have to analyze them and find meaning in that meaninglessness. In an existential novel, or in a nonsense poem, there are still literary elements to analyze.

In some interesting ways, the 1-2 essay picks up on the same concept of unknowability as the 8-9 essay, but it registers those readings as confusion, rather than as ideas to be analyzed. The essay is brief and has no quotations to analyze, nor does it answer the prompt, so it is not something to emulate, but it does show the first steps toward thinking on the page. The writer is writing toward an idea, but it becomes untethered from analyzing the poem's language, where those ideas of meaning may be explored in depth. Remember: analyze what's on the page, not a general idea that's floating around as a general philosophical musing.

HOW TO APPROACH THE OPEN ESSAY

Opinions vary on the open essay: some people love it for the chance to prepare ideas about books they've studied deeply, while others dread having to prepare for any possible topic.

The open essay is the last section of the exam, and many students don't make it to this question at all, having spent all of the time on the first two essays. Remember that you can write the essays in whichever order you like, as long as you clearly label them, so you should read through the entire set of prompts for the three essays at the beginning of the exam. The poetry and prose analysis sections are constructed out of unknowns, in that you don't know the prompts or the passages in advance. For the open essay, you have choices about how you can fill the unknowns with your own expertise, even your own favorite books. You can practice reading, thinking, and writing strategies to make that openness into an opportunity.

The College Board writes these questions so that students can select from a wide variety of literary works. They will suggest several possible plays or novels you may choose, some or many of which will be familiar from your English class reading lists. You must choose a play or a novel, not a movie or television show. In this chapter, we will recommend that you plan strategically, so that you have a few texts in mind that will be adaptable to a wide variety of questions.

In the prose and poetry section, we broke down the 40-minute timeframe into blocks for reading, writing, and editing. That 8-minute reading timeframe was very short, with limited time for reading and analysis of the themes, characters, and language. For the open section, you theoretically have days, weeks, even months to do some of the reading work that will pay off in those 40 minutes on the test day.

Obviously, you have to read books in order to write these essays, but we're talking about strategic reading that you can do during the preparatory period. First, we'll work on reading the prompts so that you learn and internalize the structure for the kinds of questions that are asked in the open section. When you learn the patterns and structures, you can practice generating them and writing your own practice essays. This way, you'll be learning the strategies for connecting your preparatory reading and thinking work to the actual writing work that takes only 40 minutes on the exam. We will also help you prepare a few trusty favorites that will be relevant to discussing a wide variety of prompts.

We can break the prompts on the open essay section down into general types of questions:

- Discuss how a particular work of literature plays with the conventions of a well-known genre . . .

- Discuss how a particular character trait, social situation, or desire affects a character's relationships with others . . .

- Discuss how a particular kind of setting affects the action and behavior in a work of literature...

- Discuss how a particular event changes how you perceive the characters or themes in a work of literature . . .

These general types of questions will ask you to analyze specific themes, concepts, character types, and social questions. You can fill in the blanks and start mixing and matching your own questions.

We can generate some possible prompts for the first bullet point by adding in specific genres or themes:

- Comic plays and novels often contain a joker, fool, or some other outsider character who is ridiculed but has secret knowledge or commentary on the situation. Discuss the complicated role that such a foolish character plays in a work of literature of your choosing.

- Tragedies often have hidden seams of comic relief or even grim humor shared among the characters. In a play or novel of your choice, discuss the ways that these comic elements amplify, alleviate, or otherwise affect the tragedy.

- They say there's no business like show business: why do many novels and plays have plots about getting together to put on a play or some other performance? In theater, they are called "plays within plays," but they exist in novels as well, as plots or subplots that revolve around all of the preparations, rehearsals, and backstage drama. What do we learn about characters by seeing them rehearse and perform inside the story?

There are many other possible ways to build a prompt from that question about genre. We're not anticipating possible questions in the hopes that you'll be able to prepare exactly the right answer before the test day. Rather, we're showing you some ways to start thinking about the structures of the language in the prompts, so that you can internalize those structures and feel comfortable tackling whatever they throw at you.

Let's practice generating more prompts with another list of general structures:

- Discuss how a particular event changes how you perceive the characters or themes in a work of literature . . .

- Discuss how a moment of unexpected violence changes the characters in a play or novel of your choice. How does it affect their relationship with each other, and how does it change their perception of themselves?

- Missed connections: an undelivered message or a missing letter can change the course of an entire story. Discuss how such a miscommunication affects the characters in a play or novel of your choice.

- Political change can often affect the everyday lives of characters who are far removed from the court or the seat of government. Discuss a novel or play in which such changes in authority have a ripple effect that changes the lives of characters in surprising ways.

You'll see that the prompts might have some variation in how they frame the questions, but they have an underlying logical structure that you can internalize so that you know what the prompt is asking you to do.

Choosing a Work of Literature

After you've read the prompt, you have to decide which play or novel you're going to choose. This choice can seem overwhelming. You may feel like there are too many options, or you may feel like none of them seems quite right. It can seem like a paradox: you can't choose when you have so many choices.

The best way to handle this paradox of choice is to prepare three plays or novels (referred to here as "texts") ahead of time that you feel confident discussing. You should pick texts from your English class that you've read, thought about, and written about extensively, so that you've already internalized the themes, concepts, character interactions, and especially the complexities of the text.

This is a very partial list, but we have found that these books are particularly rich in a variety of themes, concepts, character types, settings, and social questions. You may adapt your knowledge of them to answer a variety of prompts:

- Any Shakespeare play, especially *Hamlet, Twelfth Night*, and *The Tempest*
- *Frankenstein*, by Mary Shelley
- *The Great Gatsby*, by F. Scott Fitzgerald
- *Invisible Man*, by Ralph Ellison
- *The Sound and the Fury*, by William Faulkner
- *Jane Eyre*, by Charlotte Bronte
- *Middlemarch*, by George Eliot

Why these books? Well, it's partly personal preferences: those are books that teachers enjoy teaching because there are so many ways to read, think, and write about them. They address issues of personal identity, relationships among different people, spirituality and belief, love and loss, power struggles, failure, and fear. You could find those themes in many different kinds of books, so this is just a starting place.

In fact, you might think of this very short list of recommendations as a kind of challenge: what would your own list look like, to prove us wrong? Oh, really? Prove it. Why don't you generate four different prompts about how you see ambition, the legacies of colonialism, the role of technology in human life, and censorship in that list of your own top five book/play list. That will come out to twenty essays. They take 40 minutes each to write, so that's 800 minutes . . . and, well, this the English exam, so you'll have to do that math for us.

Then do it again. Practice for the free-response essay by generating sample prompts when you read novels and plays for class. Then reverse the process and start generating lists of other books that would be appropriate for those prompts you developed. You'll start to see which kinds of pairings you're most adept at writing. You will develop preferences for writing about particular books, so you can choose which ones to prepare the most, but you'll also gain the experience of seeing those favorites from many different perspectives.

But really, is there a guaranteed best choice?

No, there isn't a guaranteed best choice. There are "best practices" that we've already recommended, like preparing for two or three texts from your English class that you know inside and out. You'll only know what's best for you if you practice them.

Don't choose a movie or television show. Don't pretend that you've read a book because you've seen the movie or television adaptation. You may even have a lot of thoughts on how the adaptation shows the themes differently than the book or play—this exam isn't the place to work out those ideas.

Because these lists are not making claims about absolute quality, don't try to make a thing out of outsmarting them. Don't choose a really weird book, just to challenge the reader. It may seem satisfying to outsmart the exam, but just think of your own reaction when someone starts talking about a book or movie you've never seen. Your eyes glaze over. You feel disconnected. The College Board will find a reader who has read your text, whatever it may be, but if you treat the exam as a chance to prove a contrarian point, you won't have the reader on your side. You want to start with the reader's interest, and then reward it—not frustrate them with your insights that are so brilliant that only you can understand them.

Don't choose a piece of genre fiction (mystery, fantasy, science fiction, romance) or a very contemporary book or play. These books may be just as challenging and rich as the texts you read in English class, but it's less likely that a reader will be prepared to engage with you on the nuances of such a deep dive into a fantasy novel.

It's not really a question of quality, but of resources for the exam readers: they, too, have to prepare texts to grade, and they have to be strategic in what they prepare. They can't read everything, so they make it manageable by paying attention to high school reading lists, previous exams, and test preparation books that list these likely choices. They're a lot like you, it turns out—they're on your side, too.

Preparing for the Question to Come

After you've written many prompt-pairing practice essays, you'll figure out your favorite texts, characters who seem like old friends (or delicious foes), memorable settings, and even some important quotations that you can keep in your back pocket. (Not literally, of course.)

You may have your own strategies for studying for English class, and you can absolutely adapt them for studying for the exam. You may be someone who makes outlines and character maps; you may be someone who likes to collect favorite quotations and analyze them. You may be someone who likes to write a story from the perspective of a favorite character, so you may embody their deepest feelings. You may be someone who draws maps and pictures of your favorite settings. All of those strategies may be helpful: all of those strategies are ones that English teachers love to use in their classes, so that students can find different entry points into a text. (Your English teacher may not do all of those things, but you can do them yourself if you're particularly interested.) Each strategy reveals a new facet of the text and of your analysis of it: a way of thinking visually about relationships among characters, an emotional reaction that surprises you with the insights you gain from getting deep inside a character's head.

Quotation analysis and character analysis are probably the most directly applicable of those reading strategies, as you can see from the other essays on this exam. You won't be able to draw a diagram or perform a dramatic reading on the exam. You're being scored on your writing, after all. But "preparing" a text means getting in depth, and the more creative you can be with your reading and thinking, the more insights you'll have ready to deploy in your writing.

Within these constraints, there are many choices, and you can make some of those choices easier by preparing for them before the exam. We've given you reading and thinking strategies for preparing texts and internalizing the language of the prompts. In that way, you have an expansive knowledge of some favorite texts, anchored by a structural knowledge of the kinds of ways that you might fit that knowledge and preparation into a 40-minute essay. With practice, you can adapt your chosen book to fit many different possible prompts. Do you feel more prepared already?

Adapting your 40-minute timeframe for the Free-Response Essay

We told you these strategies were adaptable! For the free-response essay, you won't need to spend time reading the passage and annotating it, so you can use those 8-10 minutes to brainstorm and make a quick idea map for your essay. You know your own brainstorming strategies best—or, rather, you know your own brainstorming strategies best *from extensive practice.*

Ask: "What is the prompt asking me to do?"

Read it carefully, and recognize the patterns you've studied and internalized from your practice generating your own prompts and lists of relevant titles. Consider whether one of your prepared texts is relevant—you don't want to force an irrelevant text into a prompt, but you may be able to find a surprising link that will be fun to write as you make the case for the obscure connection. If you really don't think your prepared texts will work, find another title on the list that you read in class or on your own and which seems like a solid connection you can work with. You can practice for this somewhat disappointing event by challenging yourself in practice to write about texts you didn't like as much from class—and maybe you'll change your mind about one of them!

What is the main idea that you want to explore in your essay?

You can start your notes with two foundational questions:

- What does the prompt make you reconsider about the text you've chosen?
- What does the text you've chosen make you reconsider about the prompt?

Answer these two questions in a few notes, and you'll have some of the main ideas that you want to address in the essay. Jot down a few examples of characters, specific scenes, and even some of the key quotations you've memorized (or mostly memorized).

After your many hours of practice, you will know what kinds of notes are most helpful for you. Some students like to make an outline, while others make a concept map they've used in other classes. Strategies are most useful when you personalize them and internalize them; they're not something you can just take directly from this book and apply as a magic formula.

Write your introduction

The prompts often specify a tension or conflict. To take some of the earlier examples of sample prompts, we might find tensions between comic and dramatic elements in a tragedy, between two characters who fight unexpectedly due to underlying tensions, or between government and everyday people who are affected their political actions. If such a conflict isn't stated, it's still present—it's just up to you to articulate it.

Write an introduction in which you adapt your notes into three or four sentences about how the prompt shows you a new way to consider your chosen text. This reconsideration may be only partly true: you've studied these texts inside and out, and you were already thinking about these themes before you sat down at the exam. Remember that the exam reader wants to be surprised and challenged by your analysis, so it should read like you're discovering nuances and ideas as you write. You're taking the reader on a journey of discovery, not just of rehashing basic themes you and they already knew. Such essays will feel tired and over-rehearsed. That's not to say that you shouldn't prepare but that you should prepare to be (or act) surprised by the ideas you generate.

Write your body paragraphs

In the prose and poetry essays, we talked about "re-narrating" or retelling the passage through your own analytical language, to focus the reader's attention on seeing the passage through your eyes, as a director would do in filming a movie. That strategy is even more relevant in the open essay, because you don't have the text in front of you. You're relying on *analytical description*: describe what you're seeing, by focusing attention on specific details. Analytical description is not the same as summary, and it's not the same as close reading of quotations. It's somewhere between those two modes of analysis: you're not zoomed out to give a bird's eye summary view of the text, but you're not super-focused on particular words, either. In an analytical description, you're revealing new details of the text by reconsidering it through the analytical language you've adapted from the prompt.

Start with the most obvious connection so that you can build a foundation and gain confidence that you've chosen the right text for the prompt.

Then move on to the more complex scenes that you remember from the text, the ones that will help you find nuances in your idea. You can look at your list of notes and pick out some moments in which you can discuss such questions as:

- What does your chosen text show you about the prompt that makes it seem like an especially interesting way to address the questions the prompt is suggesting?
- What is the so-what of your connection: why is this a productive prompt-text pairing?

What themes does it help you see that you wouldn't have seen otherwise? Analyze two or three moments through these newfound realizations, realizations that wouldn't have occurred to you without the text.

Once you get to the body paragraphs, you'll see that the open essay is not that much different from the prose analysis essay. You won't be examining an unknown text for tiny nuances of language, but you will be relating your thoughts on the nuances of a known text. The distinctions between those two modes will start to feel natural the more you practice them.

Write your conclusion

For your conclusion, remember that you're not justifying your choice of texts for the prompt. You made that choice, you committed to it, and the reader wants to focus on your analysis and ideas, not your insistence that there's a connection. You're showing the value of your choice, not telling the reader about it or proving it.

You're not restating your previous points, but rather showing a resolution to the conflict or tension that you've been exploring in the previous paragraphs.

What have you reconsidered by the end of your essay? You've been preparing a few favorite texts for months, and we hope you get to write about it—so what did you learn when you studied it with the prompt?

Edit your ideas

You can use the same editing strategies from the prose and poetry essays on the open essay: check for repetitive language, cross out any notes you've made for yourself, make sure that you're spelling characters names correctly (from memory). We've seen that sometimes writers include a few more sentences of plot summary at the beginnings of their essays. It's as if they need a few lines to talk themselves into getting comfortable with their choice, like they have to justify it for a few sentences before getting to their best idea. You can almost always edit these summarizations out of your essay. The readers care about your thoughts and what you have to say. They've read the passage backwards and forwards, and don't need to be reminded of what's in it. You have a precious amount of time to have them get to know you and your thoughts—don't fatigue their reading muscles with unnecessary rehashing of text you've already been given.

OPEN ESSAY WALKTHROUGHS

Let's look at some sample essays. We won't work through them sentence by sentence as we did with the prose and poetry essays, because the writers' choices are not going to be fascinating to every reader. You may not have read the writers' chosen texts, so you don't have the same text to compare and analyze deeply, the way you did in reading Melville or Millay. For readers who haven't read *The Great Gatsby* or *The Importance of Being Earnest*, you can play along and consider what you would have written for your own essay.

Sample Open Essay Prompt 1

The travel writer Paul Theroux has written: "An island is a fixed and finite piece of geography, and usually the whole place has been carved up and claimed."

Write an essay in which you discuss a literary work that is set on an island, where the setting emphasizes divisions among characters, social classes, or cultural groups. How does the island function in the characters' senses of personal and cultural identity? How does the island setting magnify conflicts about those claims to staking one's identity or one's relationships with others?

> *Lord of the Flies*
> *The Tempest*
> *Treasure Island*
> *The Count of Monte Cristo*
> *A Brief History of Seven Killings*
> *Robinson Crusoe*
> *To the Lighthouse*
> *Twelfth Night*
> *The Island of Dr. Moreau*
> *Wide Sargasso Sea*
> *Corelli's Mandolin*
> *The Light Between Oceans*
> *A High Wind in Jamaica*
> *Foe*
> *The Summer Book*
> *The Odyssey*
> *English Passengers*
> *How the Garcia Girls Lost Their Accents*
> *The Island Under the Sea*

Sample 8-9 Essay

It may be surprising to think of F. Scott Fitzgerald's novel *The Great Gatsby* as an island tale like *Robinson Crusoe*, for we tend to think of Fitzgerald's novel as a story about sociability and city life. And yet the characters in the novel are obsessed with making distinctions among island identities in New York's East and West Egg, peninsulas in Long Island Sound. They define their social lives around the ways that the island has, in Paul Theroux's words, "carved up and claimed." The key conflict in the novel is about whether the island may be reclaimed in a shake-up of social classes: can a newly rich man without family status shift the locations of status on the island? Gatsby believes that tension lies between himself and Tom and Daisy Buchanan: if he can only possess what they possess, he may reclaim his lost love. The novel's tragedy is that it shows that those forces that carve up islands are not individual, but part of a long historical arc, longer than anyone can see from his or her own vantage point.

There is a map of West and East Egg in many editions of *The Great Gatsby*, to give readers a sense of how close, yet how far apart West and East Egg are from each other. They are neighboring peninsulas, and one may travel between them easily, but the psychic distance between them is enormous. Both Gatsby and the narrator Nick Carraway spend time gazing across the water, assessing the distance from West Egg, "the less fashionable of the two" peninsulas, to East Egg, where the houses are much larger and fancier. Gatsby has moved to West Egg because he is rich and would like to live somewhere fashionable, but he lacks the family connections to move to East Egg, where homes have been owned by families for generations. It is not as though West Egg is impoverished, not at all; instead, its shame is that it is only slightly less fashionable, and thus the distinctions are more about judgments and taste than money in one's bank account. They are not visible on a map; characters can see those distinctions because they are trained to look for them in every social situation. Gatsby's gaze is always aspirational, always trying to overcome that small distance that means everything.

Nick does not see the distinctions—until he starts to see them everywhere. His perspective on the two peninsulas changes over the course of the novel, as he sees them through Gatsby's, then Daisy's eyes. Initially he reads the map of Long Island differently, because he has his own aspirations. His distinctions are between Long Island and Manhattan, and he finds pathos in having to cross over "the Valley of the Ashes," or the industrial area between the two islands. The Valley of the Ashes is a no-man's land, a reminder of the geographic devastation of industrialization and railroad building that changed the American landscape at the beginning of the twentieth century. Now the railroad carves up the island, and those spaces have been claimed by factories. A gigantic sign for TJ Eckleberg presides over the space, an island in and of itself. It is a reminder of the past, but no one has any sense of how long it's been there or what happened to the individual man or his store—it's all just gray factories now. Nick starts to see TJ Eckleberg as a kind of judge or spiritual figure, presiding over the space as a reminder of what's lost—because no one can remember what he means. His spectacles are a symbol of perspective, and how that perspective may magnify our senses of perception and meaning.

Nick only realizes the distinctions between the different locations of Long Island when he sees them through East Egg Daisy's eyes. She is rich and always has been, so she does not even realize her own powers of perception. She does not know the meaning of what she sees. When he realizes her invisible judgments of class, taste, and family, Nick says "it is saddening to look through someone else's eyes at things you thought you knew." It means that he does not just have to adjust his vision, but also his perception of himself, his friends, and his own aspirations. Gatsby will never catch up to the Buchanans, for he is only new-rich, and can never claim the long history of family background that East Egg claims. His history can never catch up to his present, for he will always be measuring, but never measuring up.

When he sees the world through Daisy's perspective, he realizes how small he is in the grand scheme of events. At the end of the novel, Nick stands on the dock again, reassessing the distance between the peninsulas one more time. He sees his position in history: he is but a dot on a long historical timeline. He narrates a vision of the past, when Long Island was not yet carved up or claimed, when the Dutch settlers arrived on the "fresh green breast of the new world." This green land is so different from the Valley of the Ashes and the metal tracks of the railroad. He contrasts that unspoiled land: "face to face for the last time in history with something commensurate with wonder." Nick contrasts the unspoiled land with the socially stratified island, as though people were the problem because people carve and claim.

Yet that fantasy of disappearing is also complicated. That initial provocation about thinking of Gatsby as a Robinson Crusoe story reveals the shared theme among the two stories: both titular men suffer from profound loneliness on the island. Nick's fantasy takes place at about the same time that *Robinson Crusoe* was shipwrecked in Daniel Defoe's novel, in the seventeenth century. Defoe's novel traces that sailor's mixture of wonder and loneliness on the island, before it's carved up or claimed by others. Yet even he turns wonder and freshness into a map, so that he may soothe his loneliness and nurture his need to communicate with others, even if he doesn't know who those others—his future readers—might be.

Comments on the 8-9 Essay

If we had to guess, we'd imagine that this writer had written an English essay about perception in *The Great Gatsby*, remembered it, and reformulated parts of it for this exam. That's a fine strategy that shows the value of preparation. We guess that it's partly reformulated from a prior essay because it is long, and the two halves of the paragraph about T.J. Eckleburg seem disconnected. The writer makes a connection in the last sentence of the paragraph, so it looks like the writer was trying to figure the connection while writing. The language of perception, mapping, and surveying makes for strong connections throughout the essay, so the writer had good command over that analytical vocabulary.

The writer has been very diligent about using the language of the prompt in the essay, quoting Paul Theroux's words of carving and claiming at multiple opportunities. Memorizing passages worked well for the writer; although the quotations weren't totally correct, they were especially effective in the inspired final paragraph about Gatsby and Robinson Crusoe. That connection is a surprise, but the writer did a good job of showing what it revealed about the desire for connection on an island.

The paragraph about the Valley of the Ashes was a good contrast to the East Egg/West Egg distinctions, which were getting a bit long by the middle of the essay. The point about industrialization of the island sets up the final paragraph about the "fresh green breast" of the New World in a fascinating way. That passage is the key to making this essay fit into the prompt because it describes Long Island in traditional language of exotic, unspoiled locales. Most writers would probably not think of Gatsby as an island novel, but the writer has done a great job of changing one's perspective on it through strategic descriptions and quotations.

Sample 5-6 Essay

Some might say that *The Great Gatsby* is not a story about islands, but in fact it takes place on Long Island, in New York, and other parts of it take place in Manhattan, also an island. We just don't think of them as islands because they are so populace. On the other hand, we don't always think of Great Britain as an island, even though it is, but we do think of Cuba as an island. It has to do with how far away from the dominant culture they are in how they are perceived by people to be isolated or centralized.

This brings us to *The Great Gatsby*, where the characters are always judging how far apart they are from the center of society. On one peninsula of Long Island is East Egg, which is the fanciest place and the center of all of the parties, where Tom and Daisy Buchanan live. On the peninsula next to it is West Egg, which is seen as less fashionable. The characters also drive along the island, past the Valley of the Ashes, to get to Manhattan, which is seen as distant and a place where the characters can have different lives, like Tom does in his affair with Myrtle. These three places are all distant from each other and the characters change their behavior depending on which island/part of the island they are on.

This shows that *The Great Gatsby* is actually a book about three different islands/peninsulas, and should be thought of as in the same way we think about *Lord of the Flies* or *The Tempest*, for it is also about how society changes in different islands. In *Lord of the Flies*, the group's worst tendencies are exaggerated when they go to the island; this is similar to how the parties at Jay Gatsby's house are exaggerated to the extreme, where everyone is showing off their wealth and acting crazy. Interestingly, they also act crazy when they go to the hotel in Manhattan, because that is an island as well, so they see these places as places to let go and indulge their worst excesses like affairs and even violence.

This brings up the point that people spend a lot of time traveling to and from the islands, which is similar to many adventure stories. In *the Great Gatsby*, they travel to and from Long Island and Manhattan, and they pass the Valley of Ashes, which is an industrial space that they want to stay as far away from as possible because it's not aspirational like Manhattan or either of the Eggs. The eyes of TJ Eckleberg look down on the road, but it is like an island of something that used to be there that it was advertising, but now it's gone. TJ Eckleberg is like an island itself, amid the gray traffic. It is the guardian to the bridge between the islands.

In *The Tempest*, the island is thought to be a place to experiment and make a new world. In *the Great Gatsby*, Jay Gatsby thought he could make a new world and a new identity for himself out of his aspirations, and his house at first seems like a utopia for him because he can satisfy all of his desires for wealth and showing off. Then he finds a desire (Daisy) that he cannot obtain. She even comes from a different island (East Egg). In the play, the island paradise becomes impossible because of the desire for power. Gatsby and Tom struggle for power over Daisy, and the paradise of the parties and the specialness of Gatsby's paradise are ruined.

The theme of the islands is most important at the end, when the author explains the main idea of the green light. On the last page of the book, where Nick can see the place like a lush island before settlement, similar to *the Tempest*, where man views a scene that excites "his capacity for wonder." *The Tempest* is a story about wonder that gets corrupted, similar to *the Great Gatsby*'s last scene of imagining how Gatsby's own wonder has been destroyed. The "green light" is important to the island because it shows the distance from other places.

In conclusion, it is interesting to think about *the Great Gatsby* as an island novel because it makes us think about its connections to other books that it is not often compared to, like the *Lord of the Flies* or *The Tempest*. The connections make you think about the characters and behavior in a new way. The characters are seen to be isolated in their own islands, like the saying No man is an island. In *the Great Gatsby*, everyone is an island.

Sample 1-2 essay

Islands are a theme in literature because they are a confined space, and people interact in that space in complex ways. They fight over resources, whether those resources are food and water, or social issues. They argue over who owns which part of land, and those arguments lead to themes of power struggles and alienation. This happens in many novels, but I would like to look at the power struggles in The Great Gatsby, which technically applies because it takes place on Long Island. It applies because there are social issues about who lives where on the island, and who has more money. It applies because they also go to Manhattan, which is another island that is separate from Long Island. They travel over the Valley of Ashes to get there. In Manhattan, there are also struggles for resources, which have been shown in other novels that were published around the same time. Islands are a popular theme, it is clear, because they show isolation and the wish to gain more than you have.

Comments on 5-6 and 1-2 Essays

Both writers of these middle- and low-score essays seem uncertain that *The Great Gatsby* is a good choice for the essay. The 1-2 essay is so short and general that it's hard to give it more than a minimum score. It looks like the writer was unsure which text to choose, wrote a few sentences of generalizations, and finally made an attempt to choose one from memory. That means that the only specific detail is about the Valley of Ashes, which is only mentioned by not analyzed.

The writer of the 5-6 essay gains confidence after the introduction, but the quibbling over what counts as an island is not very interesting. The writer needs to make a choice of texts and move on to analysis, as the essay isn't a five-paragraph proof *that* it's an island novel. It's an exploration about what happens when you pay attention to the qualities of carving and claiming that are so complicated in novels about islands.

The writer's connections to *The Tempest* and *Lord of the Flies* are perfunctory, as the author stops short of just saying "they are similar." The connection to these extra texts is not revelatory, as it was in the 8-9 essay, for the writer doesn't develop the comparisons in a meaningful way. There may indeed be some fascinating connections between *Lord of the Flies* and *The Great Gatsby* in terms of how they show social conflicts over claiming authority on the island. Possibly. The last lines of *The Great Gatsby*, explored so compellingly in the 8-9 essay, do seem to call back to the "O brave new world" line from *The Tempest*, but this connection, too, would need a stronger motivation and analysis to justify the connection.

The problem is that none of those connections is related to one another. Each paragraph is distinct, so that there's little development of an idea other than that one can think of *The Great Gatsby* as an island novel. The ideas are superficial because they stay at the level of saying that it could be thought of that way.

Sample Open Essay Prompt 2

When an author writes a satire, some of the specific, personal targets of the satire may get lost to history, as readers may not have the same reference points or knowledge of history. Yet the best examples from the genre continue to speak to readers in later generations. Write a well-organized essay about a work of satire that has retained its relevance—or gained a new one—in a new context for contemporary readers. How does satire speak beyond its immediate time and place?

> *Candide*
> *Catch-22*
> *Animal Farm*
> *Slaughterhouse-Five*
> *The Importance of Being Earnest*
> *1984*
> *Brave New World*
> *Gulliver's Travels*
> *A Confederacy of Dunces*
> *Northanger Abbey*
> *Billy Lynn's Long Halftime Walk*
> *Vanity Fair*
> *A Bold Stroke for a Wife*
> *White Noise*
> *The Misanthrope*
> *The Master and the Margarita*
> *Pride and Prejudice*
> *One Flew Over the Cuckoo's Nest*
> *Midnight's Children*
> *Don Quixote*

Sample 8-9 Essay

"We live, as I hope you know, Mr. Worthing, in an age of ideals," the character Gwendolen announces to her paramour, Jack Worthing, at a crucial moment in Oscar Wilde's play *The Importance of Being Earnest*. Gwendolen is defending her greatest ideal—to love a man named Ernest—against the Worthing's confession that his name is really Jack, and he has been pretending to be named Ernest for convoluted, yet very funny reasons. The satire is that Gwendolyn's ideal is so silly, and yet she is ready to give up love for that inflated ideal. The satire of that silly ideal is a means to show the distortions of other Victorian era ideals, ideals about social class, gender, and what was considered good taste.

We live in an age of ideals, too, and Wilde's satire remains relevant more than a hundred years after it was first performed. Twenty-first century ideals look similar to the Victorian period because we still argue about class and gender, among many other important issues. Yet it is not just that the satirical play remains relevant, for it is a director's job to make these older plays relevant to today's audiences. It is more important to think about how the transmission of these ideals has changed, and what those changes in media and performance mean for how we interpret them. Specifically, those ideals look different on social media, for they are exaggerated even beyond what a satirical could play could imagine. The exaggerated qualities of how we behave on social media makes us feel like we're in an Oscar Wilde play all the time with how ridiculous we act. We may look to his work to see how his characters thought of themselves as <u>performing</u> those ideals, distinct from merely believing them.

In her monologue to Jack, Gwendolen goes on to explain where these ideals come from: "the monthly magazines" and "the provincial pulpits." Those places for popularizing ideals are no longer with us, for magazines are dying out and social media serves as the main source of a "provincial pulpit," or a platform not in a church. It is a significant coincidence that pulpit is another word for platform, because we think about platforms all the time. It's part of our vocabulary now: I need the biggest platform for my brand, or which platforms do you use? Gwendolyn was pointing out that then, as now, people get their aspirations and senses of identity from the media around them. They see ideals as aspirations, so they try to live up to them, and perform in a fantasy version of that life. Gwendolyn is acting in two ways: she is performing as an actress, but she is also performing for herself and for others inside the play, as the model, ideal girlfriend. Her performance shows in how she exaggerates her affection for him, until she withholds it in her monologue.

Those platforms have changed the way that we interact socially. Everyone can see our interactions, so, like Gwendolen, we are always performing. In the play, Algernon tells Jack: "My dear fellow, the way you flirt with Gwendolen is disgraceful. It's almost as bad as the way Gwendolen flirts with you." Wilde was satirizing the way that the two characters seemed to following a script and acting—badly—in a play. This line is very relatable for how we perform flirting on the platforms, with bad scripts that we know are dumb. We analyze every detail of them insistently because we have a record of them typed on the platform, for everyone to see and over-analyze, too. In the play, when Gwendolen and Cecily are obsessed with writing in their diaries, but ironically they aren't writing secrets, but rather "confessions" that are meant to be published eventually. For Wilde's characters, the satire was about testing the tension between public and private life, and the joke was funny because people knew that diaries were for private thoughts and publishing was for sharing publicly.

It seems like that tension between private and public life is no longer there because they are the same. However, it could also be that we are really anxious about the collapse of that boundary between our private and public lives, even as we go through the motions of flirting badly and publicly online. Wilde's satire reminds us that people in the past had the same worries, expressed here through jokes. Cecily and Gwendolen compare diaries to claim that they were both proposed to by "Ernest," when really they were using their diaries to perform as the woman they wanted to be. They were, in short, lying. In the lies, they could barely acknowledge that there was a gap between who they wanted to perform as, in the published form of the diary, and who they really were, which were women struggling with unrealistic goals and ideals.

Seen that way, Gwendolen and Cecily look relatable from many angles. They let us see how we are always writing in our diaries online, sharing secrets, flirtations, fantasies, and aspirational images of ourselves—our ideals. Are our ideals any sillier than theirs? Our platforms, our provincial pulpits, only give the satire a grander, more social way for those ideals to play out.

Comments on the 8-9 Essay

This is a delightful essay that could become an interesting opinion column for a high school or college newspaper, especially if the school is staging *The Importance of Being Earnest*. The "we" voice is a little bit casual and over-generalizing, although it's hard to see how that tone could have been avoided. In general, the "we" can sound like you're speaking for everyone—a problematic assumption—but the writer has reason to speak grandly in analyzing the role of satire in an age of ideals. The "we" voice sounds like an essay that would appear in one of Gwendolen's magazines, and the insights are not casual or superficial. The essay has a wonderfully satirical tone to it that Wilde would have appreciated.

This essay has a two-paragraph introduction, in which the writer has essentially reversed and adapted what you might expect and led with a quotation and then used the second paragraph to work out a complex idea. The writer does an admirable job of explaining the complicated plot in only as much detail as needed, without mentioning the other subplots and complications. The writer focuses on Gwendolen's idea and brings in other characters to show the social interactions in more detail. That focus is welcome for such a busy plot. The writer has recalled key moments in the play, with good use of short quotations to show the connections to contemporary social media style.

Sample 5-6 Essay

It is interesting to read Oscar Wilde's *Importance of Being Earnest* in today's society because it is relevant to debates about relationships and how to behave, which have changed in some ways but are also still the same as they were a hundred years ago. The satirical parts of Wilde's novel are reminders that comedy is timeless because laughing is timeless. The same jokes about how people present themselves to get married are still funny to us today because not very much has changed, especially for how foolish and idealistic people can be. The novel itself is very complicated, which is similar to how complicated people's lives still are when they are presenting one feeling and pretending to be another.

One way that it is still the same is in the expectations of how men and women are supposed to behave. The character of Lady Braxton can be seen as somewhat sexist back then, and defiantly sexist now because she tries to control how the marriages are arranged. This is seen as funny in the play because it is satirizing her strong, rigid beliefs that she forces onto other people. It is satirical because she tries to force her niece Cecilia to be silly and naive--she is forcing sexist ideas onto her, but she is doing it with a lot of power herself. This satire is even more apparent now that women are more independent, so it would seem very strange that Lady Braxton is both powerful and trying to force her niece to be someone's wife. It shows that social class is sometimes more important to people than gender balance. That is something that we are still working out ourselves, and so the satire reveals something about our lives today.

It is also interesting to see how complicated their lives are as they are trying to figure out class and gender and what it means for modern love. The novel can be seen as the ancestor to a romantic comedy in how people mix up identities and make plans that get mixed up in humorous ways. The satire is about how complicated people make falling in love, especially when they have fantasies about how things are supposed to be. This is seen with Cecilia imagining that she has to fall in love with a man named Ernest--it is her fantasy--and she then falls in love with a man just for his name. When she finds out that his name is really Jack, she doesn't love him anymore. It becomes very complicated as their names and identities get mixed up, which shows that her fantasies were more like complications than like wishes--she wants as much "drama" as possible. This is interesting for a satirical play because the characters can act as exaggerations, but there are items to recognize from contemporary life.

Sample 1–2 essay

The Importance of Being Earnest is a satirical play that is still performed today because it is still relatable. This essay is proving that it is relatable, even though it is confusing.

As a play, it is about how people flirt with each other and pretend to be something they are not. They run into trouble because their lies catch up with them. The trouble is funny, though, because the characters' lies are not important in the end. They are arguing about the importance of names, but not about their inner characters, so the lies are only on the surface.

The satire is that the surface matters too much to a character like the Mother, who cares only about appearances and marrying the right person. She judges everyone harshly. She is the character who is being satirized the most because she exaggerates everything.

The character who is the same the whole way through is Father Charles, who stabilizes everything because he can see through the lies. He is steady, which is important in a satire and in society in general.

Comments on the 5–6 and 1–2 Essays

In the middle-range essay, the writer has some good ideas that get lost in generalizations. Many of those generalizations don't serve the writer's purpose, because they could apply to any play or novel. For example, The Importance of Being Earnest is important in "today's society because it is relevant to debates about relationships and how to behave, which have changed in some ways but are also still the same as they were a hundred years ago. The satirical parts of Wilde's novel are reminders that comedy is timeless because laughing is timeless." There's an impulse to say "it's the same but it's different" and "it's timeless because all humor in general is timeless." Neither of these statements is helpful because they take away from the particular details about the play that you are trying to analyze and explain. The prompt asks you to explain the difference in time period, and why it's still relevant, so saying it's timeless creates a circular argument. It's relevant because it's timeless because it's relevant . . .

There are good ideas here, but they tend to come after a lot of generalizations. For example, the open thesis arrives at an interesting idea: "people's lives are complex when they are presenting one feeling and pretending to be another." This phrasing is a little fuzzy—how can you pretend to be a feeling?—but the idea is solid. It's familiar from many other works of literature about one's private and public personas, and The Importance of Being Earnest is a fascinating way to examine those personas and the way the characters perform them. The best sentence in the essay is the clearest one: "The satire is about how complicated people make falling in love, especially when they have fantasies about how things are supposed to be." If the writer started with this idea, there could be a lot to say about the interconnectedness of the complicated plot and the characters' ideals. Their ideals are both very simple, even silly, yet made very complicated by their performances of them.

TIP

Stay away from generalizations. We realize this is a generalization, too, but they are rarely helpful in your essay because your readers are looking for details, not statements about what's true all the time, or in all of society.

That idea is strong, but there are many places where the phrasings are vague, generalized, and sloppy. The author is over-reliant on phrases like "this is seen" and "it is interesting," which don't allow for specific insights or connections to the details being analyzed.

Both essays show the importance of remembering people's names: Lady Bracknell, Cecily, and Father Chasuble are the characters' names. (These errors seem particularly funny in essays about name mix-ups).

For the 1-2 essay, the writer seems to know parts of the play, but doesn't remember it in enough detail to give specific details. The attempt to identify satire is weak and underexplained. There are glimpses of good ideas about the importance of surfaces, but there's not much else to read in this short example.

We have been emphasizing the ability to adapt and personalize these strategies, so that you can internalize them. If, in the sample essays, you saw phrases you liked, copy them down and see if you can incorporate them into your own practice essays. They are yours to copy and adapt. If, in the sample essays, you had a better way that you would write toward the prompt, then by all means, practice writing that essay. Then do another, and another.

These essays aren't going to be the last ones you ever write, and instructors in your high school or college classes may have different strategies to recommend in the future. This isn't the final definition of an essay, an introduction, a thesis, a body paragraph—it's a set of strategies that helps you write a very specific form of an essay in 40 minutes. What matters now is what you do with the strategies, how you make them your own, so that you can ace those exams in 2 hours.

SUMMING IT UP

- You will write three essays:
  - o An analysis of a prose passage from a novel, short story, creative nonfiction, or play
  - o A literary analysis of a poem
  - o An open topic about a literary concept or theme, in which you choose a literary work from your own study that you believe best illuminates the prompt
- This section is worth 55 percent of your total score; it is weighted slightly more heavily than the multiple-choice questions.
- You will have 2 hours to write three free-response essays on test day. Aim to spend 40 minutes on each essay.
- As a general guideline, spend 8-10 minutes reading the passage and making notes, and 25-27 minutes composing your essay. For the open-response question, spend the first 8-10 minutes brainstorming.
- Each essay in Section II is scored on a scale of 0-9, for a total of 27 points. Readers use a rubric that describes the features of top-scoring, middle-range, and low-scoring essays.
- Don't just identify literary buzzwords within the prompt passage—instead identify them and discuss why the author uses them effectively.
- Use the vocabulary terms and analytical language from the question in your introduction as you're writing your main idea about what's surprising or unconventional about the passage.
- Don't restate the question or summarize it.
- Make sure to keep using the question's vocabulary and analytical language, but take ownership of it and show how it's serving your ideas as you write the essay.
- Focus on putting rich details in context, not giving a lot of general context and then a small detail.
- Make paragraph "sandwiches" of your topic idea sentence, passage quotations that have been integrated into your own sentences, analysis of those quotations and details from the passage, and the crucial so-what sentences that show why it was important to analyze those passages.
- Don't be afraid to write a couple of "so-what" sentences at the ends of paragraphs, as you may write toward your best insights.
- Write a conclusion that shows how your idea has developed over the course of the essay, not just a restatement of your previous idea: show the change; don't just tell it (or restate the question again).

PART III
THREE PRACTICE TESTS

CHAPTER 5   Practice Test 1

CHAPTER 6   Practice Test 2

CHAPTER 7   Practice Test 3

Practice Test 1

Chapter 5

ANSWER SHEET PRACTICE TEST 1

Section I: Multiple Choice

1. Ⓐ Ⓑ Ⓒ Ⓓ Ⓔ 15. Ⓐ Ⓑ Ⓒ Ⓓ Ⓔ 29. Ⓐ Ⓑ Ⓒ Ⓓ Ⓔ 43. Ⓐ Ⓑ Ⓒ Ⓓ Ⓔ

2. Ⓐ Ⓑ Ⓒ Ⓓ Ⓔ 16. Ⓐ Ⓑ Ⓒ Ⓓ Ⓔ 30. Ⓐ Ⓑ Ⓒ Ⓓ Ⓔ 44. Ⓐ Ⓑ Ⓒ Ⓓ Ⓔ

3. Ⓐ Ⓑ Ⓒ Ⓓ Ⓔ 17. Ⓐ Ⓑ Ⓒ Ⓓ Ⓔ 31. Ⓐ Ⓑ Ⓒ Ⓓ Ⓔ 45. Ⓐ Ⓑ Ⓒ Ⓓ Ⓔ

4. Ⓐ Ⓑ Ⓒ Ⓓ Ⓔ 18. Ⓐ Ⓑ Ⓒ Ⓓ Ⓔ 32. Ⓐ Ⓑ Ⓒ Ⓓ Ⓔ 46. Ⓐ Ⓑ Ⓒ Ⓓ Ⓔ

5. Ⓐ Ⓑ Ⓒ Ⓓ Ⓔ 19. Ⓐ Ⓑ Ⓒ Ⓓ Ⓔ 33. Ⓐ Ⓑ Ⓒ Ⓓ Ⓔ 47. Ⓐ Ⓑ Ⓒ Ⓓ Ⓔ

6. Ⓐ Ⓑ Ⓒ Ⓓ Ⓔ 20. Ⓐ Ⓑ Ⓒ Ⓓ Ⓔ 34. Ⓐ Ⓑ Ⓒ Ⓓ Ⓔ 48. Ⓐ Ⓑ Ⓒ Ⓓ Ⓔ

7. Ⓐ Ⓑ Ⓒ Ⓓ Ⓔ 21. Ⓐ Ⓑ Ⓒ Ⓓ Ⓔ 35. Ⓐ Ⓑ Ⓒ Ⓓ Ⓔ 49. Ⓐ Ⓑ Ⓒ Ⓓ Ⓔ

8. Ⓐ Ⓑ Ⓒ Ⓓ Ⓔ 22. Ⓐ Ⓑ Ⓒ Ⓓ Ⓔ 36. Ⓐ Ⓑ Ⓒ Ⓓ Ⓔ 50. Ⓐ Ⓑ Ⓒ Ⓓ Ⓔ

9. Ⓐ Ⓑ Ⓒ Ⓓ Ⓔ 23. Ⓐ Ⓑ Ⓒ Ⓓ Ⓔ 37. Ⓐ Ⓑ Ⓒ Ⓓ Ⓔ 51. Ⓐ Ⓑ Ⓒ Ⓓ Ⓔ

10. Ⓐ Ⓑ Ⓒ Ⓓ Ⓔ 24. Ⓐ Ⓑ Ⓒ Ⓓ Ⓔ 38. Ⓐ Ⓑ Ⓒ Ⓓ Ⓔ 52. Ⓐ Ⓑ Ⓒ Ⓓ Ⓔ

11. Ⓐ Ⓑ Ⓒ Ⓓ Ⓔ 25. Ⓐ Ⓑ Ⓒ Ⓓ Ⓔ 39. Ⓐ Ⓑ Ⓒ Ⓓ Ⓔ 53. Ⓐ Ⓑ Ⓒ Ⓓ Ⓔ

12. Ⓐ Ⓑ Ⓒ Ⓓ Ⓔ 26. Ⓐ Ⓑ Ⓒ Ⓓ Ⓔ 40. Ⓐ Ⓑ Ⓒ Ⓓ Ⓔ 54. Ⓐ Ⓑ Ⓒ Ⓓ Ⓔ

13. Ⓐ Ⓑ Ⓒ Ⓓ Ⓔ 27. Ⓐ Ⓑ Ⓒ Ⓓ Ⓔ 41. Ⓐ Ⓑ Ⓒ Ⓓ Ⓔ 55. Ⓐ Ⓑ Ⓒ Ⓓ Ⓔ

14. Ⓐ Ⓑ Ⓒ Ⓓ Ⓔ 28. Ⓐ Ⓑ Ⓒ Ⓓ Ⓔ 42. Ⓐ Ⓑ Ⓒ Ⓓ Ⓔ

Section II: Free Response

_____

_____

_____

_____

_____

_____

_____

_____

_____

_____

answer sheet

_____
_____
_____
_____
_____
_____
_____
_____
_____
_____
_____
_____
_____
_____
_____
_____
_____
_____
_____
_____
_____
_____
_____
_____
_____
_____
_____
_____

PRACTICE TEST 1

Section I: Multiple Choice

Time 1 hour • 55 Questions

> **Directions:** This section consists of selections from literary works and questions on their content, form, and style. After reading each passage or poem, choose the best answer to each question and then fill in the corresponding circle.

Questions 1–14. Read the following poem carefully before you decide on the answers to the questions.

"Written with a Slate Pencil on a Stone, on the Side of the Mountain of Black Comb," by William Wordsworth

	Stay, bold Adventurer; rest awhile thy limbs
	On this commodious Seat! for much remains
	Of hard ascent before thou reach the top
Line	Of this huge Eminence,—from blackness named,
5	And, to far-travelled storms of sea and land,
	A favourite spot of tournament and war!
	But thee may no such boisterous visitants
	Molest; may gentle breezes fan thy brow;
	And neither cloud conceal, nor misty air
10	Bedim, the grand terraqueous spectacle,
	From centre to circumference, unveiled!
	Know, if thou grudge not to prolong thy rest,
	That on the summit whither thou art bound,
	A geographic Labourer pitched his tent,
15	With books supplied and instruments of art,
	To measure height and distance; lonely task,
	Week after week pursued!—To him was given
	Full many a glimpse (but sparingly bestowed
	On timid man) of Nature's processes
20	Upon the exalted hills. He made report
	That once, while there he plied his studious work
	Within that canvas Dwelling, colours, lines,
	And the whole surface of the out-spread map,
	Became invisible: for all around
25	Had darkness fallen—unthreatened, unproclaimed—
	As if the golden day itself had been
	Extinguished in a moment; total gloom,
	In which he sate alone, with unclosed eyes,
	Upon the blinded mountain's silent top!

1. What is the poetic device employed in line 2?
    A. Consonance
    B. Paradox
    C. Symbolism
    D. Allusion
    E. Assonance

2. The poetic device employed in line 2 serves what thematic purpose?
    A. It registers the speaker's struggle to fully capture the majesty of nature with language.
    B. It establishes a poetic vantage point that will help the speaker organize the vast space.
    C. It signals the speaker's rejection of language to describe the natural landscape.
    D. It shows the speaker's mastery over nature with diction.
    E. It shows his collaboration with natural scientists to understand nature.

3. The adjective "commodious" (line 2) creates what kind of tone?
    A. Anxious
    B. Ambiguous
    C. Colonialist
    D. Scientific
    E. Grandiose

4. What does line 6 mean?
    A. The peak has been the subject of many territorial disputes.
    B. The peak is the site of many sporting events.
    C. The peak is a popular tourist attraction.
    D. The peak is a good strategic lookout.
    E. The peak has been the subject of many paintings.

5. What is the thematic function of the enjambed verbs ("Molest," "Bedim") at the beginning of lines 8 and 10?
    A. The speaker is overcome with emotion at the scene.
    B. The speaker can't quite contain the scene in poetic language.
    C. The speaker keeps getting interrupted in thoughts.
    D. The speaker is frustrated by the limitations of language.
    E. The manmade world keeps getting in the way of the view.

6. What work was the geographic Labourer performing?
    A. Mining to extract ore
    B. Writing a patriotic poem about the landscape
    C. Surveying to make a map
    D. Scouting for a military campaign
    E. Leading a group of tourists

7. The speaker voices all of these beliefs about the geographic Labourer EXCEPT
    A. he is like a poet, who composes his views of nature in solitude.
    B. he needs help from poets to put his visions into poetic language.
    C. he is heroic in his endeavors.
    D. he sees the world through the language of his own expertise.
    E. his perspective is expansive yet limited.

8. Why is the word "terraqueous" used in line 10?
   A. It calls back to "commodious" to show the whole poetic perspective.
   B. It indicates the insufficiency of simple language to describe the scene.
   C. It shows the speaker's aspiration to capture the scene with extraordinary language.
   D. It reveals the speaker's hubris in overshadowing the scene with fanciful language.
   E. It resolves the negations of "neither" and "nor" in line 9.

9. What is the shift that happens to the geographic Labourer in line 24?
   A. He goes blind.
   B. He loses his map.
   C. Night arrives.
   D. He witnesses a sunset.
   E. He enters his tent.

10. What does the circumstance in lines 23-29 mean the geographic Labourer must do?
    A. Give up his life's work.
    B. Leave the mountain.
    C. Reconsider his sensory experience.
    D. Invent new tools.
    E. Acknowledge the need for spiritual guidance.

11. The negative forms of adjectives in line 25 serve what poetic purpose(s)?
    I. They show his terror at the change in scene
    II. They show the speaker grasping for language in this shifted perspective
    III. They echo negations used in earlier lines
    A. I only
    B. II only
    C. III only
    D. I and III
    E. II and III

12. The personification of the "blinded mountain" in the last line of the poem shows all of the following themes EXCEPT
    A. the absorption of the geographic Labourer into the darkness.
    B. the deep connection between the geographic Labourer and the mountain.
    C. the expansion of a newly abstracted perspective.
    D. the rejection of empirical science for spiritual guidance.
    E. the shift from observation to reflection.

13. Which of the following ambiguous relationships is explored in this poem?
    A. Science and faith
    B. Observation and perception
    C. Religion and spirituality
    D. Man and nature
    E. Industry and nature

14. The title of the poem is "Written with a Slate Pencil on a Stone, on the Side of the Mountain of Black Comb." The choice of writing implement and surface indicate all of the following EXCEPT
    A. it is ironic to read the poem in print, given that it is said to be written in an impermanent form on a rock.
    B. it is fitting that a poem about geology should be recorded with natural elements.
    C. it shows the poet and the geographic Labourer inscribing the land for Britain.
    D. the poem was erased by the elements and Wordsworth recreated it with his imagination.
    E. it shows Wordsworth's transformation of the poetic trope of inscription in the natural world.

practice test

Questions 15–26. Read the following passage carefully before you decide on your answers to the questions.

From *The Moonstone*, by Wilkie Collins

The question of how I am to start the story properly I have tried to settle in two ways. First, by scratching my head, which led to nothing. Second, by consulting my daughter Penelope, which has resulted in an entirely new idea.

Line
5

Penelope's notion is that I should set down what happened, regularly day by day, beginning with the day when we got the news that Mr. Franklin Blake was expected on a visit to the house. When you come to fix your memory with a date in this way, it is wonderful what your memory will pick up for you upon that compulsion. The only difficulty is to fetch out the dates, in the first place. This Penelope offers to do for me by looking into her own diary, which she was taught to keep when she was at school, and which she has gone on keeping ever since. In answer to an improvement on this notion, devised by myself, namely, that she should tell the story instead of me, out of her own diary, Penelope observes, with a fierce look and a red face, that her journal is for her own private eye, and that no living creature shall ever know what is in it but herself. When I inquire what this means, Penelope says, "Fiddlesticks!" I say, Sweethearts.

10

15

Beginning, then, on Penelope's plan, I beg to mention that I was specially called one Wednesday morning into my lady's own sitting-room, the date being the twenty-fourth of May, Eighteen hundred and forty-eight.

"Gabriel," says my lady, "here is news that will surprise you. Franklin Blake has come back from abroad. He has been staying with his father in London, and he is coming to us to-morrow to stop till next month, and keep Rachel's birthday."

20

If I had had a hat in my hand, nothing but respect would have prevented me from throwing that hat up to the ceiling. I had not seen Mr. Franklin since he was a boy, living along with us in this house. He was, out of all sight (as I remember him), the nicest boy that ever spun a top or broke a window. Miss Rachel, who was present, and to whom I made that remark, observed, in return, that SHE remembered him as the most atrocious tyrant that ever tortured a doll, and the hardest driver of an exhausted little girl in string harness that England could produce. "I burn with indignation, and I ache with fatigue," was the way Miss Rachel summed it up, "when I think of Franklin Blake."

25

30

Hearing what I now tell you, you will naturally ask how it was that Mr. Franklin should have passed all the years, from the time when he was a boy to the time when he was a man, out of his own country. I answer, because his father had the misfortune to be next heir to a Dukedom, and not to be able to prove it.

35

In two words, this was how the thing happened:

My lady's eldest sister married the celebrated Mr. Blake—equally famous for his
great riches, and his great suit at law. How many years he went on worrying the
tribunals of his country to turn out the Duke in possession, and to put himself
in the Duke's place—how many lawyer's purses he filled to bursting, and how
40 many otherwise harmless people he set by the ears together disputing whether
he was right or wrong—is more by a great deal than I can reckon up. His wife
died, and two of his three children died, before the tribunals could make up
their minds to show him the door and take no more of his money. When it was
all over, and the Duke in possession was left in possession, Mr. Blake discovered
45 that the only way of being even with his country for the manner in which it had
treated him, was not to let his country have the honour of educating his son.
"How can I trust my native institutions," was the form in which he put it, "after
the way in which my native institutions have behaved to ME?" Add to this, that
Mr. Blake disliked all boys, his own included, and you will admit that it could
50 only end in one way. Master Franklin was taken from us in England, and was
sent to institutions which his father COULD trust, in that superior country,
Germany; Mr. Blake himself, you will observe, remaining snug in England,
to improve his fellow-countrymen in the Parliament House, and to publish a
statement on the subject of the Duke in possession, which has remained an
55 unfinished statement from that day to this.

There! thank God, that's told! Neither you nor I need trouble our heads any
more about Mr. Blake, senior. Leave him to the Dukedom; and let you and I
stick to the Diamond.

The Diamond takes us back to Mr. Franklin, who was the innocent means of
60 bringing that unlucky jewel into the house.

15. How would you characterize the relation-
ship between Betteredge and his daughter,
Penelope?
- **A.** Strict but loving
- **B.** Bumbling but affectionate
- **C.** Overbearing and contentious
- **D.** One-sided and stilted
- **E.** Aloof and indifferent

16. What is Betteredge using the word "compulsion" (line 8) to explain?
- **A.** His habit of recording copious details
of each day
- **B.** His slight over-embellishments of
the truth
- **C.** His desire to please people by telling
them what they want to hear
- **D.** His tendency to jump to conclusions
too quickly
- **E.** His fascination with the story

17. Based on the passage as a whole, what does the word "compulsion" (line 8) suggest about Betteredge?
    A. His mental instability
    B. His deferential servility
    C. His susceptibility to being coerced
    D. His tendency to ramble
    E. His habitual lying

18. Generally speaking, what is Betteredge's social position?
    A. Landowner
    B. Employee
    C. Disinherited relative
    D. Poor relative
    E. Lawyer

19. What is the rhetorical device that Betteredge uses in line 22 in saying "If I had had my hat . . ."
    A. Counterfactual
    B. Litotes
    C. Chiasmus
    D. Anecdote
    E. Oxymoron

20. Given Betteredge's established narrative style, the rhetorical device in lines 22-23 amplifies
    A. his contradiction of his daughter's side of the story.
    B. his tendency to jump around in time and perspective.
    C. his anxiety about concealing the truth.
    D. his sense of deference to the powerful.
    E. his talent for making a memorable entrance.

21. How would you characterize Rachel's reaction to the news about Franklin Blake?
    A. Petty and vicious
    B. Fearful and ashamed
    C. Melodramatic and duplicitous
    D. Blushing and tentative
    E. Disapproving and irritated

22. How would you characterize Betteredge's tone in relating the story of Franklin Blake, senior?
    A. Gossipy and presumptuous
    B. Penitent and anxious
    C. Chaotic and mysterious
    D. Chatty and unfocused
    E. Biased and judgmental

23. It is only at the very end of this passage that the title object of the story—the Diamond, called the Moonstone—is mentioned. Based on the details in this passage, why is this delayed revelation important?
    A. The Diamond is just a distraction from the real story.
    B. Betteredge is an unreliable narrator who is going to obscure the real story of the Diamond.
    C. The characters, including the narrator, have partial, idiosyncratic perspectives on the events of the story.
    D. No one is who they claim to be in the story, and the Diamond is a fake.
    E. The characters are cursed by the Diamond one by one.

24. Betteredge concludes that his explanation about Mr. Blake, senior, was unimportant and you shouldn't give him another thought, but it does serve which of the following purposes for the narrative?

   I. It reveals Mr. Blake, senior, to be an important character in the narrative, despite Betteredge's claims.

   II. It obliquely makes the reader pay attention to issues of inheritance and legal testimony, which are important for the main question about the whereabouts of the Diamond.

   III. It establishes Mr. Blake, senior, as the owner of the Diamond who is the victim of the crime.

   A. I only
   B. II only
   C. III only
   D. I and II
   E. II and III

25. Why is Mr. Blake's habit of "worrying" potentially important to the narrative?

   A. It reinforces the underlying anxiety and dread.

   B. It exposes the class divisions that separate the characters.

   C. It shows the importance of wrangling over details ad nauseam.

   D. It exposes Mr. Blake's abuse of his power and influence.

   E. It reveals Mr. Blake's guilt over abandoning his son, Franklin.

26. What do you learn about the notion of objective narration in this passage?

   A. Everyone has something to hide.

   B. You shouldn't trust oral testimony.

   C. Written testimony is the most objective form of evidence.

   D. All memory is subjective.

   E. Money can make anyone say anything.

Questions 27–38. Read the following two poems carefully before you decide on the answers to the questions. You will be asked questions about each poem separately, as well as questions in which you will compare the two poems by Paul Laurence Dunbar.

"Candle-Lightin' Time"

When I come in f'om de co'n-fiel' aftah wo'kin' ha'd all day,
It 's amazin' nice to fin' my suppah all erpon de way;
An' it 's nice to smell de coffee bubblin' ovah in de pot,
Line   An' it 's fine to see de meat a-sizzlin' teasin'-lak an' hot.

5   But when suppah-time is ovah, an' de t'ings is cleahed away;
Den de happy hours dat foller are de sweetes' of de day.
When my co'ncob pipe is sta'ted, an' de smoke is drawin' prime,
My ole 'ooman says, 'I reckon, Ike, it 's candle-lightin' time.'

Den de chillun snuggle up to me, an' all commence to call,
10   'Oh, say, daddy, now it 's time to mek de shadders on de wall.'
So I puts my han's togethah--evah daddy knows de way,--
An' de chillun snuggle closer roun' ez I begin to say:--

'Fus' thing, hyeah come Mistah Rabbit; don' you see him wo'k his eahs?
Huh, uh! dis mus' be a donkey,--look, how innercent he 'pears!
15   Dah 's de ole black swan a-swimmin'--ain't she got a' awful neck?
Who 's dis feller dat 's a-comin'? Why, dat 's ole dog Tray, I 'spec'!'

Dat 's de way I run on, tryin' fu' to please 'em all I can;
Den I hollahs, 'Now be keerful--dis hyeah las' 's de buga-man!'
An' dey runs an' hides dey faces; dey ain't skeered--dey 's lettin' on:
20   But de play ain't raaly ovah twell dat buga-man is gone.

So I jes' teks up my banjo, an' I plays a little chune,
An' you see dem haids come peepin' out to listen mighty soon.
Den my wife says, 'Sich a pappy fu' to give you sich a fright!
Jes, you go to baid, an' leave him: say yo' prayers an' say good-night.'

"Confirmation"

25   He was a poet who wrote clever verses,
And folks said he had a fine poetical taste;
But his father, a practical farmer, accused him
Of letting the strength of his arm go to waste.

He called on his sweetheart each Saturday evening,
30   As pretty a maiden as ever man faced,
And there he confirmed the old man's accusation
By letting the strength of his arm go to waist.

27. When is candle-lightin' time?
  A. On holidays
  B. At dawn
  C. At church
  D. At bedtime
  E. At the end of the day

28. What is the speaker doing in lines 9-16?
  A. Making dinner
  B. Praying in church
  C. Writing poetry
  D. Telling stories
  E. Drawing pictures

29. How would you characterize the speaker's tone in lines 18-20?
  A. Teasing and gentle
  B. Mocking and sarcastic
  C. Terrifying and grim
  D. Exhausted and short-tempered
  E. Rowdy and childish

30. The rhyme scheme helps establish the theme of the poem in all of the following ways EXCEPT
    A. it shows the poetry of everyday life.
    B. it shows the relationship between the family's tune (line 21) and the poet's work in composition.
    C. it reinforces the importance of repetition and ritual in the family life.
    D. it shows the long tradition of vernacular stories as a tradition of oral poetry.
    E. it shows a disregard for poetic tradition that's revolutionary.

31. What is the main source of conflict in lines 25-28?
    A. Between practical labor and poetry
    B. Between fathers and sons
    C. Between physical and mental strength
    D. Between seriousness and cleverness
    E. Between poetry and humor

32. What does "taste" mean in context in line 26?
    A. Judgment
    B. Fame
    C. Aptitude
    D. Humor
    E. Generosity

33. What is the literary device used at the end of the second poem?
    A. Synonym
    B. Homophone
    C. Epithet
    D. Reversal
    E. Allusion

34. The literary device at the end of the second poem establishes what themes?
    I. Appropriation of criticism allows for subversion.
    II. His taste is reinforced with the waste/waist rhyme pun.
    III. Cleverness is a subtler tool than polemic.
    A. I only
    B. II only
    C. III only
    D. I and III
    E. I, II, and III

35. The two poems here may be linked thematically in all of the following ways EXCEPT
    A. they claim African-American daily life and questions of identity as a valid source of poetic inspiration.
    B. they show a light touch with playful language.
    C. they expose rifts between fathers and children.
    D. they reveal some tensions between daily labor and the poetic retreat from the world.
    E. they claim ephemeral forms like shadows, bedtime stories, and puns as a valid source of poetic inspiration.

36. Dunbar called the poems in dialect "Minors" and those without dialect "Majors." What dichotomies is he exploring in making those distinctions?
    A. Formality and informality
    B. Humor and seriousness
    C. Poetry and humor
    D. Speech and writing
    E. Family and general readers

37. The dichotomies used by Dunbar are characterized by distinctions, but what makes the distinctions more complicated in the poems?

  I. The Major poem, "Confirmation," directly addresses questions of how people perceive poetic value differently.

  II. The Minor poem, "Candle-Lightin' Time," emphasizes the distinction between public and private life inside the home.

  III. The poems were likely recited by readers after they were published, which blurs some of the distinctions between oral and written poetry.

  A. I only

  B. II only

  C. III only

  D. I and II

  E. I and III

38. The question of race underlies all of those distinctions between Major and Minor poems for the following reasons EXCEPT

  A. it speaks to how Dunbar was perceived as an African-American poet who wrote in multiple registers.

  B. it signals how labels of genre and form are laden with value judgments.

  C. it claims a space for him among traditional ballad poets and others who wrote in regional dialect.

  D. it shows the pressure put on him by white publishers to write in a specific way to gain a wider readership.

  E. it shows a version of the "double consciousness" that W.E.B. Dubois (a contemporary of Dunbar's) wrote about.

Questions 39–55. Read the following passage carefully before you choose your answers to the questions. The selection is an excerpt from the novel *The Female Quixote*, by Charlotte Lennox.

The Marquis, following the Plan of Life he had laid down, divided his Time between the Company of his Lady, his Library, which was large and well furnished, and his Gardens. Sometimes he took the Diversion of Hunting, but
Line
    never admitted any Company whatever; and his Pride and extreme Reserve rendered him so wholly inaccessible to the Country Gentry about him, that none
5 ever presumed to solicit his Acquaintance.

In the Second Year of his Retirement, the Marchioness brought him a Daughter, and died in Three Days after her Delivery. The Marquis, who had tenderly loved her, was extremely afflicted at her Death; but Time having
10 produced its usual Effects, his great Fondness for the little Arabella entirely engrossed his Attention, and made up all the Happiness of his Life. At Four Years of Age he took her from under the Direction of the Nurses and Women appointed to attend her, and permitted her to receive no Part of her Education from another, which he was capable of giving her himself. He taught her to
15 read and write in a very few Months; and, as she grew older, finding in her an uncommon Quickness of Apprehension, and an Understanding capable of great Improvements, he resolved to cultivate so promising a Genius with the utmost Care; and, as he frequently, in the Rapture of paternal Fondness, expressed himself, render her Mind as beautiful as her Person was lovely.

20   Nature had indeed given her a most charming Face, a Shape easy and delicate,
      a sweet and insinuating Voice, and an Air so full of Dignity and Grace, as
      drew the Admiration of all that saw her. These native Charms were improved
      with all the Heightenings of Art; her Dress was perfectly magnificent; the best
      Masters of Music and Dancing were sent for from London to attend her. She
25   soon became a perfect Mistress of the French and Italian Languages, under the
      Care of her Father; and it is not to be doubted, but she would have made a great
      Proficiency in all useful Knowledge, had not her whole Time been taken up by
      another Study.

      From her earliest youth Arabella had discovered a fondness for reading, which
30   extremely delighted the marquis; he permitted her therefore the use of his
      library, in which, unfortunately for her, were great store of romances, and, what
      was still more unfortunate, not in the original French, but very bad translations.

      The deceased marchioness had purchased these books to soften a solitude
      which she found very disagreeable; and, after her death, the marquis removed
35   them from her closet into his library, where Arabella found them.

      The surprising adventures with which they were filled, proved a most pleasing
      entertainment to a young lady who was wholly secluded from the world; who
      had no other diversion, but ranging like a nymph through gardens, or, to say
      better, the woods and lawns in which she was enclosed; and who had no other
40   conversation but that of a grave and melancholy father, or her own attendants.

      Her ideas, from the manner of her life, and the objects around her, had taken
      a romantic turn; and, supposing romances were real pictures of life, from them
      she drew all her notions and expectations. By them she was taught to believe,
      that love was the ruling principle of the world; that every other passion was
45   subordinate to this; and that it caused all the happiness and miseries of life. Her
      glass, which she often consulted, always showed her a form so extremely lovely,
      that, not finding herself engaged in such adventures as were common to the
      heroines in the romances she read, she often complained of the insensibility of
      mankind, upon whom her charms seemed to have so little influence.

50   The perfect retirement she lived in afforded, indeed, no opportunities of making
      the conquests she desired; but she could not comprehend how any solitude
      could be obscure enough to conceal a beauty like hers from notice; and thought
      the reputation of her charms sufficient to bring a crowd of adorers to demand
      her of her father. Her mind being wholly filled with the most extravagant
55   expectations, she was alarmed by every trifling incident; and kept in a continual
      anxiety by a vicissitude of hopes, fears, wishes, and disappointments.

39. How would you characterize life on the Marquis's estate?

- **A.** Impoverished yet cozy
- **B.** Pampered yet petty
- **C.** Erudite yet cloistered
- **D.** Romantic yet dangerous
- **E.** Friendly yet guarded

40. How would you characterize the Marquis's attention to his daughter's education in the second paragraph?

- **A.** Extremely attentive in facilitating an ideal setup
- **B.** Distracted by his grief
- **C.** Overzealous in correcting her
- **D.** Whimsical in his choice of subjects to instruct her
- **E.** Pragmatic in showing her how to manage the estate

41. What are the narrator's concerns about the books Arabella finds in her father's library?

- **A.** They are in French.
- **B.** They belonged to her late mother, and the memory is too painful for him to bear when he sees her reading them.
- **C.** Arabella should be doing chores to help her father, not reading novels.
- **D.** Arabella treats the stories like they're real life and acts foolishly because she's pretending she's a character.
- **E.** The pictures inside are too scandalous for a young woman to be reading.

42. The phrase "she would have made..." (line 26) is an example of what rhetorical device?

- **A.** Hyperbole
- **B.** Counterfactual
- **C.** Imperative
- **D.** Anecdote
- **E.** Ethos

43. In context, what does "this" refer to in the sentence "... every other passion was subordinate to this" (line 45)?

- **A.** Reading
- **B.** Dancing
- **C.** Love
- **D.** Solitude
- **E.** Flirtation

44. As the narrator presents the scene, what is the main problem that Arabella faces?

- **A.** She is extremely fearful about the outside world.
- **B.** No suitors will ever get to meet her.
- **C.** She is mechanical in everything she does because she has been over-coached.
- **D.** She is melodramatic and self-absorbed because she interacts only with fictional characters.
- **E.** She cannot discern the difference between truth and lies in what she reads.

45. Why does the narrator interject with "to say better" in lines 38–39?

- **A.** To show how Arabella pretends she's in an idyllic story, but really she's just confined to her own woods and lawn
- **B.** To give another character's more objective point of view
- **C.** To explain how her father corrects her mistakes
- **D.** To show Arabella's development as a writer
- **E.** To subtly signal unreliable narration

46. The long sentence which begins "By them she was taught to believe..." (line 43) is an example of what kind of rhetorical device?

- **A.** Analogy
- **B.** Parallelism
- **C.** Hyperbole
- **D.** Tautology
- **E.** Logic

47. What is the distinction between the narrator, the author, and the protagonist in this passage?

  A. The author and narrator are adult women who are concerned for Arabella to grow up into a well-rounded person.

  B. The author is telling an autobiographical story about how she became a romance novelist, using a third-person omniscient narrator.

  C. It is unclear what the author's opinion is, but the narrator is objective.

  D. The author is showing the narrator's unreliability by showing her lapsing into the language of romance to describe Arabella's life.

  E. It is unclear what the author's opinion is, but the narrator is skeptical of Arabella's reading habits.

48. In context, what does "the insensibility of mankind" (lines 48-49) mean?

  A. The oppression of women

  B. The inability of most people to solve their own problems

  C. The disappearance of deep conversation between friends

  D. The inability to handle criticism

  E. The social tendency not to express strong emotions

49. The tone of the second half of the passage is best described as

  A. reverential.

  B. satirical.

  C. ominous.

  D. romantic.

  E. objective.

50. The narrator characterizes Arabella's "glass" (her mirror) in all of the following ways EXCEPT

  A. she looks at it too frequently.

  B. she reads the mirror like she reads her books.

  C. she has a distorted interpretation of what she sees.

  D. she is overly critical of her own appearance.

  E. she has a limited perspective on the world.

51. The mirror reflects which of the following themes?

  I. It reinforces the sense that Arabella is solitary because her own reflection is her main companion

  II. It subtly reveals that the narrator is holding a mirror, too, as a form of social commentary

  III. It shows a welcome gateway into another world of books that allows Arabella a way out of her confines

  A. I only

  B. II only

  C. I and II

  D. II and III

  E. I, II, and III

52. In context, the word "vicissitude" (line 56) conveys what about Arabella's behavior?

  A. She has suffered many tragedies.

  B. Her daily life is unpredictable.

  C. She reads a huge number of different stories every day.

  D. Her whims and desires change rapidly.

  E. Her fortunes are about to be reversed with a surprise event.

53. In context, how would you characterize the narrative's use of the adjective "trifling" (line 55)?

A. Condescending

B. Rejected

C. Whimsical

D. Gentle

E. Anxious

54. How would you characterize the narrator's opinions about reading?

A. Young women shouldn't be taught to read.

B. Instructional books on etiquette are more important than novels.

C. Fathers should read to their daughters to instill a love for the written word.

D. Getting lost in a book is both pleasurable and perilous.

E. Reading should be supervised, or readers could find inappropriate content.

55. What are the underlying ironies of the passage?

I. Readers are reading a novel about the dangers of enjoying novels too much.

II. The narrator is unreliable, so you can't trust the characterizations of Arabella.

III. The narrator is exposing readers' unacknowledged gender stereotypes by making them consider their judgments about Arabella.

A. I only

B. II only

C. III only

D. I and II

E. I, II, and III

Section II: Free Response

Time: 2 hours

The essay section of the exam lasts 2 hours, so it is recommended that you spend 40 minutes on each of the three essays on the exam. You may write the essays in any order you wish and return to work on the essays if you have extra time.

Each essay will be evaluated according to how thoroughly and clearly it addresses the question, as well as the overall quality of your writing. Please write in blue or black ink and scratch out any mistakes thoroughly and neatly. Make sure to check your spelling and punctuation so that the reader can read your essay without struggling over legibility.

The quality of the essay matters more than its length, so spend some time at the beginning of the exam planning out the ideas on your sheet of scratch paper. You may write notes on the poem in the exam booklet. Use a new sheet of paper for each essay and number them (1, 2, 3) so that the exam question is immediately obvious.

For essay 3, you should choose to write about a novel or a play of similar literary merit to those in your AP English Literature class. There are some suggestions listed, but you are not required to choose one of them.

ESSAY QUESTION 1

Why is it so much fun to love the villain? Why do audiences respond so positively to such loathsome characters? You should treat these opening lines of Ben Jonson's 1607 play, *Volpone*, as a soliloquy to analyze on its own so that you won't have to account for what happens in the rest of the plot. You may choose to focus on Volpone's self-presentation, his figurative language, his use of hyperbole, and other devices that make him a villain you love to hate. For your reference: Volpone (Vol-pon-ay if you want to say it in your head) means "sly fox" and Mosca means "the fly" or "the parasite," which may complicate your analysis of these opening lines.

Volpone, by Ben Jonson

> VOLPONE: Good morning to the day; and next, my gold:
> Open the shrine, that I may see my Saint.
> *[MOSCA withdraws the curtain and discovers piles of gold and jewels]*
>
Line | Hail the world's soul, and mine! more glad than is
5 | The teeming earth to see the long'd-for sun
> Peep through the horns of the celestial Ram,
> Am I, to view thy splendour darkening his;
> That lying here, amongst my other hoards,
> Shew'st like a flame by night; or like the day
10 | Struck out of chaos, when all darkness fled
> Unto the centre. O thou son of Sol,
> But brighter than thy father, let me kiss,
> With adoration, thee, and every relick
> Of sacred treasure, in this blessed room.
15 | Well did wise poets, by thy glorious name,
> Title that age which they would have the best;
> Thou being the best of things: and far transcending
> All style of joy, in children, parents, friends,
> Or any other waking dream on earth:
20 | Thy looks when they to Venus did ascribe,
> They should have given her twenty thousand Cupids
> Such are thy beauties and our loves! Dear saint,
> Riches, the dumb God, that giv'st all men tongues;
> That canst do nought, and yet mak'st men do all things;
25 | The price of souls; even hell, with thee to boot,
> Is made worth heaven. Thou art virtue, fame,
> Honour, and all things else. Who can get thee,
> He shall be noble, valiant, honest, wise,—
> MOSCA: And what he will, sir. Riches are in fortune
30 | A greater good than wisdom is in nature.
>
> VOLPONE: True, my beloved Mosca. Yet I glory
> More in the cunning purchase of my wealth,

Than in the glad possession; since I gain

No common way; I use no trade, no venture;

35   I wound no earth with plough-shares; fat no beasts,

To feed the shambles; have no mills for iron,

Oil, corn, or men, to grind them into powder:

I blow no subtle glass; expose no ships

To threat'nings of the furrow-faced sea;

40   I turn no monies in the public bank,

Nor usure private.

ESSAY QUESTION 2

Read this passage by Willa Cather from *The Song of the Lark* (1915). The narrator, Thea Kronberg, is lying down in the sun, enjoying the quietness of the world around her and how it makes her see new details that she would have overlooked before—not just in the scene around her, but also in her own life. Write an essay in which you discuss how Thea reflects on the tension between busyness and idleness in her life.

Thea went down to the stream by the Indian water trail. She had found a
bathing-pool with a sand bottom, where the creek was dammed by fallen trees.
The climb back was long and steep, and when she reached her little house in

Line   the cliff she always felt fresh delight in its comfort and inaccessibility. By the

5   time she got there, the woolly red-and-gray blankets were saturated with sunlight, and she sometimes fell asleep as soon as she stretched her body on their
warm surfaces. She used to wonder at her own inactivity. She could lie there
hour after hour in the sun and listen to the strident whir of the big locusts, and
to the light, ironical laughter of the quaking asps. All her life she had been hur-

10   rying and sputtering, as if she had been born behind time and had been trying
to catch up. Now, she reflected, as she drew herself out long upon the rugs, it
was as if she were waiting for something to catch up with her. She had got to
a place where she was out of the stream of meaningless activity and undirected
effort.

15   Here she could lie for half a day undistracted, holding pleasant and incomplete
conceptions in her mind—almost in her hands. They were scarcely clear enough
to be called ideas. They had something to do with fragrance and color and
sound, but almost nothing to do with words. She was singing very little now,
but a song would go through her head all morning, as a spring keeps welling

20   up, and it was like a pleasant sensation indefinitely prolonged. It was much
more like a sensation than like an idea, or an act of remembering. Music had
never come to her in that sensuous form before. It had always been a thing to be
struggled with, had always brought anxiety and exaltation and chagrin—never
content and indolence. Thea began to wonder whether people could not utterly

25   lose the power to work, as they can lose their voice or their memory. She had
always been a little drudge, hurrying from one task to another—as if it mat-
tered! And now her power to think seemed converted into a power of sustained
sensation. She could become a mere receptacle for heat, or become a color, like
the bright lizards that darted about on the hot stones outside her door; or she

30   could become a continuous repetition of sound, like the cicadas.

The faculty of observation was never highly developed in Thea Kronborg. A
great deal escaped her eye as she passed through the world. But the things
which were for her, she saw; she experienced them physically and remembered
them as if they had once been a part of herself. The roses she used to see in

35   the florists' shops in Chicago were merely roses. But when she thought of the

moonflowers that grew over Mrs. Tellamantez's door, it was as if she had been
that vine and had opened up in white flowers every night. There were memories
of light on the sand hills, of masses of prickly-pear blossoms she had found in
the desert in early childhood, of the late afternoon sun pouring through the

40   grape leaves and the mint bed in Mrs. Kohler's garden, which she would never
lose. These recollections were a part of her mind and personality. In Chicago
she had got almost nothing that went into her subconscious self and took root
there. But here, in Panther Canyon, there were again things which seemed des-
tined for her.

45   Panther Canyon was the home of innumerable swallows. They built nests in the
wall far above the hollow groove in which Thea's own rock chamber lay. They
seldom ventured above the rim of the canyon, to the flat, wind-swept tableland.
Their world was the blue air-river between the canyon walls. In that blue gulf
the arrow-shaped birds swam all day long, with only an occasional movement of

50   the wings. The only sad thing about them was their timidity; the way in which
they lived their lives between the echoing cliffs and never dared to rise out of
the shadow of the canyon walls. As they swam past her door, Thea often felt
how easy it would be to dream one's life out in some cleft in the world.

ESSAY QUESTION 3

"I love large parties. They're so much more intimate than small ones," claims Jordan Baker in F. Scott Fitzgerald's novel *The Great Gatsby*. What do we learn about the conflict between private and public life when we see characters interact at parties and other big events, perhaps especially when the parties don't turn out the way the characters expected?

The Great Gatsby
The Sun Also Rises
White Teeth
A Midsummer Night's Dream
The Age of Innocence
Mrs. Dalloway
"The Dead"
Vanity Fair
The Master and the Margarita
Through the Looking Glass and What Alice Found There
A Streetcar Named Desire
Macbeth
Americanah
Wolf Hall
Titus Andromachus
The Virgin Suicides
Pride and Prejudice
The Love Song of J. Alfred Prufrock
The Portrait of a Lady
The Masque of the Red Death

ANSWER KEY AND EXPLANATIONS

1. A	**11.** E	**20.** B	**29.** A	**38.** D	**47.** E
2. B	**12.** D	**21.** E	**30.** E	**39.** C	**48.** E
3. E	**13.** B	**22.** D	**31.** A	**40.** A	**49.** B
4. D	**14.** D	**23.** C	**32.** C	**41.** D	**50.** D
5. B	**15.** B	**24.** B	**33.** B	**42.** B	**51.** C
6. C	**16.** A	**25.** C	**34.** E	**43.** C	**52.** D
7. B	**17.** D	**26.** D	**35.** C	**44.** D	**53.** A
8. A	**18.** B	**27.** E	**36.** A	**45.** A	**54.** D
9. C	**19.** A	**28.** D	**37.** E	**46.** B	**55.** A
10. C					

Section I

1. **The correct answer is A.** The words "this commodious Seat" conspicuously repeat the "s" sound, so you are looking for the poetic device in which consonants are repeated: consonance. The easiest way to remember the definition of consonance is that it involves consonants—very similar! You might pause on assonance (choice E) because it's a similar device, but it is about similar *vowel* sounds. There are no contradictions that would form a paradox, so it's not choice B. There are no obvious symbols in these lines, so it's not choice C. It's remotely possible that the poet is making an allusion (choice D) here, but that would be a very obscure allusion that you couldn't be expected to know. The concrete answer is the right one.

2. **The correct answer is B.** This is a tricky question because there are multiple answers that echo language that is often used to analyze nature poetry by Wordsworth and other Romantic authors. It may be tempting to choose choices A or C because they indicate the Romantic theme that language is insufficient to capture the majesty of nature. Nevertheless, in the opening lines of this poem, the speaker is sure of his project to organize the landscape with poetic language like consonance—and with cartographic surveying, the subject of this particular poem. The answer is choice B: he is surveying the scene with poetic devices like a cartographer does with his own instruments. Choice D is too broad to be a good choice—it's generally true, but the question asks about the poetic device, not language in general. Choice E is basically true of the poem, but there's nothing about scientific collaboration in a poetic device like consonance.

3. **The correct answer is E.** Even if you don't know what "commodious" means, you know that it has esses and multiple syllables—it seems to be too forced a word to describe the spacious view, so you can call it grandiose. There's nothing anxious (choice A) or ambiguous (choice B) about the description. It may be tempting to answer "scientific" (choice D) if you are yourself anxious about not knowing the definition of the word because it seems to be related to the theme of the poem, but he is not using a scientific term here. Even though the poem is a celebration of English cartography, there is nothing obviously colonialist (choice C) about the description.

4. **The correct answer is D.** "A favourite spot of tournament and war" means that it's a good strategic location, so the answer is choice D. We don't know enough about the mountain to know whether it was disputed territory (choice A), but we know it's used for more than sporting (choice B), so it can't be either of those two options. The peak probably is a good tourist attraction (choice C) and painting subject (choice E) because it is such a favorite spot, but the poem doesn't mention those details.

5. **The correct answer is B.** Enjambment is the poetic device of letting phrases continue onto the next lines. This poem is in free verse, so the runover is not as obvious as it would be if there were rhymes or a strong meter. However, those two verbs stick out, so it's worth asking what purpose that enjambment serves in its conspicuousness. The enjambment calls attention to what doesn't fit into the gaze. It may be tempting to steamroll through the question with a big Romantic theme about being overcome with emotion (choice A) or the insufficiency of language (choice D), but there aren't many markers of emotion and the language isn't what's insufficient here—it's the form. "Molest" does mean to bother, but there's no obvious culprit for who or what's bothering him, so choice C isn't a good answer. There are no indications of the manmade world (choice E) in the speaker's view.

6. **The correct answer is C.** You have to have read the whole poem to understand what the geographic Labourer is up to, but there are a number of clues: the high vantage point from the mountain, his maps, and especially "his instruments of art / to measure height and distance." That's exactly what surveyors and cartographers do, so the answer is choice C. (It's not the purview of the poem to distinguish between the surveying and cartography exactly.) The speaker himself

might be writing a patriotic poem (choice B), but the geographic Labourer has his own expertise and duty. Others may have scouted for military reasons (choice D), as the speaker has mentioned, but the geographic Labourer has his own duties. Those duties do not include any mentions of mining (choice A) or guiding tourists (choice E).

7. **The correct answer is B.** These answers are relatively similar to one another, so it may be hard to distinguish among them. Fortunately, for a question that asks you to find the exception, all you have to do is find the wrong one, not judge which one is the most correct. The speaker admires the geographic Labourer (the surveyor/cartographer)—he seems to make his own poetry more like cartography, rather than saying that the Labourer needs his help in composing the scene. Thus choice B is too presumptuous: he doesn't presume to tell the cartographer how to do his job in describing the scene. He does compare himself to him in surveying space, one with a map and the other with words, so it's not choice A. He calls him a brave adventurer, so he's treating him heroically—not choice C. The cartographer sees the world as a surveyor, and by the end of the poem his perspective is limited (but not utterly destroyed), so it's not choice D or E.

8. **The correct answer is A.** Who knows what "terraqueous" means?! (It means "made of land and water.") What's most important is that it's a fancy word that calls back to the fanciness of prior unusual vocabulary. Choices B, C, and D are all tempting because they have Romantic themes in them, but there isn't sufficient evidence to weigh the best one of the three. Choice C seems to be the most tempting of those, but A is the better choice because C is so general that it could refer to any adjective in the lines, not "terraqueous" specifically. Although it

would be interesting to analyze the role of negations in the poem in choice E, that's not what this question is asking.

9. **The correct answer is C.** Darkness falls, and the most obvious answer is the correct one: it is night. The map became invisible in the darkness, but that doesn't signal that the Labourer went blind (choice A) or that he lost it (choice B). There's no mention of a sunset (choice D), and although one could infer that one took place, that's not what the question is asking. He may be in his tent (choice E), but that's not the important detail in the question about the shift. There is a clear factual answer that does not require making inferences.

10. **The correct answer is C.** This question is stealthily asking you about the theme of the poem, even though it seems to just be a factual question. Choices A, B, and D are too literal-minded, and there's no mention of any of them happening. That leaves choices C and E, and there's no mention of spirituality or any references to it. Choice C has been the clearest answer since the early questions about how the speaker organizes his perspective: from the very first question, this test has been hinting at these larger themes of sensory perception.

11. **The correct answer is E.** This question asks you to weigh the ambiguities of the three choices and choose which ones seem to be complementary. The combinations give you some clues about which options are complementary. In this case, all three options may be possible, but you don't have the option to pick options I, II, and III. The negative adjective formations of "unthreatened" and "unproclaimed" might signal terror (option I), but it's more obvious that they show him making up new words out of negations, which call back to "neither/nor" (line 9) and "unveiled" (line 11) (options II and III). Thus

the answer is choice E because it allows for both.

12. **The correct answer is D.** As with question 7, your job here is to pick the wrong statement out of five choices, not the only correct one. Choices A, B, and C are all basically correct ways to describe the effects of personification. In choice A, the object folds the person in; in choice B, the personification emphasizes their connection; in choice C, personification is the form that the abstraction of perception takes. Clearly the author of the test has a main theme in mind and is using related language in each question to help you see it. Choice E is a generalization of the main theme of the poem, the fundamental shift in the actions of the poem. Therefore choice D is the wrong option about spirituality, which isn't really present in the poem, nor is it related to the device of personification—it is the exception, and thus the correct answer.

13. **The correct answer is B.** This option echoes the similar language about perception, observation, and sensory experience that has already been used. If you were unsure about any of them you could see the pattern and work backward to make sure each answer confirmed the others. For this question, there are also obviously incorrect answers such as choices A and D, which are more like dualities or oppositions than ambiguities. There may be an ambiguous relationship between nature and industry (choice E) on a mountain where mining is taking place, but that situation isn't present in the poem. Religion and spirituality (choice C) may have ambiguous overlaps, but those overlaps aren't present in the poem, either.

14. **The correct answer is D.** This question asks you to find the incorrect option, so even if you feel unsure about making an inference or interpreting the title, all you have to do is

find one wrong detail, rather than choosing between multiple similar options. Choice A is a reasonable interpretation of the title's irony, and it matches well with choice E's interest in the genre of the poem. These two answers are so specific and literary that it would be difficult for them to be wrong. If choice E is a reasonable interpretation, that means choice C is, as well. Choice B follows a similar line of reasoning: all three are making reference to inscription, so it's unlikely that any of them is wrong. It is choice D that's the wrong answer, since it doesn't make any reference to erasure, which is the most important unique word in that answer. Choice D is not a good interpretation, so it is the correct answer.

15. **The correct answer is B.** Betteredge's long-winded narrative style can be annoying, but his daughter Penelope offsets some it with her slightly exasperated affection for her father: "Fiddlesticks!" He may be bumbling, but there is tenderness there, so the answer is choice B. Even though Betteredge may be both loving (choice A) and stilted (choice D), the paired adjectives don't match, for he seems like he could never be decisive enough to be strict, nor is he one-sided. Indeed, he seeks out her advice, so the answer can't be C or E—he's not critical of her, nor indifferent to her advice because he adopts it in order to tell the story.

16. **The correct answer is A.** This is a factual question, not an inference question, so you just need to understand how Betteredge is using a word in context. He has been describing his habit of recalling details, and although it is a confusing system that leads to over-explaining, you don't need to infer any ulterior motives in this question. Choice A is the clearest explanation of an admittedly confusing narrative style. Choices B, C, and D all jump to conclusions about him, but there's no evidence in the passage

of his over-embellishing, two-facedness, or over-interpretation. He is clearly fascinated with the story, but that's not how he's using the word "compulsion," so choice E, while somewhat tempting, is not correct.

17. **The correct answer is D.** You must make an inference or an interpretation about what his long-winded style means for him as a character. There is no textual evidence for his mental instability (choice A), being coerced by another character (choice C), or lying (choice E). These are all over-interpretations or red herrings—don't jump to conclusions! "Compulsion" doesn't seem to have anything to do with how he is treated by his employer, so choice B also seems like a stretch with no real evidence from the passage. Best to go with the descriptive choice about his rambling because you can definitely see that quality in the text.

18. **The correct answer is B.** This is a factual question that you can answer by noting the phrase "my lady" who calls him into her sitting room and explains details about visitors, so he is probably subordinate to her as her employee (choice B). He refers to other characters as Mr. and is keenly aware of their social classes and how they got that way, so he is likely observing them from a lower social position. We don't hear him talk about his land, so choice A is unlikely. The relatives discussed in the passage are the Blakes, not Betteredges, so choices C and D are not correct. While it would be technically possible for Betteredge to be his lady's lawyer, Mr. Blake senior is the lawyer mentioned in the passage, so it's not choice E.

19. **The correct answer is A.** The phrase "if I had had ... nothing ... would have" is a subjunctive + conditional phrase that indicates a counterfactual (choice A), something that didn't happen. He didn't have his hat so he

didn't toss it, but he uses the phrase to express his surprise. The verbose style is what we've come to expect from Betteredge. Choices B, C, and E are rhetorical devices that involve negation (and wordiness), so they may be tempting. Litotes (choice B) is a rhetorical device that expresses a positive with the use a double negative, like "not displeased" or "cannot disagree." A chiasmus (choice C) is a phrase that mirrors itself like "I'm tired of love, and love is tired of me," and it is usually economical—not Betteredge's style. An oxymoron (choice E) is a paradox like "pretty ugly" or "cruel to be kind," but that is not what Betteredge is saying here. Betteredge is nothing if not anecdotal (choice D), but choice A is the more precise explanation of this particular device.

20. **The correct answer is B.** These questions are testing your own tendency to jump to conclusions about Betteredge—you can start to learn something about the kinds of reading techniques that the test author wants you to pay attention to, based on the pattern of the questions asked. As in question 17, you're being tested to see if you'll jump to conclusions about Betteredge's ulterior motives, but you don't have much textual evidence for these kinds of suspicions or diagnoses in choices A, C, and D. Why does the test author keep testing your habits of jumping to conclusions? Maybe that's a theme in this passage—you might be projecting your own habits onto the annoying narrator, Betteredge! Best to go with the most descriptive choice, B, where you can clearly see that he jumps around in his narration and the test has been pointing this feature out in multiple questions. Choice E is not correct because the device was a counterfactual—he *didn't* toss his hat in the air upon hearing the good news of Blake's arrival.

21. **The correct answer is E.** We don't know much about the character of Rachel, except

that she has a strong reaction to the news about Franklin Blake: she provides several examples of his bad behavior when they were children and expresses her "indignation" and "fatigue." This question has several paired adjectives, and although a few of the full set of ten may seem to apply, you need to pick the pair in which both seem like reasonable descriptions given the little information you receive. Her irritation (choice E) is evident, as is her disapproval of his character (at least his character as a child). We don't know enough about Franklin Blake to know if she's being petty or vicious (choice A), so that is not a good option. Although she calls him a tyrant and was afraid of him as a child, her feelings don't seem to be so secretive since she is announcing them to Betteredge, so choice B is not the best option. She is using dramatic language, but we don't have any evidence that she's deceiving Betteredge here so it's not choice C. She is not tentative in expressing her displeasure, so it's not choice D.

22. **The correct answer is D.** Betteredge's introduction to the story, "two words," signal that we're in for a long digression—obviously, it's far more than two words. Therefore, choice D is the best option here because it describes the tone without jumping to conclusions. Again, the test author seems to be signaling something about what you should be paying attention to in this narrative style. Because it's such a short passage, you're not going to be able to test any suspicions you have about foreshadowing or irony—you have to go with the passage you have—so what else might be the rationale behind these questions? To test your own biases? To show you how to pay attention to the very feature that annoys you or frustrates you? Choice A is tempting because Betteredge can be gossipy, but he doesn't actually make any presumptions—he is stating facts about

what happened to Mr. Blake, not unsubstantiated rumors. Betteredge has nothing to be penitent or anxious about, so choice B is not correct. The story is not really chaotic, just long, so choice C is out. Choice E may be tempting because the narration is making you think about bias, but Betteredge offers no judgment on the Blakes.

23. **The correct answer is C.** *The Moonstone* is partly a detective story told with multiple testimonies, but you don't know that from the passage. The only answer that doesn't ask you to leap to conclusions is choice C, which is descriptive and asks you to build on the answers you've been working on. Choices A, D, and E are not supported by any details in the passage. Betteredge may be unreliable as a narrator because he is so digressive, but we don't know the motives or reasons for this narrative quirk, so B is not a good choice.

24. **The correct answer is B.** This question also tests your tendency to leap to conclusions, but it does so by asking you to pick out a likely interpretation for Betteredge's digressions, beyond just being annoyed by them. Option II gives a plausible, interesting explanation for why you've been reading so many digressions about testimony and inheritance: that's the undercurrent of the story. Options I and III make you jump to conclusions and infer material that isn't in the passage, so they are out; B is the only choice that works.

25. **The correct answer is C.** "Worrying" is what a dog does to a bone in chewing it up—Mr. Blake is a lawyer who never gives up a case as he tries to find an advantage in the argument. Betteredge will have to "worry" over the story, and the reader will have to "worry" over all of the minor details, almost like a lawyer—or a detective—would. Anxiety and dread are not noticeably present

in the narrative so far, so choice A is incorrect. There are apparent class divisions in the story so, far, but they aren't revealed by this particular word, "worrying." Choices D and E don't have enough evidence to back them up, so they are out.

26. **The correct answer is D.** These choices are relatively similar to each other, so you have to be careful in picking the one that corresponds to the narration. Narration is the key to the question that you've been preparing for in many of the other questions in this section: what have you been asked about the narrative and what have the choices taught you? Go back and look at question 23, which gives subjectivity as a possible underlying theme in the passage—that's the answer that shows the tension with objectivity in the question. The other answers are too broad and general, and don't address the style of the narration. It's not clear if Betteredge is hiding something (choice A), nor do we have much oral testimony (choice B). Penelope has a different written testimony to the events in her own diary, which she has declined to show because it is subjective—so choice C isn't a good one. Choice E may be generally true, but that's not clear from the narrative style.

27. **The correct answer is E.** The poem is set after work in the cornfield when the speaker comes home and has dinner with his family. It's possible to think that it's bedtime (choice D), but the father plays with his children and sings to them during the poem and then sends them to bed, so it's more accurate to pick choice E than choice D. Holidays, church, and dawn are not referred to in the poem.

28. **The correct answer is D.** The speaker is making shadow-puppets with his family and telling stories about them, so choice D is the best option. He turns these stories into poems (choice C), but that's not what he is

doing in this passage. One might mistakenly think he is drawing pictures, but choice E is not correct. The speaker's wife is making dinner (choice A), not the speaker. Church (choice B) is not mentioned in the passage.

29. **The correct answer is A.** The speaker is playing with his kids and telling them scary stories, but they are delighted by the bogeyman shadow, not terrified or grim (choice C). It is more apt to characterize him as teasing than as mocking (choice B) because he's not being sarcastic—everyone is in on the joke and you get the sense that this is a common story theme for the family. The scene may be slightly rowdy, but he is not childish (choice E). He and his wife may be tired, but the scene is loving and not characterized by short tempers (choice D).

30. **The correct answer is E.** This is a question that shows you all of the different ways you can interpret rhyme in a poem, beyond just describing its structure. Rhyme can give a poem all sorts of additional meaning; it may be useful to keep these interpretive strategies in mind for the essay section as you are thinking about the relationship between form and structure. The poem's rhymed couplets give a sense of the poetry of everyday life (choice A) that's repeated daily as a family tradition that can be sung casually (choices B and C). The poem is part of a long tradition of oral poetry (choice D) that can be recalled easily because of the rhyme scheme. Choice E is the least applicable answer here because it's not really simplified or revolutionary.

31. **The correct answer is A.** There are several close options here, but A is the clearest answer. The conflict is between fathers and sons, but it's not the main *source* of the conflict, so choice B is out. The poem displays humor (choice E), but that's not the conflict—it's the resolution to the conflict.

The poem is not really setting the two types of strength against each other (choice C), as there's no real mention of mental strength, nor is it setting seriousness and cleverness apart (choice D).

32. **The correct answer is C.** "Taste" can mean many different things beyond just flavor of food. Here, you're asked to pick from among meanings of the word related to poetry: a person's preferences for and talents in different "flavors" of writing. The best synonym for taste here is choice C, "aptitude": the speaker is good at writing "flavors" of clever poems. It could be choice A, judgment—like someone's taste in music—but it's not like his father wished he liked different poets, so his father isn't criticizing his judgment in poetry. Other people like the speaker's poetry, but the conflict between him and his father is not about his fame (choice B) or what other people think. The speaker uses humor (choice D) to disarm his father, but he and his father don't disagree about humor, they disagree about the usefulness of poetry. Choice E, generosity, is not discussed in the poem.

33. **The correct answer is B.** The speaker makes a pun based on a homophone (waste and waist) at the end of the poem, which allows him to appropriate his father's criticism for a clever joke. The device is about closely related sounds, not closely related meanings, or synonyms. An epithet is an apt descriptive phrase, but that device is not in play here. You could say generally that the poet reverses the criticism with his appropriative pun, but it's not as clear or obviously correct an answer as choice B. It could be an allusion to someone else's pun, but there's no evidence to suggest that.

34. **The correct answer is E.** All of the options listed are reasonable. His pun appropriates the criticism of his "waste" and turns it

into a strength of his poetic "taste," thus confirming his talent. The speaker is praised for his cleverness, so he uses cleverness as a subtle tool to subvert criticism. It would be difficult to choose one of those options for A, B, or C, and option II is a reasonable choice along with the others, so the answer is E.

35. **The correct answer is C.** As you're asked to find the exception in drawing connections between the two poems, choice C is the obvious answer because there is no rift between the father and his children in the first poem. What's most useful about the other answers, however, is that they will give you clues as to how to find deeper social and cultural meanings in the poem, as the test author is showing you all of the possibilities as reasonable interpretations. You can save up the idea of "questions of identity" (choice A), "labor and poetry" (choice D), and "ephemeral forms" (choice E) for use in later questions that ask you to make inferences and interpretations. Even if you don't know what "ephemeral" means (it means "fleeting" or "quick to disappear"), you can guess that it means something like casual or informal because it refers to bedtime stories, puns, and shadows. You already knew that the poems used humor (choice B), so you know that can't be the exception to this question.

36. **The correct answer is A.** The clearest answer to the question is A, formality and informality, although future questions will ask you to complicate that dichotomy. Both poems explore the use of humor, but humor is not set off against seriousness nor is it opposed to the general definition of poetry, so choices B and C are not correct. It would be very interesting to write about how the use of dialect complicates our notions of writing, but that idea is beyond the scope of this question, so choice D is not the best answer. Likewise, you could write an interesting essay about

how Dunbar represents the role of poetry in family life in these poems, but that's not what this question is asking, so choice E is not the best answer, either.

37. **The correct answer is E.** When you're looking at a question about dichotomies, it's best to say to yourself that *he's exploring the nuances and contradictions inside of that dichotomy*, rather than setting it up as a *total opposition*. Dichotomies are made to be complicated and explored, not just contrasted. As you're writing the free response essays, you might want to keep that complexity in mind, and the answers to this question and question 35 give you some language for articulating those nuances: "the tensions between . . .", "questions about how people perceive the dichotomies differently . . .", "blurs some of the distinctions." In this question, you're asked to find the complexity, so options I and III are obvious choices. Option II is trickier: it talks about emphasizing the distinction, which seems to move in the opposite direction as the prompt. What really seals the correct answer is that there's no option for I, II, and III, so you can choose the two most correct-seeming ones (I and III) and not worry about whether II could be correct.

38. **The correct answer is D.** This question asks you to make inferences about Dunbar's historical and social importance. The word "registers" in choice A refers to style and tone, and it basically states the fact that he wrote in both vernacular and formal style to show how he could code-switch in different racial and social contexts. Choice B also states a surface judgment about what major and minor mean—and thus who gets to be major or minor is a question related to race. You can tell that choice C is a reasonable interpretation because it would be difficult to argue with it, even if you're not familiar with particular ballad poets. Even if you

don't know the historical reference points for Paul Laurence Dunbar (or choice E, W.E.B. Dubois), you can still make some inferences on this question. Dubois is too specific a reference to be a total distraction, so choice E is probably a reasonable interpretation of the question. That leaves choice D, which leaps to some conclusions and makes statements about Dunbar's life and writing that would be hard to back up with just these two poems. It is the least good choice, so it stands as the exception and thus the correct answer.

39. **The correct answer is C.** The estate's isolation is mentioned several times, so "cloistered" is an apt adjective, yet the Marquis makes sure that his daughter has every kind of access to education and learning she could possibly have. He has set up an "erudite" life for her—even if she then chooses to explore the fantasy world of romances because she is cooped up inside. The Marquis is wealthy enough to bring in tutors, so they are not impoverished, and she is described as "secluded" so frequently that it can hardly be a "cozy" atmosphere: choice A is out. Arabella is pampered, but we don't really see any evidence of pettiness in her seclusion, so choice B is also out. Likewise, her fantasies may be romantic, but she is not in any danger because she never meets anyone else to indulge those fantasies or to be friendly with, so choices D and E are also incorrect.

40. **The correct answer is A.** The second paragraph is long and detailed, with some unfamiliar language, so this question asks you to wade through it strategically to find the main idea. You can skip some of the words you don't know; you don't need to find the significance of the capitalized nouns, even if they look strange to you. Choice B, "distracted by grief," might be tempting if you read only the first couple of sentences, but

the main idea is that he's very devoted to his daughter, so the answer is choice A. He teaches Arabella how to read and write— hardly whimsical subjects, so D is incorrect. He adores his daughter for many reasons, including her "Quickness of Apprehension," so he doesn't seem to be correcting her, as choice C suggests. Reading and writing are pragmatic subjects today, but this option speaks more to managing the estate, so E is also not a good choice.

41. **The correct answer is D.** The sentences in these paragraphs are long, so you have to read them carefully to understand what the narrator is getting at. The objections in the choices are mentioned in the passage, in one way or another, but choice D is the clearest explanation of the narrator's critique of the novels Arabella is reading. The books are "very bad translations" of French, so choice A is incorrect. Choice B is possible because the narrator mentions the Marquis's grief and his moving his late wife's books into his library, but it also neglects the rest of the passage where choice D is enumerated in detail. Choice C is not likely, because there's no mention of Arabella doing any chores at all. The "real pictures from life" mentioned in the passage doesn't refer to pictorial images, but of her imagination, the fantasy pictures in her mind as she's reading. Choice E is a misreading of that archaic use of the word "pictures."

42. **The correct answer is B.** The idea here is that Arabella would have become a serious intellectual reader had she not frittered away her reading attention on silly romances. The counterfactual shows a path that she did not take, which will indicate the course of the novel's plot. It is not a hyperbole because it doesn't exaggerate her choices or behavior, so A is incorrect. It does not tell Arabella—or readers—explicitly what they should do, so it is not an imperative

(choice C). It is more important than an anecdote (choice D), because it is the focus of the entire passage. It is not an example of ethos because it's not making a claim about Arabella that we should be persuaded by or respond to emotionally—this is a piece of fiction, not an argument about the value (or lack thereof) of romances.

43. **The correct answer is C.** "This" is an unclear antecedent: it's not immediately clear what "this" is referring to. All you have to do is track back through the long sentence to figure out what "this" means in the surrounding context: every other passion was subordinate to (less important than) love, the "ruling principle of the world." Choice A is incorrect because though she learns about love through reading romances, it is the subject matter of love she considers the main passion of the world, not reading. She has learned how to dance (choice B), but it is not as important as reading. She does not prefer the solitude of the isolated estate, so choice D is obviously incorrect. Choice E is not the best answer because she specifically refers to the notion of love, not flirtation.

44. **The correct answer is D.** This question asks you the main idea of this passage: Arabella interacts only with the characters she meets in her silly romances, so she loses touch with the outside world that she's secluded from. The clearest statement of this idea is choice D. Choice E is tempting because it voices one of the main critiques of fiction for its unreality, but Arabella's problems aren't with truth and lies, but with fantasy and reality. She is not especially fearful of the outside world (choice A) because she doesn't realize that it's different from the world inside her books. It may be the case that no real-life suitors will ever meet her in seclusion (choice B), but that's not the main problem under discussion because the narrator is more focused on her current behavior, not her

future plans. The narrator describes her fluency in her lessons and doesn't mention any over-correction on her father's part, so choice C is unlikely.

45. **The correct answer is A.** This question asks you to link a stylistic choice to a larger narrative perspective. Choice A shows the narrator correcting Arabella's perspective in the third-person narration—it's a very slight ripple in the narration that indicates some of the subtle hints of satire. Choice B is not a good choice for multiple reasons: previous questions have all indicated that the narrator has opinions, so there is no objective perspective to be found and there is no evidence of another character speaking. The father doesn't speak in the narration, so choice C is incorrect. There is no evidence of an autobiographical or unreliable narrator here, so choices D and E may be leaping to conclusions.

46. **The correct answer is B.** This question has a couple of possible answers, but you get a clue about what to focus on in the word "long": it's not just telling you where to look for the sentence, but what characterizes the rhetorical device that you're supposed to identify. *Many* sentences in this passage are very long and winding, but this question asks you to zero in on one to identify how and why it serves the narrator's purpose. You can eliminate choice A immediately because there is no comparative language to signal an analogy. "By them she was taught to believe..." is a long sentence with three clauses set off by "that": that love was the most important thing in the world, that every other passion was less important, that love causes everything to happen. This structure is an example of parallel structure, choice B, and it allows the narrator to call attention to all of the inflated ideas that delude Arabella. The long sentence emphasizes the silliness of the items it is enumerating. Arabella's

beliefs look silly when they are piled together so elaborately, but the narrator is not exaggerating how seriously she believes them, so it's not hyperbole (choice C). A tautology is a circular, repetitive argument, and while the clauses are repetitive, they are building on each other rather than proving each other as a tautology (choice D) would do. Indeed, the narrator is not making an argument based on logic, so choice E is out.

47. **The correct answer is E.** This question asks you to make an inference about the author's perspective, but that's dangerous territory in which to tread, because it can cause you to project or jump to conclusions based on a short passage. The best answer is the most cautious, descriptive answer, rather than one that tries to read too much into the relationship among the three figures. We can't really even be sure that the narrator is female, so choice A is out. Choice B reads too much into an autobiographical interpretation of the novel and is not substantiated by the text. The narrator clearly shows an opinion about romances in lines like the counterfactual "she would have been" intellectually ambitious had she not read so many "unfortunate" translations of romances. Thus choice C is not a good choice: We can't tell from this short passage whether the narrator is unreliable (choice D), so we shouldn't be too specific in prescribing narrative intention yet.

48. **The correct answer is E.** If you know about Jane Austen's *Sense and Sensibility*, you may know about the somewhat outdated use of the word "sensibility" to mean "sensitivity to strong emotions." It can be confusing because we use "sensible" to mean levelheaded and rational now. Even if you don't know the novel or the word's eighteenth-century definition—which is understandable!—you can still deduce the right answer by eliminating the obviously

wrong choices. There is no mention of the oppression of women in the passage so choice A is out. There hasn't been a problem for Arabella to solve in the narrative yet, so choice B is unlikely, too. She is alone, so she has no conversation to miss—choice C is tempting because you the reader want Arabella to have friends, but that's not what she herself is lamenting here. No one is criticizing her directly, so choice D is also incorrect. If you had to choose between choices C and E, you could think about the word "disappearance" and whether conversation had actually ever been apparent or present in her life. Choice E is the best option, for she has mistaken the strong emotions in the romance novels for the way that real people behave in daily life.

49. **The correct answer is B.** Questions 45-47 have pointed you toward reading this passage as satirical by asking you to characterize the narrator's perspective and look at stylistic details that signal judgment and mild caricature. There are no adjectives that mark it as reverent, so choice A is not a good option. The narrator has noted that Arabella faces no dangers outside of her own fantasy, so choice C is not a good option either. The passage is about the subject of romance, but it is not romantic because it is casting some subtle aspersions on Arabella's swooning, melodramatic behavior. Choice E cannot be correct because previous questions have indicated a narrative perspective, not an objective absence of one.

50. **The correct answer is D.** This question asks you to interpret a slightly archaic vocabulary word ("glass," meaning mirror) through considering the main idea of the passage. There are several clear, correct answers that have already been mentioned in previous questions: she is vain (choice A) and has a distorted interpretation of what she reads and sees (choices B and C), and she is limited

by her secluded home life. The only answer that doesn't fit is choice D, and we can guess that Arabella is so self-satisfied with being a heroine that she imagines herself to be the most beautiful girl in the world. The narrator tells us that her father believes that about her, so there's no evidence of her self-criticism. Choice D is the outlier and thus the correct answer.

51. The correct answer is C. As you have just analyzed the narrator's characterization of the glass, now you are thinking about its larger narrative function. Options I and II are reasonable notions that have been established by previous questions; indeed, one of the traditional functions of satire is to hold up a glass to society that exposes its faults. It might be tempting to pick Option III as well because that is a traditional symbolic function of a mirror, to lead into another world. However, options II and III cannot both be true because the mirror can't reflect satire AND be an escape in this passage, and the narrator has been critical of Arabella's escapist reading. That contradiction means that you can strike choices D and E. The correct answer is that it is both I and II, or option C.

52. The correct answer is D. "Vicissitude" is not a word you hear often, and you're more likely to slide over it and try to figure it out in context when you do see it in reading. Here, you can do just that and figure it out from the long string of nouns after it: hopes, fears, wishes, and disappointments. The best answer that accounts for all of those items is choice D, a series of rapid changes in those feelings. Arabella has not suffered any major tragedies, nor is her daily life unpredictable; in the narrator's eyes, it is too sheltered, too predictable, so choices A and B are out. She does read a lot, as choice C indicates, but the rest of the sentence indicates that the focus is on how the reading affects her, beyond just

its contents. It is impossible to know what's going to happen after the passage ends, so choice E is not a good option.

53. The correct answer is A. The narrator's satirical tone is becoming more and more apparent, and the word "trifling," or frivolous and unimportant, starts to expose the judgment more sharply. The sharpness of that judgment is best characterized as condescending (choice A), for it shows the narrator's sense of superiority to judge what's important or unimportant. The pairing with "vicissitudes" from question 52 also indicates the darker shadings of disapproval in the narrator's tone and vocabulary. If you are unsure about this characterization of the narrator's increasingly less subtle tone of judgment, you can also eliminate the other choices. It would be several steps too far to attribute the narrator's judgments to feelings of rejection, so that answer is incorrect. Arabella is being whimsical in her romantic fantasies, but the narrator is not, so choice C is incorrect. The narrator seems more annoyed with Arabella's overreactions than she seems caring or worried, so choices D and E are less good choices. The best answer is choice A, and it makes sense within the progression of the narration.

54. The correct answer is D. The best answer is choice D, which accounts for the elaborate rhetorical devices like the counterfactuals and grandiose parallel structures: the long sentences may not be "fun" for you to read, but they are fun and pleasurable for the narrator to deliver in a satirical tone. Although you've been seeing the increasingly sharp judgmental language of the narration, here you're confronted with several bad reductions of those judgments, which are all false answers. Choices A, B, C, and E are not supported by the narrator, who never makes a claim about what Arabella's father should do. This is perhaps the distinction between being satirical and condescending, as opposed to being paternalistic and condemnatory. The question is asking you to ease up on the judgment and find some nuance in the passage.

55. **The correct answer is A.** This question builds on previous ones about the increasingly satirical tone of the narration, but it has a tricky construction that asks you to find some subtlety and nuance. As question 54 suggests, it would be a mistake to flatten out the passage into a single strong lesson without considering the ironies—including the fact that you're reading a novel about the dangers of novel-reading. There is no evidence to suggest unreliability, so option II is unlikely and thus choices B, D, and E are out. It would be fascinating to write an essay about option III, but the evidence for that essay would come from reader responses, not solely from this passage, so option C is out. Therefore, choice A is the best answer.

Section II

Essay Question 1: Volpone, Ben Jonson

<u>8-9 Sample Essay</u>

Every villain needs an audience to feed his ego, but every villain also needs a parasite who feeds on him. Is the audience a form of a parasite, who seems to take in the villain's performance with appreciative whistles and demonstrative boos and hisses, all the while extracting something from him unwittingly? We can test that idea by considering the role of Mosca in Ben Jonson's play <u>Volpone</u>. Mosca is Volpone's first audience in his opening lines of the play: he pulls the curtain back and listens to Volpone's hyperbolic gloating about his riches. He even agrees with his boss. We don't know what will happen after these first 40 lines of the play, but Mosca's role is like the little fly that won't stop buzzing around the theater, causing the audience to be perplexed as to what his role is. He sits between the audience and their paradox of loving to hate the villain, an unstable place indeed. He is in control of the curtain.

It seems that Mosca reveals the gold, but he is really revealing a kind of golden mirror in which the audience can see themselves and their own position reflected on the stage. The dark theatre with the curtain rising is like Volpone's own vision of how the gold "Shew'st like a flame by night; or like the day /Struck out of chaos" (lines 9-10). The audience is in the same position as Volpone peering into his own opened curtain. Volpone highlights the reflective qualities of the gold and his seeing his own reflection to admire, calling it "brighter than thy father, let me kiss, / With adoration, thee," (lines 12-13). It is simple to see that Volpone sees himself in the gold; he is kissing his own reflection in self-adoration and in adoration of what he has amassed. But the audience is covetous, too, because they have come to admire the props, the set, the costumes that are like the "hoard" of "every relick /Of sacred treasure, in this blessed room" (lines 8, 13-14). Mosca sits between the audience and their reflected desires, in control of one curtain. He is an uncertain figure: is he seeing himself reflected? Is he coveting the same hoard as all of the other viewers?

Mosca's role is uncertain, caught in the middle. He gets to finish Volpone's sentence to agree with him, but what do we make of this interruption, only to agree? An interruption should be more significant. It could show a turn or a reversal, but his line "Riches are in fortune
A greater good than wisdom is in nature" (29-30) is merely a restatement of Volpone's more bombastic line. What is the function of this line that seems like an old adage or a cliche? Volpone doesn't take any notice and continues on with his speech about the depths of his villainy: he has obtained his gold through "cunning" rather than "common" (32, 34) ways, two words that sound similar enough to show the sharp distinction between Volpone's cons and others'

honest work. We may remember the other adage in play here, that cons are the most frequently conned because they are so convinced of their own powers of cunning. If there is one thing an audience loves more than a villain, it's a sudden reversal of fortune that shows the paradox in action, rather than just creating tension. The reversal is the payoff to the paradox's structural instability and tension.

But what of Mosca, who stands between the audience and Volpone, in the middle of all that tension? His name seems to indicate that he will be extracting something from the villain. It is unwise to speculate further as an essayist, yet this is the audience's job as the hold the strings of tension that create the sense of theatricality and performance. Their reactions create and maintain the tension. Volpone gives a long list of money-making ventures he eschews: "no trade, no venture," no ship speculation, and so on. With so many negations, we realize that he has nothing without his performance of the con; he needs to perform in order to make money. He needs an audience. The audience has handed over their money to the theater, but they control its fortunes.

The audience loves the villain Volpone because they are in control of his fortunes through their money and applause, whereas Mosca the minor character seems to exist in the liminal space on the threshold, and his role is uncertain. We cannot speculate on him, just like Volpone cannot speculate for riches, but we have a sure bet in Volpone.

Reader response for the 8-9 essay

This is an audacious premise of a **rhetorical question about the audience's role as a parasite,** but the author follows through to write an original, memorable answer to the question. The essay develops richness through **inspired close analysis of language from the play,** all in the service of a **strong, clear idea that develops complexity over the course of the paragraphs.** It even follows a five-paragraph format, with **a repeated structural device** of the rhetorical question as the glue between paragraphs.

What could students take from this essay as a model? **The best essays have a strong idea of what they want to do.** It seems clear that this author **annotated the text and had some critical vocabulary to make it sing.** The author **doesn't just repeat the suggestions for devices** to analyze in the original question, although they inspired the initial points about figurative language (the gold is like a mirror) and the hyperbole as an indicator of Volpone's self-aware performance.

The final line is memorable--it seems to take the weakness of some of the final lines of previous paragraphs, which drift into speculation about what will happen next, and it reverses it into a gotcha! sentence.

5-6 Sample Essay

As the person who delivers the opening speech of Ben Jonson's Volpone, the character of Volpone is both the protagonist and the villain. This puts the audience in a paradoxical position of being invested in his fortunes--literally, his gold fortunes--but also in disliking him for his obvious character flaws like greed, gloating, and sly trickery. This essay will analyze that paradox by looking at figurative language, hyperbole, and his interactions with Mosca.

Volpone is an appealing speaker who charms the audience with his cockiness and seductive figurative language. In line 11 he builds a structure of figurative language about gold as the son of the Sun (Sol), to show how brightly it glows. Who would not be attracted to such a vivid metaphor and use of figurative language? Who would not be attracted to such a beautiful sight or beautiful language. Everyone is seduced by his metaphors. He thinks of himself as a poet by referring to the Golden Age: "Well did wise poets, by thy glorious name, /Title that age which they would have the best" (lines 15-16), which shows that he is comparing himself to a poet in his own descriptions. Which he is because he is a great seducer with language.

His use of hyperbole is also seductive. He thinks gold is the best, so it deserves the highest comparisons, which means that it deserves hyperbole. He says "the best of things: and far transcending / All style of joy, in children, parents, friends, /Or any other waking dream on earth: / Thy looks when they to Venus did ascribe, / They should have given her twenty thousand Cupids." (lines 17-21). He is saying that it can only be described with the highest praise from all people, and even from "waking dreams" which he personifies as an extra audience to give that praise. He is excessive even in writing a hyperbole. Venus is a Roman goddess, so she is the height of power, and she gets an excess of Cupids in her own part of the hyperbole. It is like he is Oprah, shouting out "you get a car, and you get a car, and you get a car!" But all of the cars come to him because all of the gold belongs to him. The hyperbole is pleasing other people in its outrageousness, but it only serves him.

His selfishness is portrayed through his interactions with Mosca, who bows down to him and agrees with him. Mosca is like the sidekick on the talk show who starts the laughter when the audience isn't responding--he is the hype man, opening the curtain to reveal the gold to the audience. Mosca is such a sidekick that he is called a parasite or an insignificant fly. He only agrees with Volpone when he says "Riches are in fortune /A greater good than wisdom is in nature." He is just agreeing that it's better to be rich than wise.

The villain has to be punished in plays like this one. When you open with so much boasting, where else can you go? Volpone will probably have something happen to him that causes him to lose his gold because he is setting himself up for a heist or something. A heist would be interesting to watch because it would be like the reverse of the revelation of the gold in lines 2-3--you could get to watch him get out-foxed!

Reader response for the 5-6 essay

This is a **superficial essay where the author loses track of the essay question** about why audiences have a complicated, paradoxical relationship with characters they love to hate. The author **makes gestures toward quoting lines** but mostly **summarizes them instead of analyzing them.** By the third body paragraph, there's less attention to the main problem, as the author has lost the essay to **summarizing and describing** Mosca.

This essay question may be especially challenging, because very few students will be familiar with the play. They aren't expected to know the plot, but **they may feel anxious about speculating or filling in the gaps** of the entire rest of the plot. The stronger essays will ignore that trap because speculation will just **waste space and time that you could be using to analyze what's actually on the page.** The stronger essays will focus on the complicated language in these forty lines, because there's plenty of rich material.

In this essay, there are these charming, funny moments when the author's personality shines through the artificial, superficial essay: in comparing Volpone to Oprah and in comparing him to a talk show host's sidekick or hype man. These moments aren't exactly appropriate for the exam, but they are also places where the author **could have pursued the idea that led him to the unlikely comparisons.** What is it about Volpone's talents as a **hyperbolic showman** that make him both seductive and repellant? The essayist could have started with the idea of the hyperbole as a strategy to attract and repel with exaggerated performance, rather than relegating it to a discrete example buried in the five-paragraph format. It would have been interesting to take that idea of Mosca as the hypeman and explore what **it means for Volpone to need an audience for his performance.**

Can a villain ever be satisfied? What happens to their performance when they get what they want, and if Volpone is already at the apex, what else can he get?

1-2 Sample Essay

> In this passage from <u>Volpone</u> by Ben Johnson, the speaker is admiring his gold
> First he compares it to a Saint, showing a blasphemous, idolatrous relationship
> with the gold. You should never compare your wealth to a religious figure
> because that shows that you are worshipping the wrong thing. It symbolizes
> that he is going to get punished. Furthermore, he compares it to a ram that is
> like a nature god in line 6, so he is offending everyone with his similes. The
> speaker is offensive and likes being offensive--you can see imagine him walking
> around like he owns the place (and maybe he does).

> He continues being offensive with his metaphors in calling it sacred in line
> 14, so he is foreshadowing that he going to get in trouble. It's not enough
> for him to say that he doesn't steal or commit usury--he is still greedy, which
> is unappealing. It is not easy to like the speaker because he has so many bad
> behaviors. Therefore it is impossible to love him because you just want him to
> be punished.

<u>Reader response for the 1-2 essay</u>

This reader used the essay space to judge Volpone (who is never named, a bad sign), summarize the play's language, and speculate about what might happen, which was not a good use of the space. The essay prompt asks exam-takers to agree to part of the question--the paradox that audiences love to hate villains--in order to enter into the analysis of the play. It's **better to just agree to that initial paradox so that you can enter into the essay format on the same terms** as other authors, instead of rejecting it totally with a flat-out disagreement. **You may quibble with the terms or reject parts of them as you develop your analysis; that's how you create a complex essay** that doesn't just restate the question. By specifying the paradox, however, the instructions provide some helpful boundaries or limitations in which to frame the essay and start writing. **Those limitations actually make it easier to write because there's a starting place--a paradox**, a literary device that's worth analyzing for **the tensions it creates between audiences and actors**. The *personal opinion* of the character matters less than the analysis of HOW he acts as a villain to the other characters onstage.

Perhaps the author's strong sense of moral judgment could have served the essay well as a device for diving deeper into the paradox, instead of rejecting it outright. Why does Volpone tread into those dangerous waters of blasphemy and idolatry? Why does he risk being offensive by calling it sacred? There may be something worth analyzing in his constant push to the bounds of good taste; **perhaps that boundary-pushing creates an interesting tension with the audience?**

Essay Question 2: The Song of the Lark, Willa Cather

<u>8-9 Sample Essay</u>

As Thea Kronberg descends into Panther Canyon, she feels like she has totally new eyes to see the world. These eyes are less focused on darting around to notice day-to-day distractions; they are more focused on looking inward, meditatively, on her own life and its relationship to the natural world. One might say that she is moving from observation to reflection, a sign of inner growth. But such a characterization is too easy and reduces the scene to a kind of cliched aha! moment referenced in the first sentences of this very paragraph, full of cliches about seeing through new eyes, about the dangers of distraction. Those cliches are seductive because we want to believe in a character's inner growth. Yet there are signs that something is amiss in Thea's narration of her realization, and it is up to the reader to be both observant and reflective about how both she and we project our own desires onto the natural world.

Thea distinguishes between her vision in Panther Canyon and in Chicago by how she sees new details in nature that she would have just generalized before. She finds new ways of seeing in her stillness, the freedom from not being subject to the monotonous, pounding rhythms of urban life. Whereas before she was "hurrying and sputtering, as if she had been born behind time and had been trying to catch up," she now waits and "reflects" on her new perceptions. She has some leftover judgments in calling it "idleness" or laziness, but perhaps that judgmental language lets her sharpen the distinction between now and then.

In the stillness and quietness of nature, she can slow down and take in new details. What is striking, however, is that in claiming she can now see so much more, she makes herself into a <u>busy</u> viewer whose eyes are always on. If roses were just roses in Chicago, now she sees not only the moonflowers above Mrs. Tellamantez's door, but also "masses of prickly-pear blossoms she had found in the desert in early childhood, . . . grape leaves and the mint bed." This may be a welcome change for Thea, but it's not as much of a change from the "hurrying from one task to another" in her past. In quotes like that one, we see that she can't actually stop being a busy viewer, no matter how much she wishes she could slow down. This makes her habits of reflection somewhat suspect--not because she is lying, but because she is still over-thinking and processing like a busy person would. She is not as still as she thinks she is.

It is unclear if Thea realizes how much of a pathetic fallacy she is committing when she says "how easy it would be to dream one's life out of some cleft in the world" like Panther Canyon. Perhaps she does realize that it's a fallacy; after all, she says it's easy. She projects her own prior "timidity" onto the swarm of swallows who don't break out of their familiar flock. The function of the pathetic fallacy is not just a fallacy or an error, however; it is Thea's vehicle or tool for contemplation. She uses the pathetic fallacy of imagining herself a color or a sensation in the landscape as a tool for getting outside her head. She is using contemplation like a tool, like a busy person would--she <u>must</u> reflect, she <u>must</u> learn, grow, and change from these reflections. Reflection becomes instrument. Her "effort" is not "undirected" but instead directed toward describing everything in elaborate poetic detail!

Clearly, that "fallacy" of effort and projection does not ruin the passage, but it does suggest that these natural reveries are not diametrically different than what she used to be like. She reflects with this tool, which signals that she has some control over it. The world is not swimming over her; she is projecting herself onto it. It is a kind of guided meditation that allows for more control than she's saying in ecstatic quotes like "her power to think seemed converted into a power of sustained sensation." The appeal of a line like that one is undeniable, for we want to have those kinds of sublime encounters with nature. The language is seductive because we take on that power when we contemplate it as readers. As readers, we also want to go with characters like Thea Kronberg on a journey, so we project ourselves onto her to find our own paths, like she projected herself onto nature. It is easier to identify with a novel's character than with heat or color, but we should not pretend that we are ever wholly.

After all, human perception and language shapes our encounters with the natural world. We are always busy making metaphors and poetry out of our visions, even when we think we're being idle.

Reader response for the 8-9 essay

This is an ambitious essay that impresses with its elegant integration of well-chosen quotations and the author's desire to philosophize beyond the easy dichotomy of busyness and idleness in the quotation. The author has constructed a dynamic structure by pointing out the limitations of the dichotomy in the first paragraph, before diving into the text to find evidence of tensions in the language, not just evidence of one "side" or another. That tension creates the insight about how Thea is still busy, even as she thinks she's idle, because she is still processing and thinking as she's reflecting. The simple statement, "she is not as still as she thinks she is" is a simple, clear articulation that is a nice stylistic change from some of the pontification and overly complex sentences.

The author is astute in saying that she uses description as a tool--it's a clever of inversion of the writer's toolbox of examining discrete literary devices like diction, imagery, tone, etc. Instead of using that writer's toolbox to analyze the scene, the author locates that same toolbox in Thea's own reflective toolkit. She too is using tools to process the world, like the student is processing the passage.

This inventive analysis allows the author to ask the big "so what" question about why we want to believe Thea as she reflects in such beautiful language that Cather uses. The author has identified projection as a tool like pathetic fallacy, and so zooms out to consider how readers project themselves onto books, as Thea has projected herself onto the natural world. This is an ambitious move that prompts some big-picture pontification and generalization, but it's a believable argument that allows for a sophisticated reading of the passage.

The author's work is an interesting model because it resists the either/or approach to find complexity, and the passages reflect a nuanced reading. If students were going to imitate this author's "moves" it might work best to say:

A. **Identify the paradox in the question**—we're never fully idle when we're writing because that activity takes not just reflection but creation.

B. **Analyze two or three fragment quotations that illustrate the shades of gray in that paradox**: e.g., even a beautiful description of flowers is still full of details that needed work to be observed.

C. **Analyze another quotation that shows a full literary device** like the pathetic fallacy, but show how the device has nuances in it, not just that the author employs it. How does the device show a surprising effect beyond what it normally does as device, e.g., how does the poetic fallacy act as an engine for generating more descriptive language and grandiose insights about power?

D. **Take apart the most grandiose quotation in the passage** by showing that it has more shades of meaning than just "grand reflection of an idea." Here the author picks the quotation about "power" and reads it skeptically—the power is not just natural reflection, but human-generated action of description, not idleness

E. **Discuss the "so what" of this revelation that the scene is more complex** than it appears.

5-6 Sample Essay

In Willa Cather's novel, *The Song of the Lark*, we learn the lesson with Thea Kronberg that we all need to step back and smell the roses sometimes. Not just roses--also moonflowers, mint, and other kinds of vegetation. Cather makes an argument for the value of sensory perception in this passage, for Thea has never realized so much about herself as when she is paying attention to what she sees, hears, feels, smells, and tastes. She would not have been able to pay that kind of attention if she was still as busy as she used to be; therefore, it is important to slow down and really see the world. Cather uses sensory details, diction, and other literary devices in order to show this point.

Thea uses all five senses in this passage. She starts by saying that her newfound attention is on "fragrance and color and sound, but almost nothing to do with words." She can see the swallows, hear the cicadas, smell the different flowers, feel the sunlight, and taste food. The change in her senses are all obvious in this quote: "It was much more like a sensation than like an idea, or an act of remembering. Music had never come to her in that sensuous form before. It had always been a thing to be struggled with." She is now better at just sensing in the moment rather than worrying about it or struggling with it. This improvement is clear in the vivid sensory details.

Thea's diction shows complexity in long sentences like the one in the paragraph above, and also in this quote: "she could become a mere receptacle for heat, or become a color, like the bright lizards . . . she could become a continuous repetition of sound, like the cicadas." The long sentences show the way the details fit together in a long train of thought. Probably in Chicago she would not have written such a long sentence with so many details. This shows her change in mind that came because she slowed down.

The other literary device she uses in addition to diction and sensory details is the pathetic fallacy, or seeing her own emotions reflected in nature. She does that in several places like with the cicadas, the laughing aspens, and the birds in the last paragraph. She wouldn't have been able to do that if she were busy because she wouldn't be looking closely enough to see what she was thinking.

These three devices show the value of Cather's argument about the need to slow down. Thea Kronberg only learns her true inner self when she slows down.

Reader response for the 5-6 essay

This is a partly competent essay that seems to be **hampered by the artificial set-up of the five-paragraph structure and a lack of analysis**. The author seems to be **ticking off boxes** of devices to list and quotations to summarize rather than analyze.

The author has picked out some interesting details of the natural descriptions, but seems unsure how to connect those details to the question that the prompt is asking about busyness. **Without that**

clear connection, the author summarizes the question instead of analyzing it, **repeating phrases** like "the need to slow down."

The author **overuses cliched language** like "stop and smell the roses" (although the comparison with the other flowers is clever) and "true inner self." That cliché stands out for its blandness in a passage that describes one's growing self-awareness in such vivid language.

One way that the author could make a significant change in the essay's setup is use a phrase like **"Cather shows the tension between idleness and busyness," instead of saying that she's making an argument** or proving a point. Novels rarely prove points or arguments--essays do that, but rarely do novels make such a black-and-white case a lesson. If the author were looking for tensions, there's one in the chosen quotation about the way that Thea used to struggle with music--that word "struggle" indicates a kind of tension that would allow for deeper analysis of the surrounding language and a more complex, detailed analysis.

The last two paragraphs are all summary and no quotations; for an essay that asks for close analysis of language, **summary is not enough, especially when illustrating a literary device** like the pathetic fallacy. The laughing aspens were an apt example to pick out, but they're brushed over quickly.

<u>1-2 Sample Essay</u>

You shouldn't be busy all the time, but you shouldn't be lazy either. You have to find a happy medium, the way that Thea does in the passage. She starts off busy hiking, but she finally slows down and enjoys nature without thinking too much. We need that kind of balance, as the author shows in her descriptions and literary devices.

She talks about being hurried and anxious until she gets into the canyon and sits on the blanket. She needs to find a happy medium between working and playing, so she can take time every day to go on a hike and "listen to the whir" of her thoughts. She needs to slow down and start hearing the "music" of nature.

The use of the passive voice in the line "was never highly developed" shows that she is not in full command of her life because it is running her, not the other way around. Therefore, she needs to relax in nature, like she does in the last paragraph when she sees the birds and realizes that it would be "easy to dream one's life out in some cleft in the world."

<u>Reader response for the 1-2 essay</u>

This essay shows an author who has run out of time and who is reading the passage quickly and writing just a short blurb. The author shows a superficial reading with the **artificial set-up of the two opposed poles that need to find a "happy medium."** Not only does the author artificially devise those two poles, but the **"happy medium" is a cliché that generalizes any complexity** that might be explored in an essay. The author quotes only **single words that, by themselves, are not useful for analysis.** The author does not attempt analysis, so the single word quotations just look like a last-minute attempt to fulfill the prompt.

Essay Question 3: Reader's Choice

<u>8-9 Sample Essay</u>

Audiences are familiar with the public banquet scene in Act III of *Macbeth*, after Banquo has been murdered and the newly powerful title character can barely contain his conflicted feelings in front of the assembled group and Lady Macbeth. In fact the audience has seen another banquet scene that is less public during Macbeth's memorable private soliloquy, "if it twere well it were done quickly." The stage directions show that people are setting up another banquet around him as he schemes--such is the life of a Scottish thane, always hosting people and then worrying about the power dynamics on display. These two scenes illustrate the complicated private and public reactions caused by these elaborate displays of power and deference. They mean that the characters must be performers two times over: they are performing intricate acts of power struggles and betrayals for each other in the hall, while they are also performing for the audience. The audience sees the struggle to reconcile those two over-lapping performances. Most of the time, the actors cannot see it themselves.

In a soliloquy like Macbeth's in Act I, he is speaking directly to the audience as an aside--he is both private and public in this iconically theatrical device. Macbeth turns over his scheming to kill Duncan and seize power. He notes the duplicity of his action when he says that he is in "double trust" as a subject and a kinsman. This duplicity and double trust extends to his position as an actor on a stage who is sharing his inner thoughts with an audience that is both present and absent--it's not as though he acknowledges the audience when he is not performing a soliloquy. No, it's the act of soliloquizing, of performing, that brings up the "double trust" because it casts doubt on reality.

Macbeth seems to be most uncertain of the double trust and the problem of his having to perform when he has to act self-consciously for others. He is thoughtful in his soliloquy in Act I, but it all falls apart in Act III, scene 4 when he has to perform as though he doesn't know that Banquo has been murdered. He shows his conflict when he says at the beginning of the scene: "Ourself will mingle with society / And play the humble host." He has never liked having to perform humbleness in front of society in order to maintain power dynamics, but now that illusion is starting to crumble onstage in front of him. Having destroyed the terms of his "double trust" of kinship and service in his murderous actions, he does not know what his identity is. He starts to see the ghost of Banquo in the banquet hall--<u>or is it a manifestation of his own guilt at being unable to handle the breakdown of the "double trust" facade</u>? The ghost treads a similar kind of "is this real?" situation for the audience that the soliloquy did: they seem to be seeing something that the actors don't. The ghost problematizes the public/private distinction because it appears to Macbeth in the privacy of his own madness onstage, but that madness is also public to the audience. The other characters cannot perceive the source of this strangeness, but they, too, notice that something is going wrong.

Lady Macbeth is the character with the least conflict between private and public with a gracious performance of being a gracious hostess who can cover for her husband. She literally covers up his bad behavior with the "sauce" of ceremony--she is trying to return to the familiar performance space of elaborate kinship rituals. She does not realize that Macbeth can no longer function inside that performance space.

Macbeth is not as much of a play about acting as, say, Hamlet, but it does make commentary on the nature of having to perform deference. Is the deference to those about to be murdered, like Duncan and Banquo, or are Macbeth and Lady Macbeth also anxious about their performance for those they cannot fully see--the audience who are like ghosts?

<u>Reader response for the 8-9 essay</u>

This essay rambles a bit, especially in the third paragraph, but it's a strong idea that shows command of sophisticated ideas about performance and meta-theater (theater about the function of performance among the characters, or theater about theatricality). It would not be surprising if this were an **adaptation of a class essay assignment** about this subject of performing soliloquies, for the author seems to have **remembered key details and fragments of quotations that fit her argument** about the role of performance in Macbeth. Some of the seams of the adaptation show, but it is still ambitious and interesting to read.

The author starts with a clear structure of comparing two separate scenes and showing how the themes of the play change from Act I's soliloquy to Act III's public banquet. The author **pushes beyond the basic distinction** that a soliloquy is private and introduces the key idea, that the Macbeths are always aware of their own performances of schemes and betrayal, always conflicted by that constant performance and self-awareness. The author adds an even more interesting complexity by **implicating the audience** in this vexing self-awareness.

This is a complex juggling act, to be sure, and it's not always successful. It is, however, interesting and ambitious, and it led me to reconsider the play through this compelling lens that illuminates new ideas. The essay loses some momentum in the Lady Macbeth paragraph, where there's less detail and analysis, but the (fragment) quotation about the sauce of ceremony is a thoughtful way to bring the analysis back to **her initial articulation of her analytical lens** on the play in the essay's introductory paragraph.

<u>5-6 Sample Essay</u>

To address the question of how a party scene reflects the conflict between public and private behavior, we may look at how the banquet scene in Macbeth relates. It relates because it is a conflict between Macbeth's private guilt about ordering Banquo's death, and it takes place in public as he is at a banquet where Banquo is supposed to be a guest. Before the banquet starts, the murderers tell him and he is greedy for the power that Banquo had, but he is also stunned by the extreme situation. The conflict occurs when he sees a ghost of Banquo, but others cannot see the ghost. His public and private feelings are in conflict, which you can see in his diction, Lady Macbeth's reaction, and the reaction of the other characters.

Macbeth's diction shows his conflict in multiple different ways. His famous line "if it were done then twere well done quickly" about the need to kill Banquo occurs in the first act of the play, long before the banquet scene, but it is an interesting foreshadowing of his conflict that will show up later. Macbeth is private in this example of a soliloquy and he can express his feelings clearly. In public, after the murder, he is much more muddled in his thoughts and language, to the point that people cannot understand what he is saying.

Lady Macbeth is stronger in her will and behaves the same in private and public, so she is a contrast to her conflicted husband. At the banquet, she reassures the guests that Macbeth is ill, so that explains his odd behavior. She is very conscious of appearing to be in control, and in private she thinks of herself in control, so she is not conflicted the way that Macbeth is.

The theme of hospitality connects to this theme about public and private behavior because you should treat guests in public the way you would treat them in private. Lady Macbeth and her husband try to pretend that they are treating their guests well, and they even say that if Banquo had been forgotten, it would have been "unbecoming." This is a pun on Banquo not "becoming," or not being alive anymore--not <u>being</u>. The other characters don't know that; they think she is just being polite and talking about good behavior. They make a big production out of the banquet, but it is a display of their power and their desire for more power, not a statement of being kind or generous. They are publicly behaving as being generous, but in private they seek power. Banquo's ghost is the form that the disconnect takes because it shows the gap between private and public, but the ghost is something between those two places, neither one or the other. The ghost at the party is troubling because the party is excessive. It is too public because Macbeth's haunted behavior is even more noticeable at a party, than it would be in private. It is too private, though, because only Macbeth and the ghost are in this netherworld. Even the audience is unsure what they are seeing. This is the conflict between private and public.

<u>Reader response for the 5-6 essay</u>

This essay takes a while to get going, but the author makes some interesting, original points in the last paragraph. It is **hampered by the artificial set-up of the five-paragraph essay with three disconnected body paragraphs about different ideas.** The author could have taken some time to **free-write or make a concept map about how his ideas connected to one another**, where he could have **started with his strongest ideas about hospitality** rather than writing toward them. Of course, it's better for an essay to gain steam than to lose it--the author was clearly thinking while he was writing.

The author's best ideas are about the notion of Macbeth's "unbecoming" behavior in the public banquet paired with his private anguish about Banquo's "unbecoming" through death. This is an interesting, **specific example that would have been even stronger with more context,** but it is still a striking word to point out.

There are a number of **run-on sentences and comma splices that show the author jamming together ideas.** That process shows the author's thought process, but some of that material can stay on scratch paper or get revised with **more definite punctuation** in a quick revision. **It's also less elegant to keep saying "this relates"**--it's clear that it relates, or the author wouldn't be writing it. The goal in sentences like those is to show the relationship, not just to tell it. **We don't just say "this is evidence!" in a court case; we take the audience/readers through it.**

1-2 Sample Essay

> In private, Macbeth can make up schemes with murderers and Lady Macbeth, but in public he must pretend that he is loyal. This problem comes to a head in the banquet scene of Macbeth, when he sees the ghost of Banquo, who he has just ordered to be killed. The ghost represents the conflict between private and public because he can only be seen as a private torment for Macbeth of how he was supposed to be loyal but he wasn't.

Reader response for the 1-2 essay

This is a very brief essay that looks like the author ran out of time and just left notes. The essay is not structured in any way, nor is there development of a thesis, point-of-view, or exploration of themes and how they relate back to the essay question. It seems like the essay writer ran out of time—be sure to pace yourself on test day so you aren't left with only a few minutes to write your final essay.

Practice Test 2

ANSWER SHEET PRACTICE TEST 2

Section I: Multiple Choice

1. Ⓐ Ⓑ Ⓒ Ⓓ Ⓔ   15. Ⓐ Ⓑ Ⓒ Ⓓ Ⓔ   29. Ⓐ Ⓑ Ⓒ Ⓓ Ⓔ   43. Ⓐ Ⓑ Ⓒ Ⓓ Ⓔ

2. Ⓐ Ⓑ Ⓒ Ⓓ Ⓔ   16. Ⓐ Ⓑ Ⓒ Ⓓ Ⓔ   30. Ⓐ Ⓑ Ⓒ Ⓓ Ⓔ   44. Ⓐ Ⓑ Ⓒ Ⓓ Ⓔ

3. Ⓐ Ⓑ Ⓒ Ⓓ Ⓔ   17. Ⓐ Ⓑ Ⓒ Ⓓ Ⓔ   31. Ⓐ Ⓑ Ⓒ Ⓓ Ⓔ   45. Ⓐ Ⓑ Ⓒ Ⓓ Ⓔ

4. Ⓐ Ⓑ Ⓒ Ⓓ Ⓔ   18. Ⓐ Ⓑ Ⓒ Ⓓ Ⓔ   32. Ⓐ Ⓑ Ⓒ Ⓓ Ⓔ   46. Ⓐ Ⓑ Ⓒ Ⓓ Ⓔ

5. Ⓐ Ⓑ Ⓒ Ⓓ Ⓔ   19. Ⓐ Ⓑ Ⓒ Ⓓ Ⓔ   33. Ⓐ Ⓑ Ⓒ Ⓓ Ⓔ   47. Ⓐ Ⓑ Ⓒ Ⓓ Ⓔ

6. Ⓐ Ⓑ Ⓒ Ⓓ Ⓔ   20. Ⓐ Ⓑ Ⓒ Ⓓ Ⓔ   34. Ⓐ Ⓑ Ⓒ Ⓓ Ⓔ   48. Ⓐ Ⓑ Ⓒ Ⓓ Ⓔ

7. Ⓐ Ⓑ Ⓒ Ⓓ Ⓔ   21. Ⓐ Ⓑ Ⓒ Ⓓ Ⓔ   35. Ⓐ Ⓑ Ⓒ Ⓓ Ⓔ   49. Ⓐ Ⓑ Ⓒ Ⓓ Ⓔ

8. Ⓐ Ⓑ Ⓒ Ⓓ Ⓔ   22. Ⓐ Ⓑ Ⓒ Ⓓ Ⓔ   36. Ⓐ Ⓑ Ⓒ Ⓓ Ⓔ   50. Ⓐ Ⓑ Ⓒ Ⓓ Ⓔ

9. Ⓐ Ⓑ Ⓒ Ⓓ Ⓔ   23. Ⓐ Ⓑ Ⓒ Ⓓ Ⓔ   37. Ⓐ Ⓑ Ⓒ Ⓓ Ⓔ   51. Ⓐ Ⓑ Ⓒ Ⓓ Ⓔ

10. Ⓐ Ⓑ Ⓒ Ⓓ Ⓔ   24. Ⓐ Ⓑ Ⓒ Ⓓ Ⓔ   38. Ⓐ Ⓑ Ⓒ Ⓓ Ⓔ   52. Ⓐ Ⓑ Ⓒ Ⓓ Ⓔ

11. Ⓐ Ⓑ Ⓒ Ⓓ Ⓔ   25. Ⓐ Ⓑ Ⓒ Ⓓ Ⓔ   39. Ⓐ Ⓑ Ⓒ Ⓓ Ⓔ   53. Ⓐ Ⓑ Ⓒ Ⓓ Ⓔ

12. Ⓐ Ⓑ Ⓒ Ⓓ Ⓔ   26. Ⓐ Ⓑ Ⓒ Ⓓ Ⓔ   40. Ⓐ Ⓑ Ⓒ Ⓓ Ⓔ   54. Ⓐ Ⓑ Ⓒ Ⓓ Ⓔ

13. Ⓐ Ⓑ Ⓒ Ⓓ Ⓔ   27. Ⓐ Ⓑ Ⓒ Ⓓ Ⓔ   41. Ⓐ Ⓑ Ⓒ Ⓓ Ⓔ   55. Ⓐ Ⓑ Ⓒ Ⓓ Ⓔ

14. Ⓐ Ⓑ Ⓒ Ⓓ Ⓔ   28. Ⓐ Ⓑ Ⓒ Ⓓ Ⓔ   42. Ⓐ Ⓑ Ⓒ Ⓓ Ⓔ

Section II: Free Response

_____

_____

_____

_____

_____

_____

_____

_____

_____

answer sheet

PRACTICE TEST 2

Section I: Multiple Choice

Time 1 hour • 55 Questions

> **Directions:** This section consists of selections from literary works and questions on their content, form, and style. After reading each passage or poem, choose the best answer to each question and then fill in the corresponding circle.

Questions 1-13. Read the following poem carefully before you decide on the answers to the questions.

From "A Japanese Wood-Carving," by Amy Lowel.

High up above the open, welcoming door
It hangs, a piece of wood with colors dim.
Once, long ago, it was a waving tree
Line   And knew the sun and shadow through the leaves
5   Of forest trees, in a thick eastern wood.
The winter snows had bent its branches down,
The spring had swelled its buds with coming flowers,
Summer had run like fire through its veins,
While autumn pelted it with chestnut burrs,
10   And strewed the leafy ground with acorn cups.
Dark midnight storms had roared and crashed among
Its branches, breaking here and there a limb;
But every now and then broad sunlit days
Lovingly lingered, caught among the leaves.
15   Yes, it had known all this, and yet to us
It does not speak of mossy forest ways,
Of whispering pine trees or the shimmering birch;
But of quick winds, and the salt, stinging sea!
An artist once, with patient, careful knife,
20   Had fashioned it like to the untamed sea.
Here waves uprear themselves, their tops blown back
By the gay, sunny wind, which whips the blue
And breaks it into gleams and sparks of light.
Among the flashing waves are two white birds
25   Which swoop, and soar, and scream for very joy
At the wild sport. Now diving quickly in,
Questing some glistening fish. Now flying up,
Their dripping feathers shining in the sun,
While the wet drops like little glints of light,
30   Fall pattering backward to the parent sea.

Gliding along the green and foam-flecked hollows,
Or skimming some white crest about to break,
The spirits of the sky deigning to stoop
And play with ocean in a summer mood.
35   Hanging above the high, wide open door,
It brings to us in quiet, firelit room,
The freedom of the earth's vast solitudes,
Where heaping, sunny waves tumble and roll,
And seabirds scream in wanton happiness.

1. What is being described in the first fourteen lines of the poem?
    A. The intricacies of the design
    B. The emotions stirred up by the art
    C. The speaker's childhood
    D. The tree before it was carved
    E. A favorite spot in nature

2. The characterizations of the tree in lines 6-10 are
    A. unconventional yet pleasing.
    B. brilliant yet grounded.
    C. familiar yet hackneyed.
    D. marvelous yet earthy.
    E. subtle yet strong.

3. What is the shift in scene in lines 15-18?
    A. From the forest to the home
    B. From the storm to the home
    C. From the forest to the sea
    D. From the storm to the sea
    E. From the sea to the home

4. The most important contrast between lines 20-34 and the opening lines are that these later descriptions are
    A. blue and silver.
    B. dynamic and unpredictable.
    C. marine and avian.
    D. carved and artistic.
    E. beautiful and mysterious.

5. The "patient, careful knife" in line 19 is an example of what poetic device?
    A. Personification
    B. Antithesis
    C. Oxymoron
    D. Synesthesia
    E. Foreshadowing

6. What is the most important purpose that the device in question 5 serves in the poem?
    A. It dulls the contrast between the artist's calmness and the scene's wildness.
    B. It pairs with the woodcut's insistence in telling its own story outside of human conventions.
    C. It indicates the sensory confusion in the wild, salty sea.
    D. It exemplifies the relationship between humans and the natural world.
    E. It signals the shift in the scene from the sea to the home.

7. Why doesn't the wood-carving "speak of mossy forest ways"?
    A. It wants to find beauty elsewhere in the sea.
    B. It prefers its life as a piece of driftwood.
    C. It does not want to remember the trauma of the storm that broke its limbs.
    D. It prefers the sea image depicted on its surface to its initial tree form.
    E. It rejects language in favor of images.

8. Lines 33-36 each end with similar vowel sounds, a poetic device called
   A. assonance.
   B. consonance.
   C. alliteration.
   D. synesthesia.
   E. internal rhyme.

9. The language in lines 33-36 serves all of the following thematic purposes EXCEPT
   A. it creates harmony for the wood-carving with its resting spot above the door.
   B. it makes sounds reverberate in the memory, from the sea into the room.
   C. it imposes some order on the scene to take it from the wild sea into the enclosed room.
   D. it adds a poetic shaping quality to the scene, to pair with the shaping quality of the knife.
   E. it shows the over-arching importance of the human eye in composing the scene.

10. What best describes the colors on the wood-carving?
    A. Faded
    B. Vivid
    C. Dark
    D. Embellished with silver
    E. It is unknown from the information in the passage

11. What is the literary device used to describe a work of art in this poem?
    A. Metaphor
    B. Simile
    C. Ekphrasis
    D. Monologue
    E. Apostrophe

12. How would you best characterize the relationship between the carving's medium (wood) and the images depicted on it?
    I. The wood's solidity is contrasted with the sea's changeability.
    II. The wood changes shape through human imposition, while the waves shift with the unpredictable forces of wind.
    III. The wood-carving becomes disenchanted with the cliched language used to describe the seascape, just as it did with the forest.
    A. I only
    B. II only
    C. I and II
    D. II and III
    E. I, II, and III

13. The author of this poem, Amy Lowell, went on to write the preface to a book called *Some Imagist Poets*, in which she listed the essential goals of the Imagist movement: "to present an image .... We are not a school of painters, but we believe that poetry should render particulars exactly and not deal in vague generalities, however magnificent and sonorous." What do the Imagist poet and the wood-carver share?
    I. The ability to remake nature according to their own desires
    II. The ability to shape the meaning of the wood through poetic devices and carving
    III. The concern for the intricacies of surface details
    A. I only
    B. II only
    C. I and III
    D. II and III
    E. I, II, and III

14. If you were going to write an essay form of this poem, which would NOT be a good title?

- **A.** Carving Open a Poem
- **B.** The Beauty of Autumn
- **C.** The Story of a Knife
- **D.** How to "Sea" an Image
- **E.** High Up Above the Open, Welcoming Door

Questions 15-29. Read the following passage carefully before you decide on your answers to the questions.

From *New Grub Street*, by George Gissing

One day at the end of the month [Marian] sat with books open before her, but by no effort could fix her attention upon them. It was gloomy, and one could scarcely see to read; a taste of fog grew perceptible in the warm, headachy air.

Line Such profound discouragement possessed her that she could not even maintain
5 the pretence of study; heedless whether anyone observed her, she let her hands fall and her head droop. She kept asking herself what was the use and purpose of such a life as she was condemned to lead. When already there was more good literature in the world than any mortal could cope with in his lifetime, here was she exhausting herself in the manufacture of printed stuff which no
10 one even pretended to be more than a commodity for the day's market. What unspeakable folly! To write—was not that the joy and the privilege of one who had an urgent message for the world?

Her father, she knew well, had no such message; he had abandoned all thought of original production, and only wrote about writing.

15 She herself would throw away her pen with joy but for the need of earning money. And all these people about her, what aim had they save to make new books out of those already existing, that yet newer books might in turn be made out of theirs? This huge library, growing into unwieldiness, threatening to become a trackless desert of print—how intolerably it weighed upon the spirit!

20 Oh, to go forth and labour with one's hands, to do any poorest, commonest work of which the world had truly need! It was ignoble to sit here and support the paltry pretence of intellectual dignity. A few days ago her startled eye had caught an advertisement in the newspaper, headed 'Literary Machine'; had it then been invented at last, some automaton to supply the place of such poor
25 creatures as herself to turn out books and articles? Alas! the machine was only one for holding volumes conveniently, that the work of literary manufacture might be physically lightened. But surely before long some Edison would make

the true automaton; the problem must be comparatively such a simple one.
Only to throw in a given number of old books, and have them reduced, blended,
30 modernised into a single one for to-day's consumption.

The fog grew thicker; she looked up at the windows beneath the dome and
saw that they were a dusky yellow. Then her eye discerned an official walking
along the upper gallery, and in pursuance of her grotesque humour, her mocking
misery, she likened him to a black, lost soul, doomed to wander in an eternity of
35 vain research along endless shelves. Or again, the readers who sat here at these
radiating lines of desks, what were they but hapless flies caught in a huge web,
its nucleus the great circle of the Catalogue? Darker, darker. From the towering
wall of volumes seemed to emanate visible motes, intensifying the obscurity; in
a moment the book-lined circumference of the room would be but a featureless
40 prison-limit.

But then flashed forth the sputtering whiteness of the electric light, and its
ceaseless hum was henceforth a new source of headache. It reminded her how
little work she had done to-day; she must, she must force herself to think of
the task in hand. A machine has no business to refuse its duty. But the pages
45 were blue and green and yellow before her eyes; the uncertainty of the light was
intolerable. Right or wrong she would go home, and hide herself, and let her
heart unburden itself of tears.

15. How would Marian characterize her job as a writer?
  A. A privilege, even when it's a difficult day
  B. A career she's pursuing to gain fame
  C. A creative outlet that's better than being a critic
  D. A pointless, yet undemanding job
  E. A daily task of drudgery

16. What is the literary device employed in the phrase "a taste of fog" (line 3)?
  A. Simile
  B. Metonymy
  C. Synesthesia
  D. Hyperbole
  E. Oxymoron

17. What is the best way to describe the imagery in Marian's visions in this scene?
  A. Vivid scenes that will become part of her novel
  B. Disillusioned daydreams
  C. Revelations of insight
  D. Fantasies of future fame
  E. Imaginative storytelling

18. All of the following adjectives might describe Marian's opinion of "writing about writing" (line 14) EXCEPT
  A. postmodern.
  B. commodified.
  C. derivative.
  D. pointless.
  E. uninventive.

19. The imagery associated with the "trackless desert of print" (line 19) indicates Marian's vision of
   A. the Internet.
   B. a world without writing.
   C. books without readers, only writers.
   D. inspiration without realization.
   E. the obliteration of the library.

20. Why is it unlikely that Marian will quit her job to take "any poorest, commonest work"?
   A. She's not strong or healthy enough to take another job.
   B. She has found the inspiration for her own novel.
   C. Her father won't let her be downwardly mobile in the social register.
   D. She's being condescending in imagining that writing is the worst job one can have.
   E. She secretly loves writing, even if she complains about it.

21. What is the Literary Machine?
   A. A device for making new books by combining sections of older books
   B. A device for holding books
   C. A device for reading books quickly
   D. A device enabling the library to store books for patrons more efficiently so it's less unwieldy
   E. A device for writing books, like an early version of the computer

22. "Some Edison" (line 27) is an example of what rhetorical device?
   A. Anecdote
   B. Metaphor
   C. Simile
   D. Zeugma
   E. Metonymy

23. We can infer all of the following about the function of the Literary Machine in the narrative EXCEPT
   A. it serves as satire of the social concerns of the time.
   B. it is foreshadowing that it will eventually replace Marian's job in the novel.
   C. it is prescient for imagining the future of technology.
   D. it shows the problem that advertising is more flash than substance.
   E. it is a commentary on the changing nature of labor in industrial society.

24. When Marian uses the word "hapless" (line 36) she is
   A. condemning others for being mindless workers.
   B. describing the official's shared sense of drudgery.
   C. complaining about how miserable she is.
   D. voicing fear that such a vision could come true.
   E. counting herself as one of the unlucky ones.

25. What is the image she's conjuring in the sentence "volumes seemed to emanate visible motes" (line 38)?
   A. The fog is taking vaguely human shape.
   B. Flying bugs seem to be swarming around the room.
   C. Specks of dust seem to be swirling around the room.
   D. The books are growing in size to become like walls.
   E. The room seems to be growing bars like a cage.

26. What are the ironies of Marian's vision that she does not realize?

    I. In day-dreaming, she is more creative than when she is working.

    II. In the obscure fog of her vision, she comes up with vivid images.

    III. They occur in the library, where writers are inspired by all of the literature that surrounds them.

    A. I only

    B. II only

    C. III only

    D. I and II

    E. II and III

27. How would you characterize the tone in the sentence: "A machine has no business to refuse its duty." (line 44)?

    A. Pessimistic, yet inspired

    B. Driven, yet unconfident

    C. Sardonic, yet resigned

    D. Bitter, yet hopeful

    E. Gritty, yet creative

28. The phrase "the uncertainty of the light" (line 46) is what kind of literary device in this passage?

    A. Pathetic fallacy

    B. Oxymoron

    C. Synesthesia

    D. A collective noun

    E. Antithesis

29. What does "the uncertainty of the light" (line 46) indicate?

    I. A light turning on in the stacks, interrupting her dark fantasies and creating yet another unwanted sensory stimulus

    II. A manifestation of the saying "a light bulb goes off in her head," which indicates that she may be having a breakthrough idea

    III. An allusion to Thomas Edison, the inventor of the light bulb mentioned earlier in the passage, and a marker of how technological inventions bring as many headaches as they do efficiencies

    A. I only

    B. II only

    C. III only

    D. I and II

    E. I and III

Questions 30-43. Read the following poem carefully before you decide on your answers to the questions.

Prologue, David Garrick from Oliver Goldsmith's play, *She Stoops to Conquer*

Excuse me, sirs, I pray—I can't yet speak—
I'm crying now—and have been all the week.
"'Tis not alone this mourning suit," good masters:
Line "I've that within"—for which there are no plasters[1]!
5 Pray, would you know the reason why I'm crying?
The Comic Muse, long sick, is now a-dying!
And if she goes, my tears will never stop;
For as a player, I can't squeeze out one drop:
I am undone, that's all—shall lose my bread—
10 I'd rather, but that's nothing—lose my head.
When the sweet maid is laid upon the bier,
Shuter[2] and I shall be chief mourners here.
To her a mawkish drab of spurious breed,
Who deals in sentimentals, will succeed!
15 Poor Ned and I are dead to all intents;
We can as soon speak Greek as sentiments!
Both nervous grown, to keep our spirits up.
We now and then take down a hearty cup.
What shall we do? If Comedy forsake us,
20 They'll turn us out, and no one else will take us.
But why can't I be moral?—Let me try—
My heart thus pressing—fixed my face and eye—
With a sententious look, that nothing means,
(Faces are blocks in sentimental scenes)
25 Thus I begin: "All is not gold that glitters,
"Pleasure seems sweet, but proves a glass of bitters.
"When Ignorance enters, Folly is at hand:
"Learning is better far than house and land.
"Let not your virtue trip; who trips may stumble,
30 "And virtue is not virtue, if she tumble."
I give it up—morals won't do for me;
To make you laugh, I must play tragedy.
One hope remains—hearing the maid was ill,
A Doctor comes this night to show his skill.
35 To cheer her heart, and give your muscles motion,
He, in Five Draughts prepar'd, presents a potion:
A kind of magic charm—for be assur'd,
If you will swallow it, the maid is cur'd:

---

1   bandages
2   Shuter is playing the role of Hardcastle.

But desperate the Doctor, and her case is,
40   If you reject the dose, and make wry faces!
This truth he boasts, will boast it while he lives,
No poisonous drugs are mixed in what he gives.
Should he succeed, you'll give him his degree;
If not, within he will receive no fee!
45   The College YOU, must his pretensions back,
Pronounce him Regular, or dub him Quack.

30. From what position in the theater is the speaker speaking in this prologue?
   A. Playwright
   B. Actor
   C. Critic
   D. Rival playwright
   E. Audience member

31. Who are the "sirs" in line 1?
   A. The rest of the theatrical company
   B. Playwrights he's asking to write better comedies
   C. Directors he's asking to put on more skilled productions
   D. The patrons who finance productions
   E. The audience

32. Who is the "sweet maid" in line 11?
   A. An actress "player" in a tragic play
   B. The Muse of Tragedy, performing her role to audience acclaim
   C. The Muse of Comedy, who is ailing and needs to be revived
   D. An actress "player" in a comic role, who will come back to life in a reversal
   E. A male "player" disguised for a female role

33. In lines 8-14, the speaker is critical of the type of plays he calls "mawkish" and "spurious," which most closely mean
   A. emotional and realistic.
   B. devastating and cruel.
   C. satirical and dark.
   D. maudlin and contrived.
   E. spectacular and expensive.

34. What are the ironies of lines 8-14?
   I. People were laughing at a tragedy.
   II. The genre has died the same kind of contrived death that he criticizes.
   III. The speaker can't cry for her death because he's not a good tragic actor.
   A. II only
   B. III only
   C. III only
   D. I and III
   E. II and III

35. How do you imagine the speaker's tone in lines 25-30?
   A. Gradually gaining confidence
   B. Finally inspired
   C. Exaggeratedly grandiose
   D. Authoritative and respectable
   E. Wise and kind

36. Generally speaking, what does he need?

A. Money to put on a production

B. A good comedy to perform in

C. A replacement actor from the audience

D. A source of inspiration

E. An actress to serve as leading lady

37. The rhyme "do for me" / "tragedy" in lines 31-32 serves all of the following purposes EXCEPT

A. its stiltedness matches with the tragic clichés he was just reciting badly.

B. it shows how the unwitting effects of his grief.

C. it makes the audience laugh at the bad rhyme, which helps to set up the play.

D. it heightens the self-deprecation in the speaker's prologue.

E. it shows them bending rules in a playful way, just like they bend the rules of the genre.

38. In the analogy of theater to medicine in lines 34-46, what do the Five Draughts refer to?

A. The senses

B. The muses

C. The charms

D. The acts of the play

E. The beverages

39. Who is the Doctor in the analogy?

A. The hero

B. The villain

C. The playwright

D. The audience

E. The actor in disguise

40. What is the best paraphrase of line 40?

A. If you miss the point and treat the comedy as satire.

B. If you don't like the play and refuse to laugh.

C. If you miss the point and treat the tragedy as comedy.

D. If you recognize the actor in disguise and ruin the surprise.

E. If you don't like the play and retaliate against the playwright.

41. In context, what are "pretensions" in line 45?

A. Claims to the play's quality

B. Insistences that he's a good actor

C. Disguises that the actors wear

D. Criticisms of the play

E. Arguments among the theater company

42. In the extended analogy, what is a quack?

A. A comic actor who can't make the audience laugh

B. A tragic actor who can't make the audience feel deep emotions

C. A director who can't get good performances out of his actors

D. A comic playwright who can't make the audience laugh

E. A playwright who can't transform sentiment into stirring art

43. In this example, the prologue serves which of the following purposes?

A. It defends against criticism of the play.

B. It acknowledges the audience's power.

C. It uses pathos to appeal to the audience.

D. It threatens the audience with retaliation.

E. It criticizes rival theater companies.

Questions 44-55. Read the following passage carefully before you decide on your answers to the questions.

My Brilliant Career, by Stella Maria Sarah Miles Franklin, known as Miles Franklin. For reference, the narrator's name is Sybylla.

Every night unfailingly when at home M'Swat sat in the bosom of his family and speculated as to how much richer he was than his neighbours, what old Recce lived on, and who had the best breed of sheep and who was the smartest
Line at counting these animals, until the sordidness of it turned me dizzy, and I
5 would steal out under the stars to try and cool my heated spirit. This became a practice with me, and every night I would slip away out of hearing of the household to sing the songs I had heard at Caddagat, and in imagination to relive every day and hour there, till the thing became too much for me, and I was scarcely responsible for my actions. Often I knelt on the parched ground
10 beneath the balmy summer sky to pray—wild passionate prayers that were never answered.

I was under the impression that my nightly ramble was not specially noticed by any one, but I was mistaken. Mr M'Swat, it appears, suspected me of having a lover, but was never able to catch me red-handed.

15 The possibility of a girl going out at night to gaze at the stars and dream was as improbable a thought for him as flying is to me, and having no soul above mud, had I attempted an explanation he would have considered me mad, and dangerous to have about the place.

Peter, junior, had a sweetheart, one Susie Duffy, who lived some miles on the
20 other side of the Murrumbidgee. He was in the habit of courting her every Sunday and two or three nights during the week, and I often heard the clang of his stirrup-irons and the clink of hobble-chain when he returned late; but on one occasion I stayed out later than usual, and he passed me going home. I stood still and he did not see me, but his horse shied violently. I thought he
25 would imagine I was a ghost, so called out:

"It is I."

"Well, I'll be hanged! What are ye doin' at this time ev night. Ain't yuz afraid of ghosts?"

"Oh dear no. I had a bad headache and couldn't sleep, so came out to try if a
30 walk would cure it," I explained.

We were a quarter of a mile or so from the house, so Peter slackened his speed that I might keep pace with him. His knowledge of 'etiquette did not extend as far as dismounting. There is a great difference between rudeness and ignorance.

Peter was not rude; he was merely ignorant. For the same reason he let his
mother feed the pigs, clean his boots, and chop wood, while he sat down and
smoked and spat. It was not that he was unmanly, as that this was the only
manliness he had known.

I was alone in the schoolroom next afternoon when Mr M'Swat sidled in, and
after stuttering and hawing a little, delivered himself of:

"I want to tell ye that I don't hold with a gu-r-r-l going out of nights for
to meet young men: if ye want to do any coortin' yuz can do it inside, if it's a
decent young man. I have no objections to yer hangin' yer cap up to our Peter,
only that ye have no prawperty—in yerself I like ye well enough, but we have
other views for Peter. He's almost as good as made it sure with Susie Duffy, an'
as ole Duffy will have a bit ev prawperty I want him to git her, an' wouldn't like
ye to spoil the fun."

Peter was "tall and freckled and sandy, face of a country lout", and, like
Middleton's rouse-about, "hadn't any opinions, hadn't any ideas"[3], but possessed sufficient instinct and common bushcraft with which, by hard slogging,
to amass money. He was developing a moustache, and had a "gu-r-r-r-l"; he
wore tight trousers and long spurs; he walked with a sidling swagger that was
a cross between shyness and flashness, and took as much pride in his necktie
as any man; he had a kind heart, honest principles, and would not hurt a fly;
he worked away from morning till night, and contentedly did his duty like a
bullock[4] in the sphere in which God had placed him; he never had a bath while
I knew him, and was a man according to his lights. He knew there was such
a thing as the outside world, as I know there is such a thing as algebra; but it
troubled him no more than algebra troubles me.

This was my estimation of Peter M'Swat, junior. I respected him right enough
in his place, as I trust he respected me in mine, but though fate thought fit for
the present to place us in the one groove, yet our lives were unmixable com-
modities as oil and water, which lay apart and would never meet until taken in
hand by the omnipotent leveller—death.

Marriage with Peter M'Swat!

Consternation and disgust held me speechless, and yet I was half inclined to
laugh at the preposterousness of the thing...

---

3   The phrases in quotations are from an Australian poem called "Middleton's Rouseabout," by Henry Lawson,
which begins "Tall, freckled, and sandy / Face of a country lout . . ." about a man who has no "opinions or
ideas," with few aspirations in life.

4   A steer

44. When the narrator grows annoyed with M'Swat's nightly conversation topics and says she can hardly stand the "sordidness," she is objecting to all of these qualities EXCEPT
    A. his bragging.
    B. his gossiping.
    C. the dirty details of livestock.
    D. the smallness of country life.
    E. his speculations on her romantic life.

45. What does "having no soul above mud, had I attempted an explanation he would have considered me mad, and dangerous to have about the place" mean?
    A. I wanted to commune with nature.
    B. My reasons will remain obscure.
    C. I'm forming a plan to escape.
    D. I was out doing things he shouldn't know about.
    E. My fantasies are embarrassing to talk about.

46. What is the contrast between the narrator's spoken dialogue and her inner narration in the passage?
    A. Her dialogue is in dialect, and her inner narration is grandiloquent.
    B. Her dialogue is sparse, and her inner narration is verbose.
    C. Her dialogue is sassy, and her inner narration is sassier.
    D. Her dialogue is in dialect, and her inner narration is plainspoken.
    E. Her dialogue is comic, and her inner narration is serious.

47. She adopts that tone in her narration for all of the following reasons EXCEPT
    A. she wants to sound smarter and more sophisticated.
    B. language gives her power, when she has very little real power over her day-to-day life.
    C. she is a stickler for proper etiquette.
    D. she thinks she's better than the M'Swats and wants to distinguish herself from them.
    E. she prefers the space inside her own head to what's around her.

48. What does she mean when she describes Peter: "it was not that he was unmanly, as that this was the only manliness he had known" (line 36)?
    A. Peter is rude and vulgar to women.
    B. Peter is condescending to women.
    C. Peter has never had to consider his own behavior seriously.
    D. Peter takes care to reject his father's overbearing example.
    E. Peter is never rude or condescending, and his father teases him for it.

49. As noted in the footnotes, the narrator is quoting a poem called "Middleton's Rouseabout," about an Australian "country lout" who works as an unskilled laborer and doesn't distinguish himself in life. The refrain about him is that he "hadn't any opinions, hadn't any ideas." Why does she use the poem to describe Peter?

    A. She sees him as a stereotypical guy who will never rise above his station in life.

    B. She wants to demonstrate to him that she can understand his situation.

    C. She wants to show the many facets of his personality.

    D. She wants to hint at his literary sensibilities, even though he seems to lack them.

    E. She cannot imagine what goes on inside his head, but she wants to understand him.

50. What are some of the ironies underlying the narrator's long description of Peter?

    I. When she quotes the poem and M'Swat in her description, she has to shift her style back and forth to account for those multiple registers of dialect and high-mindedness.

    II. Her list of Peter's qualities is longer than M'Swat's list at the beginning of the passage, and it grows just as gossipy.

    III. She is showing that she has paid attention to every detail of Peter's behavior, and she may be in love with him.

    A. I only

    B. II only

    C. I and II

    D. II and III

    E. I, II, and III

51. What is the best description of the word "bushcraft" (line 49) as the narrator uses it?

    A. A complimentary way of describing Peter's money-making skills

    B. A mean-spirited way of characterizing the M'Swat family's traditions

    C. A dismissive way of describing Peter's outdoor skills

    D. A blushing way of describing Peter's horse-riding skills

    E. A neutral way of describing Australian spiritual beliefs

52. When Sybylla characterizes Peter as "a man by his own lights," what are the tensions underneath her appraisal?

    I. She uses a colloquial term that Peter himself might use.

    II. You could say that his father has the same qualities.

    III. Even though she looks down on him, Sybylla herself tries to live by her own conscience and desires.

    A. I only

    B. II only

    C. III only

    D. I and II

    E. I and III

53. The narrator describes the possibility of M'Swat's understanding her behavior with the phrase "as improbable a thought for him as flying is to me." (line 15) She describes Peter with a similar comment: "He knew there was such a thing as the outside world, as I know there is such a thing as algebra; but it troubled him no more than algebra troubles me." (lines 56-58) Why does the narrator assess people with the literary device of imagining improbabilities and counterfactuals—what they don't or can't believe, rather than what they might or do?

A. She wants to teach them how to be more cultured and intellectual, but they refuse her condescending attitude.

B. She is offended by their beliefs, so she inserts her own narration.

C. She wants them to understand her, but they refuse to do so.

D. She believes they have sparse interior lives, so she fills those gaps with her own ideas.

E. She imagines these conversations because she is so lonely with the M'Swats.

54. How do you think the narrator means the word "respected" in the second-to-last paragraph?

A. Dutifully

B. Grudgingly

C. Ashamedly

D. Mournfully

E. Adoringly

55. Why is it striking that Sybylla tells Peter that she is not a ghost when she sees him late at night?

A. She spends her time on the margins of the scene, observing rather than interacting.

B. She wants to get her revenge on M'Swat in the next life.

C. She is imagining what will happen after she and Peter are dead.

D. She wants to float above the scene like a spirit when she is praying.

E. She is always inside of other people's heads, trying to imagine what they are thinking.

Section II: Free Response

Time: 2 hours

The essay section of the exam lasts 2 hours, so it is recommended that you spend 40 minutes on each of the three essays on the exam. You may write the essays in any order you wish and return to work on the essays if you have extra time.

Each essay will be evaluated according to how thoroughly and clearly it addresses the question, as well as the overall quality of your writing. Please write in blue or black ink and scratch out any mistakes thoroughly and neatly. Make sure to check your spelling and punctuation so that the reader can read your essay without struggling over legibility.

The quality of the essay matters more than its length, so spend some time at the beginning of the exam planning out the ideas on your sheet of scratch paper. You may write notes on the poem in the exam booklet. Use a new sheet of paper for each essay and number them (1, 2, 3) so that the exam question is immediately obvious.

For essay 3, you should choose to write about a novel or a play of similar literary merit to those in your AP English Literature class. There are some suggestions listed, but you are not required to choose one of them.

ESSAY QUESTION 1

Read the following poem carefully and write a well-organized essay in which you discuss the speaker's preferences—and prejudices—for listening to music in different locations. How does setting affect the way that he hears? You may choose to analyze his diction, imagery, and use of comparison, although you are welcome to discuss other features, as well.

"Lines Composed in a Concert-Room," by Samuel Taylor Coleridge

> Nor cold, nor stern, my soul! Yet I detest
> These scented Rooms, where to a gaudy throng,
> Heaves the proud Harlot her distended breast
> In intricacies of laborious song.
>
> These feel not Music's genuine power nor deign
> To melt at Nature's passion-warbled plaint;
> But when the long-breathed singers up-trilled strain
> Bursts in a squall--they gape for wonderment.
>
> Hark! the deep buzz of Vanity and Hate!
> Scornful, yet envious, with self-torturing sneer
> My lady eyes some maid of humbler state,
> While the pert Captain, or the primmer Priest,
> Prattles accordant scandal in her ear.
>
> O give me, from this heartless scene released,
> To hear our old Musician, blind and gray,
> (Whom, stretching from my nurse's arms I kissed,)
> His Scottish tunes and warlike marches play,
> By moonshine, on the balmy summer-night,
> The while I dance amid the tedded hay
> With merry maids, whose ringlets toss in light.
>
> Or lies the purple evening on the bay
> Of the calm glossy lake, O let me hid
> Unheard, unseen, behind the alder-trees,
> For round their roots the fisher's boat is tied,
> On whose trim seat doth Edmund stretch at ease,
> And while the lazy boat sways to and fro,
> Breathes in his flute sad airs, so wild and slow,
> That his own cheek is wet with quiet tears.

Line (at line 4)
5
10
15
20
25

But O, dear Anne! when midnight wind careers,
And the gust pelting on the out-house shed
Makes the cock shrilly on the rain-storm crow,
To hear thee sing some ballad full of woe,
Ballad of ship-wrecked sailor floating dead,
Whom his own true-love buried in the sands!
Thee, gentle woman, for thy voice re-measures
Whatever tones and melancholy pleasures
The things of Nature utter; birds or trees
Or moan of ocean-gale in weedy caves,
Or where the stiff grass mid the heath-plant waves,
Murmur and music thin of sudden breeze.

ESSAY QUESTION 2

Prose analysis from "The Library Window," by Margaret Oliphant

Margaret Oliphant was a prolific 19th-century novelist best known for her domestic fiction and her ghost stories. Write an essay about this passage's extended conversation about "the library window." Why do the characters argue about it in this passage? How is it a kind of metaphor for the work of interpretation, in which we wonder over what an object "really means" in a text? What other purposes might the mysterious window serve in this passage?

It was, and still is, the last window in the row, of the College Library, which is opposite my aunt's house in the High Street. Yet it is not exactly opposite, but a little to the west, so that I could see it best from the left side of my recess. I took
Line it calmly for granted that it was a window like any other till I first heard the
5   talk about it which was going on in the drawing-room. "Have you never made up your mind, Mrs. Balcarres," said old Mr. Pitmilly, "whether that window opposite is a window or no?" He said Mistress Balcarres, and he was always called Mr. Pitmilly, Morton: which was the name of this place.

"I am never sure of it, to tell the truth," said Aunt Mary, "all these years."

10   "Bless me!" said one of the old ladies, "and what window may that be?" Mr. Pitmilly had a way of laughing as he spoke, which did not please me; but it was true that he was not perhaps desirous of pleasing me. He said, "Oh, just the window opposite," with his laugh running through his words; "our friend can never make up her mind about it, though she has been living opposite it
15   since— "

"You need never mind the date," said another; "the Leebrary window! Dear me, what should it be but a window? Up at that height it could not be a door."

"The question is," said my aunt, "if it is a real window with glass in it, or if it is merely painted, or if it once was a window, and has been built up. And the
20   oftener people look at it, the less they are able to say."

"Let me see this window," said old Lady Carnbee, who was very active and strong-minded; and then they all came crowding upon me—three or four old ladies, very eager, and Mr. Pitmilly's white hair appearing over their heads, and my aunt sitting quiet and smiling behind.

25   "I mind the window very well," said Lady Carnbee; "ay: and so do more than me. But in its present appearance it is just like any other window; but has not been cleaned, I should say, in the memory of man."

"I see what ye mean," said one of the others. "It is just a very dead thing without any reflection in it; but I've seen as bad before."

30   "Ay, it's dead enough," said another, "but that's no rule; for these hizzies of
women-servants in this ill age—"

"Nay, the women are well enough," said the softest voice of all, which was Aunt
Mary's. "I will never let them risk their lives cleaning the outside of mine. And
there are no women-servants in the Old Library; there is maybe something
35   more in it than that."

They were all pressing into my recess, pressing upon me, a row of old faces,
peering into something they could not understand. I had a sense in my mind
how curious it was, the wall of old ladies in their old satin gowns all glazed with
age. Lady Carnbee with her lace about her head. Nobody was looking at me or
40   thinking of me, but I felt unconsciously the contrast of my youngness to their
oldness, and stared at them as they stared over my head at the Library window.
I had given it no attention up to this time. I was more taken with the old ladies
than with the thing they were looking at.

"The framework is all right at least, I can see that, and pented black—"

45   "And the panes are pented black too. It's no window, Mrs. Balcarres. It has been
filled in, in the days of the window duties: you will mind, Leddy Carnbee."

"Mind!" said the oldest lady. "I mind when our mother was marriet, Jeanie: and
that's neither the day nor yesterday. But as for the window, it's just a delusion:
and that is my opinion of the matter, if you ask me."

50   "There's a great want of light in that muckle room at the college," said another.
"If it was a window, the Leebrary would have more light."

"One thing is clear," said one of the younger ones, "it cannot be a window to see
through. It may be filled in or it may be built up, but it is not a window to give
light."

55   "And who ever heard of a window that was no to see through?" Lady Carnbee
said.

ESSAY QUESTION 3

Free Response

When you see a character reading a book inside a novel or a play, you may experience a moment of recognition: they're doing what I'm doing! You might see them struggle to read, fall in love with a character, learn lessons, even misinterpret what they're reading!

Write an essay in which you explore a character's relationship with reading inside a novel. What do you learn from seeing someone else's habits of interpretation spelled out for you as you yourself are trying to interpret the text? You should pick a novel or a play that depicts a multifaceted, complicated, or otherwise rich reading experience, so that you have some tensions and complexities to analyze in interpreting a fictional character's reading habits.

Catcher in the Rye
Frankenstein
Oliver Twist
Don Quixote
The Sorrows of Young Werther
Invisible Man
The Narrative of Frederick Douglass
I Capture the Castle
The Hours
Hamlet
Twelfth Night
Sense and Sensibility
Northanger Abbey
If On a Winter's Night a Traveler
The Book Thief
The Book of Lost Things
The Curious Incident of the Dog in the Nighttime
Great Expectations
People of the Book
Possession

ANSWER KEY AND EXPLANATIONS

1. D	11. C	20. D	29. E	38. D	47. C
2. C	12. C	21. B	30. B	39. C	48. C
3. C	13. D	22. E	31. E	40. B	49. A
4. B	14. B	23. B	32. C	41. A	50. C
5. A	15. E	24. E	33. D	42. D	51. C
6. B	16. C	25. C	34. E	43. B	52. E
7. D	17. B	26. D	35. C	44. E	53. D
8. A	18. A	27. C	36. B	45. B	54. B
9. E	19. C	28. A	37. B	46. B	55. A
10. A					

Section I

1. **The correct answer is D.** The answer to this question is stated directly in line 3: "once, long ago, it was a waving tree," but it may be tempting to get caught up in the descriptive language. Choices B, C, and E feel like familiar answers to a question about nature poetry—memory, emotions, favorite spots—but they are actually pointing readers toward a reversal in line 15 that will reject those timeworn associations with nature. The intricate design (choice A) is not described until later in the poem.

2. **The correct answer is C.** If you read these opening lines and thought, "I know *exactly* that feeling of autumn in the woods!" then this poem knows it. The interplay between the sun and shadow, the branches bent by snow in the winter, the pelting acorns—these are all conventional descriptions of trees and forest that are so familiar that they are hackneyed, or clichés. The descriptions may be pleasing, but they are hardly unconventional, which makes choice A incorrect. The positive adjectives in choices B, D, and E may be true of these lines—and it's okay to like them!—but they aren't the best answers for guiding you to the poem's main idea about breaking free from convention.

3. **The correct answer is C.** The poem rejects the conventional descriptions of the forest in favor of the "salt, stinging sea!" In line 1, the wood-carving "lives" above the doorway, but it prefers to indulge in the image of the sea depicted on its surface, rather than its prior life as a tree. You can strike all of the home possibilities in choices A, B, and E. There was mention of a storm in line 11, so this is a technical possibility, but the scene shifts back to the sunlit woods in the next two lines and the focus of those lines is mostly on the forest, not the brief storm. Choice C is a better choice than D.

4. **The correct answer is B.** The familiar seasonal rhythms of the forest give way to images of the dynamic, thrashing sea, where the birds swoop unpredictably and the waves are always changing in the wind. Choice D describes the wood carving in the most general terms, but there's no contrast and no focus on the content of lines 20-34 about the sea. Choice E is also much too general to be a good choice. Choice C is a contender because there are marine and avian elements in the lines, but the question asks you to choose the *most important* contrast. Similarly, the scene may be blue and

silver (choice A), which contrasts with the green and sunlight in the opening lines, but that's not the most important contrast, either. Choice B is the most important change that takes place in the poem.

5. **The correct answer is A.** You may eliminate the obvious wrong answers: a patient knife is not an example of antithesis or oxymoron because the adjective and noun aren't obviously opposed to each other. It is not a case of mixed sensory adjectives so it is not synesthesia, nor is it a case of foreshadowing because the knife doesn't play a role later in the poem. You can eliminate all of those answers and be sure about the correct choice, A, personification. A warning, however: This can be a difficult question because it can be hard to sort out the differences between metonymy, synecdoche, and personification. Some writers don't make a strong distinction between metonymy and synecdoche or say that synecdoche is a special case of metonymy, or that personification is also a special case of metonymy. In general terms, metonymy is a device in which a writer substitutes a word with a closely associated word, like a ruling party may be called "the Crown" because rulers wear crowns. Synecdoche is a device in which a writer substitutes a word for a whole with a word for a part of it, like you might call your car "your wheels," and wheels are part of a car. Personification can be a special form of metonymy in which, in the case of this question, a patient, calm wood-carver is substituted with his handy knife. If there were a different set of answer choices for this question and you saw "metonymy" but not "personification," you would be correct to choose metonymy because the knife is associated with the wood-carver and takes on his calmness and patience.

Unless there is a very obvious distinction to be made between those devices in a passage, the exam will probably not make you choose among the three devices. If you're asked to identify that kind of device, you will probably see only one of them among choices. (To add to the confusion, not all personification is metonymy: a storm may be personified with a name, but that name isn't substituting for a particular person associated with the storm.) To reiterate: the best choice here is A, but you probably won't have to agonize over so many fine distinctions on your own exam.

6. **The correct answer is B.** This question asks you to identify the *function* of the literary device: what does the personification highlight in the poem? Throughout these answers, we've been referring to the wood-carving as though it were an entity itself, personifying it even before question 5 appeared. The personified knife carves the personified wood, so the correct answer is choice B. You can eliminate choice E because the shift to the home happens later in the poem, and we're still out at sea. You might pause on choice A as you assess the relationship between the calm wood-carver and the wild scene, but the personified knife isn't dulling the scene. If anything, it's sharpening it. Choice C describes the image of unpredictable sea, but the personification of the knife doesn't create any notable sensory confusion. Choice D is basically true, but, as with question 4, you're not trying to find the most general answer but the most specific, important one. Multiple choice exams don't reward generalizations; that recommendation is true of the essay part of the exam, as well. You are better off looking for the important idea, instead of trying to find an answer that's almost always true, no matter the context.

7. **The correct answer is D.** The wood-carving fantasizes about the sea carved on its surface and prefers those fantasies to what it knows from its old life in the familiar forest. In this preference, the poem signals its deeper meaning to champion aesthetics, art, and

artifice over one's "natural" state. Choice A is too general to be a good choice. Choice B misreads the poem: the wood-carving has an image of the sea carved on its surface, but it was never a piece of driftwood. Choice C would be a potentially interesting, though strange, companion poem for the wood-carving to narrate, but there's no evidence in this poem that it was affected emotionally by the storm. Choice E is the most tempting alternative because the poem does proceed in many images of the sea; nevertheless, the shifts in the poem aren't from language to image, but from images of the forest to images of the sea. It's still a poem, so language is its medium for describing those images.

8. **The correct answer is A.** The repetition of the "oo" vowel sounds is a form of assonance. It's relatively common for the exam to ask you to distinguish among assonance, consonance, and alliteration in answer choices because those distinctions are clear-cut (unlike those blurrier lines between other rhetorical devices). It's easy to remember the distinction because consonance involves similar consonants, so assonance refers to similar vowel sounds. Alliteration involves similar sounds at the beginning of a word, so it is not the correct choice here. Synesthesia is a mixing of the senses, but that's not the device you're looking for in the question about similar sounds. It is not a case of internal rhyme among words inside a line, so choice E is also incorrect. You have a clear correct answer in choice A.

9. **The correct answer is E.** You are looking for the EXCEPTION in this question, so the correct answer will be the one that seems least appropriate. In looking at the possibilities, it seems difficult to take exception with choices B, C, and D because they seem to add a thoughtful layer of interpretation to the poem. They help us interpret what the assonance resolves in the poem and what it adds to our understanding of the scene.

Choices A and E seem to be a bit more of a stretch, but, again, it is hard to argue with the idea of harmony in the sounds—especially since there is no counter-example to find. Choice E is the outlier because it overstates the role of human perception in a poem that is mostly concerned with how wood-carvings and knives might tell their own stories.

10. **The correct answer is A.** The answer is stated in line 2 of the poem—"a piece of wood with colors dim"—but you may have missed it in the many shifts of tone and mood throughout the poem. It's important to go back and read the poem all the way through as you're moving to make more interpretations of the poem's larger meaning, otherwise you may not be able to answer the question and go with choice E. If you don't go back, you may be tempted to go for an answer that reflects the more vivid or sparkling imagery of the rest of the poem. This question was just to check that you can find the details!

11. **The correct answer is C.** Ekphrasis is the rhetorical term for a description of a work of art inside a poem, which often expands the story to get the "inside view" of what's happening in the depicted scene. Here we get to zoom into the image to see it like a movie instead of just a still image. The poem is not a metaphor nor an extended comparison to something else in simile form. Despite all of the personification and perspective, the wood-carving is not actually speaking in a monologue. An apostrophe is the poetic form in which a writer addresses a person, object, or idea as though he were speaking directly to it abstractly: "O Death," or "Twinkle, twinkle little star" are both apostrophes. In this case, the poet is not addressing the wood-carving directly; she is describing its image in ekphrastic form.

12. **The correct answer is C.** This question asks you to choose the best set of answers, to show that there may be more than one

correct answer or meaning. In this case, options I and II are similar to one another in describing the way the wood changes shape and meaning, but you don't have to choose between them. Why not both? Option III is not a good choice because there are waves and seagulls in the final two lines, so there's no rejection of the sea. You can thus eliminate it and the choices that contain it (D and E), so choice C is the correct answer.

13. **The correct answer is D.** This question gives you some information about the literary movement of Imagism that Amy Lowell embraced in her later poetry. This poem is a good example of an extended Imagist poem—sometimes her poems could be just two lines long, a very brief image! As with question 12, there are multiple options that may be correct, and you have to choose the right set of them. The quotation tells you that option I is wrong because Lowell specifically rejects the idea of grandiose statements about nature; option I is also too presumptuous because we don't have any sense of the wood-carver's desires. You can strike choices A, C, and E. Option II may seem like a reiteration of option I, but it's much more specific to "the" wood in the poem, not wood or nature in general. Lowell asked for specificity in the question's quotation; that's a scale that the patient, careful wood-carver can work on. Option III resembles the question's quotation for its attention to particular images, the wood-carver's métier. Options II and III complement each other, so the answer is choice D.

14. **The correct answer is B.** Some of these are cheesy titles, no doubt, but only one of them is the wrong answer. That choice won't be based on the quality of the title, but on whether it's relevant to the discussion of the poem. Choice B is the least relevant title because it's about autumn, and the wood-carving doesn't want to talk about seasonal beauty in the forest. The silly wordplay in

choices A and D may make you groan, but they're not incorrect choices. Choice E repeats the phrase from lines 1 and 35, so it's an apt title for an essay. Choice C picks up the personification device from line 19, so it could work, too, especially to talk about the relationship between the poet's craft and the wood-carver's craft.

15. **The correct answer is E.** The character Marian describes her job as "exhausting herself in the manufacture of printed stuff which no one even pretended to be more than a commodity"—in other words, drudgery. She repeats several related adjectives throughout the passage: discouraged, intolerable, condemned. Choices A and D are each only half-correct: she finds the work pointless and is having a difficult day, but she also finds it overly demanding and explicitly rejects the idea that it's a privilege. She has given up on the idea of fame (choice B), and she has stopped thinking of it as a creative outlet (choice C), comparing it more to a kind of intellectual factory-work.

16. **The correct answer is C.** The "taste of fog" is an example of synesthesia, or the mixing up of the senses—here, the mixing of taste and sight/touch—which signal her addled frame of mind in the passage. Although Marian has an excruciating headache, "a taste of fog" is not a hyperbole because she is not intentionally exaggerating for rhetorical effect. It is not an oxymoron because the phrase doesn't contain opposites—taste and fog may be different senses, but they aren't opposed. It's not a simile because it's not directly comparing two things, and it's not an example of metonymy because taste isn't replacing an idea commonly linked with fog. Synesthesia is the clear answer about sensory confusion.

17. **The correct answer is B.** As we saw in question 16, Marian is disillusioned with her writing career, and her daydreams show the

intensity of that feeling of drudgery. She does not gain any insights (choice C) from these visions; one imagines that she has similar visions every day, yet she is "condemned" to return to it over and over again. She has given up the idea of fame (choice D). It is entirely possible that the author of this novel, George Gissing, has taken Marian's fantasies from his own experience as a disillusioned writer and turned them into this novel (choices A and E)—but that information is not present in this passage. Choice B is the best answer here.

18. **The correct answer is A.** Several of these choices are very similar, but it's your job to pick the EXCEPTION, so you can eliminate the choices that are near synonyms. Marian feels condemned to her job of research and writing, yet she looks to her father's job as a critic as derivative, pointless, and uninventive (choices C, D, and E). Critics merely recycle other bits of writing into new forms of writing, she thinks; they are the first stage of the robotic Literary Machines she will go on to imagine as those who perpetuate the cycle of commodification, of turning writing into something just to be sold (choice B). That leaves the correct answer, choice A, as the best exception. It may be tempting to call this novel about the pointlessness of writing "postmodern," but that term does not yet exist in the nineteenth century, so Marian wouldn't use it to describe her own situation, nor her father's position as a critic! Indeed, writers have been writing about the drudgery of writing for a long time—that anxiety was not invented recently.

19. **The correct answer is C.** Marian's vision of this vicious cycle of print production is bleak: the library's shelves will become unwieldy with books that no one will ever read for their substance or meaning, except to make new books out of them. She is not describing a world without books (choice

B) or the destruction of the library (choice E), but the opposite. She has given up on inspiration (choice D), so that is not one of her concerns here. Choice A is a cheeky choice—this story does seem very prescient of our current times!—but choice C is more in keeping with the specific imagery of the passage.

20. **The correct answer is D.** It may be difficult to make an inference here, but it's easier to eliminate the incorrect answers. We can strike choice E, because each preceding question has emphasized just how much Marian dislikes her job, and there's no reversal indicated in the passage that might indicate inspiration (choice B)—it ends in tears. We don't have enough information about Marian's father to ascribe any motives to him, so choice C is out. Although she is clearly sick of her job, the focus of the passage is on her job, not on her health, so choice A is too much of a stretch. Those eliminations leave choice D, and although we don't have any other comparisons to jobs in the passage, her disdain for her father's position as a critic indicates her limited perspective on what's considered an "acceptable" job.

21. **The correct answer is B.** This question asks you to distinguish between Marian's frustrated projections and the reality outside the library. Choice B copies the language directly from the passage: the Literary Machine is a device for holding books. She imagines that it's a device for making books out of old books (choice A), only to say "Alas!" Choices C, D, and E—a device for reading quickly, an automated cataloging system, and a computer—are machines that would increase efficiency, to be sure, but they are not what's in the advertisement. Again, it's striking how prescient this book from 1891 could be!

22. The correct answer is E. "Some Edison" is an example of metonymy because she has replaced "inventor" with a closely related phrase—Thomas Edison, the most famous inventor of the time, the inventor of the light bulb. Marian's fantasies are very similar to what Edison imagined for the future, where work would become automated, thanks to efficient machines. It is an example of metonymy in the same way that we'd say "Hollywood gives us unrealistic fantasies," where Hollywood stands for the film industry. It is not an example of personification because there's no object being replaced: she's replacing one person with a proper name. Some may call it an eponym, the replacement of a noun with a person's name, but that term is used more often to show how we derived the name for Kleenex® or Xerox® products from the companies that created them. An epithet is also sometimes used to show this kind of replacement, but it tends to do so with an adjective, not another noun: Muhammad Ali was "the Greatest," so sportswriters sometimes replace his name with that phrase.

It was noted earlier that it is unlikely that you'll have to decide between two devices that overlap unless the distinction is clear-cut. Here, you probably wouldn't get metonymy, synecdoche, personification, eponym, and epithet as five of the answer choices. The exam may give you misleading answers that come from common misunderstandings, but it's probably not going to ask you to make fine-grained rhetorical differentiations among closely related devices, unless the distinction is (or should be) obvious.

In this case, you can answer the question by eliminating the wrong answers. She is not comparing two items, so it is not a simile or a metaphor. It is not a short example, an anecdote. It is not a zeugma, a figure of speech in which an adjective or a verb is used playfully and figuratively to apply to more than one noun in the phrase. An example might be: she gave you her heart and her lunch, where lunch is literal and heart is figurative. Choice E is the best answer.

23. The correct answer is B. This question effectively asks you to assess which forms of prescience and foreshadowing you can identify based on the information inside the passage. It is not asking you to predict what comes next in the novel because you don't have that information. Choice B is the most unlikely outcome (especially given that you have no way of knowing what comes next in the novel), and thus the EXCEPTION that the question is asking you to find. Choices A, C, and E are reasonable inferences about the novel's social concerns and the satirical edge to Marian's vision of writing as machine-work. The idea about advertising in choice D is a reasonable choice for interpreting the passage; indeed, the next inference one might draw is that those kinds of advertisements are part of the vast volume of stuff that is written but which is not important to actually read.

24. The correct answer is E. Hapless means unfortunate, and Marian's sense of being unable to extricate from the situation is palpable in her figurative language of unlucky flies stuck to a web. She is not condemning others (choice A), for she feels that they are all condemned to the same situation, with little recourse to change. The other options are tempting because they are similar and generally true, but they aren't specific to the word "hapless" in the question. The official (choice B) is also a "lost soul, doomed" to be stuck in the library, but "hapless" refers specifically to the faceless group of readers like herself. She has been complaining for the entire passage, so choice C is not specific enough to be a good answer to this vocabulary question. Her vision is dark and scary (choice D), but "hapless" isn't an indicator of her fear—it's more about her feeling stuck.

25. **The correct answer is C.** Motes are flecks of dust and other tiny bits of matter—you can imagine that an old library might be full of them. To emanate is to appear from a source. This is a vocabulary question in disguise, so the main goal is to find the answer that indicates dust emitting from the shelves. Marian has conjured up plenty of crazy fantasies of flies ensnared in webs and lost souls, but the other choices do not involve flecks of dust.

26. **The correct answer is D.** Here you have to identify the irony or ironies of this passage, for there may be more than one good option listed. Option I seems like a good choice, for her vision has shown the originality of her perspective, missing from her professional work. Option II is also a good choice because it plays with the notions of fog and vividity—and the first question about this passage called your attention to the use of synesthesia as a poetic device. Option III may be tempting because it describes how we normally think of libraries as fantasy spaces for intellectual growth. However, the passage has been suggesting something different: that libraries are not sources of inspiration, but rather of oppressive bulk that no one will ever read. They are monuments to over-producing stuff, not sites of inspiration. You may quibble with this characterization of the passage by saying that literature (not the hack-writing Marian refers to) *should* serve as an inspiration. Nevertheless, the answer choices don't let you select all three options, so you have to go with the choice that contains the two best possibilities: choice D.

27. **The correct answer is C.** These answers have many similarities, so it may be difficult to choose the best one. To begin

the elimination, you should look at all ten adjectives listed and try to find single ones that don't seem to fit—inspired (choice A), hopeful (choice D), and creative (choice E) are all adjectives that are sorely missing from Marian's perspective in this passage. You can strike those three because you're looking for a pair of adjectives. (Arguably, she has been creative and inspired in imagining this elaborate scene, but she doesn't realize that, as question 26 points out.) We don't really see a lack of confidence as her problem in this passage, so choice B is not a good fit, either. She is being sarcastic or sardonic in her cynical, mocking extension of the idea of the Literary Machine from earlier in the passage. The word "resigned" may trip you up because we tend to associate it with quitting a job, but it also means that she has acquiesced to a situation without wanting to.

28. **The correct answer is A.** Marian has projected her feelings upon the light, so it is an example of pathetic fallacy. She can't make a decision to quit, but she doesn't know how she can go on. The gloom in the library has matched her own inner sense of gloom; the suddenness of the light signals her own uncertainty about her intolerable future. It is not a case of oxymoron or antithesis because uncertainty and light aren't opposed to each other, nor is it a case of synesthesia because uncertainty isn't a sensory feeling. Although "an uncertainty of light bulbs" would be a creative way to describe a group of light bulbs in a collective noun, that is unlikely to ever gain popular use!

29. **The correct answer is E.** Here you are asked to interpret the function of the light bulb: is it symbolic, allusive, literal, or some combination of these? Option I describes the literal events of the scene in sensory terms: the light flashes, her headache grows worse from the intensifying stimuli around. Option II gives you the possibility of a revelation,

but such a moment doesn't occur in these last sentences, so you can strike choices B and D. Option III seems like it may be a stretch—we can't ask Gissing if he meant to allude to Edison twice in the passage—but the explanation for its function is a reasonable one, as it sets up a tension between innovation and frustration. Such an interpretive possibility doesn't seem tangential or unrelated to the passage. It is the kind of creative interpretation that would serve you well on the essay section because it allows you to draw interesting connections to other parts of the passage in context. If you wanted to pursue this idea in an essay, you'd have to frame it in terms of what it lets you understand about larger concepts like innovation, sensation, and work. You wouldn't write a sentence like "The phrase 'an uncertainty of light' is a reference to Thomas Edison" and be done with it—you'd have to explain why that insight is important for understanding the rest of the passage.

30. **The correct answer is B.** This is a difficult passage to understand for modern readers because we aren't as used to formats in which someone addresses the audience before a play starts. There's also a lot of old-fashioned words and clever wordplay. For these reasons, the exam is going to lead you through simpler questions to help you get a handle on some of these theatrical terms and conventions so that you can answer progressively more complicated interpretive questions about the passage. The speaker tells you the correct answer "as a player . . ." in line 8, and even though you may not have heard actors referred to as "players" before, the lines around it make it clear that he and Shuter (named in the footnote) and Ned are actors in the play. You may have heard the word in context in *Macbeth*: "Life's but a walking shadow, / A poor player that struts and frets his hour upon the stage, and then is heard no more" or read about the Player

King and Queen who perform the play within a play in *Hamlet*. If you're really not sure about the answer to this question, it's a good strategy to skip it and get some clues for answering it by looking at the rest of the questions in the section, which differentiate the playwright, audience, and other actors more clearly. You will start to get some of that language about "players" defined for you in context, starting in question 32.

31. **The correct answer is E.** As in question 30, the speaker gives you the answer later in the passage, in line 32: "To make you laugh . . ." and then in the extended metaphor about "if you reject the dose" (40) and "YOU must his pretensions back" (45). If you are stumped by the strangeness of the language, it may be worth it to try to eliminate some obvious wrong answers and then return to these questions with more context from the rest of the passage and exam. The question of who "you" is becomes clearer as the prologue goes on.

32. **The correct answer is C.** The speaker gives you the answer in line 6: "The Comic Muse, long sick, is now a-dying! / And if she goes, my tears will never stop . . ." If you're having a hard time reading the lines and understanding who he's referring to, try to track the pronouns: if there's a "sweet maid," then where are the other female-identifying pronouns in the surrounding lines? The Comic Muse is referred to as "she" in the preceding lines, and the speaker says he is not good enough an actor to be able to cry: "as a player, I can't squeeze out one drop." If you're unsure what "bier" means, then you can get some information from the next line, where there are "mourners," so you know it must be sad. The actor is saying that he and the other players are ill-suited to playing tragedies because they can't cry on cue. They need to revive the Comic Muse (hopefully,

with this play) so that they can continue to act in the theater.

33. **The correct answer is D.** The following line "who deals in sentimentals" can help you answer this question, even if you don't know what "mawkish" means. Sentimental means emotional, so that adjective eliminates choices C and E. Choice B, "devastating and cruel," is not usually described as sentimental, either. You can eliminate choice A because "realistic" doesn't square with the adjective "spurious," which means false. The best answer is choice D, maudlin and contrived, which fit with the critiques of sentimental movies that we watch even today, so it's not as unfamiliar as it seems to be. As the speaker has been noting that he can't cry on cue, he is showing that he doesn't want a maudlin, sentimental story—he wants a rousing comedy!

34. **The correct answer is E.** The options to choose from use words like "contrived" (which you saw in question 33) and proposes that a genre has died and the actor cannot cry for it (which you saw in question 32). These questions can't contradict each other: what can you take from 32 and 33 together? Options II and III present the situation in clear language: the speaker disdains sentimental plays, but he's staged a sentimental death scene for the Muse of Comedy, only to show that he can't cry for her death. There's no mention of the audience laughing in lines 8-14—although he asks them to laugh later—so Option I is unlikely. There's no choice for options I, II, and III all together, so you know that you have to make a choice of the best combinations. The correct combination of options is choice E.

35. **The correct answer is C.** Here the actor is proclaiming lines from those "mawkish," "spurious," "sentimental" plays, along with famous lines from tragic plays, just to show the audience what a bad actor he is.

You can imagine his tone as exaggeratedly grandiose—he is being like Polonius in *Hamlet* when he delivers his advice, but he is mixing up all of the advice so that it comes out as nonsense. The advice is hard to imagine being authoritative (choice D) or wise (choice E), so you can strike those options. It would be silly if he were gaining confidence from delivering clichés, so choice A is also not a good option. The problem is that those lines don't inspire his comic gifts, so choice B gives you the opposite. With these descriptions of the actor's tone, the shape of the passage starts to become clearer, one hopes, and you're getting a sense for the peculiarities of historical humor.

36. **The correct answer is B.** If you read questions 30-36 together, you can start to get a good sense of what's happening in the passage, even if the language mystifies you. The Comic Muse is sick, so he needs to revive her with a play to perform in so that he and his friends can act in their preferred genre. He can elicit laughs by acting poorly when he tries to proclaim serious lines from other plays. You can eliminate choice A because there are no mentions of money, and choice D is too general to be a useful answer. No one has actually died on the stage—just the genre of comedy—so he doesn't need a replacement actor (choice C) or actress (choice E). The answer is in the shift at line 33: "One hope remains!" and he introduces a "Doctor" who can cure the Comic Muse . . . with a new play to stage for the audience. Thus, the answer to the question is that he needs a good comic play to perform in, choice B.

37. **The correct answer is B.** The rhyme is self-consciously bad, so you need to find the choice among the answers that does not indicate this self-consciousness or the inside joke of "killing" the Comic Muse with bad acting. Choices A, C, D, and E each make reference to the play's jokes, while choice B

seems to still believe that we're watching a tragedy. Therefore, choice B is the outlier and the correct answer.

38. **The correct answer is D.** The Five Draughts—the cures for the ailing Comic Muse—are the five acts of the play. He has only mentioned two muses, Comedy and Tragedy, and there are nine Muses, not five, so choice B is unlikely. He has not made reference to the five senses (choice A), so they are also not the best choice. Neither choice C nor D makes sense in the extended metaphor that he will draw in lines 34-46, so the best answer is choice D. In five acts, the upcoming comedy will try to cure its dying Muse.

39. **The correct answer is C.** As you've gradually been figuring out the context and meaning of the unfamiliar theatrical terms in this passage, this question might allow you to go back to questions 30 and 31 to sort out who's speaking to whom: The actor is introducing a new play. Who can best cure the ailing Comic Muse but a playwright who has composed the play the audience is about to view? If you're still unsure, you can eliminate the less likely choices of hero and villain because those figures haven't been mentioned yet. The audience is the group being addressed and asked to judge the Doctor, so choice D is unlikely. The playwright and the actor could be the same person, but you wouldn't be asked to make that determination—that would be a very specific historical detail to recall without any textual evidence. (David Garrick was indeed an actor, director, and playwright, but he is serving only the role of actor in this prologue.)

40. **The correct answer is B.** "If you reject the dose, and make wry faces" means that the audience may reject the play and refuse to laugh. "Wry" means mocking or unimpressed. He is saying that the Comic Muse

may have a desperate, incurable ailment, if the audience doesn't laugh at the new play—so they have an incentive to laugh, lest Comedy be gone forever! Choices A and D mention satire and disguises, but neither has been important to this prologue, so they are not good options. Choice C repeats his game from earlier in the passage, when he acts so melodramatically that the tragedy becomes comic—one hopes the playwright has a better production to show the audience than that goof. Choice E is a possibility, but "making wry faces" is not much of a retaliation. Choice B is the best option.

41. **The correct answer is A.** It's useful to figure out who "his"/"him" is referring to in the line "YOU, must his pretensions back / Pronounce him Regular, or dub him Quack." *He* is the Doctor, and "you," the audience, are being asked to assess his worthiness as a doctor of the Comic Muse—that is, as a playwright. We might say the College is the theater itself, where he is being assessed. Therefore, the audience is assessing choice A, the claims to the play's quality. His/him/he does not refer to the actor delivering the prologue, so choice B is incorrect; the criticisms (choice D) of the play will be the *judgments* of those pretensions. A pretense may be a disguise (choice C) in other contexts, but not here; there haven't been any mentions of arguments among the theater company, so choice E isn't supported by the passage.

42. **The correct answer is D.** The Doctor (the playwright) has been given but one task here, to cure the Comic Muse. A doctor who makes false claims for his cures is called a quack. Thus there is only one good choice: the playwright who can't cure the Comic Muse with a good comedy has failed at his job and is a quack. Choices A and B about actors don't follow from that Doctor analogy, which focuses on the playwright. There are no directors (choice C) mentioned directly in the passage; as noted earlier, even today

we remember playwrights from that period more than we do directors. The playwright isn't being asked to play multiple registers, so choice E is asking too much!

43. **The correct answer is B.** It may seem unfamiliar today to read such a direct appeal to the audience in a prologue, for we now treat the prologue as something more neutral, used for scene-setting or general introduction. In this situation, the audience would probably be familiar with the theater company, their previous productions, the playwright's last success or bomb, and so on. Going to the theater to see a comedy was a social experience, with lots of inside jokes between the actors, playwrights, and members of the audience that showed the strength of the social bonds inside the theater. You can get a sense of that idea from the speaker's self-deprecating humor at the beginning of the prologue, the inside jokes about the other actors' abilities, and the direct address to the audience to judge the playwright's success. That's their power. The other options here don't work as well: the audience is being asked to judge the playwright, which doesn't defend (choice A) against criticism—it may even invite it as a joking reaction. The "tragic" death of the Comic Muse was not an example of pathos (choice C), or an appeal to strong emotion, because it was intended as a joke. There are no threats against the audience or rival companies (choices D and E)—this was a jovial environment where the jokes on the playwright warm up the audience, helping them enjoy the play and laugh a little more easily.

44. **The correct answer is E.** Sent to live in the country, the narrator Sybylla gives a long list of all of her host M'Swat's nightly conversation topics until she cannot bear the "sordidness" any longer. We tend to use "sordid" to refer to something sleazy, but she is mostly just objecting to the tedium of so many details about country life—who

has bigger sheep, who has more sheep, etc. Choices A, B, C, and D all describe features on that list; his speculations about her romantic interest in Peter don't come until later in the passage, so the best choice is E.

45. **The correct answer is B.** Sybylla's narrative style is distinctive, and this question sets up a series of questions about how to interpret her idiosyncrasies. Her description of her motives is evasive—yet she has no reason to evade the readers she is addressing. It's more likely that she likes to hear how these words sound as she's authoring her own life. Indeed, Miles Franklin wrote *My Brilliant Career* while she was still a teenager, mostly for her friends' entertainment, before submitting it to a publisher. (You would not need to know that in order to answer the question, but still: she was in high school!) Choices C, D, and E aren't supported by the passage, for she has just described her walks as a way to remember her home in Caddagat and to pray that she can get out of the country. She doesn't want to explain the walks further, so the answer is choice B.

46. **The correct answer is B.** Sybylla rarely speaks in dialogue in this passage, filling it instead with her own verbose narration, rich with her 50-cent vocabulary. She rarely picks a short word, if a long one like "consternation" or "presumptuousness" will work instead. One gets the feeling that she has read these words more often than she has spoken them aloud--or heard them spoken aloud. Her short, formal dialogue, like "It is I," contrasts with the M'Swat men's use of dialect. You can strike the options that suggest she uses dialect (choices A and D). "It is I" and her headache explanation are hardly sassy or comic (choices C and E), so those choices are incorrect, too.

47. **The correct answer is C.** Choosing the outlier here is relatively easy. Although Sybylla goes on to discuss Peter's etiquette,

the reason for her verbosity is that she uses language aspirationally. Choices A, B, D, and E are all versions of that explanation: her narrative voice is self-consciously writerly because she wants something better than where she is. That tone can be supercilious and condescending (choices A and D), or it can be authorial (choices B and E). Choice C is the only one that doesn't fit.

48. **The correct answer is C.** As Sybylla goes on to describe Peter's habits, she notes that he does not question the gender roles around the house. His mother does his chores for him, but he does not even notice the effort, for why would he? That's what he thinks is normal. She takes care to say that he is only ignorant, not rude, so choices A and B are incorrect. Sybylla likes Peter more than she likes his father, but she does not characterize him as rejecting his father's example, so choices D and E are incorrect. Choice C is the best option.

49. **The correct answer is A.** The snippets of the poem that Sybylla quotes, taken with the bits in the footnote and question text, don't give a flattering picture of the Middleton Rouseabout as a poetic subject. Choices B, C, D, and E indicate far more generosity of spirit to Sybylla than she merits in this description—she has no real desire to understand Peter's inner life more than she describes here. Interestingly, Miles Franklin sent *My Brilliant Career* to the "Middleton Rouseabout" poet Henry Lawson, so he wrote the preface for the book to celebrate a remarkable writing achievement for a teenager. (He worked as a roustabout for some years before becoming a writer.)

50. **The correct answer is C.** For those romantics who detect a crush: there's no romance between Sybylla and Peter. You don't need to know that for this passage, but it does go to show that you would be jumping to conclusions if you went for option III.

There's no textual evidence to support that possibility, unless you wanted to read against her strong "consternation" in the last line of the passage. Such a reading would echo M'Swat's own jumping to conclusions, and the passage is aligned squarely against him. You can eliminate the choices with option III, choices D and E. The other two options in this question have more interesting tensions to explore in Sybylla's descriptive abilities and her language. Sybylla is a keen observer of details, mostly centered around solidifying the stereotype of him in the "no opinions, no idears" mode that she quotes. In observing so keenly, she starts to echo M'Swat's assessments of his neighbors—a dip into her own sordidness, though she would hardly say so. Sybylla's fragmentary quotations of the poem's dialect "idears," together with her imitation of M'Swat's "g-u-r-r-l" are striking in a narration filled with so many aspirational words. As option I suggests, they show the mix of highbrow aspirations and country language that she hears and digests every day. They show her ability to switch between those registers. Options I and II are the most interesting tensions to consider in this passage, so the answer is choice C.

51. **The correct answer is C.** "Bushcraft" is an Australian term for outdoor skills, a term that's guessable from the context of the passage about how he might make money through hard slogging. From that description, it seems like choices A and C are the best possibilities, and Sybylla's characterization is not very complimentary. Her tone in the whole passage is dismissive, so choice C is the clear answer.

52. **The correct answer is E.** Sybylla takes pains to say that she respected Peter, but her condescension seems to be getting in the way of her seeing some of the ironies in her dismissal of him. These ironies aren't

going to fully reverse the way she feels about him, but they add some complexity to her narration. First, we can strike Option II because we don't get any indication that the elder M'Swat goes his own way: Sybylla notes that he is obsessed with his family's standing compared to others, and he tries to intervene (mistakenly) to tell her she can't have Peter because she's not wealthy enough. Those objections do not sound like an independent spirit, so we can strike all choices with Option II: B and D. Option I points out that "a man by his own lights" is a colloquial phrase, and it's not hard to imagine Peter using it. Option III points out that such a phrase describes Sybylla herself, although if she were adapting it for her own narration, she would come up with a longer way to say "she plays by her own rules." These are reasonable complexities to find in Sybylla's characterization of Peter, so we can pick choice E. They don't jump to conclusions; they are notes about her tone, not her intentions or motives. From the phrasing of these options, you might note some of the ways you can discuss these kinds of tensions and complexities in narrative language and tone without insisting that you know a character's inner motivations, even in a first-person narration. Indeed, Sybylla herself warns against trying to do that. Some of those writing strategies that may be useful for the essay section include using phrases like "the tensions in her language indicate a conflict between" or "her description becomes complicated when we notice that even though...."

53. **The correct answer is D.** Sybylla's verbose counterfactuals about what the M'Swat's cannot think are the most striking part of her narration, so this question is asking you to infer the meaning behind this unusual device. Choices A, B, and C are not supported by the passage, because she has no desire to understand them more deeply, nor for them to understand her. She is content with being annoyed most of the time—it helps her feel superior. Choice E is a strong possibility, for Sybylla *is* lonely on their farm and does fill up that space with her narration. However, the word "conversations" is not quite the right description of this device, for she is not imagining dialogue or back-and-forth with them about their opinions or interests. She is imagining their dumb silence, what they don't know—rather than what they might say. Choice D is a better description of that narrative device and its purpose.

54. **The correct answer is B.** When Sybylla says that she and Peter respected each other, she has a sharp tone behind it. The adverb that best modifies this verb is definitely "grudgingly," because it's clear that she doesn't have much respect for him. Choice A is a slight possibility, but Sybylla rarely feels duty in this passage—it's more apt to say that she holds grudges.

55. **The correct answer is A.** This question asks you to make an inference about the relationship between Sybylla's narration and her brief dialogue with Peter. Sybylla would perhaps rather be a ghost than be trapped on the farm, so she spends her time observing and trying to interact with them as little as possible. You can eliminate the heavy-handed explanations like choices B and C. She stays grounded when she is praying, "[kneeling] on the parched ground," so choice D is not a good choice. Choice E is a strong possibility, except that, as question 53 asks, she is not really trying to understand other people. She is content to project her own feelings onto them, because she believes they are boring blanks. The best answer here is choice A: that she stays on the margins, where she can project all the more easily.

Section II

Essay 1: "Lines Composed in a Concert-Room," by Samuel Taylor Coleridge

8-9 Sample Essay

In "Lines Composed in a Concert Room," by Samuel Taylor Coleridge, it is difficult for the modern reader to ignore the word "Harlot" in the first stanza. Coleridge's speaker says that he "detest[s] / These scented Rooms, where to a gaudy throng, / Heaves the proud Harlot her distended breast," as though it were the female singer's "laborious song" that were distracting him. Nonsense: he is leering at her. It is difficult to ignore this gross objectification of female singers, especially when Coleridge's speaker seems to build an entire argument out of it. He prefers "the merry maids, whose ringlets toss in light" in nature, or, best of all, his "dear Anne" a "gentle woman" who sings ballads that are simple and evocative. He may praise Anne for her natural simplicity, but why does that praise have to follow so much objectification of other women?

The direction of this critique is not just a 21st-century gender studies criticism of Coleridge; rather, it is useful for thinking about how we always bring our context with us as we experience poetry and song. Contemporary female readers may bring their own enlightened distaste for leering to the poetry anthology; Coleridge's speaker brought his sexism to the concert hall. Context matters: our environments and preferences are things we build. The thrust of the poem seems clear, as the speaker makes a basic distinction between how he prefers to hear music: in a natural setting as opposed to an artificial concert hall. That opposition seems fitting for a Romantic poet. Yet his distinction is too simple, for the speaker is blind to the ways in which he constructs <u>both</u> spaces: it is not that one is artificial and the other is not, but that both are highly artificial spaces, constructed by the poet's eye and ear. Ironically, the best example of that construction comes from his praise for Anne's natural singing, as she "<u>remeasures</u> / Whatever tones and melancholy pleasures / The things of Nature utter." Anne reconstructs Nature with her own human voice: she is making, constructing, artificing nature.

It may even be possible to say that Anne and the speaker do similar work in artificing nature, for the speaker could be said to "re-measure" nature with his own rhyming lines in the poem. He creates a complex rhyme scheme that begins ABAB, only to add in an extra ABACB CDCEFE in the following two stanzas, adding an extra predictive rhyme in each stanza--"re-measuring" the structure with more counter-point as he goes along. This is a poem that's highly attuned to creating an artificial, complex structure and context out of rhyme; it is a celebration of artifice, even as he claims to disdain such a structured situation when he listens to music. Is there such a strong difference between music and poetry here?

The speaker seems to think that he is merely an observer in these listening spaces, either as a leering, snobby critic in the concert hall where he wants to be "released," or an appreciative lounger when he is listening to Anne. The passage with the Musician, a male singer of Scottish folk ballads, furthers this idea, for he remembers the old man in the context of a constructed parenthetical statement: "(Whom, stretching from my nurse's arms I kissed,)." This parenthetical could not be more artificial as a structure inside a poem--we see the parentheses around it but could never hear them.

He constructs these listening spaces with his eyes and ears, picking up on the tiny details of the "long-breathed singers up-trilled strain / Bursts in a squall." These details aren't noticed by the "prattl[ing]" audience members who aren't listening to her, so they may as well not exist until he details them in his own rhymed context of criticism. Like a tree falling in a forest with no one around to hear it, a singer with bad melisma doesn't know she is bad until it is heard and remarked upon: listening takes two people to create a context. The speaker is not merely passive: he makes these scenes with his discerning ear.

That is why his obnoxious leering gaze matters: it is like a "male ear" form of the "male gaze." (The blind Musician only underscores this idea.) John Berger says that the entire history of art is about this subject: "Men look at women. Women watch themselves being looked at." In this poem, men hear women and construct the scenes for assessing them, all the while thinking that they are merely telling it like it is. The concert hall is artificial. Natural voices are the best. No, the male ear is constructing these scenes and then denying their own role in that construction. There's no way out for the female voice but to be heard without being listened to.

Reader response for the 8-9 essay

One of the reasons this essay is admirable is that the author begins with something that bothered her about the poem—the use of the word "Harlot"—and used that anger to write an interesting essay. The essay isn't merely a takedown of Coleridge or the speaker for being sexist, though; she doesn't spend it "proving" an uncontroversial point and amassing evidence for it in lines from the poem. Instead, she lets that initial frustration motivate her to dig deeper into the question of how men listen to women in the poem. A less sophisticated essay might just be about sexism in this poem; this essay is about gender and the construction of a listening space. That's a rich concept to develop in only a short time, so the author must have been thinking about the subject in her own life of listening to popular music. (That's a fine way to practice thinking about gender in poetry or representations of art: practice analyzing them in the popular culture you consume.)

The author builds the concept of the "constructed listening space" by paying close attention to language in the poem, especially that crucial word "re-measure." That word ends up being very useful for the argument! Again, a less sophisticated essay might read: he uses language about measurement in the poem and leaves it at that observation, whereas this essay takes that attention to diction and uses it to develop her own argument and idea. The author's idea dominates the essay, and the close-reading scaffolds it, instead of it being mere surface observations.

The attention to rhyme is also compelling, although the author could have spent more time discussing how that elaborate structure worked and explained it in more detail.

The detail about the Musician allows her to add in a slightly complicated example of a male singer; without him, the essay would have felt like she was conveniently skipping over evidence that didn't support her claim about the objectified women. Having to account for him also lets her make an interesting point about the constructed space of parentheses inside the nurse's arms: a highly original reading!

There are many insights and remarkable ideas in this essay, with a compelling line of argument to the end with the John Berger quotation. A fitting conclusion.

<u>5-6 Sample Essay</u>

Samuel Taylor Coleridge's poem "Lines Composed in a Concert Room" shows his preference for natural beauty. He is inside a concert hall, but the audience all around him is more concerned with socializing and being seen than listening to the music, ruining the experience for him. In this poem, he argues that we should listen to nature instead of to recorded music. You can even say that we should make our own music out of nature, the way that Anne does in the last stanza. He uses diction, rhyme scheme, and the example of Anne to make his argument for how nature is better than fakeness.

In the concert hall, everyone is watching themselves instead of listening. The performer is full of "Vanity" and even "Hatred," and the audience feels the same way. They have reason to hate her, for she is not a good singer. The speaker quotes that it sounds like she is "burst in a squall." The speaker also quotes, "These feel not Music's genuine power," even if she was a good singer they would still not being paying attention because the concert hall is so cramped. Even the Priest does not listen to the music, even though he should.

In contrast, the speaker says he likes being "unheard" and "unseen" when he is out in nature on the lake. He can remember fond times of hearing a blind musician sing. The blind musician is not vain like the concert hall singer, so the speaker is drawing a connection between seeing and hearing. It is best not to be to self-conscious when you are listening or when you are singing, so that you can enjoy the music. Everyone in the concert hall could learn that lesson better from this poem.

The rhyme scheme in the poem seems simple at first, but it becomes more complicated as he adds more lines to the stanzas. This shows that he can find beauty not just in the simplicities of nature but also make something beautiful out of simple language that becomes more complicated. He uses rhymes such as "sneer" and "ear" in the second stanza to show how people are listening badly in the concert, but then he starts to show "pleasure" in the listening by rhyming it with "measure." This shows that he can listen better in nature (where the pleasure takes place) but he can also make measures of lines in the form of stanzas. The rhymes become pleasing to him, instead of obnoxious.

Finally, it is the example of Anne who shows that you can mix human song and nature. She is the compromise between nature and human voices because she is so unaware of herself. She does not realize the speaker is paying attention to her in lines like "birds or trees / Or moan of ocean-gale in weedy caves, / Or where the stiff grass mid the heath-plant waves, / Murmur and music thin of sudden breeze" because she is literally lost in nature. There's no description of her, just of the nature that surrounds her. It is best when she fades into the background and it is not about her but her music. This is the opposite to the concert hall, where they are obsessed with being seen in the audience. Here, the only audience is the grass and birds.

The speaker starts the poem opposed to human voices, but he ends it feeling like he has found a compromise when he can listen to Anne in nature. What's important is that there is no stage to perform on, but nature to be embedded in like you are part of it. The best way to listen is not to be aware that it's artificial, when you internalize the rhymes and rhythms instead of being aware of them so much.

Reader response for the 5-6 essay

There is a good idea here about the way that seeing and listening work together, and the author is beginning to think about the way those ideas work in complex ways throughout the poem. The mention of the lines about "unseen, unheard" is a good foil to the opening lines about the constant surveillance in the concert space. It might be a good idea to start with a larger concept about the complicated relationship between seeing and hearing, to shift the reader outside of the obvious points of opposing art and nature, or artifice and nature.

The problem is that those obvious art vs. nature dichotomies limit the essay to being a THESIS ANTITHESIS SYNTHESIS (or compromise, in the example of Anne) essay. The author uses the language of "argument," as though Coleridge were constructing an essay rather than a poem. It would be more productive to use a phrase like: "The speaker's perspective changes," or "The speaker sets up an opposition and then finds tensions in it." Those kinds of analytical phrases would be more useful than framing the poem as an argument. The three paragraphs don't relate to one another—each one seems like just an example, rather than the development of a more interesting, original theme in considering that possible tie between seeing and hearing.

The author can continue to work on integrating quotations into his or her analysis. The author misreads some lines about "Hatred" and "Vanity." That problem could be addressed by trying to quote more substantial fragments--phrases, rather than single words. Single words can be useful for analyzing AFTER you've quoted a line and given context, but they have a way of losing context when they are just single words floating around in the paragraph. The author tries to use a more substantial quotation from the end of the poem, and that's a good start, but there's little analysis of the language in those final lines of the poem, so that passage remains undigested.

The mention of "recorded music" in the opening paragraph is an odd mistake that the author could have checked in editing, but it doesn't really detract from the essay.

<u>1-2 Sample Essay</u>

This poem is about art and nature, and how you find the best kinds of art from the natural world, not the world of people. At the same time, the poem is full of rhymes, which are not natural. There is a contradiction between the author's use of rhymes and his dislike of human voices, because rhymes only happen from human voices. It is unclear what he wants, or if there is a happy medium between the two.

This is shown in the first paragraph about the concert hall and how bored he is, and how bad the singer is. Her voice "bursts." He feels suffocated. He doesn't want to be indoors or listening to her. He quotes, "O give me, from this heartless scene released." He wants to be outside in nature. This is shown by the last paragraph where he describes "trees" and "grass" that he can listen to in the wind. He likes the sound of nature and quotes "The things of Nature utter; birds or trees." Utter means that that is all he wants.

Nevertheless, nature doesn't contain rhymes, but the poet is using rhymes to talk about nature. What does he want: art or nature? Can he have both? That is the question left open by this poem.

<u>Reader response for the 1-2 essay</u>

This essay is very short and superficial. The author makes an attempt at integrating quotations into the essay and picks some good possibilities, but there is little analysis. The author's main idea about the absence of rhyme in nature is confusing. It almost seems contrarian to make a point like this, because it seems to ignore the kind of contract that a poet makes with the genre: there are long traditions of poems about nature and art that use rhyme. It's not a contradiction to use rhyme in a poem about the pleasures of nature.

At the same time, that tension is always underlying these poems, and I wonder if the student might be convinced (outside of the exam structure) that paying attention to the subtleties of rhyme might enhance their understanding of how a poet comments on his own use of artifice to order the natural world. In this essay, that idea isn't possible because it's so brief, but there may be a way to turn this contrarianism into poetic attention. Maybe!

Essay 2: "The Library Window," Margaret Oliphant

<u>8-9 Sample Essay</u>

During her career as a novelist, Margaret Oliphant wrote different genres of novels, from domestic novels about "women's issues" to ghost stories. In her short story "The Library Window," the majority of the story seems to be taken up by a never-ending conversation among old people at a nursing home of sorts, as they bicker about whether a window across the street is really a window. Is it painted over? Is it a door? Is it boarded up? The narrator is visiting her elderly aunt, who explains: "the oftener people look at it, the less they are able to say." This essay will interpret that conversation as a deeper inquiry on the question of genre: how is a story constructed by its frame, then filled in with reader interpretations? Margaret Oliphant's career writing domestic fiction and ghost stories will serve as a frame for the essay, for "The Library Window" seems to take on elements of both genres, depending on how you look at it, just like the titular window.

As the elderly people argue about whether it's a window, a high door, a boarded-up window, or some other architecture feature, they start to intersperse these observations with bits of family history and events they have witnessed in their own lives. Lady Carnbee brings her domestic squabbles into the argument: she doesn't mind about the window, but she is nursing resentments with Jeanie: "Mind!... I mind when our mother was marriet, Jeanie . . ." Another lady wants to use the window to comment on how there are no good servants anymore: "for these hizzies of women-servants in this ill age . . ." They have been practicing two kinds of observation all those years: observation of the window, and observation of each other's domestic concerns. In these parts of the conversation, the story feels like a drawing story of manners about the minutia of everyday life. The window allows them to attach their attention onto an object, then to filter their everyday concerns through that question. It must be a window of sorts, because it is a marker of domestic life.

However, it might be more ambiguous than a simple domestic window into everyday observation. Its middle, ambiguous position is that of <u>screen</u>, instead of window. Instead of being able to look through it to see inside the Library or other house on the street, the characters can only look at the blankness to project their own opinions. The narrator herself projects her own feelings of comparison: "she felt unconsciously the contrast of my youngness to their oldness . . ." With the narrator's added comparison perspective, the library window is a screen to project one's anxieties about age, or servants and class, or family resentments. The narrator remarks on this projection: "I was more taken with the old ladies than with the thing they were looking at." These old women become a kind of architectural feature themselves: "the wall of old ladies in their old satin gowns all glazed with age. Lady Carnbee with her lace about her head." The content of their conversation doesn't matter when the window is just a screen for projections, for the important thing is the viewer's subjectivity.

One might say that when the window is a screen, the story becomes more complex than just a domestic fiction; it becomes a psychological fiction that became popular at the beginning of the twentieth century with Sigmund Freud.

There is less evidence of his psychology in this passage, but it is a possibility worth considering.

However, it might be easier to see the psychological ambiguities by looking at it as a genre of a ghost story, which Margaret Oliphant was a major author of. She is mixing the components of the domestic story about marriages and servants with the more ambiguous stories about ghosts. Ghosts can serve as markers of psychology because they are projections. They are not solid like a screen, but diaphanous and changing, just like the window may be, itself. In this passage, Oliphant does not say either way whether this is a ghost story, but the elderly people's arguments may be interpreted as arguments about seeing the super- natural. They call it a "dead thing" and yet they try to see if it's still active, like they are trying to detect a ghost. One character says: "It is just a very dead thing without any reflection in it" but others see the reflection. The questions sound like a ghost story: what is it? Are they seeing the same thing?

Ghost stories are fundamentally stories about interpretations and what they say about us, as Freud says in the Interpretations of Dreams. If one could continue reading this story, would the answer ever be revealed or would it go on forever? What kind of genre story would it turn into after it's a domestic fiction or a ghost story? The reader's own interpretations have the power to make it become another genre, like it's a window of text that we see through to see our own ideas.

<u>Reader response for the 8-9 essay</u>

This is a very long, very interesting essay. The author tends to ramble a bit and the Sigmund Freud tangent is perhaps not necessary because it gets away from the text, but it shows significant thinking on the page.

The author sets up a compelling initial framework around the idea of the window in different genres of fiction. It was not necessary for exam-writers to work with that brief bit of biographical material, but this is an inspired reading. (It may be too brief for the reader's desire to find Freud in it.) That strong structure is a traditional five-paragraph essay, but the idea develops significantly from paragraph to paragraph, so each idea seems to relate to the next one. The essay does not have the sense that the author has three distinct ideas and has fit them into boxes; rather, it seems as if the essay builds from the consideration of the domestic, then the ambiguous screen (a good middle paragraph), and finally to the ghost story.

There are some repetitive passages and unwieldy sentences, but this author was clearly inspired by the prompt.

<u>5-6 Sample Essay</u>

In Margaret Oliphant's short story, "The Library Window," the characters argue about whether a window is actually a window. Not very much else happens, which makes the reader wonder why it's a story. The narrator is in the same situation of wondering why she is listening to the old people argue, so we identify with her. When she remarks that listening to them makes her feel her age, the point of the story becomes clear. This is a story about the fear of death, and the conversation about the window is to stall off death for the elderly residents across the street. This idea might sound like an over-interpretation, but there are three pieces of evidence: the black paint (pent), the "memory of man" mentioned by one of the characters, and the length of the conversation.

The characters use the symbolism of black paint to show, but not tell, that the window symbolizes death. They say that it has "black pent" on it. It is also high up, which could symbolize that it is not part of the earth anymore. The symbolism is ambiguous, just like the window.

The reason for this ambiguous interpretation is that it's a lot like Waiting for Godot or another existential play, which are all about the fear of death. The existential questions that the characters are asking about the "memory of man" is like what one would discuss in Godot or even Rosencrantz and Guildenstern Are Dead. This could be a play and it would be an interesting way of designing a set, where you'd only see them looking out a curtain, but you wouldn't see what they're looking at. That would show the audience that we'll never be able to know for certain.

This is a story about the fear of death because the old people are all afraid of dying. The main character cares about them, especially her aunt, and does not want them to die. So she keeps the story going to stall off death. If they keep guessing, maybe the story will never end.

Reader response for the 5-6 essay

This essay runs out of steam, in part because it can't sustain a thoughtful development with such a strong overstated interpretation at the beginning. "The Library Window" seems to be more about *competing* interpretations and the unresolvability of those questions, instead of just one idea: the fear of death. When the author makes a one-way claim like that, there's not much room to test related ideas. Everything gets filtered into that particular interpretation, and the evidence for that idea seems thin. The interpretation becomes overdetermined.

Another problem with the essay is the lack of textual evidence that might support this reading. The fragmentary quotations don't serve the author well. "Black paint" is hardly enough to hang this kind of interpretation on. It may be that the author realized the lack of textual evidence that could be quoted and analyzed and went for digressions instead.

The digressions show someone who's interested in existential philosophy and has some kind of reference point for comparing this story's confusion with existential drama. It's an unusual reading, and perhaps outside of this exam there's more to say by comparing the whole story with Beckett's writings. It's an unlikely pairing, but who knows? The comparison doesn't serve the author as well, though, because it becomes a long digression about how to perform the story as a play, which doesn't have anything to do with what's on this exam page. The author needs to stick to what can be analyzed from the language on the sheet of paper, instead of imagining what it could look like in some other imaginary context.

<u>1-2 Sample Essay</u>

> In the short story, "The Library Window," the characters are in a ghost story, in which they keep seeing something outside the window, but they aren't sure what it is. It is a very interesting ghost story because it doesn't seem like one. You don't ever see the ghost. That's what makes it a ghost story, though. You never know what the answer could be. It seems like this story is just one day in a lot of years where they're having the same conversation. They are locked in a kind of eternal question because they can't go outside to look at it.
>
> The answer comes from the lady who says it's a "delusion." That's the secret to the ghost story, they have been making it all up in their heads like a collective delusion that everyone sees the same imaginary thing. This is a story that looks like a story about nothing, then a ghost story, and then it becomes apparent that it is all a delusion that they will keep talking about forever.

<u>Reader response for the 1-2 essay</u>

This is a short essay without textual evidence, except for one word: "delusion." That's a good word to analyze in depth, because it's potentially interesting to showing the unresolvability of the story's main question. However, without more analysis from the text, these two brief paragraphs look more like misguided summary of the story.

In the very brief item written, the author makes an interesting point that it's a ghost story that doesn't seem like a ghost story. Perhaps the author was inspired to write that after reading the biographical material in the prompt. The author might be able to pursue this kind of question in a longer essay with more evidence.

Essay 3: Free Response

<u>8-9 Sample Essay</u>

> The first thing for modern readers to know about *Sense and Sensibility* is that in Jane Austen's time, "sensible" means too romantic and emotional, not level-headed and wise. Marianne is the sensible sister who seems to believe she lives in a love poem that she may read and perform with great emotion; whereas her sister Elinor is the rational, logical one. This contrast is too simple, however. Instead, it is instructive to pay attention to how the two sisters re-read poems and letters, for those reading habits are more complicated than they appear to be. Both sisters are obsessive re-readers, for they each believe that re-reading will somehow show them a new interpretation, or even, just slightly, shift the situation into their favor.

Indeed, it is in their reading habits that we can see problems in the overly simple contrast, for Elinor is not the wholly rational reader she appears to be. She is not a credulous reader; she is very attentive to details. Early in the novel, we see her reading the offer of the small house carefully, where she notes the rent and the proximity to others, and she looks it over carefully before making her decision. She is used to dotting her i's and crossing her t's. She applies the same attentiveness to her emotions, however guardedly she keeps them. She reads and re-reads the letters to Edward Ferrars obsessively, making small inferences from his shared details, which add up into her picture of the man she loves but cannot quite approach. Nevertheless, she makes a large mistake in interpreting that he is already spoken for; it is only a personal interaction late in the story that solves her misinterpretation, when she cannot hide behind letters anymore. This complication does not mean that she is a bad reader, but rather that she over-relies on her normal, even admirable mode of re-reading carefully with too narrow a focus that limits her vision beyond the written page. Her strength in reading becomes her weakness: she is too careful an interpreter to take risks as a reader.

Her sister Marianne also over-relies on her reading talents because they bring her such pleasure and praise. She is a skilled reader of poetry because she reads it and performs it so often, and she admires others who have similar talents. She criticizes Edward Ferrars for how he "read with so little sensibility." Her initial paramour, Willoughby, on the other hand, is an "exquisite" reader, who "was exactly formed to engage Marianne's heart." Marianne's sensibility comes not just from her habit of mirroring her reality to what she reads in a love poem, but in the very notion that reading is a form of mirroring. To use a word that is somewhat taboo: she wants reading to be relatable, so she makes it relate to her life by seeing the page as a mirror that she may look at again and again as she re-reads poems and situations through her sensibility.

There are limitations to this mode of reading, however. After Marianne and Willoughby part, she "read nothing but what they had been used to read together." She wants to recreate those reading experiences that made her fall in love with him, to freeze the past by reading. At the same time, she is a romantic, sensible reader who feels transformed by books, so she knows that they are dynamic. Books and poems do change as we read them; we become different people as we grow up, read more, experience new things. Marianne and Elinor each seem to want <u>nothing</u> and <u>something</u> to change as they read. They want their cherished prior interpretations to remain the same, while the current situation to change through some new interpretation that will reveal itself through another glance at the poem or letter. Wouldn't it make as much sense for re-reading to reveal to Marianne that Willoughby the exquisite reader was mirroring her not because he was "exactly formed to engage [her] heart," but rather as a seduction trick? He may not have completely realized it, too, as mirroring behavior was so crucial to his exquisite reading performances.

Marianne screams as she reads Willoughby's letter confessing that he did not mean to hurt her. He writes that he did not mean to make her think that he cared for her more than he did--he did not mean to be such an exquisite reader or performer. Crucially, Austen notes that Marianne "read it again and again," for that is the Dashwood sisters' reading habit. She writes multiple notes to him to make the situation different--she is trying to re-read the situation and re-write it so that she may not be as hurt this time around. Willoughby has stopped mirroring her, however, so her re-reading is like looking only at herself, and not at her exquisite partner.

What of Jane Austen's own obsessive re-readers? It is well known that people love to read Austen's novels and mirror the characters, like they are Marianne. They can use the books as models for how to fall in love with a Darcy from *Pride and Prejudice*. Or perhaps they are cautious readers like Elinor, careful readers who want the novels to remain the same artifacts whenever they pick them up again. Whichever sister we read into, we should know that our re-readings will always be slightly different.

Reader response for the 8-9 essay

This is a lovely essay that shifts expectations a bit because it focuses on Elinor's reading habits, rather than Marianne's, which are more dramatic and obvious to see shift. Marianne's habits do appear as an instructive contrast, but it is a nuanced portrayal of both characters' habits rather than a black-and-white opposition of the two sisters.

The essay gets out of that oppositional approach by focusing on a shared habit: re-reading. That concept lets the author compare and contrast scenes that one has read many times before (fittlingly enough). The idea that one's strengths become one's weaknesses in re-reading is lovely and helps cast the characters into new perspectives.

From the author's use of brief quotations, it seems like this is a subject or a novel that she has prepared for the exam, which was a wise choice. That preparation allowed for a long, nuanced analysis.

5-6 Sample Essay

In *Sense and Sensibility* by Jane Austen, the character of Marianne often gets too involved in the love poetry she is reading. The reader can relate with her because she loves to read, but she also needs to look up from her book sometimes and realize that people are not characters. She mistakes it for reality and doesn't realize that people act different in books than they do in real life. She is an example of sensibility, she was a too romantic and emotional. The love poems distract her from the sense she needs to make good choices. She falls in love with the wrong person and doesn't see the right person. She needs to learn the lesson to be a better reader so she can progress as a character. This lesson is seen in her abilities, the comparison with her sister, and the changes in her behavior and choices.

Marianne is admired for her ability to sing, play piano, and recite poetry. These abilities come from her creativity and emotions. She is good at making other people feel the emotions that are overflowing from her, she is a performer. Willoughby is similar at being able to perform for people; Marianne falls in love with him because he can recite poetry with emotion, too. He is a complex character because he is too good at making people believe his performances, he has seduced others with his behavior, which Marianne finds out too late. Performers have a gift for making other people feel emotions. Sensibility is a problem when they feel too much without thinking. Therefore Marianne needs to be better at reading people who are good at reading poetry, that's a complicated way of saying she needs to not believe performances and start understanding human nature.

Marianne needs to be more like her sister, who is the character with sense from the title. Her sister needs to pretend more that she is in one of Marianne's love poems and stop being so hesitant. They both need to become better readers. Her sister is right to be distrustful of Willoughby for being a seducer, but she is also not trusting enough of other people and keeps them at a distance, they are opposites in this way. If Marianne is always performing, her sister Elinor is always hiding behind her common sense. Hiding is a form of reading, and you can see that in the role of the other sister Margaret, who surprises people in the map room where she is hiding and reading a book of maps at the same time. Margaret is like the blend of the two sister because she can talk to people and show off, but she still likes to read for learning and sense, like Elinor. She is the happy medium.

Marianne needs to change, and she does so by becoming a better reader of people. She sees through Willoughby's performances and starts to look beyond her first reactions to Colonel Brandon. It's like Willoughby is an actor, but Brandon is a book you can't judge it by its cover or the first chapter, you have to keep reading it to understand it. There is more to him than meets the eye.

This is a book about people becoming better readers, so it makes sense that Jane Austen was trying to show people how to become better readers themselves. She wants people to read the novel and see these characters for their flaws and their positives, and how they resolve them into becoming better readers of human nature. Therefore, reading is not just for books, it can also be for reading people.

Reader response for the 5–6 essay

The writer often seems to be writing *toward* interesting ideas, which is understandable in a timed essay. The idea of reading books and reading people would be a good way organize the whole essay, and the writer even seems to realize that strength because it shows up in the conclusion. It's underdeveloped, however, because the idea is used only to judge Marianne and Elinor, rather than to show the different ways it manifests in the novel.

The essay is limited by the artificiality of the five-paragraph structure and the notion that there needs to be a lesson or a judgment of the characters—a "should" for Marianne. The essay confines Marianne's behavior, the comparison with Elinor (and Margaret), and Marianne's changes to one paragraph each, making it difficult to show the interrelationships between the characters, or how each character changes.

It's also a concern that the author is getting some ideas from the movie version of the novel, because the anecdote about Margaret's hiding and reading the atlas is, to my knowledge, not in the novel.

Because the author is clearly interested in the film adaptations, she might be able to work in a small mention into an expandable, refocused essay around her clearest idea. That essay might be structured as follows:

1. Introduction: Reading books is like reading people.

2. Marianne is good at reading poetry and people and responding to them engagingly.

3. Willoughby is very good at reading poetry and people, yet he is all performance without reciprocation, and this is where Marianne runs into a conflict because she sees only the performance part at first. This paragraph would build on the previous only, rather than being a totally different idea.

4. Contrast Marianne with Elinor, who is more guarded about reciprocation.

5. The idea has developed into the concept of being a reciprocal reader who can be a flexible, adaptable, even skeptical (for Marianne) reader of people and books.

6. Show how the idea of reciprocity relates to our readings of Austen's novels as they're adapted, reciprocally, by filmmakers, other novelists. Champion the role of adaptation as transformation while staying grounded, just like Marianne and Elinor have to adapt their expectations while staying grounded.

<u>1-2 Sample Essay</u>

People love to read books by Jane Austen and imagine that they are the characters. They learn about the characters by pretending they are being them as they are reading about them. However, reading Sense and Sensibility by Jane Austen today is different from the past because the characters aren't relatable anymore. The two sisters Ella and Mary are the title characters. They each represent a different emotion, so someone is supposed to identify with Ella or Mary as their favorite when they are reading. They love to read letters and books, but we don't read the same books anymore, so it's hard for us to understand what they enjoy. From the general reader's point of view, the book is hard to understand because it's like people telling about their favorite book or movie, but others don't have the same experiences to compare to or relate to. Books about the pleasure of reading are supposed to be universal because you can read the book the same way a character does, but Sense and Sensibility is not successful in conveying a universal reading experience. It is not universal because the characters read letters and we don't, the characters read books that we don't know about anymore, and they use diction that is outdated, so it is hard to identify with them.

The characters send letters to each other. They wait for each other's letters and it's like waiting for people to write back today, except it's a shorter period of time. It is similar, but hard to relate to waiting so long. The book is not told in letters like some other books from then, but the whole book is based on this waiting period that we don't experience anymore. Therefore the reading experience is unlike ours, which makes it hard to relate to the characters.

They also read poems and books that we don't read anymore, so it is hard to understand what they are reading. For instance, Maria reads love poetry, but the diction in those poems is hard to understand so we would not have the same sense of falling in love with it. Maria relates to these poems, but times have changed and they do not have the same importance anymore. This makes it hard to relate to her. It is almost ironic that she relates to what she reads by believing she's in a love poem, but we don't understand what she's relating to, so she is unrelatable. Jane Austen is an author that everyone wants to read, but they don't really read her--they just identify with the characters that they see elsewhere. It is ironic that a book about reading isn't really read, just liked in a shallow way. If they had to read it, they might not actually identify with the characters because they seem so far away.

Reader response for the 1-2 essay

The writer's carelessness in not referencing the characters by the correct name further illustrates the writer doesn't want to write about *Sense and Sensibility* and would have more success with a different book. **Use the essay to write about a book you feel prepared to write about because you have a lot to say—not one that you didn't understand or like. It's hard to explore the nuances in a negative because you keep looking for evidence to prove your dislike: everything becomes evidence of unrelatability or lack of "success." At the same time, there's no specific scenes or moments to be analyzed and so the writer gets stuck generalizing to prove the dislike, rather than analyzing moments where there may be "relatability" to be found.** This mode might be better suited to a polemical review, rather than a timed essay in a literature exam—even then it's a superficial reading of the book.

On the question of relatability, that word shows up frequently in this essay—repetitively, nearly compulsively—yet it's not clear what it means to the author. The author is using it as though it were obvious what relatability means to a "general reader," but if the author's point is that reading is subjective, then **it doesn't make sense to use a blanket term like "relatable" without some explanation.** It becomes a crutch, an overused term for the author, and it limits the specificity of the analysis. (That and the lack of specific examples from the novel.)

Practice Test 3

Chapter 7

PRACTICE TEST ANSWER SHEET

Section I: Multiple Choice

1. Ⓐ Ⓑ Ⓒ Ⓓ Ⓔ   15. Ⓐ Ⓑ Ⓒ Ⓓ Ⓔ   29. Ⓐ Ⓑ Ⓒ Ⓓ Ⓔ   43. Ⓐ Ⓑ Ⓒ Ⓓ Ⓔ

2. Ⓐ Ⓑ Ⓒ Ⓓ Ⓔ   16. Ⓐ Ⓑ Ⓒ Ⓓ Ⓔ   30. Ⓐ Ⓑ Ⓒ Ⓓ Ⓔ   44. Ⓐ Ⓑ Ⓒ Ⓓ Ⓔ

3. Ⓐ Ⓑ Ⓒ Ⓓ Ⓔ   17. Ⓐ Ⓑ Ⓒ Ⓓ Ⓔ   31. Ⓐ Ⓑ Ⓒ Ⓓ Ⓔ   45. Ⓐ Ⓑ Ⓒ Ⓓ Ⓔ

4. Ⓐ Ⓑ Ⓒ Ⓓ Ⓔ   18. Ⓐ Ⓑ Ⓒ Ⓓ Ⓔ   32. Ⓐ Ⓑ Ⓒ Ⓓ Ⓔ   46. Ⓐ Ⓑ Ⓒ Ⓓ Ⓔ

5. Ⓐ Ⓑ Ⓒ Ⓓ Ⓔ   19. Ⓐ Ⓑ Ⓒ Ⓓ Ⓔ   33. Ⓐ Ⓑ Ⓒ Ⓓ Ⓔ   47. Ⓐ Ⓑ Ⓒ Ⓓ Ⓔ

6. Ⓐ Ⓑ Ⓒ Ⓓ Ⓔ   20. Ⓐ Ⓑ Ⓒ Ⓓ Ⓔ   34. Ⓐ Ⓑ Ⓒ Ⓓ Ⓔ   48. Ⓐ Ⓑ Ⓒ Ⓓ Ⓔ

7. Ⓐ Ⓑ Ⓒ Ⓓ Ⓔ   21. Ⓐ Ⓑ Ⓒ Ⓓ Ⓔ   35. Ⓐ Ⓑ Ⓒ Ⓓ Ⓔ   49. Ⓐ Ⓑ Ⓒ Ⓓ Ⓔ

8. Ⓐ Ⓑ Ⓒ Ⓓ Ⓔ   22. Ⓐ Ⓑ Ⓒ Ⓓ Ⓔ   36. Ⓐ Ⓑ Ⓒ Ⓓ Ⓔ   50. Ⓐ Ⓑ Ⓒ Ⓓ Ⓔ

9. Ⓐ Ⓑ Ⓒ Ⓓ Ⓔ   23. Ⓐ Ⓑ Ⓒ Ⓓ Ⓔ   37. Ⓐ Ⓑ Ⓒ Ⓓ Ⓔ   51. Ⓐ Ⓑ Ⓒ Ⓓ Ⓔ

10. Ⓐ Ⓑ Ⓒ Ⓓ Ⓔ   24. Ⓐ Ⓑ Ⓒ Ⓓ Ⓔ   38. Ⓐ Ⓑ Ⓒ Ⓓ Ⓔ   52. Ⓐ Ⓑ Ⓒ Ⓓ Ⓔ

11. Ⓐ Ⓑ Ⓒ Ⓓ Ⓔ   25. Ⓐ Ⓑ Ⓒ Ⓓ Ⓔ   39. Ⓐ Ⓑ Ⓒ Ⓓ Ⓔ   53. Ⓐ Ⓑ Ⓒ Ⓓ Ⓔ

12. Ⓐ Ⓑ Ⓒ Ⓓ Ⓔ   26. Ⓐ Ⓑ Ⓒ Ⓓ Ⓔ   40. Ⓐ Ⓑ Ⓒ Ⓓ Ⓔ   54. Ⓐ Ⓑ Ⓒ Ⓓ Ⓔ

13. Ⓐ Ⓑ Ⓒ Ⓓ Ⓔ   27. Ⓐ Ⓑ Ⓒ Ⓓ Ⓔ   41. Ⓐ Ⓑ Ⓒ Ⓓ Ⓔ   55. Ⓐ Ⓑ Ⓒ Ⓓ Ⓔ

14. Ⓐ Ⓑ Ⓒ Ⓓ Ⓔ   28. Ⓐ Ⓑ Ⓒ Ⓓ Ⓔ   42. Ⓐ Ⓑ Ⓒ Ⓓ Ⓔ

Section II: Free Response

_____

_____

_____

_____

_____

_____

_____

_____

_____

answer sheet

answer sheet

PRACTICE TEST 3

Section I: Multiple Choice

Time 1 hour • 55 Questions

> **Directions:** This section consists of selections from literary works and questions on their content, form, and style. After reading each passage or poem, choose the best answer to each question and then fill in the corresponding circle.

Questions 1–11. Read the following poem carefully before you decide on the answers to the questions.

"Delight in Disorder," by Robert Herrick

A sweet disorder in the dress
Kindles in clothes a wantonness;
A lawn about the shoulders thrown
Line   Into a fine distraction;
5   An erring lace, which here and there
Enthrals the crimson stomacher;
A cuff neglectful, and thereby
Ribbons to flow confusedly;
A winning wave, deserving note,
10   In the tempestuous petticoat;
A careless shoe-string, in whose tie
I see a wild civility;--
Do more bewitch me, than when art
Is too precise in every part.

1. How is the word "kindles" being used in line 2?
   A. Judgmentally, to mean that he's beginning to get annoyed
   B. Figuratively, to mean that it sparks interest
   C. Anxiously, to mean that he wants to help
   D. Carelessly, to mean that he is messy
   E. Sympathetically, to mean that he won't judge

2. "Erring" pairs with "here and there" in line 5 to produce
   A. alliteration.
   B. antithesis.
   C. false rhymes.
   D. internal rhymes.
   E. repetition.

3. "A cuff neglectful" (line 7), "a tempestuous petticoat" (line 10) and "a careless shoe-string" (line 11) are examples of what rhetorical device?
   A. Synecdoche
   B. Simile
   C. Hyperbole
   D. Antithesis
   E. Ellipsis

4. "Careless shoe-string" (line 11) is an example of what poetic device?
   A. Alliteration
   B. Assonance
   C. Jargon
   D. Epithet
   E. Consonance

5. "Enthrals" (line 6) has a double meaning in the poem. It means that the bodice's strings
   A. get tangled in her dress and trip her lover.
   B. barely fasten her dress and charm her lover.
   C. decorate her dress and please her lover.
   D. clash with her dress and annoy her lover.
   E. cover her dress and mystify her lover.

6. All of the following statements about the couplets in the middle of the poem are true EXCEPT
   A. they are examples of inverted diction.
   B. taken together, they are examples of parallel structure.
   C. they are deceptively disordered because they form a set of similarities.
   D. the sense of the descriptions runs over from line to line like the lover's shawl
   E. they are in iambic pentameter appropriate for a sonnet

7. The poem proceeds in rhymed couplets, but the rhymes in lines 3-4 ("thrown"/"distraction"), 5-6 ("there"/"stomacher"), 11-12 ("tie"/"civility") pair a monosyllable with a polysyllable to produce slant rhymes. What is the effect of these pairings?
   I. They signal his criticism of the couplet form as a limiting form for poetry.
   II. They show his inattention to detail, similar to his lover's own fashion mishaps.
   III. They produce harmony in mistakes.
   A. I only
   B. II only
   C. III only
   D. I and III
   E. II and III

8. The speaker's tone is best described as
   A. playful, yet controlled.
   B. loving, yet judgmental.
   C. chaotic, yet appreciative.
   D. silly, yet sarcastic.
   E. noncommittal, yet self-conscious.

9. The oxymoron in the title of the poem does all of the following EXCEPT
   A. match the similar device in the phrase "wild civility."
   B. show off the same poetic ostentatiousness as his lover's dress.
   C. lend the poem a firm underlying structure of repetitive contradiction.
   D. reveal the speaker's unacknowledged ambivalence.
   E. use alliteration to unify the seeming paradox.

10. The speaker is comparing fashion to art because

A. the contrast between the two shows that fashion is frivolous compared to great sculptures and paintings.

B. he is showing the similarities between his lover and a figure in a painting.

C. neither fashion nor art can compare to the beautiful imperfections of nature.

D. he is complicating the idea that the eye always prefers symmetry and order in appearance.

E. he is writing a critique of the objectification of women and wants them to be able to dress how they wish.

11. What do you infer is his lover's opinion about her disordered dress?

A. She is ashamed of her inferior clothing.

B. She and her partner play out a mutual flirtation.

C. She is unaware that he is looking at her so closely.

D. She is pushing back at his criticisms and insisting on her independent style.

E. She is an artist who cares more for her work than her appearance.

Questions 12–27. Read the following passage carefully before you decide on your answers to the questions.

From *Shadowings*, by Lafcadio Hearn

The characteristics of many kinds of palm have been made familiar by pictures and photographs. But the giant palms of the American tropics cannot be adequately represented by the modern methods of pictorial illustration: they must

Line be seen. You cannot draw or photograph a palm two hundred feet high.

5 The first sight of a group of such forms, in their natural environment of tropical forest, is a magnificent surprise,—a surprise that strikes you dumb. Nothing seen in temperate zones,—not even the huger growths of the Californian slope,—could have prepared your imagination for the weird solemnity of that mighty colonnade. Each stone-grey trunk is a perfect pillar,—but a pillar of

10 which the stupendous grace has no counterpart in the works of man. You must strain your head well back to follow the soaring of the prodigious column, up, up, up through abysses of green twilight, till at last—far beyond a break in that infinite interweaving of limbs and lianas which is the roof of the forest—you catch one dizzy glimpse of the capital: a parasol of emerald feathers outspread

15 in a sky so blinding as to suggest the notion of azure electricity.

Now what is the emotion that such a vision excites,—an emotion too powerful to be called wonder, too weird to be called delight? Only when the first shock of it has passed,—when the several elements that were combined in it have begun to set in motion widely different groups of ideas,—can you comprehend

20 how very complex it must have been. Many impressions belonging to personal experience were doubtless revived in it, but also with them a multitude of sensations more shadowy,—accumulations of organic memory; possibly even vague

feelings older than man,—for the tropical shapes that aroused the emotion have a history more ancient than our race.

25   One of the first elements of the emotion to become clearly distinguishable is the æsthetic; and this, in its general mass, might be termed the sense of terrible beauty. Certainly the spectacle of that unfamiliar life,—silent, tremendous, springing to the sun in colossal aspiration, striving for light against Titans, and heedless of man in the gloom beneath as of a groping beetle,—thrills like

30   the rhythm of some single marvellous verse that is learned in a glance and remembered forever. Yet the delight, even at its vividest, is shadowed by a queer disquiet. ... You stare at the towering lines of the shape,—vaguely fearing to discern some sign of stealthy movement, some beginning of undulation. Then sight and reason combine to correct the suspicion. Yes, motion is there, and life

35   enormous—but a life seeking only sun,—life, rushing like the jet of a geyser, straight to the giant day.

During my own experience I could perceive that certain feelings commingled in the wave of delight,—feelings related to ideas of power and splendor and triumph,—were accompanied by a faint sense of religious awe. Perhaps our

40   modern æsthetic sentiments are so interwoven with various inherited elements of religious emotionalism that the recognition of beauty cannot arise independently of reverential feeling. Be this as it may, such a feeling defined itself while I gazed;—and at once the great grey trunks were changed to the pillars of a mighty aisle; and from altitudes of dream there suddenly descended upon me

45   the old dark thrill of Gothic horror.

12. The use of the second-person address "you"
   A. familiarizes the scene for the reader by making it appeal to a general perspective.
   B. judges the reader for trying to take a photograph of the trees, despite his admonition.
   C. immerses the reader in an alien environment with no warning or guide.
   D. gives the reader a bird's-eye view of the scene.
   E. recounts a dream in which the writer wasn't sure who or where he was.

13. What is the effect of directing the reader's vision "up, up, up through abysses of green twilight" (lines 11-12)?
   I. It amplifies the sense of enormous scale of the trees compared to the human viewer.
   II. It enhances the sense of disorientation because you normally look down into an abyss.
   III. It exposes how the narrator is tricking the reader with unreliable narration.
   A. I only
   B. II only
   C. III only
   D. I and II
   E. I, II, and III

14. In the second paragraph, what does the word "capital" (line 14) refer to, specifically?
    A. A large city gleaming in the distance
    B. The green fronds (leaves) at the top of the tree
    C. A bird that's sitting at the top of a tree
    D. The money that palm growers use to build the plantation
    E. The height of the writer's imagination

15. What is the extended metaphor of colonnades and other nouns in the second paragraph?
    A. Natural
    B. Spiritual
    C. Supernatural
    D. Architectural
    E. Military

16. In the phrase "that were combined in it," (line 18) what does "it" refer to?
    A. Shock
    B. Vision
    C. Emotion
    D. Delight
    E. Complexity

17. "Terrible beauty" is an example of what literary device?
    A. Oxymoron
    B. Synesthesia
    C. Synecdoche
    D. Fallacy
    E. Cacophony

18. What is the best description of the effect of all of the dashes and interruptions in this description?
    A. Fear
    B. Distraction
    C. Drowsiness
    D. Ineffability
    E. Delusion

19. What does the repetition of the word "weird" in the phrases "weird solemnity" (line 8) and "too weird to be called delight" (line 17) help the author convey?
    A. His confusion about if what he is seeing is real or an illusion
    B. His sense of the sublime, of feelings that exceed the limitations of language
    C. His paranoia about the spirits he senses around him but cannot see
    D. His annoyance at how others have described the trees inaccurately
    E. The insufficiency of words to convey their majesty the way an image could do

20. What is the source of the "shock" he mentions in line 17?
    A. The "azure electricity" he mentioned earlier
    B. The spooky trees that seem to be still but are moving slightly
    C. The terror at being left alone
    D. The nausea that has overtaken him
    E. The emotional realization of the complicated network of nature

21. What sensory effect does "undulation" bring to the description?
    A. Immense growth
    B. Slight swaying
    C. Shimmering light
    D. Overwhelming scent
    E. Swirling mist

practice test

22. "Queer disquiet" (lines 31-32) is an example of what poetic device, and what does it help the author establish?
   A. Synesthesia that shows his confusion of sight and sound
   B. Assonance that gives a sense of the strange mix of sound and silence around him
   C. Psychological jargon that shows his grandiosity and his losing touch with reality
   D. Consonance that crystallizes a moment of revelation
   E. Alliteration that gives a sense of his declamatory tone

23. The line about "heedless of man in the gloom beneath as of a groping beetle" (line 29) helps the writer express his
   A. sadness about the eventual extinction of the trees.
   B. anger at humans for cutting down the trees without appreciating them.
   C. awe at how insignificant humans are compared to the gigantic, ancient trees.
   D. disgust at the oppressive nature that's overwhelming him.
   E. deep, abiding love for all creatures, even the seemingly insignificant.

24. What does "aspiration" (line 28) refer to?
   A. The writer's dreams of success
   B. The tremendous height of the trees
   C. The personification of the trees
   D. The movement of the leaves in the breeze
   E. The writer's palpable sense of longing

25. What is "a life seeking only sun" (line 35)?
   A. The human desire for joy
   B. The writer's quest for illuminating knowledge
   C. A personification of the tree's photosynthesis process
   D. An unusual ghostly form that lives in the sun, not the shadows
   E. The spiritual revelation the author seeks

26. The word "perhaps" in the phrase "[p]erhaps our modern æsthetic sentiments are so interwoven" (lines 39-40) helps the author
   A. express his sense of uncertainty and dislocation in the jungle.
   B. propose a theory for his nearly spiritual sense of wonder.
   C. suggest a course of action to find a way out.
   D. reveal to readers that he has been hallucinating all along.
   E. sum up his description of the scene's beauty.

27. With the phrase "Gothic horror" in the final sentence, the author
   I. concludes his extended architectural metaphor: the tree canopy is like the arched ceiling of a Gothic cathedral.
   II. follows through with the foreshadowing about the ancient spirits that seem to be lurking in the forest, as they finally become visible to him and the reader.
   III. reveals he has been deeply absorbed in reading a scary story and has projected his fears onto the scene.
   A. I only
   B. II only
   C. III only
   D. I and II
   E. I and III

Questions 28–42. Read the following poem carefully before you decide on your answers to the questions.

"On Recollection," by Phillis Wheatley

MNEME[1] begin. Inspire, ye sacred nine,
Your vent'rous Afric in her great design.
Mneme, immortal pow'r, I trace thy spring:

Line Assist my strains, while I thy glories sing:
5 The acts of long departed years, by thee
Recover'd, in due order rang'd we see:
Thy pow'r the long-forgotten calls from night,
That sweetly plays before the fancy's sight.
Mneme in our nocturnal visions pours
10 The ample treasure of her secret stores;
Swift from above the wings her silent flight
Through Phoebe's realms[2], fair regent of the night;
And, in her pomp of images display'd,
To the high-raptur'd poet gives her aid,
15 Through the unbounded regions of the mind,
Diffusing light celestial and refin'd.
The heav'nly phantom paints the actions done
By ev'ry tribe beneath the rolling sun.
Mneme, enthron'd within the human breast,
20 Has vice condemn'd, and ev'ry virtue blest.
How sweet the sound when we her plaudit hear?
Sweeter than music to the ravish'd ear,
Sweeter than Maro's entertaining strains
Resounding through the groves, and hills, and plains.
25 But how is Mneme dreaded by the race,
Who scorn her warnings and despise her grace?
By her unveil'd each horrid crime appears,
Her awful hand a cup of wormwood bears.
Days, years mispent, O what a hell of woe!
30 Hers the worst tortures that our souls can know.
Now eighteen years their destin'd course have run,
In fast succession round the central sun.
How did the follies of that period pass
Unnotic'd, but behold them writ in brass!
35 In Recollection see them fresh return,
And sure 'tis mine to be asham'd, and mourn.
O Virtue, smiling in immortal green,
Do thou exert thy pow'r, and change the scene;

---
[1]   The Muse of Memory
[2]   Phoebe is associated with the moon

Be thine employ to guide my future days,
40   And mine to pay the tribute of my praise.
Of Recollection such the pow'r enthron'd
In ev'ry breast, and thus her pow'r is own'd.
The wretch, who dar'd the vengeance of the skies,
At last awakes in horror and surprise,
45   By her alarm'd, he sees impending fate,
He howls in anguish, and repents too late.
But O! what peace, what joys are hers t' impart
To ev'ry holy, ev'ry upright heart!
Thrice blest the man, who, in her sacred shrine,
50   Feels himself shelter'd from the wrath divine!

28. The first two words "Mneme begin" are an example of what poetic convention?

A. Invocation

B. Fragmentation

C. Inscription

D. Antithesis

E. Authority

29. In context, what does "spring" mean in line 3?

A. Season

B. Leap

C. Source

D. Surprise

E. Song

30. The repetition of "I" rhymes like nine, design, night, flight, and sight in the first six couplets serves all of the following purposes EXCEPT

A. it employs traditional imagery of inspiration by the muses to write poetry.

B. the I/eye homophone emphasizes personal vision.

C. it gives the poem a traditional rhyme and metrical structure.

D. the light of inspiration is enhanced through its conspicuous absence.

E. the repetition of night in lines 7 and 12 shows the poet exhausted for inspiration.

31. In lines 9-16, the poet is

A. singing.

B. crying.

C. flying.

D. dreaming.

E. writing.

32. In context, what is a "pomp of images" (line 13) that Phoebe displays?

A. A vivid spectacle

B. A carefully edited scene

C. A deliberately deceptive vision

D. A foreboding shadow

E. A pleasing medley

33. Phillis Wheatley was taken from West Africa as a slave when she was a child. How does she shift the meaning of Mneme as a muse in line 25?

   A. She is no longer solely a classical source of poetic inspiration but now a figure who brings traumatic memories.

   B. She adjudicates the clash between Wheatley and older British poets who have written in the mode of invocation before.

   C. She cannot be a poetic source of inspiration because the memories she brings are traumatic ones.

   D. She and Phoebe depart Wheatley's vision abruptly when the scene becomes traumatic.

   E. Wheatley must claim her own poetic voice separate from Mneme.

34. How is the shift in line 25 reflected in her style?

   A. Her use of iambs shows the back-and-forth pattern of her struggle with Mneme for authority.

   B. Her use of use of formal language shows her deference to classical authority.

   C. Her use of variable pentameter reflects her ambivalence about the classical form.

   D. Her use of free verse reflects her insistence on finding her own voice.

   E. Her use of iambic pentameter reflects her joining her own voice to classical forms.

35. The rhyme "appears/bears" in lines 27-28 is the only slant rhyme in a poem full of couplets. The slant rhyme does all of the following EXCEPT

   A. signal disorientation from Mneme's "cup of wormwood."

   B. introduce another competing muse of history and resistance.

   C. expose a fissure in the relationship between poet and muse.

   D. show her resisting the orderly power of the muse.

   E. show her growing into her own poetic authority to be creative.

36. How would you characterize the relationship between Mneme and the speaker in lines 25-36?

   A. At a standoff

   B. In productive tension

   C. Mutually beneficial

   D. Familiar

   E. Maternal

37. In line 35, what does "them" refer to?

   A. Poetic authorities

   B. Poetic abilities

   C. Traumatic historical events

   D. Acts of resistance

   E. Disagreements

38. Wheatley's description of memories "writ in brass" (line 34) refers to the slave bracelets used to trade slaves. Why does she connect these two forms of writing: the contract and the poem?

I. Written as poetry, the memories themselves may induce the same trauma as the inscribed bracelets.

II. The slave bracelets serve as a marker of collective memory, as a form of historical objects, and her writing is another form of record.

III. Writing is not a neutral activity, for the same power of inscription that a poet claims is also used to claim the authority to mark someone for sale.

A. I only

B. II only

C. III only

D. I and III

E. I, II, and III

39. The repetition of the word "enthron'd" in lines 19 and 41 serves to emphasize all of the following ideas EXCEPT

A. memory has protected the poet from trauma.

B. memory is not just external to the poet as a Muse, it is within herself.

C. the power of Memory is made stronger by combining with the force of spiritual Virtue.

D. recollection is a public act for everyone to contend with history.

E. spiritual authority is important for leading a moral, ethical life.

40. What kind of realization does Wheatley call for at the end of the poem?

A. Political revolution

B. Spiritual awakening

C. Collective activism

D. Poetic rejection of old forms

E. Individual self-reflection

41. The shift in emphasis in lines 43-50 signals

I. a poet's act of creative resistance is not just personal, but part of a spiritual movement.

II. the means by which one learns from history by synthesizing memory and spiritual grace.

III. the rejection of classical models of memory for religious authority.

A. I only

B. II only

C. III only

D. I and II

E. I and III

42. Who is likely the intended audience for this poem?

I. Readers who know the classical conventions of poetry and mythology

II. Political activists who want anti-slave-trade anthems to sing in the streets

III. Readers of religious poetry who are opposed to the slave trade

A. I only

B. II only

C. III only

D. I and II

E. I and III

Questions 43–55. Read the following passage carefully before you decide on your answers to the questions.

Villette, by Charlotte Brontë. The narrator, Lucy Snowe, is on board a ship traveling from England to Belgium, where she meets Ginevra Fanshawe, a young woman who lives in the village of Villette in Belgium.

"Do you like Villette?" I asked.[3]

"Pretty well. The natives, you know, are intensely stupid and vulgar; but there are some nice English families."

Line   "Are you in a school?"

5   "Yes."

"A good one?"

"Oh, no! horrid: but I go out every Sunday, and care nothing about the *maî-tresses* or the *professeurs*, or the *élèves*, and send lessons *au diable* (one daren't say that in English, you know, but it sounds quite right in French); and thus I get

10   on charmingly . . . . You are laughing at me again?"

"No—I am only smiling at my own thoughts."

"What are they?" (Without waiting for an answer)—"Now, *do* tell me where you are going."

"Where Fate may lead me. My business is to earn a living where I can find it."

15   "To earn!" (in consternation) "are you poor, then?"

"As poor as Job."

(After a pause)— "Bah! how unpleasant! But *I* know what it is to be poor: they are poor enough at home—papa and mamma, and all of them. Papa is called Captain Fanshawe; he is an officer on half-pay, but well-descended, and some

20   of our connections are great enough; but my uncle and godpapa De Bassom-pierre, who lives in France, is the only one that helps us: he educates us girls. I have five sisters and three brothers. By-and-by we are to marry—rather elderly gentlemen, I suppose, with cash: papa and mamma manage that. My sister Augusta is married now to a man much older-looking than papa. Augusta is

25   very beautiful—not in my style—but dark; her husband, Mr. Davies, had the yellow fever in India, and he is still the colour of a guinea; but then he is rich, and Augusta has her carriage and establishment, and we all think she has done

3   Villette is the Belgian village where the second half of the novel is set, modeled in part on Brussels.

perfectly well. Now, this is better than 'earning a living,' as you say. By the way, are you clever?"

30 "No—not at all."

"You can play, sing, speak three or four languages?"

"By no means."

"Still I think you are clever" (a pause and a yawn).

"Shall you be sea-sick?"

35 "Shall you?"

"Oh, immensely! as soon as ever we get in sight of the sea: I begin, indeed, to feel it already. I shall go below; and won't I order about that fat odious stewardess! *Heureusement je sais faire aller mon monde.*[4]"

Down she went.

40 It was not long before the other passengers followed her: throughout the afternoon I remained on deck alone. When I recall the tranquil, and even happy mood in which I passed those hours, and remember, at the same time, the position in which I was placed; its hazardous—some would have said its hopeless—character; I feel that, as—

45 *Stone walls do not a prison make,*
Nor iron bars—a cage,

so peril, loneliness, an uncertain future, are not oppressive evils, so long as the frame is healthy and the faculties are employed; so long, especially, as Liberty lends us her wings, and Hope guides us by her star.

50 I was not sick till long after we passed Margate, and deep was the pleasure I drank in with the sea-breeze; divine the delight I drew from the heaving Channel waves, from the sea-birds on their ridges, from the white sails on their dark distance, from the quiet yet beclouded sky, overhanging all. In my reverie, methought I saw the continent of Europe, like a wide dream-land, far
55 away. Sunshine lay on it, making the long coast one line of gold; tiniest tracery of clustered town and snow-gleaming tower, of woods deep massed, of heights serrated, of smooth pasturage and veiny stream, embossed the metal-bright prospect. For background, spread a sky, solemn and dark blue, and—grand with imperial promise, soft with tints of enchantment—strode from north to south a
60 God-bent bow, an arch of hope.

---

4   "Fortunately, I know how to get my own way."

Cancel the whole of that, if you please, reader—or rather let it stand, and draw thence a moral—an alliterative, text-hand copy—

Day-dreams are delusions of the demon.

Becoming excessively sick, I faltered down into the cabin.

43. Which adjectives best describe Lucy's part in the opening dialogue?
- **A.** Witty and urbane
- **B.** Confessional and intimate
- **C.** Tense and guarded
- **D.** Pompous and judgmental
- **E.** Sentimental and self-pitying

44. The dialogue between Lucy and Ginevra Fanshawe on the ship reveals all of the following EXCEPT
- **A.** Ginevra's tendency to talk without thinking.
- **B.** Lucy's tendency to think more than she talks.
- **C.** Lucy's idealism.
- **D.** Ginevra's sense of entitlement.
- **E.** Lucy's reason for leaving home.

45. How would you characterize Lucy's reaction to Ginevra's long story about her family in lines 17-29 [(After a pause)—"Bah! how unpleasant!......are you clever?"]?
- **A.** Confusion at the digressions and numerous details
- **B.** Empathy for her suffering
- **C.** Reflection on her own precarious situation
- **D.** Annoyance at the girl's prattling
- **E.** Gratitude for Ginevra's advice to be hopeful

46. What are some inferences to draw from Ginevra's cutting remarks about the inhabitants of Villette, the appearance and ethnicity of her family members, and the appearance and behavior of other people onboard the ship?
- **I.** Ginevra is a stand-in for the author, who casts a satirical eye on society around her.
- **II.** With her relentless external judgments, she serves as a foil to the more inward-focused Lucy.
- **III.** Many characters in the novel, not just Lucy, lack agency to live the lives they want to live.
- **A.** I
- **B.** II
- **C.** I and III
- **D.** II and III
- **E.** I, II, and III

47. Ginevra's use of French phrases reveals her
- **A.** disdain for the English language.
- **B.** attempts to be fashionable.
- **C.** intellectual aspirations.
- **D.** attempt to shame Lucy.
- **E.** moodiness.

48. What is the best way to describe Lucy's tone in the lines that begin "When I recall the tranquil, and even happy mood . . ." (lines 41-42)?
- **A.** Euphemistic
- **B.** Epigrammatic
- **C.** Polemical
- **D.** Moral
- **E.** Circuitous

49. The two lines of verse she quotes further emphasize her interior monologue's
    A. precision.
    B. lyricism.
    C. misery.
    D. haughtiness.
    E. persuasiveness.

50. The exalted diction in Lucy's interior monologue reveals her
    A. embellishing of her prospects.
    B. religious vision.
    C. willful ignorance of Ginevra's warning.
    D. fear for the future.
    E. ambition to be rich.

51. Why does Lucy use the passive voice in her vision of how "the faculties are employed" (line 48)?
    A. She is giving advice that readers may follow themselves.
    B. She is recalling from a story about someone else's experiences.
    C. She can imagine her future only in idealized terms, without herself at the center.
    D. She herself lacks the "faculties" to follow through on these plans.
    E. She wants to sound more objective by removing her subjective perspective from the experience.

52. What kind of extended metaphor is Lucy building in her description of the gold and blue vision?
    A. Maritime
    B. Archaeological
    C. Ornamentation
    D. Astronomical
    E. Sculpting

53. The seasickness serves all of the following thematic purposes EXCEPT
    A. it reverses the direction of her vision from upward to downward.
    B. it grounds her generalized vision in her own embodied experience.
    C. it reminds her of the reality of the world around her.
    D. it punishes her for being too hopeful.
    E. it adds an edge to her rich sensory description.

54. The direction to "cancel . . ." (lines 61-64) asks the readers to
    A. stop reading the novel and look to a religious text instead.
    B. reconsider their opinion of Ginevra.
    C. follow the advice of the author.
    D. reconcile the beauty of her description with a contradiction.
    E. reject novels for the alliterative beauty of poetry.

55. Lucy's direct address to the reader serves what purposes?
    I. It shows the unreliability of her narration because she is liable to make changes.
    II. It extends the metaphor of her vision into the related realm of annotation.
    III. It gives her some subjectivity, which she immediately contests as she tries to fade away.
    A. I only
    B. III only
    C. I and III
    D. II and III
    E. I, II, and III

Section II: Free Response

Time: 2 hours

The essay section of the exam lasts 2 hours, so it is recommended that you spend 40 minutes on each of the three essays on the exam. You may write the essays in any order you wish and return to work on the essays if you have extra time.

Each essay will be evaluated according to how thoroughly and clearly it addresses the question, as well as the overall quality of your writing. Please write in blue or black ink and scratch out any mistakes thoroughly and neatly. Make sure to check your spelling and punctuation so that the reader can read your essay without struggle over legibility.

The quality of the essay matters more than its length, so spend some time at the beginning of the exam planning out the ideas on your sheet of scratch paper. You may write notes on the poem in the exam booklet. Use a new sheet of paper for each essay and number them (1, 2, 3) so that the exam question is immediately obvious.

For essay 3, you should choose to write about a novel or a play of similar literary merit to those in your AP English Literature class. There are some suggestions listed, but you are not required to choose one of them.

ESSAY QUESTION 1

James Weldon Johnson was a poet, novelist, lawyer, diplomat, and civic leader in the National Association for the Advancement of Colored People (NAACP). His poem "Lift Ev'ry Voice and Sing" was promoted as the "Negro National Anthem." The most well-known of his novels, *The Autobiography of an Ex-Colored Man*, was first published anonymously in 1912.

Read the following poem closely and write a well-organized essay in which you discuss how Johnson characterizes conflicts among different forms of authority in this poem. Those entities vying for authority may include: nature, science, religious authority, the poet himself. How does Johnson animate these conflicts? What are the terms they argue about? Are the conflicts resolved—or exacerbated—by the end of the poem?

"The Word of an Engineer," by James Weldon Johnson

> "She's built of steel
> From deck to keel,
> And bolted strong and tight;
> In scorn she'll sail
> The fiercest gale,
> And pierce the darkest night.
>
> "The builder's art
> Has proved each part
> Throughout her breadth and length;
> Deep in the hulk,
> Of her mighty bulk,
> Ten thousand Titans' strength."
>
> The tempest howls,
> The Ice Wolf prowls,
> The winds they shift and veer,
> But calm I sleep,
> And faith I keep
> In the word of an engineer.
>
> Along the trail
> Of the slender rail
> The train, like a nightmare, flies
> And dashes on
> Through the black-mouthed yawn
> Where the cavernous tunnel lies.
>
> Over the ridge,
> Across the bridge,
> Swung twixt the sky and hell,

Line
5

10

15

20

25

On an iron thread
Spun from the head
30 Of the man in a draughtsman's cell.

And so we ride
Over land and tide,
Without a thought of fear—
Man never had
35 *The faith in God*
That he has in an engineer!

ESSAY QUESTION 2

Vernon Lee was the pen name of Violet Paget, an essayist and short story writer in Victorian England. "Against Thinking," Lee's essay excerpted here, is one of her nonfiction essays, yet she uses many of the same writing techniques that you might find in a novel or a play. After you read her work carefully, write your own essay about how Lee incorporates elements of fiction, poetry, and/or drama into her nonfiction essayistic style. Be specific about which imaginative literary elements you see, by using quotations from her essay paired with specific illustrations of how those features pair with literature or drama. *Why* does she incorporate these literary techniques into an essay about the trouble of communicating ideas to other people?

Your task is to analyze her style and argue for the function of her most distinctive features, so you may want to consider her use of allusions, diction, style, and personification. You may choose other stylistic features that jump out at you, as well. Be sure to also give an example of a literary work that uses similar devices, so that you can illustrate how Lee adapts those devices for her own uses.

"Against Thinking," by Vernon Lee

As towards most other things of which we have but little personal experience (foreigners, or socialists, or aristocrats, as the case may be), there is a degree of vague ill-will towards what is called *Thinking*. It is reputed to impede action,

Line to make hay of instincts and of standards, to fritter reality into doubt; and the
5   career of Hamlet is frequently pointed out as a proof of its unhappy effects. But, as I hinted, one has not very often an opportunity of verifying these drawbacks of thinking, or its advantages either. And I am tempted to believe that much of the mischief thus laid at the door of that poor unknown quantity *Thinking* is really due to its ubiquitous twin-brother *Talking*.

10   I call them twins on the analogy of *Death* and *Sleep*, because there is something poetical and attractive in such references to family relations; and also because, as many people cannot think without talking, and talking, at all events, is the supposed indication that thinking is within, there has arisen about these two human activities a good deal of that confusion and amiable not-caring-which-

15   is-which so characteristic of our dealings with twins. But *Talking*, take my word for it, is the true villain of the couple.

Talking, however, should never be discouraged in the young. Not talking *with them* (largely reiteration of the word "Why?"), but talking among themselves. Its beneficial effects are of the sort which ought to make us patient with the

20   crying of infants. Talking helps growth. M. Renan, with his saintly ironical sympathy for the young and weak, knew it when he excused the symbolists and decadents of various kinds with that indulgent sentence, *Ce sont des enfants qui s'amusent*[5]. It matters little what litter they leave behind, what mud pies they make and little daily dug-up gardens of philosophy, ethics, literature, and

25   general scandal; they will grow out of the need to make them and meanwhile,

---

[5]   They are children having fun.

making this sort of mess will help them grow. Besides, is it nothing that they should be amusing themselves once in their lives (we cannot be sure of the future)? And what amusement, what material revelry can be compared with the

30   great carouses of words in which the young can still indulge? We were most of us young once, odd as it appears; and some of us can remember our youthful discussions, our salad-day talks, prolonged to hours, trespassing on to subjects, which added such a fine spice of the forbidden and therefore the free! The joy of asking reasons where you have hitherto answered school queries; of extem-

35   porizing replies, magnificent, irresponsible, instead of laboriously remembering mere solutions; of describing, analyzing, and generally laying bold mental eyes, irreverent intellectual hands, on personalities whose real presence would merely make you stumble over a chair or drop a tea-cup! For talking is the great equalizer of positions, turning the humble, the painfully immature, into judges with rope and torch; and in a kindlier way allowing the totally obscure

40   to share the life of kings, and queens, and generals, and opera-singers; which is the reason that items of Court news or of "dramatic gossip" are so frequently exchanged in omnibuses and at small, decent dinner-tables.

Moreover, talking has for the young the joys of personal exuberance; it is all honeycombed, or rather, filled (like champagne) with the generous gaseousness

45   of self-analysis, self-accusation, self-pity, self-righteousness, and autobiography. The poor mortal, in that delusive sense of sympathy and perfect understanding which comes of perfect indifference to one's neighbour's presence, has quicker pulses, higher temperature, more vigorous movements than are compatible with the sober sense of human unimportance. In conversation, clever young

50   people vain, kindly, selfish, ridiculous, happy young people actually take body and weight, expand. And are you quite sure, my own dear, mature, efficient, and thoroughly productive friends and contemporaries, that it is not this expansion of youthful rubbish which makes the true movement of the centuries?

ESSAY QUESTION 3

The word "nostalgia" has opposition in its word roots: *nostos* means home, but *algia* means pain. The word mixes familiarity with tinges of distress: no wonder it is such a ripe theme for literature. Characters may indulge in nostalgia for their childhoods when life seemed simpler, or they may look back at other moments to freeze a point when everything seemed to have more promise and possibility. Those indulgences may be bittersweet, however, as characters realize that they cannot relive those moments. In your essay, you should devise an answer to the following question:

The Great Gatsby
In Search of Lost Time
When We Were Orphans
Absalom, Absalom!
The Remains of the Day
The Sound and the Fury
One Hundred Years of Solitude
The Age of Innocence
Death of a Salesman
To the Lighthouse
Dandelion Wine
Ignorance
The Reluctant Fundamentalist
The Virgin Suicides
Cannery Row
The Ice Storm
A Tree Grows in Brooklyn
Like Water for Chocolate
The Way We Live Now
Little Dorrit

ANSWER KEY AND EXPLANATIONS

1. B	11. B	20. E	29. C	38. E	47. B
2. D	12. C	21. B	30. E	39. A	48. E
3. A	13. D	22. D	31. D	40. B	49. B
4. E	14. B	23. C	32. A	41. D	50. A
5. B	15. D	24. B	33. A	42. E	51. C
6. E	16. C	25. C	34. E	43. C	52. C
7. C	17. A	26. B	35. B	44. E	53. D
8. A	18. D	27. A	36. B	45. C	54. D
9. D	19. B	28. A	37. C	46. D	55. D
10. D					

Section I

1. **The correct answer is B.** The verb "kindles" is being used figuratively; you may know the word "kindle" from kindling for firewood or kindling a spark to start a fire. He's saying that her slightly disarrayed outfit sparks his interest. He is not being judgmental (choice A) or anxious (choice C). He likes the disarray. That arousal means he's not writing the poem out of sympathy (choice E), but desire. It might be tempting to say that he must be careless (choice D), too, but the poem is more about him looking at a woman, so we don't know the state of his own dress.

2. **The correct answer is D.** "Erring" pairs with "here and there" to produce internal rhymes in the line. It's repeating the "er" sound in both vowel and consonant form, which means that the poet is playing with assonance (repeated vowels) *and* consonance (repeated consonants) here to produce the internal rhyme. It would be unlikely that you'd have to choose between internal rhyme, assonance, *and* consonance in a selection of answers because the internal rhyme is produced by the combination of the other two. (If one of those other two showed up

on this particular answer selection, the *best* answer would be internal rhyme because it accounts for the multiple devices in use here.) It's more likely that you'll have to choose between assonance and consonance because those are distinct devices. It's not a case of alliteration because that device uses repetition in the first syllable; repetition is too general to be the right answer here. It's not a false rhyme because those are imperfect rhymes at the ends of lines. It's not an example of antithesis because that device pairs two opposites to emphasize contrast. Here, "erring" has multiple meanings: not just of being wrong, but of meandering or wandering, like the laces in her dress that are trailing down.

3. **The correct answer is A.** "A cuff neglectful," "a tempestuous petticoat," and "a careless shoe-string" are all examples of a part representing the whole, or a synecdoche. Those items themselves are not neglectful, tempestuous, or careless: their owner is. There are, arguably, other interpretations of this device; for example, one could say that Herrick is personifying the petticoat rather than using it as a synecdoche. As

with question 2, you will probably not have to make these small distinctions: either the answer will be clear-cut, or you will be asked to choose the best answer among the answer choices. The petticoat itself could be personified, but the cuff and the shoe-string are more obviously cases of synecdoche. The four other answer choices don't work: there's no comparison for it to be a simile, there's no pause for an ellipsis, it's not an obvious exaggeration for a hyperbole, nor are those objects and adjectives opposed for an antithesis. You have a clear choice in A.

4. **The correct answer is E.** "Careless shoe-string" has many devices attached to it for such a minor item! The repeated s-sounds create consonance, or repeated consonants. Note here that assonance is listed among the answer choices: the distinction between assonance and consonance is clear, so you can easily choose between them. (The distinction between internal rhyme and assonance was less clear in question 2.) It is not an example of alliteration because alliteration depends on repeated sounds in the first syllables of the words; whereas, the repeated s-sounds appear in -less and then tie to shoe and string. It is not an example of jargon because the words are relatively common and not examples of specialized knowledge. You might pause on choice D, epithet, if you remember that an epithet is usually an example of an adjective-noun pairing, but epithets usually describe the qualities inherent in the noun. Even if they're difficult to keep tied, we don't normally think of carelessness as a quality that defines shoe-strings.

5. **The correct answer is B.** A "stomacher" is a piece of fabric that is tied to the mid-section, kind of like a corset. The laces in the woman's stomacher are not fully tied, causing provocative gaps that charm the speaker. You can eliminate the other choices by what's not mentioned in the poem: the

speaker doesn't trip on the strings (choice A), nor is there any mention of clashing designs that might be annoying (choice D). The speaker is excited, not mystified (E), by those gaps. The stomacher is a kind of decoration, and the speaker is pleased (choice C), but this choice is much too general and doesn't adequately describe the specific qualities of "enthral" as a word with a double meaning here.

6. **The correct answer is E.** Here you are looking for the EXCEPTION among all of the answer choices, so you know that four of the possibilities are correct and there's one outlier. The lines are only four feet (four iambs: a LINE / a-BOUT / the SHOUL- / ders THROWN) long, so they are in iambic tetrameter, not pentameter. Even if you immediately counted those syllables and figured out the right answer, it's worth pausing on the other four choices just to see what the test is telling you about what it considers the correct way to interpret these lines. The rest of the choices are good examples of how the poet is using these devices to add structure and order to a poem that says it's about disorder. The repetition of synecdoches creates parallel structure of phrases with similarities in inverted diction (choices A, B, and C). The sense of the descriptions runs over from line to line, much like the shawl falling over her shoulders (choice D). That's a lot of structural work for those devices to do!

7. **The correct answer is C.** The list of all of the ways that Herrick is creating order in question 6 should give you some clues for understanding this question: fundamentally, this poem is more about order than disorder, despite the title. He is not rejecting the couplet (option I): the slant rhymes *call attention to the value* of the couplet as a form that's special to the couplet. The charming cases of disorder exalt the couplet, rather than denouncing it. With so many poetic

devices in play, you can see that Herrick is anything but careless (option II). Thus, the only good option is III, where you see that he's creating harmony with the repetition. The correct choice is option III only, or choice C.

8. **The correct answer is A.** The playful disorder in the poem is superficial; beneath it all, the speaker is controlling the scene with his poetic devices. You can also eliminate the adjectives in the pairs that don't seem to fit: although there's a trailing lace or a slant rhyme here and there, there's no chaos (choice C) in the poem's tight structure. There's little judgment or sarcasm in the poem, so choices B and D are not a good fit, nor is the speaker apparently self-conscious himself (choice E).

9. **The correct answer is D.** Here you are looking for another exception among four correct answers, and many of the previous correct answer choices will give you clues as to how the test is leading you to interpret the poem. The previous four questions have each pointed out that the disorder in the poem is really example of ordering through poetic devices, so these answer choices will point to a similar line of interpretation. Choices C and E echo that interpretation of the oxymoron as a structural device. Choices A and B both point to other similarities in the poem: in other poetic devices and in the main subject. The only outlier is choice D, which asks you to interpret the poem as ambivalent. None of the previous questions has pointed toward uncertainty or mixed feelings, so this one is the outlier.

10. **The correct answer is D.** Choice D proposes that he is "complicating" the traditional idea of order as pleasing: "complicating" is a classic interpretive word that works well in essays as a way for you to insist that a situation isn't simple or black and white. In these kinds of literature exams, it rarely means that

it muddles the situation in a bad way—it's usually used as a positive term to show the newly revealed depths of the text. They want you to be clear in discussing complexity—which may be a daunting task, but terms like these can help you put those interpretive moves into analytical language. When you see this word in an answer choice, it's a good one to consider because it's unlikely that the test is proposing an incorrect way of seeing more deeply into the situation. (It's possible, of course, but, if so, there would likely to be other synonyms in the other answer choices like: adds nuance, deepens, leaves unresolved . . .) Among these answer choices, you can strike choices A and B because there are no paintings mentioned, and there's no contrast with the natural world, so choice C is also incorrect. The speaker is not writing a critique of objectification here (choice E)—especially not since there are so many objects that are taken as part of the woman's whole in the poetic device of the synecdoche in these poem.

11. **The correct answer is B.** This question may be tricky if you are not inclined to make inferences, or if you tend to read poems by forming an opinion or judgment about the speaker. You may be unimpressed with the speaker's ogling of her gaping stomacher and playful flirtation—it may read a little gross to you. However, this question is asking for an interpretation, not a judgment or an opinion of the poet. That means you have to pay attention to the stylistic devices themselves, and the questions have given you many clues of how to interpret the mutuality and playfulness of the poem's tone. The synecdoches, assonance, and rhymes show a tight structure of mutuality in the poem: every problem gets resolved with a perfect imperfection. Thus, the best inference is that the woman is an equal partner; they have a kind of rapport, even if we can't hear her speaking back in her own voice in this poem.

You may also eliminate the more obviously incorrect answers: we don't know much about her identity, so choices A and E are incorrect. We don't hear from her, so choice D is also not a good option. It's possible that she doesn't know that her laces are trailing, but because we never see the situation from her perspective, we can't know what she sees (choice C). It may seem like it's hard to interpret all of those eliminations, or to see why B is correct, but C isn't. Another way of thinking about it is that the test won't ask you to prove a negative (she can't see . . .) but it might ask you to interpret from the devices. With that logic, choice B is better supported by those frequent pairs and mutual resolutions.

12. **The correct answer is C.** This passage is from an essay, not a piece of fiction, so there are no characters to analyze here. Hearn is describing palm trees in a tropical forest, so he uses the second-person "you" to immerse readers in the unfamiliar, dense scene. This isn't a choose-your-own adventure story where you can perform actions of your own volition—he guides your vision with significant control of how and where to look—so there's no possibility that you are taking a photo (choice B). He is emphasizing the *unfamiliar*, while choice A describes the opposite. He asks readers to look up at the trees, so they are under the canopy, not above it (choice D). Choice E is possible, but there's no textual evidence to support the dream hypothesis.

13. **The correct answer is D.** This question builds on question 12; through the particular antithetical detail of looking *up* into the abyss of trees, Hearn increases the disorientation. Options I and II well describe the effect of this particular reversal of normal perspective: it's a reminder of the enormous scale and its disorienting effects. You may want to read more into the narrative voice, but there's no

evidence that he himself is unreliable, even if the scene around you is disorienting.

14. **The correct answer is B.** Hearn is using "capital" to describe the palm trees as building elements. A capital is the flourish at the top of a column, like the fronds at the top of the palm tree. Capital can have other, more familiar, meanings in other contexts, but here it doesn't refer to a city, money, or a more abstract kind of height. It's not a bird, either.

15. **The correct answer is D.** As with question 14, this question is asking you about specific architectural terms, such as "capital" and "colonnade." Even if you don't know those particular terms (and you can figure out capital from context in question 14), Hearn gives you the more recognizable comparison of a tree trunk to a gray pillar. (A colonnade is a grouping of columns, referring to the grouping of trees in the scene.) You can use pillar and capital to give you choice D. It's unlikely that it's a natural metaphor: the scene itself is in nature, so there's no metaphor to be detected. The other options may be tempting to describe such a strange scene that might be spiritual or supernatural (choices B and C), but Hearn uses mostly adjectives and verbs to get those feelings across. Colonnade, pillar, and capital are all specific nouns tied to a specific metaphor.

16. **The correct answer is C.** It's difficult to keep track of Hearn's nouns; he uses them as obscure signposts as he winds his way through the sentences to describe this dense forest. If you trace the word "it" back to the beginning of the paragraph, you can see that "the emotion" is the main idea he's describing. That same word applies the examples of "it" in these references: "shock of it," "combined in it," "how very complex it must have been," and "revived in it." Hearn is speaking in terms of the

sublime, or the Romantic notion of awe and trembling before a scene that excites emotions too complex to be pinned down. The other choices might seem plausible if you're reading the passage quickly, but "the emotion" is the main antecedent of the rest of the references in the rest of the paragraph.

17. **The correct answer is A.** "Terrible beauty" is an oxymoron, another signal that Hearn is writing about the sublime. For Romantic writers, who were used to describing the awe-inspiring mountains of the Alps or grand storms, such scenes could not just be described as beautiful—they inspired complex feelings of fear and terror. Hearn is writing a hundred years later than the Romantics, but he is applying those theories of the sublime to the jungle (where Wordsworth and Coleridge had not visited). The Romantics and their inheritors of the sublime knew that it was not a fallacy, but rather the basis of all creative tension in their art. The device is not an example of synesthesia (blended sensory descriptions) or synecdoche (where the part stands for the whole). It may be cacophonous in the jungle, but we don't get a sense of it in the phrase "terrible beauty."

18. **The correct answer is D.** In question 16, you had to follow one of these sentences back to the beginning of the paragraph to trace the antecedent for the word "it" in the paragraph's description of the intense emotions aroused by the sublime tropical scene. That is not the only winding sentence; this question asks you to interpret why these sentences might be so long and twisty. Several of the possible choices may be partially correct: there are elements of fear and distraction in his description as he keeps finding new terrors. But the best answer is choice D, ineffability, as he keeps turning back on descriptions to qualify them or add new details. Ineffability fits well with

the hints of the sublime in the other questions. Choices C and E aren't good options because they aren't mentioned in the text.

19. **The correct answer is B.** Following the markers of the sublime in question 17's oxymoron and question 16's and 18's too-complex, twisty emotions, we can see that Hearn is hammering home the idea that these feelings are too intense to be described fully. He can only give partial views through these literary devices. Choice B is the skeleton key for questions 16–22: it identifies the main idea of the tropical sublime. Choice E initially looks like the very definition of the sublime: "the insufficiency of words . . ." but he has specifically said that photographs *cannot* capture their majesty. Choices A, C, and D are not supported by the text, for there's no annoyance or obvious paranoia, nor is there a question of what's illusory in the scene, for it's all emotion, not tricks or delusions.

20. **The correct answer is E.** The shock comes from the realization of the immensity of the natural world and all of the emotions it stirs up. Shock may come from electricity in other contexts (choice A), but here you just need to trace the source to the main grammatical antecedent—the emotion—rather than building a metaphor. There are probably elements of fear in the description (choices B and C), but you're looking for the best description of the main idea of the passage.

21. **The correct answer is B.** The answer to the question is in the preceding phrase: "some sign of stealthy movement, some beginning of undulation," but it might be difficult to parse the twisting sentences. *Undulation* means slight swaying. Choices A, C, D, and E refer to other examples of sensory overload in the passage, but you are being asked about only one specific word in this question.

22. **The correct answer is D.** "Queer disquiet" is an example of consonance, the repetition of the "qu" consonants. You may not believe that it crystallizes a moment of realization, but you don't have any other correct choices among the selections. Arguably, the realization is one of the smallness of man among the gigantic trees. This question might be tricky because the descriptions of the functions are more tempting than the specific poetic devices named. It's not an example of assonance or alliteration (choices B and E), although those explanations of its function are in keeping with what you've been interpreting so far. You may be annoyed by his verbosity, but that phrase is not a marker of his confusion or grandiosity (choices A and C).

23. **The correct answer is C.** The word "awe" might be a good signal that you're working in the language of the sublime in this passage. Anger and disgust (choices B and D) are not present in the passage, and there's little sense of love (choice E). There's no mention of trees being cut down (choice A). Awe is the best word to tie back to the sublime.

24. **The correct answer is B.** Aspiration is another word that has different meanings depending on the context. Although there has been plenty of figurative language in this passage, the context here is literal: the aspiration is the enormous height of the trees. The human senses of the word—to mean ambition or achievement—don't work here, for the author's own ambitions aren't discussed (choice A), and the trees are mostly strange, not human (choice C). You shouldn't mix up aspiration and respiration to mean breathing. The author has many longings (choice E), but aspiration is not the right word to describe them.

25. **The correct answer is C.** Here is the figurative version of question 23. "Aspiration" literally described the height of the trees. They are seeking the sun to grow higher, so the best answer is also the strangest: "a life seeking only sun" describes the plants' photosynthesis as a kind of arboreal desire. Hearn was writing without extensive knowledge of botany, so he was speaking figuratively rather than scientifically. (You might be asked to differentiate a palm tree's photosynthesis on a different exam, but here we can just go with his figurative language.) Even with some quibbles about biology, you can eliminate the other answers because only one refers to the trees. "A life" refers to the trees, not to humans (choices A and B) or spiritual elements (choices D and E).

26. **The correct answer is B.** After obliquely referring to the theory of the sublime so frequently in the preceding lines, Hearn wants to add his own theories of spiritual aesthetics to the paragraph. "Perhaps" lets him move into theorizing, even pontificating mode, and his sentences will remain twisty to take you through his complex thoughts. He is not expressing ambivalence (choice A) but instead building to his grandest idea of Gothic horror, as though he creates an imaginative space for himself in a tropical cathedral. We don't see evidence of his hallucination, so choice D is not supported by the text. It may be tempting to pick choice E, but "summing up" is not the best description of his tone here, nor has he been describing beauty, but something more ineffable and sublime.

27. **The correct answer is A.** Option I is the best description of how the architectural metaphors resolve into creating a tropical Gothic cathedral in the forest. The other two options are not supported by the text: it would be fascinating if the spirits were real (option II), but they seem to be mostly just part of his sense of the deep history of the place. Similarly, although he has been

twisting the reader's perspective around in so many complex sentences, we don't have any sense that the narrator is actually unreliable (option III). Remember, this is a piece of prose nonfiction, not a novel. It's safest to pick the clear description of the main idea here, instead of trying to interpret more, and choose only option I, or choice A.

28. **The correct answer is A.** "Mneme begin" is a classic example of a poet's invocation of her muse, the muse of Memory. That invocation will become complicated in the following lines, but with this opening line, Wheatley places herself in a long poetic tradition of poets like Virgil and John Milton, who invoke the muses to give them the powers to describe the scene in poetry. Despite the short phrasing, it is not an example of fragmentation: the brevity is part of the convention. Inscription is a different device that usually refers to reading an inscription on a building or a gravestone, although the act of inscription itself will become important later in the poem. It is not an example of antithesis because she's not setting opposed ideas against each other. You might say that she is claiming authority by invoking the Muse in this way, but that is only an effect of the device, not the name of the device itself.

29. **The correct answer is C.** This question asks you to identify the meaning of a common word in the context of the poem, just to check your understanding of diction that may be unfamiliar to you. You can trace the subject of "spring" back to Mneme, for the poet traces the source, or spring, of her inspiration back to the Muse. The spring is like the source of water in a hot springs. It is not referring to a season, a jumping motion, or a surprise—all legitimate meanings of the word, just in other contexts. She is going to use Mneme's song to write a poem, but she is looking for the source of inspiration, not the song itself.

30. **The correct answer is E.** You are looking for the exception here, and choice E is an obvious choice because the poem continues for thirty more lines after those repetitions of "night" in lines 7 and 12, so she's not exhausted so early in the poem. As with the other questions that ask you to find the EXCEPTION, you should look to the four correct answers as clues to help you with future questions, for the exam has told you that all of those interpretations are reasonable. You should keep in mind those ideas about the importance of the poem's adherence to formal rules from classical models, as well as how the speaker uses imagery to build her vision.

31. **The correct answer is D.** She is asleep, as noted by the phrase "in our nocturnal visions pours" and the footnoted reference to Phoebe, who is associated with the moon. Mneme has come in dream form to inspire. You may be tempted to follow the line of singing from line 4 or more generally writing, but the question asks you about a specific passage, so it's important to pay attention to that specific request.

32. **The correct answer is A.** Phoebe is the mythological figure associated with radiance; together with Mneme, she displays a vivid spectacle of memories. "Pomp" means something like a spectacle or parade. In the phrase "a pomp of images," we don't get any sense of deception (choice C) or foreboding (choice D), although there will be a significant shift in the following lines. Your choices may come down to A or B, but there's no mention of Phoebe (or Mneme) editing these scenes—that's for the poet to do herself, as a means of composition. They are the source, but she must craft the visions.

33. **The correct answer is A.** These answers are all similar to one another, so you must pick the one that best describes the situation. Choice A gives you a useful structure:

"Mneme is not solely . . . but also" which would allow you to see the ongoing tension between Mneme's poetic inspiration and the poet's trauma that define a course for Wheatley's voice in the rest of the poem. The other choices are too limiting: she does not reject Mneme (choice E), nor does Mneme reject her (choices C and D). Choice B is another possibility because it describes a conflict that could be potentially productive, but she is not really the judge of that conflict.

34. **The correct answer is E.** Wheatley generally uses iambic pentameter so that she may claim her own position in the formal classical tradition. She is joining her own distinctive voice and set of memories as a freed slave with the poetic forms that white poets have dominated. Other poets wrote about recollection--and her slightly later contemporaries like William Wordsworth would go on to write about the subject as well--but none showed the complex relationship between memory and trauma, tied to the national past, like she did. Among these answer choices, B and D are too heavy-handed interpretations. Not every line may sound like obvious iambic pentameter to you, but there's no textual evidence to suggest ambivalence (choice C) on her part—indeed, the formal rhyme and meter are ways for her to tap into a collective experience with poetry, history, and literary memory. Choice A is a possibility, although iambs rarely signal struggle; they're more about regularity. Choice E is the best answer to show Wheatley's style.

35. **The correct answer is B.** This question builds on the previous one by looking at a particular line and example of slight variation for you to interpret. It gives you four correct answers, and it's worthwhile to check those interpretations against question 34 and later questions to make sure that you're on the right track with your readings. The exception is the only one that is obviously

not supported by the text: there's no new Muse introduced in the poem (choice B). That means that you can continue reading the poem as evidence of Wheatley's creative tension with Mneme—a tension that is not debilitating (see the next question) but productive, for it allows her to find her own voice and style (choices C, D, and E).

36. **The correct answer is B.** "Productive" tension is the key to this exam's interpretation of the poem. The possibility of mutual benefit is not supported by Wheatley's lines about memory and trauma—benefit is the opposite word to use there. But they are not at a standoff, either, for Wheatley continues to write the poem and gains authority from her recasting of Mneme's power for her own uses. Choices D and E are not good descriptions of the relationship, either.

37. **The correct answer is C.** If Wheatley can be said to have a thesis in this poem, it is in these lines, about the tension between trauma and recollection. The memories of the slave trade may be called back in Recollection, to serve as a corrective to history that's been forgotten. The word "them" lets her link traumatic memories and history together; when those memories become history, then their memory can become part of the national consciousness so that the shame and mourning in line 36 may become collective, not just personal, memory. "Them" is a strategically unclear antecedent that may make you think she's referring to previous poets or her own abilities (choices A and B), or to disagreements and conflicts more generally (choices D and E), but in fact it joins together two larger concepts of memory and history.

38. **The correct answer is E.** This question asks you to interpret the meaning behind her invocation of the slave bracelets. They are markers of trauma, to be sure, as option

I suggests. It's important to pay attention when a poet mentions any kind of writing, for poets are especially attuned to acts of inscription in letters, gravestones, monuments—and, here, in Wheatley's poems, in the metal slave manacles used to trade slaves. This is a reference that other classical poets would not be able to make, so here it shows her using the classical form to comment on how those bracelets must join those other inscriptions in literature, in history. The work of inscription, she says, is not merely poetic: it is also an economic act of claiming authority over others, of inscribing a contract (option II). Seen through her poem, the inscriptions are not only personal memory but also a national, historical memory of the slave trade. This is a poem that flows in the iambic pentameter of celebrated poets, but it questions the very activity of writing for how it marks authority, as option III suggests. There is little to argue with in any of these three interpretations of those lines, so choice E is correct.

39. **The correct answer is A.** Memory has no protective powers in this poem, for the main idea is how Wheatley takes control of the Muse herself and turns her work into a national, spiritual project so that "in ev'ry breast, and thus her pow'r is own'd." Thus, Recollection is not protective but provocative, and choice A is the outlier among four reasonable interpretations of the final lines. Memory is "enthron'd" inside people (choice B) and should be combined with Virtue for a spiritual project of grace (choices C and E). The poem turns it from a personal sense into a public one (choice D).

40. **The correct answer is B.** There is some ambiguity in the poem: has everyone been sleeping? Who is awakening? In these lines, Wheatley turns to those who have not combined Recollection and Virtue and have not been saved by grace; they are still slumbering. Spiritual awakening is the key to the final lines of the poem, for it is what allows people to see their collective relationship to one another as spiritual beings who can be saved. The other options may be secondary goals of collective action (choice C) or the end of the slave trade—which was often advocated by religious groups of abolitionists, who used Wheatley's poems in the movement.

41. **The correct answer is D.** This question asks you to specify how Wheatley explains the spiritual awakening. Option II is clearly a good choice, for it builds on the work you did in question 38 about how she wants to build historical memory. Option I is also a reasonable interpretation of the poem that is difficult to argue with. Option III is the one that seems less certain, for she is not rejecting any other models of memory, nor is it specified what those would be, anyway. You can be sure of options I and II—and there is not an answer choice for all three to be correct—so choice D is the best answer.

42. **The correct answer is E.** The references to mythology and the classical conventions of poetry indicate Wheatley's own education; among abolitionists who promoted her work, she became the most well-known former slave poet in America in the eighteenth century. Thus, option I is a good choice that pairs well with option III, the religious abolitionists who joined spiritual and political activism. Although many abolitionists wrote anthems to be sung in the streets, there's some contradiction between those classical references and an anthem to be sung in the streets. Option II is less likely. Choice E is the best pairing of options here.

43. **The correct answer is C.** It may be useful for you to annotate the passage like a dialogue if you can't follow who says what. Lucy says very little in her exchange with Ginevra. She

can barely get a word in, but she also doesn't say much about her own background. This guardedness is a puzzling part of her character throughout the novel. After you figure out who's saying what, you can eliminate the adjectives that apply more to Ginevra than to Lucy: judgmental, confessional, and sentimental (choices B, D, and E). There's no indication of Lucy's wit, even if Ginevra thinks she must speak multiple languages (choice A). The best answer is indicated in her tendency to respond in single words or very short sentences: choice C.

44. **The correct answer is E.** Choices A and B are apparent immediately: Ginevra and Lucy are conversational opposites who mostly talk and mostly listen, respectively. Lucy is idealistic (choice C) for her desire to set off abroad without a plan or connections in Belgium. Ginevra, on the other hand, is materialistic and looking for the most strategic way to get ahead (choice D). What we never learn in this passage is Lucy's reason for leaving. It is not clear if Ginevra has trampled on those reasons with her own story, or if Lucy has some unspoken reason for not explaining herself. What seems clearer in the passage is that in her idealism, she wants to look ahead, not behind her.

45. **The correct answer is C.** Lucy listens to Ginevra's long story and does not offer immediate sympathy or reaction—Ginevra just keeps talking. After the younger woman has gone inside the boat, Lucy reflects on "the position in which I was placed; its hazardous—some would have said its hopeless—character." Although she does not make specific connections to Ginevra's loquacious anxiety about her marriage prospects, she sees some kind of kinship between them as young women who are subject to precarious fortune. Lucy seems to have no family, no money, no prospects other than her idealism. Even if you're not sure that she

draws connections to Ginevra's story, you can eliminate the other answers: Ginevra is not really suffering (choice B), except perhaps in her own mind. Even if *you're* annoyed by Ginevra, there's stronger textual evidence for Lucy's reflectiveness (choice C) than for her annoyance (choice D). Lucy draws her hope from her own idealism, not from Ginevra's advice (choice E).

46. **The correct answer is D.** Ginevra's long speech is annoying, perhaps, but it draws attention in the passage because it is so different from Lucy's own self-reflection and terseness. This question asks you to infer why that contrast in tone might be important for the themes of the novel. We don't have any evidence that Ginevra is a stand-in for the author, so option I is not good, and you can strike choices A, C, and E that contain it. Nevertheless, Ginevra can still serve an important role even if she is not a stand-in for the author; here, she serves as Lucy's opposite who reveals her defining qualities through opposition (option II). Ginevra's speech also signals a theme that Lucy reflects on later in the passage, about how to take agency and get what you want (as the young girl says haughtily in French). This theme is clearly important to Lucy, and Ginevra's speech widens the world to show that other characters may also be struggling to be agents in their own lives. Thus, options II and III are the best pair, and you can select choice D.

47. **The correct answer is B.** Ginevra answers this question when she tells Lucy that she shouldn't refer to the *diable* (devil) in English but that "it sounds quite right in French." She calls the residents of Villette "vulgar," which signals her own class anxieties even though her family is poor because her father is an officer at half-pay. She is not learning the lessons for intellectual reasons, exactly (choice C), but so that she may act

cosmopolitan and fashionable. That desire isn't directed at anyone in particular, not even Lucy, so choice D is also not a good pick.

48. **The correct answer is E.** Lucy's reflections meander all over the place as she keeps interrupting herself to pin down exactly what she's feeling: fear, anxiety, danger, hopelessness, etc.? Her thoughts are circuitous; by following them through all of those fears, anxieties, and hazards, she might arrive at Hope at the very end of that paragraph, after a lot of twists and turns. We don't see her trying to find more positive words for those fears, so choice A is incorrect. Epigrammatic means witty and brief, the opposite qualities displayed in this paragraph. Polemical means argumentative, but while she may be arguing with herself, she is not constructing an argument to be defended strenuously. Her language may have moral qualities, but its twists and turns are the more important parts of this tone to analyze.

49. **The correct answer is B.** Lucy has nearly succumbed to the fears and hazards that preoccupy her in the beginning of her interior monologue, but she draws strength from remembered lines of poetry that allow her to reframe the scene not as a prison, but as a place to stand, or even to pull herself up and steady herself. The poem reveals the lyricism of her vision that pulls her away from the circuitous meandering of her fears, toward a steadier, more inspiring vision of Hope. The poem negates the misery she might feel. She is not persuading anyone but herself here, so that's not the best option. There's no evidence for her haughtiness or precision in the passage (choices A and D); indeed, her verbosity indicates she is not the most precise thinker and has to work her way toward ideas, rather than pinning them down immediately.

50. **The correct answer is A.** In her idealism and hope, Lucy is literally embellishing her vision with gold edges. She has been working her way through her fears for the future (choice D), but the question is asking you about her exalted diction, not her meandering style (addressed in question 48). When the question gives you "exalted" as a clue, you can pick an answer that has a positive, heightened answer to match it, like "embellishing." There are no obvious markers of a religious vision (choice B) or an ambition to be rich (choice E). Ginevra hasn't issued a warning, so choice C is also not a possibility.

51. **The correct answer is C.** The previous questions have indicated that the theme of agency is important to this passage, so this question asks you to find that theme in a particular example of Lucy's inward-facing style. She cannot see herself actually taking specific actions in the future; she can only imagine the general, idealized version of what one ought to do. She is not giving general advice (choice A); rather, she is trying, incompletely in this passage, to find her own position in this imagined future. Although she quotes a poem, there's no mention of her reading a story (choice B) in order to figure out what she must do. We don't yet know if she has the ability to finally take action (choice D), but she has the rest of the novel to try to do so! Choice E makes reference to a desire for "objectivity," but this passage is all about her subjectivity, for it ends with her own personal vision (and her subjective experience being ill--the scene affects her in particular). Indeed, most literary passages will not ask you to find "objectivity" because few narrators ever pretend to being objective; novels are better for exploring the vastness and changeability of perspective and subjective experience.

52. The correct answer is C. With her mentions of gold tracery and embossing, she is talking about adding ornamentation to some kind of surface—as a form of embroidery, probably. As noted in question 50, she is literally embellishing her vision with these artistic flourishes. Although the colors may match a maritime or astronomical vision of the sky or sea (choices A and B), the main metaphor of tracing and embossing is specific to ornamentation.

53. The correct answer is D. As question 51 points out, Lucy loses her own self in her vision, preferring those ornaments to her own specific abilities. When she becomes ill, it reminds her that she is not just a visionary who can look toward that beautiful future, but a human on a boat. Choices A, B, C, and E all point to that subjective, embodied sensory experience. Choice D is an overstatement and a judgmental interpretation of the passage, and we don't want to overstep those bounds. It's the outlier among those answer choices, so it is the correct answer here.

54. The correct answer is D. This question may be more difficult than the previous one, for it asks you to interpret a strange moment when Lucy speaks directly to the reader. We are used to her visionary language, which she introduced by noting that she would be sick later on. The direct address to the reader is a surprise: what does it mean? You will be in the best position if you can read it for its ambiguities; indeed, it is so unexpected and strange that you can't determine its meaning at the end of this selected passage. Choice D uses the interpretive language to suggest that you can "reconcile" the contrasts between her visionary language and the sensory details of her vomit. That word is useful in literary analysis, for it shows an interpreter who can work between extremes, rather than choosing between them as a judgment or a strong dichotomy. Choices A and E are too extreme, and they are not supported by the text. Ginevra has left the scene by now (choice B), so it is unlikely that she is important to this address to the reader. Choice C may be tempting, but there's nothing to suggest that Charlotte Brontë herself is speaking here or that this is some evidence of a correction that could never be made. No, the act of correction has to be meaningful in and of itself.

55. The correct answer is D. In the previous question, the exam asked you to interpret the meaning of Lucy's direct address to the author; this question builds on that idea by asking you to use the action to interpret something about her character (and not just its function in the novel). You know that you're looking for her subjectivity, as suggested in option III. You know that the embellishment of her vision is important to notice, and option II suggests a reason why: from embellishing we see her asking the reader to cross out, or perform their own tracery on the text. She is finding her own form of subjectivity in writing metaphors, even if it's incomplete in this passage. Recall the question about writing in Phillis Wheatley's poem: whenever an author makes reference to writing in a text, especially in something as strange as a direct address to the reader, it's significant. Option I is the only question mark here: we don't see any evidence of her unreliability in this passage, even if she is passive and not as garrulous as Ginevra. Options II and III are the best interpretations, so choice D is correct.

Section II

Essay 1: "The Word of an Engineer," by James Weldon Johnson

<u>8-9 Sample Essay</u>

The first thing to notice about James Weldon Johnson's poem "The Word of an Engineer" is the quotation marks around the first two stanzas. Who is speaking? Based on the title, we can infer that it is the engineer. What happens in the third stanza, however? Who is speaking once the quotation marks have disappeared? And who is speaking in the final three italicized lines at the end of the poem? These are formatting questions, questions that could have been settled by someone other than Johnson himself, like an editor or a typesetter. They seem too incidental to base an entire interpretation upon. However, they also reveal the smaller conflicts of authority in the poem, the ones less visible than those more obvious conflicts between engineers and religious authorities that are italicized so noticeably in the last stanza.

Johnson cannot settle that eternal conflict between science and religion, nor between nature and art--two overly familiar conflicts. He sets those aside and takes on the very notion of words as a source of authority, where he himself may be considered the heavy favorite as a poet. Johnson is writing a poem about the "word of an engineer," but it is his "words of the poet" that are the most important to the poem.

The words of the poet are in control of the narrative, in control of guiding the reader's interpretations. The poet lets the engineer speak first about "the builder's art" (line 7) with hyperboles like "Ten thousand Titans' strength" (line 12). That hyperbole sounds like an advertisement. It contrasts with the more ambiguous similes and metaphors later in the poem, presumably in the poet's own voice, in which the train is "like a nightmare" (21) or a bridge is "an iron thread / Spun from the head / Of the man in a draughtsman's cell" (28-30). That imagery is literally more open-ended, like a "black-mouthed yawn" (23) into a tunnel of ambiguity, for the speaker must weigh his own imagistic words of terror against the "word of an engineer" that vouches for them. The ambiguity lies between trust and fear--the poet has to accept that he feels some combination of both emotions as he's riding on a train through a tunnel or over a bridge.

That sense of ambiguity is the middle ground of the poem, between the word of an engineer and the word of a poet. If the engineer carves the land with metal, the poet carves the space on the page that follow his own structural logic of rhyme--yet he turns that logic against the engineer. The poem has a regular rhyme scheme of AABCCB in each of its stanzas. The B rhymes are remarkable for how they at first create a strong structure--like a covered tunnel--for the CC rhymes. This structure is given by the quotation in the first two stanzas, but Johnson starts to introduce doubt and ambiguity through his own rhyme choices. He makes the pairs sinister: "sky and hell / draughtsman's cell," (27-30) "thought and fear / engineer" (33-36). Even the structure itself is wobbly: "shift and veer/ engineer" (15-18). The poet appropriates the rhyme structure--indeed, the entire theme of sturdy structure--and then turns it into a vehicle of doubt, rather than a strong train or ship. The poet has used his own words to show the limitations of the engineer's words. The poet chose the terms of that conflict and where it could take place: in a poem, on the printed page.

Yet do these semantic conflicts matter? Who cares about a conflict of authority between a poet and an engineer, carried out on the poet's home arena? The smaller conflicts of authority in this poem are about who's speaking on the page, for the written word is more durable than a ship or an train. The "Ice Wolf" once "prowl[ed]" the seas, but that ship became obsolete. The railroads them-selves are forms of writing on the landscape--forms of italics across America--indeed, we know many of the tracks of trolleys and smaller rails by how they've been paved over with roads, so that the engineer's marvels are no longer as visible as they once were. That perspective looks far into the future from John-son's time, of course, but that is Johnson's point: the engineers work on a short time of consciousness about the novelty and immediate power, but those powers are "shift[ing] and veer[ing]," not stable.

The italicized three lines at the end of the poem call attention to how we take the "word" of an engineer as faith, which seems like a rejection of religious authority. However, the deeper value of "words" has already been established by Johnson in the rhymes and metaphors: who controls words but poets? The word of an engineer can be reformatted, manipulated, and controlled by the poet. He gets to have the last word in his italics, not the engineer, whose creation is too bulky to be adapted in such a way.

<u>Reader response for the 8-9 essay</u>

The author of this essay had a clever idea, and the essay reads like a very smart response to a dare to interpret the smallest marks of quotation marks and italics. The author seems to be reaching a bit in the conclusion of the essay, and trying very hard to follow through on the promises made in the introduction, but the rest of the essay shows a remarkable command of analysis of language and rhyme, and a thoughtful way of framing the essay around the notion of the poetic métier of words.

What is admirable about the poem is the author's rigor and care in reading the smallest details in the poem. The readings of similes, metaphors, and "sinister" rhymes are attentive and well cited.

The paragraph about obsolescence takes the author's problem about not knowing the "Ice Wolf" and turns it into a thoughtful reading of what we do and don't know based on written records. The engineer's work is less durable, the essay suggests, than the records about it. Stuff breaks, but written records are as durable as the poem is, as it was written a hundred years ago. The author argues that the words of the poem have aged more durably than the specific trains, tunnels, bridges constructed by engineers of the same period. That's a lot to pin on the "Ice Wolf," but it's not a bad reading. It's an admirable paragraph, in fact, for it looks toward interpretation of larger themes, beyond the small details observed in the other two body paragraphs.

5-6 Sample Essay

In "The Words of an Engineer," by James Weldon Johnson, we see the conflict between multiple people/things/ideas. Those conflicts include: between nature and science, between science and religion, and poetry and science. These conflicts overlap like a Venn diagram to show the ways that they can meet in the middle, to form a resolution in this poem.

The first conflict, between nature and science, is shown in the ways that the author uses negative imagery to describe the way that the engineer's have affected the land. The engineer's inventions "prowl" (14) the landscape like a burglar, or they are "like a nightmare" (21). The sky is cut in half by an "iron thread" that creates a "hell" below (26). These are negative imagery that shows the poet's opinion of the engineer against the nature; it is a kind of machine version of the pathetic fallacy, where the engineer puts their rational emotions on the scene to carve it up into black yawns and hell, but then they aren't rational anymore. They are destroying the landscape with pollution and taking resources.

The next conflict is between science and religion, as seen in the last stanza, in which the poet writes; "Man never had / The faith in God / That he has in an engineer!" (33-36). This shows that the author's opinion that we trust engineers more than God, which is true when we start building really big machines that seem all-powerful. He is saying that we have faith that ships won't sink or bridges won't collapse (even though they do sometimes), but we have these doubts about whether God exists. This is the role of the ambiguity of doubt in the poem, that we can accept debate about God in poems and philosophy, but we don't accept doubt about engineers. The poet is saying that we have deep trust in engineers, but actually this is a superficial idea because the engineers never have to be tested with doubt, whereas God survives doubt and debate for centuries. God can live in the gray area, but engineers are mostly black-and-white: either it works or it doesn't. So while the poet talks about faith, he doesn't talk about the role of doubt.

This poem is about the overlaps between conflicting ideas, to try to find the middle ground for them. The poet tells the story of how the conflicts to take place by setting the scene in quotes like "in faith I keep," which mixes up science and religion so that they'll be in conflict (line 17). He uses the word faith deliberately. It is like he is creating a kind of trial like the Scopes Trial, which took place around the same time at the beginning of the 20th century. He is a lawyer, so it makes sense that he would put them up against each other. What this means is, the poet is like the ringmaster who is creating the conflicts.

They are eternal, but we don't have to accept that they are always in conflict. We don't have to make them fight, which he knows as a diplomat.

Reader response for the 5-6 essay

This essay has a lot of ideas, and the author strikes upon a very interesting idea about whether engineers can support the weight of doubt the way that religious debates have grown stronger over time through contending with so much doubt. That's a very interesting idea that the author might test with the imagery about the blankness of the engineering spaces—like yawns, or threads—that don't seem strong enough to support the weight of doubt. Such a reading would be very attentive and creative.

The author doesn't quite get there, though, because that idea is more like a philosophical tangent than an idea tied to specific language in the poem. There are many sentences that seem to be gesturing toward an idea, without clear language of expression. In sentences like "This is the role of the ambiguity of doubt," the author is less certain of how to integrate quotations or how to discuss the complex ideas that are bubbling beneath the surface here. It might be useful to use phrases like "The speaker uses figurative language of doubt in metaphors such as 'the iron thread'..." or "The phrase 'and faith I keep' is ambiguous because . . . " These are simpler phrases that might help the author do the kind of philosophy that comes naturally in the last two paragraphs.

The essay ends on an interesting note about Johnson's own position as a "ringmaster" or lawyer who can "try" these oppositions like a lawyer (apparently drawing on the biographical material about Johnson's life as a diplomat). This information is really interesting and would be fascinating to test out in a longer essay that's not on the exam; the ambition is admirable, even if it falls flat in the conclusion here. One lesson might be that the author should focus more on the poem itself, instead of on the more general ideas.

1-2 Sample Essay

In the poem "The Word of an Engineer," the author contrasts religion and science. The author proves that science is religion in each stanza. The ship can sail through seas that no one thought were able to navigate. The train can go faster than a horse. You might think that he is saying that one is better, but really he is showing that science is a kind of religion for how we believe in it. Thats why he says that we have more faith in engineers than religion, because they are now the same.

The first evidence that they are the same is how in the author uses similes and metaphors to compare them. The quote "like a nightmare" show that they become the same thing when you think or worry about them: science can be a nightmare when it is like Frankenstein, or religion can be a nightmare like in poems about hell, which is mentioned in the poem, too.

"Hell" is another place where they become the same thing. The bridge goes across the sky and divides it, which show how engineers create religion with their manufacturing. The bridge creates an idea of hell.

Finally, they show that they are the same in the way that they both come from your mind when they are "Spun from the head." Some people say that all of Religion is spun from someone's head, and the poem agrees that engineers ideas are also spun from someone's head.

It is interesting that there is no conflict after all, for science and religion have been shown in the poem to be the same. They are both able to be authorities because theyre power comes from the same place. It is not clear if religion is a kind of science, or if science is a kind of religion that you believe in with "faith," but they are the same.

<u>Reader response for the 1-2 essay</u>

The author misunderstands the poem and proceeds from the wrong idea from the start. Instead of seeing Johnson's deliberate play with calling the faith in engineers as a kind of religion, the author takes that idea as a fact that must be "proved" with very superficial readings of the poem. It looks like the author tried to find three examples of proof for this specious logic and tried to construct the paragraphs of a brief five-paragraph essay. The problem is that the small snippets of the poem are cherry-picked to "support" a thesis that doesn't make sense.

A few lessons from this essay: Read the poem closely for tone and irony before you decide what the main meaning is. Don't cherry-pick tiny fragments to "prove" an idea.

Most important, if the question asks you to analyze the conflicts, then it's asking you to work through oppositions and tensions, rather than trying to show that they're "the same." This essay doesn't address any conflicts because the author has steam-rolled over all of the material that the essay question asked for in the analysis. Insisting that two opposed ideas are "the same" is usually an overstatement that doesn't pay off.

Essay 2: "Against Thinking," by Vernon Lee

<u>8-9 Sample Essay</u>

At first, it is off-putting to read Vernon Lee's essay "Against Thinking," because it seems like it's rambling and improvised. She writes in nearly interminable sentences that are full of lists, digressions, parentheses, and asides. It seems possible that the "essay" is just the unedited record of her random flights of fancy as she was talking without taking a breath. She is writing about how we often mistake Talking for Thinking, because they are twins and we are frequently experiencing "that confusion and amiable not-caring-which-is-which so characteristic of our dealings with twins." Talking is "the more ubiquitous twin-brother" who masquerades as though he were Thinking, but he is just taking up all the air in the room. She even calls Talking the "villain" twin. If Talking is the villain, it seems Vernon is playing the villain of her own essay, making the reader hate her talkative style.

After considerable confusion and frustration, the reasons behind her rambling style become clearer in a subtle, sneaky revelation. In the first paragraph of this essay, there are hints to Lee's game: she is using the elements of drama--a form made of talking--to construct her essay about Talking and Thinking. The reader may have been frustrated when they believed they were reading an essay, but it opens up when it is considered to be a form of drama, in the tradition of the dramatic monologue and the reversal in the Shakespearean comedy. Lee has pulled a kind of dramatic bait and switch, to play with the reader's expectations about Talking and Thinking--which makes them start thinking about form, style, and even identity.

The key to this interpretation is her mention of Hamlet, the prince of the rambling monologue. Hamlet is an example of a dramatic character who thinks too much. As Lee puts it: "the career of Hamlet is frequently pointed out as a proof of its unhappy effects." Hamlet's soliloquies are full of the same rambling qualities as in Lee's essay, like parenthetical aside to the audience in a line like "(Though this is madness, there is method in it.)" He has over-thought his plan in that scene with the players, and it backfires on him because he starts talking too much and ruins the plan. Lee is not writing a critique of Hamlet, though; she is taking her cues from him. In the opening sentence, she uses those same stylistic features for her own version of the monologue: "As towards most other things of which we have but little personal experience (foreigners, or socialists, or aristocrats, as the case may be)..." This digression in the very first sentence is a demonstration of how difficult it is to follow someone's train of thought when you are not inside their head. The monologue is evidence of "the generous gaseousness of self-analysis, self-accusation, self-pity, self-righteousness, and autobiography." People start talking to try to communicate, but it only exaggerates the situation. It is easier to understand Lee, when you start to imagine her acting as Hamlet in the midst of a talkative monologue about what he is thinking.

There is more Shakespeare in the rest of her essay, because she has used one of Shakespeare's most famous devices of mixed-up twins. In *Twelfth Night* and other plays, the twins Viola and Sebastian get mixed up for one another, causing comic misunderstandings. The comic misunderstandings sound a lot like the way that "talking is the great equalizer of positions, turning the humble, the painfully immature, into judges with rope and torch; and in a kindlier way allowing the totally obscure to share the life of kings, and queens, and generals, and opera-singers." Lee has described the plot of a Shakespearean comedy like *Twelfth Night* or *The Comedy of Errors*. The twin reversal story causes mix-ups, frustrations, confusions--interactions, in short. Lee writes: "In conversation, clever young people vain, kindly, selfish, ridiculous, happy young people actually take body and weight, expand." The Talking Twin causes people to break out of their monologues and talk to one another. When Lee lets the Talking Twin take over in her writing, she creates a performance of exposing readers' social stereotypes about what should count as "proper" writing. Their judgments about gender might also become clear as people judge her as a silly rambling woman.

Lee plays the villain, then, in making people wish they could have more familiar, staid Thinking, only to pull off her mask and reveal the performance of Talking, Talking, Talking to expose your prejudices about style. Readers may have been muttering under their breath, talking to themselves about how frustrating her essay is to read. Lee addresses them at the end: "are you quite sure," she asks, "dear, mature, efficient, and thoroughly productive friends," that your own talking isn't adding to that which you say you disdain, the talking rather than reflecting on your own habits?

Reader response for the 8-9 essay

The author has a wonderful idea for reading Vernon Lee's essay as though it were a dramatic monologue, so that she may use the conventions of monologue and dramatic reversal to comment on style as a kind of performance. Her reading of Hamlet's digressions as compared with Lee's is inspired and thoughtful. The essay question asked for specific details from other forms of imaginative writing, and this essay delivers those in large quantity. The paragraph about twins in *Twelfth Night* is less persuasive because there are fewer specific details that connect the play and Lee's sentences. The author seems to realize that problem and starts to generalize about the role of the Twin plot, and so finds a way out of that problem relatively gracefully.

It is also admirable that the author constructs the essay around a feature of Lee's style that was initially off-putting. The author sets up the reconsideration with remarkable deftness in the opening paragraph by using so many "dramatic" vocabulary words. That paragraph sets up a thoughtful thesis paragraph about the function of the dramatic elements in Lee's style. The reconsideration approach allows for a dynamic structure: one gets the sense that the author is discovering little nuggets in Lee's sentences that were initially confounding. Some essays might try to prove that Lee is a good or bad stylist; this essayist tries to change the initial perception with some reflection.

That's a good gambit to follow in writing these kinds of essay exams: How can I show my reconsideration of an idea, to see how it's more complicated than it initially appeared?

5-6 Sample Essay

In her essay entitled, "Against Thinking," the author Vernon Lee has a very unusual style of writing like she is talking too quickly at a coffee shop. It seems like she is writing her thoughts as they come to her in a free-write. This style makes sense because she is arguing "against thinking" and for talking, so she decides to write how she talks, without revising or going back to look at what she wrote. She writes more about living life in the moment, which is an idea that we see characters in novels like *On the Road*. Whereas, essays make arguments and support them. Thus, she has a paradox of writing an essay that doesn't have any of the same goals of an essay. It makes a kind of paradoxical sense that she has to use other genres to write an essay that is not an essay.

She says that most people who want to be great thinkers have to go through a phase of talking about their ideas before they produce anything. She quotes about the "litter they leave behind, what mud pies they make and little daily dug-up gardens of philosophy, ethics, literature, and general scandal; they will grow out of the need to make them and meanwhile, making this sort of mess will help them grow." This essay is a mess that helps her "grow" as a writer, so it makes sense that it is rambling and all over the place.

Lee's essay is similar to Jack Kerouac's novel/autobiography *On the Road*, which he typed onto one continuous sheet of paper as he traveled around the United States and Mexico. He wrote it like a letter to his friend, Neal Cassady. In the novel, they have the names Sal and Dean Moriarity, and it is like they are talking to each other the whole time about such subjects as jazz, sex, drugs, Eastern religion, travel, and many other subjects. In *On the Road*, the value of talking is expressed in the quote where he says that he likes "the mad ones" who love to talk until they are worn out, like a firework that is brilliant until it's dead. Or it is like a jazz musician who talks through improvising. Most jazz improvisation isn't recorded, it's another form of art that's "against thinking," and more like a way of just being creative without worrying about someone else judging it. Jazz musicians are like the people who are talking to practice in Vernon Lee's essay—that is how they grow. They are "the mad ones."

This idea about *On the Road* is a demonstration of how an essay can be about throwing ideas out there "like mud pies" because it's more about creativity and ideas, and not about making the ideas pretty or acceptable for other people. Vernon Lee doesn't care about people understanding her, she just wants to show that talking matters more than arguing in a formal way. She is more like Sal and Dean than anyone could have realized.

Reader response for the 5-6 essay

This author is onto a great idea in the first paragraph about how Lee is writing an essay that doesn't appear to be a conventional essay, so she has to look to other genres of writing for inspiration. That argument would make for an excellent essay, if it were backed up with detailed analysis of how elements from those genres appear in her style. That was the essay question, in fact.

Instead, the author gives a perfunctory quotation and then writes her off with a superficial reading of Lee's essay. The author underestimates Lee's style in saying that she "doesn't care" about style, only about random ideas or improvisation. It's a mistake to believe that "Against Thinking" was just free-writing that she didn't revise. It's also not a good strategic move on the author's part: Lee's essay was picked for the exam for a reason, so it makes sense to take it seriously as a passage to analyze in depth. Lee's style, though unusual, is also highly stylized as an embellished, thrilling conversational style. The essay question asked students to analyze that style, to not take it for granted.

The connection to *On the Road* is unexpected and could be useful as a minor example, but it takes up too much space in the essay, because the writer seems more interested in writing about the pleasures of Kerouac's novel than analyzing Vernon Lee's style. The essay goes off on a digression and doesn't recover.

If the author wanted to pursue the idea of *On the Road*, she might make some connections between Sal and Dean as "twins" who are at odds about experience and reflection, in some of the same ways that the twins of Talking and Thinking square off in Lee's essay. Sal and Dean have many conversations that seem to upend social conventions in some of the same ways that Lee describes in her essay; if one were really good at quoting Kerouac's style about "the mad ones," one could also compare their digressive habits. (One could do something similar by thinking about Walt Whitman's "Song of Myself," perhaps.) Any of those approaches would be a way to get this essay back on track—just remember to focus on the passage itself, and not on a summary of a totally different work.

1-2 Sample Essay

> This essay uses elements of other imaginative works like drama, literature, and poetry, which makes it hard to read because it is a combination of so many different styles. The author is critical of Thinking, saying that Talking is better because it is an easier way to communicate. After reading this essay, I would recommend that the writer take some of her own advice and practice communicating her ideas more clearly. She can eliminate some of the poetic or rambling parts of her style so that others can understand her more clearly.

> I think that is the point of this essay, though, that we will never be able to communicate with each other clearly. The author is just making that idea in an annoying, melodramatic way. In a quote that begins "I call them twins on the analogy of *Death* and *Sleep*," she puts in too many examples from poetry to make her point clear--why does there need to be an analogy or twin characters in an essay? She wants to make it seem more interesting by adding elements of literature, drama, and/or poetry, but it just makes it more confusing.

> For example, she can cut out the extra words and synonyms in a quote like "It is reputed to impede action, to make hay of instincts and of standards, to fritter reality into doubt." All she is really saying is that thinking is wasteful, but she ironically wastes a lot of words in order to get there. That is the irony of this essay about the problems of talking to others, we can't understand her.

Reader response for the 1-2 essay

This essay is limited by the author's opinion, rather than analysis, of the passage. The task of the essay is to analyze the literary elements of Lee's essay, and although the author repeats the essay prompt twice, the author is more interested in judging and even "editing" the passage. This judgment limits what the author can do in more than one sentence or paragraph: there's nowhere to go, because the only idea here is that the essay is "annoying" or overwritten.

As with the 5-6 essay, the author needs to work more strategically here, and enter the essay under the agreement that the passages are worth analyzing in depth, not just dismissing. The 8-9 essay author started with a statement of skepticism about Lee's style; however, the rest of the essay answered the question in depth by relating it to dramatic works that illuminated Lee's unusual style. The 5-6 essay author made a gesture toward doing that with the mention of *On the Road*, although that comparison could have been more focused on textual comparison with Lee's sentences.

This author doesn't even make a gesture toward specifying any literary texts that it resembles. It may be helpful to list a few possibilities, for those who are taking the sample exam and are frustrated by Lee's style. You could draw comparisons between her work and:

- examples of characters who talk rather than listen
- examples of elaborate interior monologues or first-person narrations
- unreliable narrations
- dramatic soliloquies
- comic monologues
- comic poems that play with language in a self-conscious way

Essay 3: Free Response

8-9 Sample Essay

In Ray Bradbury's short story "The Third Expedition," the archaeologist-rocketman Hinkston is asked a crazy question: can two societies on two different planets, hundreds of years apart, evolve at the same rate to produce exactly the same culture, architecture, technology, and even songs? Hinkston and the other scientists are stunned to land on Mars in the 2030s and see that it looks exactly like the 1950s midwest, down to the music playing. They experience a sense of nostalgia, of coming home to a familiar space, but it is understandably confusing. To solve the confusion, they try to use their scientific backgrounds and habits of observation and experiment, leading to the story's conflict between science and nostalgia.

They would seem to be opposed, for science is rational but nostalgia is a feeling. Science forms impersonal theories, while nostalgia tells personal stories. In "The Third Expedition," from *The Martian Chronicles*, Bradbury complicates those oppositions by showing that the scientists succumb to the Martians' nostalgia trap because of their scientific backgrounds, not in spite of them. The two ways of understanding the world are more linked than they seem. Both scientific observation and nostalgia depend on intense observation of sensory details, and they each depend on using past information to help make sense of the present. In this way, science becomes the paradoxical way of enhancing one's sense of nostalgia--and thus of falling right in the trap set by the Martians' nostalgic glue-trap for the scientists to get stuck in.

At first, each of the scientists sees the nostalgic world through his own field of science. The plant expert notices that the flowers were created in a laboratory on earth in the 20th century, so it would be unlikely that the exact same plant would be made on Mars 80 years later, especially in the thinner air. The archaeologist Hinkston wants to see this new world through his own desire to find a kind of map for civilization, where they follow similar patterns. Speaking as a scientist, he says "we have the proof before us, we just have to verify it." Each nostalgic detail that they take pleasure in seeing, hearing, touching, tasting (like the lemonade), is a way that he verifies his theories. Hinkston says that he doesn't know "whether to laugh or cry," because either option would be incredible. Either they are getting to relive happy memories of the past, or they are getting to achieve their scientific fantasies of discovery of a grand theory. He loves conducting this scientific research and exploration because it lets him indulge in both his nostalgia and his ambition.

Hinkston is talented at creating theories, depending on the new information he comes across. This is another way that nostalgia and science are similar: they are both about making sense of those sensory details with narratives about how they came to be. Hinkston never stops coming up with alternate theories of how the Martian Midwest came to be, showing how generative that habit of rearranging information, observations, and hypotheses can be. Faced with the other scientists' skepticism, he abandons the theory of convergent evolution on Mars. He proposes the idea that the reason the Martian town appears to be frozen in the 1950s is because it is the work of 20th century scientists who started building rockets earlier than anyone knew. They wanted to escape the wars of the 20th century, so they built rockets and went to Mars. He also comes up with another theory that it's all a delusion of these 20th century explorers who were nostalgic for earth and remade Mars. He doesn't realize that he is projecting his own nostalgia and delusion onto his proposed hypothesis. He never hits on the best hypothesis, that it's a trap designed to hit their psychological weaknesses via nostalgia. They confuse their nostalgic indulgence with their own heightened abilities for observation and hypothesis.

Finally, what of that second root word in "nostalgia," about pain. We don't see the deaths of the scientists, only their graves. All of Hinkston's theories have an underlying root--not just of his ambition to come up with grand theories, but of his desire to cure pain. He comes up with psychological theories about humans leaving earth to protest World War I and World War II because he wants previous scientists to have found a way to escape suffering and death. When they see their relatives, they wonder if they've found a cure for death, grief, and suffering, even if they know it's implausible. They want a cure for grief. They think they've found it, not realizing that they've entered into that familiar pain all over again.

Reader response for the 8-9 essay

This essay takes a creative, independent approach to the free response question by looking at an unusual form of nostalgia: scientific observation in Ray Bradbury's *The Martian Chronicles*. Bradbury's novels are full of nostalgia and science fictional detail, and this essay brings those two kinds of details together under a plausible argument about the nostalgic elements of scientific observation. It's a well-argued essay with compelling readings of details from "The Third Expedition"—one wonders if the essay might expand to consider this idea in other short stories from the collection.

In the final paragraph, the author seems to write toward a connection with the exam question about the "pain" root of nostalgia. Nevertheless, the author recovers with a memorable final idea about the desire for a cure for grief.

For those students who wish to emulate an essay like this one, it may be useful to follow the author's format of showing that two seemingly opposed concepts are not as opposed they appear, and to frame the argument as: "in fact, these two opposed ideas actually enhance each other." That format is as familiar as dramatic irony: love and hate actually produce stronger emotions; ambition and fear actually intensify both feelings; a scientific view of nature actually enhances one's powers of observation. With that "formula," the author was able to construct this argument to create a compelling reading of the short story.

<u>5-6 Sample Essay</u>

> The story 'The Third Expedition" in The Martian Chronicles by Ray Bradbury is an example of nostalgia that is both pleasurable and dangerous. In the story, the scientists who are going to Mars are surprised when they land that Mars looks like the United States, specifically Illinois, from the 1950s. It looks like what they remember or what they heard about the past, since some of them are younger and can only imagine what it would have looked like when theyre grandparents lived there. Then they see their grandparents and other family members, which is confusing but also exciting. It is like the past is living on Mars. It is the pleasurable part of coming home and seeing the people you miss and most want to see.
>
> However, one of the scientists is not as sure as the others. He is the one who the memories seem to be most important to because they come from his childhood, when he can remember songs and Victorian houses, and other items from the past. It seems to convenient to him. His dilemma in the nostalgia is whether to find it pleasurable or painful. He doesn't want to destroy the good times that the other scientists are having with their families, but he also doesn't know whether it is a trick.
>
> The reason it might be a trick is that the Martians might "hate" the Americans. That is the word he uses: hate. Hate is a painful emotion that contrasts with pleasure, that is the form that the pain and pleasure contrast takes in this story. The reason that they would hate the Americans is that they could construct some kind of mirage of all of their happy memories to trick them and then they could use that mirage against them. They could make themselves appear like the grandparents and brothers, and then use the nostalgia as a trap. That is what the main scientist whose memories are the main mirage realizes, but it is too late. He tries to escape by saying he is going to get a glass of water, but the

Martians tell him that he doesn't want a glass of water and that is the last that is heard of him.

The next scene is of the Martians around the graves of all of the scientists. The trick worked, and the main Martian is a contrast to the scientist because he has executed the plan. The reason that he is a contrast is that he can shift his face to appear like a memory. Whereas, the scientist cannot shift his memories because he is too nostalgic. The memories are unchanging for him because of the nostalgia, and that is the weakness that the Martians exploit.

There are other short stories in the Martian Chronicles that contain the theme of nostalgia. For example, in the story The Fire Blooms, the priest compares the sight of the rockets going to Mars to his nostalgia for the fireworks on the 4th of July when he was growing up. He uses this nostalgia to make a decision about whether he should go to Mars. He knows that it will not be like going home to the past, but he uses the nostalgic sense of familiarity to help him see what he wants. Bradbury shows in this story that the nostalgia makes him make the wrong decision because he is making decisions based on a fantasy.

In the narration in "The Third Expedition" and "The Fire Blooms," Ray Bradbury calls nostalgia a "myth," showing that it is not real but it is powerful for the scientists and for Father. He shows but doesn't tell that it is painful and dangerous too.

<u>Reader response for the 5-6 essay</u>

The author has chosen a good text to work with in *The Martian Chronicles*. This is an essay with a lot of detail, but most of that detail is summary of "The Third Expedition." The author has the beginning of an idea in contrasting "pain" with the Martians' "hatred" (which might be a form of extracting pain from the humans), but that idea isn't really explored in the essay. The author would have had more success with analysis of the story, rather than just stating the examples of nostalgia in the plots of the two stories and restating the exam question.

In the fourth paragraph, there's another potentially interesting idea about how one might be able to change one's nostalgia. The author mentions that the Martian in charge is able to shift his face, referring to how the Martians seem to shift away from their human forms once the scientists have been killed. The author notes that the Martian is able to change, but the scientist is not. The scientist's memory stays the same, which makes him susceptible to the nostalgia trick. This idea is potentially compelling for thinking about how nostalgia can change shape, like the Martians themselves. With less plot summary and perhaps a comparison to another story in the volume, the author might be onto something.

(Note that the title of the second story is "The Fire Balloons," not the "The Fire Blooms.")

<u>1-2 Sample Essay</u>

The theme of nostalgia is explored in Ray Bradbury's novel The Martian Chronicles. There are many stories about humans going to Mars expecting it will be like their hometowns on Earth. Why they believe that is irrational, but they do believe it. Their nostalgia gets in the way of rational thinking about what Mars will really be like. It is ironic that the scientists become the most irrational thinkers.

Ray Bradbury has different characters who are nostalgic in the stories. The scientists in "The Third Expedition" are nostalgic for the towns they grew up in, and they don't even become suspicious when it starts to seem too perfect. They aren't using their brains when they see their old relatives who died a long time ago, even though they are supposed to be conducting a scientific exploration. All of the characters act like this. It makes more sense that the priest in another story might act like this, because he sees the world through his personal beliefs. The priest decides to go to Mars because they need people who believe in the new colony. But even he is overcome with the deleterious effects of nostalgia.

Bradbury gives a counterexample when he talks about the beings that actually live on Mars without human contact. In the story with Ylla, there is no nostalgia at first because Yll and Ylla have had no human contact. Their pain doesn't start until Ylla meets one of the Earth explorers who brings his pain with him. The counterexample shows the argument best: nostalgia is a negative emotion that leads people to act against their best interests.

The message in the stories is simple: Humans shouldn't impose their nostalgia onto other planets. We've already screwed up one Earth, so they should not make other planets in our own wishes and memories of the past.

<u>Reader response for the 1-2 essay</u>

The author of this essay uses the prompt to make an argument about whether nostalgia is good or bad, and in so doing misses the point of Bradbury's nostalgic scientists and how they meet their doom on Mars. In giving the root words of *nostalgia*, the question sets up a *tension* between home and pain. A more successful essay would have dealt with the scientists' *conflicting* desires for home and their exploration, between their "rationality" and their human qualities (including their desire to beat death and see loved ones again). This author rejects all of those tensions, in a misreading of Bradbury's ingenious blending of nostalgia for the past and interest in what the future might look like. The takeaways from this black-and-white, judgmental essay are that you should resist trying to find a single "should" from the essay, and one should find the complex parts of the stories instead of trying to show that they're simple.

On a stylistic note, it's important to name the stories and give more details from "The Fire Balloons," for even some explanation of details might help you find those complexities that you need to write a longer, more nuanced essay.